A Billion Years of Sex Differences

A Billion Years of Sex Differences

How Evolution Shaped the Minds of Men and Women

Steve Stewart-Williams

FORUM

FORUM

First published in Great Britain by Forum,
an imprint of Swift Press 2026

9 8 7 6 5 4 3 2 1

Printed and bound in Great Britain by CPI Group (UK) Ltd, Croydon CRO 4YY

A CIP catalogue record for this book is available from the British Library

ISBN: 9781800756472
eISBN: 9781800756489

MIX
Paper | Supporting responsible forestry
FSC® C013604

For Jane, always

Contents

Acknowledgements

Most books have a single name on the cover, but no book is truly the work of just one person. This book is no exception. Many people helped shepherd it from a blinking cursor in an empty Word document to the finished product you hold in your hands. Without them, the journey would have been a lot shorter – but only because it would have ended before it began.

So, some thank-yous are in order! First and foremost, thanks to Jane, India, and Darwin for their patience and encouragement, and for serving as sounding boards for ideas, arguments, and alternative wordings, whether they wanted to or not. I owe you more than I can say.

My deepest gratitude goes to my agent, Christy Fletcher at United Talent Agency, and my publisher, Mark Richards at Swift Press. Their belief in my work and tireless advocacy helped keep the book alive and moving forward.

Thanks to all my colleagues in the School of Psychology at the University of Nottingham Malaysia for providing such a supportive, stimulating, and fun environment to work in. A special thanks to Andy Chan and Steve Janssen for defending my academic freedom when it was under threat (long story; see Chapter 1). And a special, special thanks to my fellow members of the School of Psychology staff rock band, the Psychic Armpits: Polly Chen and Miflah Hussain, plus our manager, fashion advisor, and art director Christine Leong. (The band name is another long story.)

On top of that, I'd like to thank the many others who contributed their expertise, encouragement, or constructive scepticism, or who otherwise helped me to the finish line: Musa al-Gharbi, Angelos Antonatos, John Barry, April Bleske-Rechek, Paul Bloom, Michael Britt, Diana Broccardo, David Buss, Jimmy Carr, Stephen Ceci, Laurie-Maude Chenard, Logan Chipkin, Nicholas Christakis, Kai Li Chung, Cory Clark, Jerry Coyne, Sabhbh Curran, Alan Davison, Rolf Degen, Marieke de Vries, Janet Dreyer, Lucie Ewin, Emma Finn, Alexander Graul, Katie Greally, Julie Gunz, Lewis Halsey, Martie Haselton, Rob Henderson, Harold Herzog, Carole Hooven, Rosemary Hopcroft, Jeremy Hopes, Coleman Hughes, Victoria Hunt, Iona Italia, Kathryn Jarvis, Lee Jussim, Scott Barry Kaufman, David Keeble, Razib Khan, Ruth Killick, Louisa Gee Ling Lee, Claire Lehmann, Louise Liddon, Ricardo Lopes, David Lubinski, Pablo Malo, Paul Marsden, Geoffrey Miller, Yascha Mounk, James Nuzzo, Rebecca Owens, Lionel Page, Steven Parton, Steven Pinker, Helen Pluckrose, Jess Price, Sam Reynolds, Matt Ridley, Larry Rifkin, Sally Satel, David Schmitt, Yael Schonbrun, Timur Sevincer, Todd Shackelford, Daniel Sharp, Michael Shermer, Sarah Shrubb, Rob Sica, Jack Smyth, Christina Hoff Sommers, Beatrice Stewart, Jolyon Stewart, Andrew Stewart-Loughnan, Will Storr, Josh Szeps, Andrew Thomas, Andy Thomson, Barbara Williams, Brian Williams, Wendy Williams, Chris Williamson, Colin Wright, Xiu Ling Wong, Claire Yoo, and Cathy Young.

Finally, a quick shout-out to Mike Alborough: Although you didn't help with this book, you did help with the last one, and I misspelled your name in the Acknowledgements. Consider this a belated correction. Sorry, Mike!

Steve Stewart-Williams
University of Nottingham Malaysia
December 2025

1
A Can of Worms
Everything You Wanted to Know About Sex Differences but Were Too PC to Ask

> Nothing in life is to be feared, it is only to be understood. Now is the time to understand more, so that we may fear less.
>
> Marie Curie (attributed)

> Rather than rejecting biological differences, we must seek to reveal the nonsense in the arguments that brain and behavioral sex differences justify discrimination, segregation, and differential treatment of the sexes.
>
> Sheri Berenbaum (2017), p.254

Falling in Love with Sex Differences

In 1998, I fell in love. Awkwardly, I was on my honeymoon at the time. You see, I'd fallen in love in 1997 as well, with the woman who was now my wife. We'd married the week before, and were now travelling around New Zealand, my home country, seeing the sights. But we also had some spare time, and I spent a lot of it reading a book I'd picked up on a whim: *The Moral Animal* by Robert Wright.[1]

People often talk about how a book changed their life, and sometimes they just mean 'I really liked it'. But *The Moral Animal* really did change my life. It was my introduction to the field of evolutionary psychology, and reading it set the course of the rest of my career. It was the ideas contained between the covers of this book that I fell in love with on my honeymoon.

The basic idea of evolutionary psychology is simple and compelling. Humans are animals, and like every other animal, from beatles to bonobos, we're products of evolution by natural selection. This applies to our bodies, of course, but it also applies to our minds. Just as eyes evolved for vision and wings for flight, so too the basic constituents of the mind evolved to achieve their own adaptive ends: Hunger evolved to motivate us to eat; fear evolved to motivate us to escape from danger; lust evolved to motivate us to have sex. Ultimately, the mind is a collection of drives and devices 'designed' by natural selection to help us stay alive and have offspring, while also helping our genetic relatives to stay alive and have offspring – or, what amounts to the same thing, to help us to pass on our genes.

And this doesn't just explain our most basic desires and motivations. The evolutionary framework explains many of the central features of what it means to be a human being: why we find some people more attractive than others; why we fall in love; why we get so upset if the person we're in love with gets involved with someone else; why we're more likely to risk life and limb to help genetic relatives than unrelated individuals. On top of all that, it explains many enduring differences between the sexes.[2]

From what I've said so far, you might think I'm saying that I fell in love with evolutionary psychology, and that would be true to a point. But what I really fell in love with, above all else, was the evolutionary psychology of sex differences. I hadn't been particularly interested in sex differences before I came across the evolutionary approach; afterwards, I was hooked. In a single stroke, it explained many of the recurring female–male differences we see in the world around us, and which otherwise seem arbitrary and puzzling: differences in sexual behaviour, in the things people want in a mate, in aggression, parental inclinations, and so on. From the moment I grasped the evolutionary explanation for these and other common gender gaps, I found it hugely intellectually satisfying. I got the same feeling I did as a kid when I first understood how the phases of the moon work: Everything just clicked into place. But the click was even more satisfying this time, because the a-ha moment was about something we all encounter in everyday life, and which matters a lot to most people: differences between men and women.

So, I fell in love: with sex differences, with the logic of the evolutionary explanation for sex differences, and with the sense that evolutionary psychologists had made genuine progress in explaining a fundamental aspect of human life. As everyone knows, though, the course of love is never smooth, and over the following years and decades, my relationship status with evolutionary psychology switched to 'It's complicated'. There are various reasons for this.

The first is that love can sometimes blind you to the imperfections of the object of your affection. As I immersed myself in the field, I slowly but surely came to the view that its approach to sex differences, though definitely on the right track, was in need of a serious makeover. Much of that makeover is now complete. In many ways, the field as it exists today is very different from the one I met in the 1990s. It's grown and matured – and in the process, my early infatuation with the area has given way to a more realistic, deeper love.

A second complication is that not everyone reacted to the evolutionary psychology of sex differences in the way I had. Whereas for me it was love at first sight, many took an instant dislike to the whole project. In their view, sex differences – if they exist at all – are largely a product of discrimination and socialization. As such, abolishing the differences is the only path to gender salvation: Trucks and dolls should be gender-neutral toys; engineering and teaching should be gender-neutral jobs – and evolutionary psychology, which downplays the unjust origins of society's gender gaps, should be banished to scientific purgatory. With attitudes like these running in the background of people's thinking, the field was pelted with criticisms and widely demonized. To be sure, some of the criticisms were fair, and helped us refine our ideas. But many were not, and partly as a result of the unfair criticisms, many misunderstandings about evolutionary psychology now have wide circulation in the culture. You probably have some yourself.

A third complication is the mirror image of the second. Sex differences minimizers are always in the foreground of evolutionary psychologists' attention, because the minimizers are their main academic foes. But minimizing sex differences isn't the only way to get sex differences wrong. Some people – including, to be fair, some evolutionary psychologists – make the equal but opposite mistake: They massively exaggerate the differences, and the extent to which they're irreversibly locked into human nature.[3] More than that, some people *moralize* the differences, arguing not only that the sexes differ, but that they *should* differ. Although this view has little institutional power in the West today, it was the dominant trend historically and still has cultural momentum. Indeed, the attempt to minimize or deny the differences is largely a reaction to the traditional view. As we'll soon see, however, both the sex differences minimizers *and* the sex differences exaggerators fall foul of the current science.

A fourth and final complication is that the minimizers and the exaggerators both create serious problems for individuals and society as a whole. With these positions dominating the public discourse, almost everyone gets sex differences wrong: laypeople, policymakers – even many scientists. But getting sex differences *right* really matters. It matters for our dating lives, our parenting lives, and our work lives. It matters for solving the social problems that plague us, from domestic violence to sexual harassment to disparities in the workplace and home. It matters for reducing discrimination, not just against women but against men. And it matters for our physical health and our mental well-being. By taking the science of sex differences seriously, we can set a new course to a better world.

It's for all these reasons that I decided to write this book. I see the book as at once an ode to a loved one, a progress report from the frontlines of a rapidly evolving science, the case for the defence of that science against its academic prosecutors, and a deep dive into the personal and cultural implications of the knowledge that that science has produced. I've got an aim, a hope, and an expectation for the book. My aim is to upload everything I've learned about sex differences over the past quarter-century from my brain into these pages, so you can download it into your own brain. My hope is that the book will do for you what *The Moral Animal* did for me in the 1990s, while taking into account what we've learned in the interim. And my expectation is that having read this book, you'll never see men, women, or society the same way again – not because I'm so great, but because the science is. If you're not ready for that, you might want to consider pausing the download and putting the book aside, at least for a while. Don't say I didn't warn you!

The Science of Human Sex Differences

What sex differences are we talking about, are these differences real, and where, if they are, did they come from? These are difficult questions: questions that have stumped some of the greatest minds of the ages. This is partly because there are no easy answers, and partly because the discussions around these issues have often been so fraught. But although the questions are difficult, they're not beyond our scientific reach, and in the last few decades in particular, we've made substantial progress in answering them. Let's begin our exploration of the answers with what I call the *standard-issue sex differences*: a collection of female–male differences that profoundly shape our lives and societies, and which form the backbone of the rest of the book.

STANDARD-ISSUE SEX DIFFERENCES

- Men are larger and stronger than women; women can perform miracles (they can make new life).
- Girls develop faster than boys and hit puberty earlier; boys, after taking a more leisurely path to puberty, make a more rapid beeline to the grave: They age faster and die younger.
- Most men are primarily attracted to women; most women are primarily attracted to men.
- Men are often more interested than women in casual, no-strings-

attached sex; women are often choosier about their sexual partners.
- Men often place more weight than women on a romantic partner's looks and youthfulness; women often place more weight than men on a partner's social status and ability to accrue resources.
- Men corner the market on violence, risk-taking, and other antisocial antics; women are more involved in childcare.
- Men tend to be more interested than women in things and gadgets; women tend to be more interested than men in people.
- Men tend to have somewhat better spatial skills; women tend to have somewhat better verbal and social skills.
- Boys engage in more play-fighting, and usually prefer toy weapons and vehicles to dolls; girls engage in more play-*parenting*, and usually prefer dolls to weapons and vehicles.
- Males are more prone to ADHD, autism, and substance abuse; females are more prone to depression, anxiety, and most eating disorders.

Now, it's fair to say, I think, that a lot of people would bristle at this list. Many would argue that, leaving aside the undeniable physical and developmental differences, it's basically a compilation of antiquated stereotypes of the sexes: the kind of stereotypes that your drunken grandfather might spout at a family gathering while everyone cringes and stares at their shoes.

It is true that many of the claims are stereotypes, in the sense that they're widely held beliefs. It's also true that most of these stereotypes have been around for a long, long time. However, we can't just assume without checking that people's stereotypes are false. On the contrary, given how often most people interact with members of both sexes, we might expect that sex stereotypes will tend to be accurate. More than that, we might argue that the mere existence and persistence of the stereotypes constitutes suggestive evidence that the differences they depict are real – especially given that they're remarkably similar from culture to culture.[4]

Fortunately, we don't need to rely on intuition here. We now have more than a century's worth of research on sex differences, and we've mapped out the territory quite well – much better, in fact, than most people realize.[5] And contrary to the view that the unwashed masses are simply hallucinating the differences, many of your granddad's stereotypes turn out to be surprisingly accurate. This is an example of a common phenomenon that the social psychologist Lee Jussim dubbed *stereotype accuracy*.[6]

Sure, plenty of people exaggerate the size of the differences. But at least as many do the reverse: They *underestimate* how much men and women differ. And the average stereotype of both sexes tends to be close to the mark.[7]

A Typology of Sex Differences

Next question: How big are the sex differences in our species? By way of an answer, let me introduce a three-part typology which will help organize our later discussion.

1. **Mars-and-Venus Sex Differences.** Named after John Gray's pop-psychology book *Men Are from Mars, Women Are from Venus*, Mars-and-Venus sex differences are close to dichotomous: Males are this way, females are that, and exceptions are virtually non-existent. The best examples in our species are physical traits such as penises and beards in men, and vaginas and lactation in women.
2. **Mars-and-Venus-Plus-Exceptions.** These are sex differences where most men possess one trait and most women possess another, but a non-trivial number of men and women are exceptions to the rule. Sexual orientation is a good example: Most men are primarily attracted to women, and most women primarily attracted to men, but exceptions – people who are primarily attracted to the same sex – are not especially rare.
3. **Fuzzy or Statistical Sex Differences.** These are differences involving

modest gaps in the average scores for each sex – that is, in the central tendencies of a broad distribution of scores – with the distribution for one sex overlapping substantially with that for the other. An example is the sex difference in life expectancy: The average life expectancy is higher for women than men, but both sexes die at every age, and plenty of men live longer than plenty of women.

Spoiler alert #1: Most human sex differences fall into bucket three; they involve modest discrepancies in the central tendencies of highly overlapping distributions. This is an important point, so I'll repeat it: *Most human sex differences involve modest discrepancies in the central tendencies of highly overlapping distributions*. These words are worth repeating because many misunderstandings about evolutionary psychology stem from a failure to appreciate this point. A lot of people, for instance – including both enemies of the field and overexcited fans alike – are convinced that, according to evolutionary psychologists, women are monogamous whereas men are promiscuous; women alone are choosy about their mates, whereas men will sleep with anything that moves; and men only care about a potential mate's looks, whereas women care only about the size of a man's wallet.

None of this is what evolutionary psychologists claim! *Both* sexes, in their view, have the psychological 'machinery' for long-term, committed relationships *and* for casual sex, and although men tend to be more interested than women in the latter, the sexes don't particularly differ in their interest in the former. *Both* sexes, not just women, are choosy about their committed, long-term partners; it's mainly only in early courtship and for casual liaisons that we see a difference between the sexes in choosiness. And *both* sexes, not just men, care a fair amount about a prospective partner's looks; men just care a little more, on average, in long-term, committed relationships (in casual relationships, women care at least as much as men).[8] Similar qualifications apply to caricatured versions of the rest of the standard-issue sex differences.

The Nature and Nurture of Sex Differences

Of course, to say that the sexes differ in certain ways is to say nothing about the causes of the differences. It's certainly not to say they're innate. Where, then, do the standard-issue sex differences come from?

This question turns out to be two questions rolled into one. Question number one is: To what extent are the differences due to nature, and to what extent to nurture? And the first thing to say about *this* is that learning, socialization, and culture clearly play a role in shaping the standard-issue sex differences. If they didn't – if the differences were entirely due to nature – they'd presumably be invariant across cultures and times, which they're not.

So, the issue isn't whether nurture is involved in shaping the differences; it's whether nurture is the whole story. Spoiler alert #2: For most of the sex differences we'll be discussing, the answer is a resounding no. As a complete explanation for the differences, the sociocultural approach has holes in it big enough to drive a gender-neutral truck through. Among other things, the differences often appear in an embryonic form early in the lifespan; they're found across cultures even when the culture pushes against them; they've been linked to prenatal hormonal exposure; and they're comparable to differences found in other species – species with a similar evolutionary backstory to our own. The convergence of these very different lines of evidence adds up to a near-watertight case that, when it comes to explaining most sex differences, nurture alone can't cut it. Nature matters as well.

So much for the first question. The second is: Given that there's an innate component, why? Where did it come from? This brings us to the heart of what I fell in love with all those years ago: the evolutionary explanation for differences between the sexes. Here's the gist. Although both sexes evolve to pass on their genes, the best way to do this sometimes differs for each sex. The main reason it differs is that, in most species, males can potentially produce more offspring than females. A male that has, say, three sexual partners in a breeding season could end up with three litters of offspring. A *female*, on the other hand, that has three sexual partners in a breeding season will probably end up with no more litters than she would if she'd only had one. This is largely because, in most species, females invest more time and resources into each new offspring they produce. In mammals, for instance, females get pregnant, females give birth, and females manufacture milk for the young. In contrast, males' contribution to the baby-making enterprise is often just a sperm donation.

The asymmetry in maximum offspring number turns out to be the key to unlocking the mystery of sex differences. The logic is easiest to see in highly sexually dimorphic species like peacocks and red deer. (*Sexual dimorphism* is biologist-speak for sex differences; *di* means 'two' and *morph* means 'form'.) In most dimorphic species, a minority of males sire the bulk of the offspring in any given mating season, whereas the majority sire few or even none. For males in this situation, any trait that increases their chances of being one of the lucky few that hits the reproductive jackpot is likely to be selected – in other words, the genes underlying the trait will tend to be passed on to more offspring than competing genes, causing the trait to become increasingly common over the generations. What kind of traits are we talking about? For peacocks, they include a huge, flashy tail to seduce the peahens; for red deer stags, they include a big, strong body and massive antlers to fight off rival males; and for many species, they include an unquenchable thirst for mates, a desire to show off to impress potential mates, and an aggressive disposition to motivate male–male combat over territory, status, and ultimately (you guessed it) mates.

For females, on the other hand, traits such as these are generally less useful, because females can't greatly increase the number of offspring they produce by mating with multiple partners. A better policy for females in most species is to be ultra-choosy about which males they mate with. Choosy females – females that hold out for males with the best genes or the healthiest tail feathers or the largest territories – are likely to have more surviving offspring than their less discerning sisters. As such, the genes underpinning their choosiness have a good chance of going viral in the gene pool.

To be clear, males and females aren't *thinking* about how to get their genes to go viral; they're just acting on their built-in desires. But why do they have those built-in desires in the first place? *That's* the question that the evolutionary approach aims to answer. The answer it gives is that it's because genes that happened to nudge development toward those outcomes typically found themselves copied into more new bodies, and eventually crowded out competing variants.

The Ape That Thought It Was a Peacock

In short, many common sex differences trace back to the maximum number of offspring that each sex can produce. This is the idea that really clicked for me on my honeymoon: the idea I fell in love with. If you're anything like I was when first encountering it, you've already started wondering about how this framework might apply to one particular species we both have a special connection to: our own. This turns out, however, to be a trickier question than it first appears.

Humans, you see, are oddities of the animal kingdom. In most species, females alone are choosy about their mates, while males alone compete for as many mates as possible. As a result, males evolve sexual ornaments like the peacock's tail, and weaponry like the deer's antlers. Humans aren't like that. We have what's called *mutual mate choice*: In our species, *both* sexes are choosy about their long-term mates, and *both* compete among themselves for the best mates on offer. For that reason, *both* sexes have their equivalents of the peacock's tail *and* the deer's antlers. Indeed, when it comes to physical attractiveness, *females* in our species have the larger 'peacock's tail': a reversal of the usual pattern found in nature.[9] It's all very weird.

Another important difference between us and most of our animal cousins is that sex differences in our species tend to be less pronounced and profound. This is an area where evolutionary psychologists sometimes go off the rails: They talk as if human sex differences are huge, when in general, they're relatively modest (emphasis on the 'relatively'). As I and my colleague Andrew Thomas have argued, this is because humans evolved to fall in love and form pair bonds, and because both sexes, rather than just the females, evolved to invest in their young.[10] This reproductive arrangement lowered the ceiling number of offspring that most men could produce, bringing it closer to the ceiling for women. And as that happened, it ushered in a corresponding reduction in the magnitude of sex differences in our species. Pair bonding and biparental care are rare in the animal kingdom, and especially among mammals. But they're not unique. In fact, in birds, they're the norm. This means that, in our primary approach to making babies, humans are more like the average bird than the average mammal.[11] Again: all very weird.

Now, don't get me wrong; men and women are clearly not carbon copies of each other. Some sex differences are genuinely large, including – unsurprisingly – the sex difference in whether one is primarily attracted to men or women. Many sex differences are modest throughout most of life, but large in early adulthood. And many sex differences are larger among the minority at the extremes than the majority in the middle: the shortest and tallest, for instance; the most aggressive and the least.[12] Still, when it comes to sexual dimorphism, humans are swimming in the shallow end of the pool compared to most of our fellow mammals. And rather than contradicting an evolutionary explanation for the differences, that's exactly what an evolutionary explanation predicts for us, given our penchant for pair bonding and biparental care.[13]

The War on Sex Differences

The evolutionary explanation for sex differences is deeply satisfying in the way that the best scientific theories always are – *if*, that is, you're not horrified by the idea of evolved sex differences. As mentioned already, though, some people are genuinely horrified. Many suffer from what we might call *dimorphism dysphoria*: They're deeply uncomfortable with the suggestion that men and women differ above the neck, and especially with the possibility that the differences might come from nature rather than nurture.

This discomfort underlies what I call the *war on sex differences*. This 'war' – yes, it's an overstatement – can be seen in every nook and cranny of modern life, from parents fretting about their daughter's love of dolls, to bans on gender stereotypes in children's textbooks and ads on TV, to efforts to achieve a 50:50 sex ratio in every desirable profession where men outnumber women. In fact, as I'm writing these words, even the grammar checker on my word processor is getting in on the act: Whenever I use the phrase 'men and women', it warns me that I should avoid these gendered terms, and consider using 'people' instead. Not a helpful suggestion when I'm writing a book about sex differences . . .

In certain circles, then, sex differences are about as welcome as the plague. Needless to say, not everyone feels this way; if they did, there'd be nothing for those who *do* feel this way to wage war on. And as I pointed out earlier, some people lean in the opposite direction: Rather than playing down or denying the differences, they hype them up and moralize them. Thus, as we dig deeper into these issues, it would be useful to equip ourselves with some technical terms to help bring order to the chaos.

We'll start with a pair of terms coined by the psychologists Rachel Hare-Mustin and Jeanne Marecek, who argued that two major biases distort the discussion of sex differences: the *alpha bias* and the *beta bias*.[14] The alpha bias is the tendency to exaggerate sex differences; the beta bias is the tendency to minimize them. Both can be found in the culture, but it's fair to say, I think, that in the modern Western world, the beta bias has the upper hand.

Nowhere is this truer than in my own natural habitat of academia. Many academics are wary of sex differences, and some have an intellectual allergy to them.[15] According to an old joke, everyone knows that men and women are different . . . except social scientists.[16] Plenty of research reveals the truth in the jest. One study, for instance, found that social scientists are more likely than civilians to chalk up sex differences to nurture rather than nature, and that this even extends to differences between hens and roosters.[17] As we'll see later, even when it comes to humans, the evidence sides with the civilians, making this one area where laypeople have a firmer grasp on reality than many alleged experts – and one area where academia seems to impair people's understanding of the world rather than improving it.

Certainly, in some corners of the academy, sex differences are sexy, and we find the alpha bias rather than the beta. This is true, I have to say, of my own field of evolutionary psychology.[18] But evolutionary psychology is an outlier, and in general, the beta bias rules the roost.[19]

I'll give you an example. When psychologists and psychology textbook writers discuss sex differences in brain, mind, or behaviour, they're usually quick to stress that most of the differences are small, that individual differences within each sex dwarf the average differences between them, and that overlap between the sexes is enormous. Most of the time, this is true. The problem, however, is that it's also true of the vast majority of findings in psychology, and yet the warning label is only ever attached to the sex differences.[20] Why? Presumably because those issuing the warnings want to downplay the differences. It's a risky game, though; if sex differences are too small to matter, then most findings in psychology are too small to matter, because most fall within a similar range.[21] And although most sex differences are small, some, as I've mentioned, are large: among the largest effects in psychology. *That* little factoid rarely gets much airtime. But it should. After all, while it's clearly possible to overestimate the differences, it's also possible to underestimate them. The fact that psychologists tend to warn against the former but not the latter suggests that the motivation is to minimize the differences, rather than just get the estimates right.

For a neutral observer, the distaste for sex differences might seem somewhat perplexing. For the bulk of human history, most people accepted that the sexes were different, and weren't the slightest bit perturbed by it. Today, many people *are* perturbed – perturbed enough, in some cases, that they'd happily banish from polite society anyone who floats the idea. How can we explain this?

The short answer, I think, is politics. The influence of politics can be seen in the fact that, while academics generally exhibit the beta bias, on certain topics, they mysteriously become immune to it. The gender pay gap is a case in point. Rarely do academics feel a compunction to point out that the gender pay gap is relatively modest these days, that variation in earnings within each sex dwarfs the average difference between them, and that overlap in men's and women's earnings is vast. But if variation and overlap imply that sex differences in brain, mind, and behaviour aren't really real or important, they equally imply that sex differences in *earnings* aren't really real or important – and the same for sex differences in power, privilege, and many other areas central to the activist worldview. The inconsistency in the treatment of the gaps has a political explanation, not a scientific one: The overlap argument is levelled selectively against differences the levellers want to minimize.

Many exceptions to the beta-bias rule can be captured by adding two further biases to our list: the *gamma bias* and the *delta bias*, both proposed by the psychologists Martin Seager and John Barry.[22] The gamma bias has two parts. The first is the tendency to highlight sex differences that put women in a better light than men, while minimizing those that do the opposite. No one's too bothered, for instance, by the idea that women are better multitaskers than men, but they would be if the difference went the other way. (Women probably *aren't* better multitaskers, by the way; both sexes are fairly atrocious at multitasking.) In my own research, I've found that people rate fictitious studies showing that men draw better, lie less, or are more intelligent than women as lower in quality, more harmful, and more worthy of being censored than otherwise identical studies showing that women do better than men in these domains.[23]

The second part of the gamma bias is the tendency to highlight gender gaps where women are disadvantaged and need assistance, but to minimize those where men are. An example is the tendency to treat sexual victimization and intimate partner abuse as problems only ever suffered by women, when in fact a significant minority of victims are men.[24] In such cases, ironically, the same people who usually downplay sex differences flip the script and greatly exaggerate them.

So, that's the gamma bias. The delta bias, in contrast, involves disparaging traditional sex differences but praising non-traditional ones: Sleeping around is bad when men do it, for instance, but wonderful when women do – and vice versa for stay-at-home parenting. As with the gamma bias, the influence of the delta bias can be seen in the scientific literature. One example concerns research on leadership aspirations. Analyses of publication bias suggest that psychologists are happy to publish papers finding that women have stronger leadership aspirations than men, but often leave papers finding the reverse languishing in the file drawer, unpublished and unacknowledged.[25]

Where do the gamma bias and delta bias come from? One possibility is that they stem from our growing awareness of the historical mistreatment of women and our desire to put things right. Another is that they reflect a deep-seated tendency to be more concerned about girls' and women's welfare than boys' and men's. And a third possibility is that it's a combination of both: perhaps the latter amplified by the former.[26] Regardless of the ultimate answer, however, the war on sex differences is primarily a war on *traditional* sex differences and differences favouring men. See Table 1 for an overview of the four biases discussed in this section.

Table 1 Four Biases That Distort Our Understanding of Sex Differences

Bias	Description
Alpha Bias	The tendency to exaggerate sex differences
Beta Bias	The tendency to minimize sex differences
Gamma Bias	The tendency to minimize sex differences that put men in a better light or imply male disadvantage, while highlighting those that do the opposite
Delta Bias	An aversion to traditional sex differences, and a preference for the reverse

Again, I don't want to overstate the antipathy to sex differences; if there weren't academics researching the topic, I wouldn't have the source material to write this book. At the same time, though, we also shouldn't *underplay* the antipathy. When it comes to sex differences, the attitude is often 'Don't go there'. In some cases, people may quietly accept that the sexes differ in certain ways, but feel that it's rude to point it out, just as it's rude to point out that someone's put on a little weight. In other cases, people may doubt the differences and find themselves uncomfortable with the whole topic, but grudgingly accept that people have the right to explore it. But then there's a third, more extreme reaction. A vocal minority see positing sex differences as more than a mere faux pas or difference of opinion, and view it instead as a moral transgression. For individuals in this camp, the idea that the sexes are naturally identical has become a sacred belief. Disagreement is seen not as an honest mistake or interesting challenge to be evaluated, but as sacrilege. And the typical response to sacrilege isn't a tolerant appreciation of the wonderful diversity of human lifeways: 'Well, I'm not *personally* into sacrilege, but if other people are, who am I to judge?' Instead, the typical response is to censor, to silence, to cancel, punish, and shun.[27]

This can make doing research on sex differences somewhat uncomfortable: You're never quite sure when a claim you've made in an article or interview will come back and explode in your face. Everyone working in the area knows about the scandals involving former Harvard president Lawrence Summers, former Google programmer James Damore, and former Harvard professor Carole Hooven: all 'former' because they challenged certain sacred shibboleths related to sex and gender. And everyone knows that, if they're not careful, they might be next in the firing line. I've always tried to write carefully and sensitively on this subject, but I've still managed to accumulate some war stories. For example, an academic paper I wrote with Lewis Halsey about sex differences in STEM sparked a minor online controversy and got me reported to my university's diversity, equity, and inclusion (DEI) administrators.[28] I was lucky; the complainants had misrepresented the paper, and in any case, the university has strong protections for academic freedom. But the story doesn't always end so happily. Shortly after that little kerfuffle, a course on human nature and politics at Sciences Po university in Paris, which showcased work by myself, David Buss, Nicholas Christakis, Jonathan Haidt, Steven Pinker, Michael Shermer, and others, was cancelled after a small number of students complained (most apparently loved it).[29] I know I'm not alone among sex differences researchers in wondering sometimes whether I should have stuck to a less controversial topic . . . like politics or religion. I joke, of course, but this *is* a serious problem. If we want to make the world a better place, we need good science – but that's impossible if scientists are afraid to diverge from the pre-specified conclusions of an academic political monoculture.[30]

Are Sex Differences Sexist?

We've got several elephants in the room already. We'll get to them all eventually. For now, though – and to postpone being cancelled till at least Chapter 9 – let's address the largest elephant: sexism.

For many people, generalizations about the sexes are inherently sexist. The main reason, I suspect, is a concern that such generalizations inevitably imply that one sex is inferior to the other. More precisely, the concern is that they imply that *women* are inferior: a possible example of the gamma bias. This would be bad enough at the best of times, but attributing the differences to evolution makes it a thousand times worse. After all, if the differences are natural in any sense, argue the critics, that would imply that they're good – or if not good, then permissible, or if not permissible, that we're stuck with them till the end of the world. Long story short, evolutionary explanations for sex differences clash with the goals of feminism, and threaten to roll back the progress of women.

Of course, even if evolutionary explanations really did have these terrible implications, that wouldn't imply that they're false. Reality is under no obligation to conform to the way we want it to be. Fortunately, however, evolutionary explanations don't have these terrible implications.

Before exploring why not, it's only fair to acknowledge that people's concerns about these issues don't just come out of nowhere. Our species has a long history of seeing women as inferior, and such views have sometimes infected our science. The most jarring example that I know comes from a nineteenth-century French scientist named Gustave Le Bon, who wrote that, sure, *some* women are as intellectually distinguished as the average man, but such women are as rare as two-headed gorillas so can basically be ignored.[31] And not only do we have a long history of holding sexist beliefs of this kind, we have a long history of using arguments from nature to justify keeping women down. The most jarring example of *this* that I know comes from Napoleon Bonaparte, who reportedly stated that, 'Nature has made [women] our slaves . . . [T]hey are nothing but machines for producing children.'[32] With a track record like this, it's easy to see why people are wary of evolutionary explanations for sex differences. The fear is that they'll put us on a slippery slope to seeing intellectually distinguished women as two-headed gorillas, and treating all women, one-headed or two, as mere child-producing machines.

But like I say, the idea that evolutionary explanations support such a scenario is entirely misguided. For a start, even if it were true that the science shows that women are inferior to men in certain domains, or that women are naturally better suited to certain traditional roles, this wouldn't imply that these things are good or even inevitable. The idea that it *would* involves two common fallacies of reasoning. The first is the *naturalistic fallacy*: the fallacy of assuming that what's natural is necessarily good. This assumption is fallacious because, outside certain theological worldviews, we have precisely zero reason to equate *natural* with *good*, or *unnatural* with *bad*. Indeed, much that we consider bad is perfectly natural – think famine, disease, and death – while much that we consider good goes explicitly against nature: think medicine, flood barriers, and extending our moral concern beyond family, tribe, and species. No one should be taking their moral marching orders from the whims of natural selection. On the contrary, doing the right thing often involves actively resisting selection's diktats.[33]

That's all very well and good, you might say, but it's of little consolation if resistance is futile, and we're stuck with the hand that natural selection dealt us. This brings us to our second fallacy, which I call the *fixed-forever fallacy*. Contrary to widespread opinion, the fact that a trait or sex difference has an evolutionary origin doesn't imply that it's immutable. My favourite way to capture this idea is to say that *our genes push us in certain directions, but our genes aren't the only things shaping us, and thus we can often push right back*. Admittedly, pushing back might not always be easy, and in some cases, we might decide that, on balance, we shouldn't do it – not because it goes against nature, but because it would do more harm than good. Still, the fact remains that an evolutionary perspective doesn't imply that change is impossible. And if we decide that we do want to change things, we're more likely to succeed if we understand their true origins than if we bury our heads in the sand.

So, even if the science of sex differences really did show that women are inferior, this might not be the end of the world. The good news, however, is that the science of sex differences absolutely *doesn't* show that women are inferior. Several arguments converge on this conclusion, but perhaps the most important is the idea that *differences don't imply deficiencies*. As sex differences expert Diane Halpern put it, everyone agrees that men's and women's genitals are different, but no one would argue that either sex's genitals are *superior*.[34] The same applies to many psychological sex differences.

As soon as we absorb this point, the whole debate starts to look very different. Many argue that it's sexist to say, for example, that women are more parental than men, or that women are more interested in working with people and less interested in working with things. But the accusation can be turned on its head. The idea that such claims are sexist only makes sense if we tacitly assume that the female-typical tendencies are inferior. Why else would it be disparaging to women to say that more women than men exhibit these tendencies? But if women really are more parental than men, or if they really are more interested in working with people, then we're taking a negative view of traits that are more characteristic of women than men.[35] *That's* sexist! It implies that we don't accept or respect women as they actually are. It's also *androcentric*: It treats men as the measure of all human beings – the yardstick against which women should be judged.[36] Ironically, this is exactly what the feminist philosopher Simone de Beauvoir railed against in her book *The Second Sex*, one of the founding documents of second-wave feminism.[37]

There's another irony here as well. We live in an age where, quite rightly, we encourage people to accept and celebrate differences and diversity, and yet we get outraged whenever anyone points any out. Not exactly tolerance of diversity! Get it tattooed on your forehead: Differences are not deficiencies.

Or at any rate, they're not *necessarily* deficiencies. One response to this argument might be to say, fine, when it comes to preferences and tastes, differences don't imply deficiencies. But when it comes to abilities and talents, or to traits that are universally valued or despised, differences may indeed imply deficiencies. In fact, this is virtually true by definition. It's the idea that the sexes might differ in traits like these that keeps a lot of people up at night. To be more precise, it's again the idea that women might come off worse in such comparisons. As Halpern observes, the unspoken, somewhat sexist assumption is that 'if the truth were known, females would be found to be "less" – less smart, less able, less strong, or less of whatever society values'.[38] She calls this the *women-have-less fallacy*.

And it *is* a fallacy. To begin with, for many important traits, men and women don't particularly differ. There are no average sex differences in IQ, for instance (much to the surprise and disappointment of both sexes).[39] And where the sexes do differ on valued traits, women come out on top at least as often as men. Men have a slight edge on most tests of spatial ability; women have a slight edge on most tests of verbal ability and social skills. Men are physically stronger; women have stronger immune systems and live longer. Men throw better; women have better fine-motor control.[40] All in all, the science of sex differences doesn't have an axe to grind with women.

Indeed, if anything, it has an axe to grind with men. I remember a male student in one of my evolutionary psychology courses complaining during a class discussion that, in every lecture, he had to endure a long litany of negative generalizations about men: They're more likely to be unfaithful, they're more prone to violence, they're less involved parents, and so on. He had a point, although again, the fact that the news is unwelcome doesn't mean the news isn't true. What the complaint does highlight, however, is that if evolutionary psychology paints a more negative picture of either sex, it's not necessarily women – not, at least, unless you think that infidelity and violence are good things, whereas being a good parent is bad.

In a sense, though, the whole discussion is moot. If sex differences are sexist, then reality is sexist, because sex differences are real. Those who don't like this need to take it up with Mother Nature, not with the scientists reporting on Mother Nature's handiwork. Those scientists might not like the differences any more than you do. And whether they like them or not, the differences aren't their fault, any more than the morning news is the fault of the journalists who write the headlines.

We Need to Talk About Sex Differences

Let me indulge a brief fantasy: Everyone who reads the last section agrees with every last word I wrote. In this fantasy world – this wonderful utopia – would the critics of sex differences research hang up their hats and withdraw their opposition, their concerns about the research allayed?

Probably not. Many would still worry that, even if my rebuttals are correct in principle, not everyone will get the memo, and claims about sex differences will continue to have pernicious effects. Most people will exaggerate the differences, and many will also moralize them, treating them as goals or ideals rather than mere statistical generalizations. We know they will because we know that, throughout history, people have routinely done just that. And we know as well that, throughout history, exaggerating and moralizing sex differences has had extremely harmful consequences.

You might be surprised to hear that I agree: People all too easily exaggerate and moralize sex differences, and doing so produces many harms. It creates social pressure to conform to exaggerated stereotypes of the sexes, and intolerance of those who don't: stay-at-home dads, women who put career before kids, and other gender rebels. It leads us to discriminate against women and against men, treating them not as individuals but as instantiations of the statistical properties of their sex. It leads us to overlook or stigmatize gender-atypical problems, such as ADHD, autism, and drug abuse in females, and depression, eating disorders, and sexual victimization in males.[41] And it leads us to underestimate the extent to which gender gaps in society are still shaped by bias and barriers, thus failing to identify remaining injustices that could otherwise be dismantled.[42]

Given these very real harms, the question many people have is this: What the hell are we doing? Why would we want to risk talking about and researching sex differences?

It's a good question, but I think I've got a good answer. In fact, I think I've got two. The first is that even though the risks are real, the sexes *do* differ on average, and we can't just lie about that. What we should do instead is *tell the truth carefully*. We should emphasize at every turn that the gaps are generally modest, that they're rarely set in stone, and that they're statistical trends, not life goals or moral imperatives.[43]

My second answer is that exaggerating and moralizing sex differences isn't the only mistake on the menu, and isn't the only mistake that causes harm. Minimizing and denying sex differences – or moralizing the *absence* of sex differences – can cause various harms as well. It creates social pressure to *reject* traditional gender roles, effectively replacing one gender straitjacket with an equally restrictive unisex or gender-role-reversed one. It leads to failures of cross-sex mindreading that create unforced errors in our dating lives, family lives, and work lives. It leads us to overlook physical and mental-health problems that manifest differently in one sex than the other, including heart attacks, autism, and ADHD in females, and depression and anxiety in males.[44] It leads to misguided practices such as testing drugs on men only, thereby potentially putting women's lives at risk.[45] It hobbles our ability to solve our most pressing social problems by blunting our understanding of the true causes of those problems; as policymakers like to say: *Wrong diagnosis, wrong cure*. And it leads us to *overestimate* the role of gender bias in shaping the modern world, with downstream harms such as pouring time and money into interventions that don't work, pressuring people to make life choices that don't mesh well with their preferences, and inadvertently reversing the direction of discrimination rather than eliminating discrimination altogether.[46]

With dangers of erring in either direction, how can we navigate a safe passage through the minefield? I hope the answer is obvious. We have no responsible choice but to take a Goldilocks approach to the issue, striving to walk the thin pink-and-blue line between exaggerating and minimizing sex differences: the alpha bias and the beta. Once again, if we want to make the world a better place, our best bet is to ensure that our picture of the world is accurate.

What Should We Do About Sex Differences?

Of course, making the world a better place involves more than just establishing accurate knowledge. We also need to decide what we're going to do with that knowledge once it's in our possession. How, in other words, should we deal with sex differences?

As I see it, there are three main approaches. I call them *gender-role traditionalism*, *gender-role progressivism*, and *gender-role individualism*.

1. **Gender-Role Traditionalism**. Sex differences are natural and good, and thus ought to be preserved and protected. If society starts deviating from the gender roles bequeathed to us by God or nature, we should make every effort to restore things to their natural state, just as we'd restore a broken bone to its natural state by putting it in a cast.

2. **Gender-Role Progressivism**. Gender gaps in society have nothing to do with inherent differences between the sexes, and everything to do with discrimination and sexist socialization. As such, we should make every effort to wipe all sex differences from the face of the planet – or even to reverse them to make up for past injustices.
3. **Gender-Role Individualism**. We shouldn't seek to impose any gender outcome on the world. We should instead seek to establish a level playing field, then let the gender outcomes set themselves as an emergent effect of individuals making informed decisions about what would suit them best.[47] Unless sex differences are products of discrimination or cause demonstrable harm, progressives have no more right to eliminate them than traditionalists have to enlarge them.

The science of human sex differences can't tell us which approach is best, because that's ultimately a matter of values rather than facts. But it can help us to evaluate the empirical assumptions associated with each position. And it turns out that both the traditionalist and progressive positions butt heads with the modern science.

To start with, contrary to gender-role traditionalists, sex differences in our species tend to be fairly modest, and exceptions to the rule are not especially exceptional. As a result, insisting that everyone conform to an off-the-rack gender role for their sex inevitably means that some people will be forced into roles that don't suit them, or excluded from roles that do. That's unlikely to be a recipe for happiness.

At the same time, contrary to gender-role progressives, sex differences are not just products of discrimination and socialization; nature plays a part as well. For that reason, some differences may never be completely eradicated – not, at any rate, without draconian interventions that limit people's freedom and potentially make them miserable. Such interventions may be modern-day equivalents of earlier efforts to force gay people to be straight or left-handers to use their right hands: a progressive form of conversion therapy. Like it or not, in some cases, we may need to learn to live with the differences.

In fact, in some cases, we might even positively welcome them. Sex differences, you see, are often larger, rather than smaller, in societies with better living standards and greater gender equality.[48] Yes, you read that correctly: *Sex differences are often larger, rather than smaller, in societies with better living standards and greater gender equality* – perhaps because in nations meeting those specs, people have more opportunity to pursue their own interests and do what suits them best. This raises the intriguing possibility that, rather than being indicators of a sexist or oppressive society, sex differences may sometimes be indicators of the opposite: a comparatively free and fair one (emphasis on the 'comparatively').[49]

As you've probably guessed, my preferred approach is gender-role individualism. The spirit of this approach can be captured in just four words: Let people be themselves! If they defy traditional gender norms, that's fine. But if they *conform* to traditional gender norms, that's fine too. In the absence of harm or injustice, we should let people do their own thing.

That's not to say, however, that we should just do nothing. On the contrary, we should do everything we can to eliminate bias and barriers, to introduce everyone to every option, and to empower people to pursue whatever options they prefer. Importantly, though, having done this, we should respect men's and women's decisions about their own lives and how they want to live them, even if this doesn't result in gender parity in every area – *or* result in traditional, non-overlapping gender roles.[50] People are ultimately going to be happier if they can chart their own course through life.

With these cautions and qualifications in mind, we're ready to take the next step in our journey. If we really want to get to grips with sex differences, we should probably know exactly what we mean by 'sex' and exactly what we mean by 'differences'. That's what we'll tackle in Chapter 2.

2
What's the Difference?
The Landscape of Human Sex Differences

What Are We Talking About?

Imagine you've signed up to be a participant in a psychology experiment. You're sitting outside the lab, waiting to be called in, when another participant arrives, sits down next to you, and strikes up a conversation. After a few minutes of pleasant chit-chat, a head appears from behind the lab door, and a research assistant invites you in. 'Guess what?' says the assistant, guiding you to a small cubicle. 'The experiment has already begun. We're interested in people's memories of everyday events. The person you were talking to outside is actually another research assistant, pretending to be a participant. We now want to know how much you remember about them.' The assistant then gives you a pop quiz about the person and your interaction.

How well do you think you'd do? Perhaps you'd remember the colour of the person's shoes or their eyes – but perhaps not; maybe you didn't notice. Perhaps you'd remember the first thing the two of you talked about – but again perhaps not; maybe it slipped your mind. One thing, however, that you'd almost certainly notice and remember is the person's sex: whether they were female or male. It would be a rare person indeed who didn't – who, when quizzed about it later, said 'You know what? I don't remember if the person was a man or a woman. I don't think I noticed.' Almost everyone does notice, immediately and automatically. In a sexually reproducing species, it would be surprising if it were otherwise.

But what exactly is it that we're noticing? What, in other words, defines *female* and *male*? We know that the sexes must differ in some ways, because if they didn't, we could never tell them apart. What does it mean, though, to say that they differ? And are the differences large, small, or somewhere in between?

These are the questions we'll address in this chapter. In doing so, we'll remain steadfastly agnostic about where the differences come from. So, if you find yourself thinking 'Yes, but these differences could all be due to learning and culture' – you're right; they could be! In fact, learning and culture are almost always a big part of the story. But are the differences *just* due to learning and culture? That's a question for later.

What Is Sex?

We've all got a good working knowledge of what the words *female* and *male* mean. We rarely make mistakes in deploying these concepts. But as with most of our words, few of us have explicit definitions of the terms. We're pointing at something with *female* and *male*, but that something is shrouded in fog. Let's do some defogging. What exactly defines sex?

This turns out to be a difficult question. To answer it, I propose we run through a series of possible definitions, ruling out those that don't make sense, and making our way in the process to one that does.

A logical place to start would be to ask how we identify people's sex in everyday life. And the answer, of course, is that we do so via immediately observable attributes such as facial appearance, body shape, voice pitch, clothes, and hairstyles. Here, then, is our first attempt at a definition: Sex is defined by attributes such as these.

Could this definition work? I won't beat around the bush; the answer is a definite no. The most obvious problem with it is that humans aren't the only animals that come in female and male varieties – most do – and yet no other animal exhibits the same sex differences as us in facial appearance, body shape, or voice pitch, let alone in clothing or hairstyles. This tells us something important, namely that we need to draw a distinction between traits that enable us to *identify* members of a category and traits that *constitute* the category in the first place. Hairstyles and the rest help us to identify people's sex, but they don't define what sex is. We need to dig deeper.

At this point, a lot of people leap to the conclusion that sex is defined by certain anatomical features usually hidden beneath our sex-specific clothing – most notably, penises for males and vaginas for females. This is a big improvement on our first definition, if for no other reason than that it doesn't just apply to humans. Again, though, we're still not home and dry. That's because, although *many* species have these gadgets, most do not. In only 3% of birds, for instance, do the males come equipped with penises.[1] In the rest, both sexes have a unisex opening called a *cloaca*, which they press together during mating in a manoeuvre known rather charmingly as a *cloacal kiss*. Nonetheless, the 97% of penis-free birds still have females and males, as do most species bereft of penises. Odd though it might sound, penises and vaginas, no less than clothing and hairstyles, are *indicators* of sex in some species, rather than defining characteristics in all.

Perhaps now you're getting impatient. 'Obviously', you might want to say, 'sex is defined by sex chromosomes: XX for females, and XY for males.' I sympathize with the impatience, but unfortunately this doesn't cut it either. Not all species with sexes have the XX/XY system. Our friends the birds, for instance, have a ZZ/ZW system: Individuals with two Z chromosomes develop into males, whereas individuals with a Z and a W develop into females. Other groups depart even more radically from the XX/XY protocol. For example, in most ants, bees, and wasps, fertilized eggs develop into females, while unfertilized eggs develop into males. (This has the rather bizarre consequence that males have grandfathers but not fathers, and that virgin births are commonplace.) More than that, many species dispense with chromosomal sex determination altogether. In many turtles and crocodilians, for instance, sex is determined by the temperature of the egg: Warm eggs develop into males; cold eggs develop into females – or vice versa, depending on the species. What all of this tells us is that XX and XY don't define sex any more than do fertilized vs unfertilized or warm vs cold. Instead, XX and XY are part of the mechanism guiding the *development* of sex in some species.

Feeling confused? Well, the good news is that biologists long ago found the definitive answer to the question 'What is sex?' and it turns out to be quite straightforward. What's the one thing that females and males can do together that they can't do on their own or with members of the same sex? The answer, of course, is that they can produce offspring via sexual reproduction. And what do all females and all males contribute to offspring, regardless of whether they're humans, birds, butterflies, or even plants? The answer is that they contribute sex cells, also known as *gametes*. Now the important point. In the vast majority of sexually reproducing species, gametes come in two distinct forms: large and small. The large ones are called eggs; the small ones are called sperm. In some species, individual organisms make both types of gametes. In many, though – including most animals – individuals come in two distinct types: one specializing in eggs, and the other in sperm. And *that's* how biologists define sex. Individuals designed to produce eggs during the reproductive phase of life are females; individuals designed to produce *sperm* during the reproductive phase of life are males. End of story.

The gamete definition of sex is the only definition that works for all sexually reproducing species. And it clears up a lot of confusion. How do we know that XX mammals, ZW birds, and honeybees born from fertilized eggs are all female? Simple: Because they all produce eggs. How do we know that *XY* mammals, *ZZ* birds, and honeybees born from *unfertilized* eggs are all male? Simple again: Because they all produce sperm. We sometimes assume that female mammals are female because they have XX chromosomes, whereas male mammals are male because they have XY chromosomes. But it's the other way around: XX chromosomes are female chromosomes because they give rise to female mammals – mammals that produce eggs – whereas XY chromosomes are male chromosomes because they give rise to male mammals: mammals that produce sperm. The same applies to female vs male sex organs, hormones, and sex-typical behaviour: We only know which are female and which are male because of their association with either egg production or sperm production, respectively.

And there's nothing arbitrary about putting gametes at the centre of the definition, above sex chromosomes, sex organs, sex hormones, and other sex-linked traits. On the contrary, the fact that gametes come in two basic types is the ultimate explanation for the fact that the sexes *have* different sex chromosomes, sex organs, and sex hormones to begin with: All these attributes evolved to facilitate reproduction via either eggs or sperm. Whichever way you cut it, sex is ultimately about gametes.

The Case for the Sex Binary

We've now got definitions of *female* and *male* that work not only for human beings, but for every sexually reproducing species on the planet. We can't rest on our laurels just yet, though. In pursuing these definitions, we've assumed without question the validity of the female–male distinction and the binary concept of sex. Some, however, question this assumption. The questioners fall into two main camps: reformers and abolitionists. Reformers want to preserve the concept of sex but reconceptualize it as a spectrum rather than a binary. Abolitionists want to dismantle and discard it; in their view, *female* and *male* are merely arbitrary social constructs, or even ideological impositions of Western colonial powers designed to justify bias.[2] The common core of both positions is the conviction that the simple female–male binary is no longer fit for purpose.

At first glance – and, as we'll see, at later glances as well – this all seems rather implausible. Every culture has the concepts of *female* and *male*, and every language has synonyms for words assuming these concepts: *boy* and *girl*, *man* and *woman*, *aunt* and *uncle*.[3] Sure, some cultures also have categories for people who don't quite fit the expectations associated with their sex. But all have the Big Two categories of *female* and *male*. The most plausible explanation for this cross-cultural universality is that the categories track something real in nature, which people everywhere find it useful to track. And not just people! Other animals, including dogs and elephants, spontaneously categorize humans in terms of these supposedly arbitrary social constructs.[4]

Still, to be fair to the critics of sex, several lines of evidence do seem to challenge the validity of the female–male distinction. Let's consider three. We'll start with what are called *intersex conditions*. These are anomalies of sexual development in which individuals have a mixture of female-typical and male-typical traits. Perhaps the most striking example is a condition known as *complete androgen insensitivity syndrome* or *CAIS*. (Androgens are hormones like testosterone that, although found in both sexes, have higher levels in males, and play a central role in male development.) People with CAIS have XY sex chromosomes and (undescended) testicles pumping out testosterone. Normally, people with this setup would develop male-typical bodies. However, the cells of people with CAIS are completely unresponsive to testosterone, so they develop *female*-typical bodies instead. In fact, because most females produce *some* testosterone, and because most females' cells *are* responsive to this hormone, people with CAIS are in some ways more feminine than most females, despite their XY chromosomes: They often have no body hair, for instance, and virtually no body odour.

Intersex conditions aren't just found in humans. A particularly memorable nonhuman example, seen in some birds, insects, and crustaceans, is *bilateral gynandromorphism*. For individuals with this syndrome, one half of the body develops as male, while the other develops as female. In gynandromorphic cardinals, for instance, one half has the colourful courtship plumage of the male, while the other has the low-key camouflage gear of the female. Similarly, in gynandromorphic stag beetles, one half has the antler-like mandibles of the male, while the other has the more modest and practical mandibles of the female. According to the critics of sex, whether in birds, insects, or humans, intersex conditions pull the rug out from underneath the binary concept of sex.

That's the first challenge. The second comes from a fascinating group of species known as *hermaphrodites*. Hermaphrodites come in two flavours: simultaneous and sequential. Simultaneous hermaphrodites are species where each individual produces both eggs and sperm, rather than one or the other. Earthworms, slugs, and most snails are simultaneous hermaphrodites, as are a large majority of plants. *Sequential* hermaphrodites, in contrast, are species where each individual has just one sex but, at a certain point in the lifecycle, some undergo a spontaneous sex change. Clownfish are the poster boys of sequential hermaphroditism – or rather, they're the poster *boys* at birth, but the poster *women* in later life. All clownfish, you see, start out as males, but then some later change into females. Specifically, when the group's current alpha female dies, the highest-ranking adult male transforms into a female: the new alpha. Nemo from the movie *Finding Nemo* was a clownfish; if the movie had been ethologically accurate, then when Nemo's mum was killed by a barracuda, his father would have turned into his mother and taken one of the remaining males as her new mate. Strangely, the filmmakers skipped over this detail of clownfish life history.

You might be wondering why this kind of thing doesn't happen in our species or any other mammal. Why, for example, don't all gorillas start life as females, then metamorphosize into silverbacks when they're large enough to fight for a harem? The answer is that the sexes are too differentiated in mammals, and the plumbing is much too complex.[5] Nonetheless, according to the critics of sex, the fact that sequential hermaphroditism happens at all is another challenge to the traditional sex binary.

The third and final challenge is that, in virtually every species, we see enormous variation within each sex – more, the critics argue, than our binary sex concepts can accommodate. The best examples are species where there are more than just two basic types. In bluegill sunfish, for instance, we see one type of female but *three* types of male: big parental males who defend a territory and a harem of females; small sneaker males who lurk near the outskirts of the big male's territory and occasionally zip in to fertilize some of the females' eggs; and medium-sized female mimics who, because they look like females, can easily infiltrate the harem and fertilize some eggs without risking the wrath of the dominant male. Distinct male morphs are rare among mammals. As it happens, though, they're found in one of our closest living relatives, the orangutans. Male orangutans come in two types: giant males with long hair and decorative cheek flanges, and smaller 'Peter Pan' males, stuck in a kind of perpetual adolescence for as long as there's a giant male in the area.

You've probably noticed that, with both the bluegills and the orangutans, I'm still talking about just two sexes: female and male. The critics, however, would argue that this arbitrarily shoehorns non-binary variation into a binary mould. Why not say that bluegills have four sexes, whereas orangutans have three? And although distinct morphs provide a particularly attention-grabbing version of the challenge, the general argument applies even to boring species like our own, which only have two basic morphs. In all such species, we see a huge amount of diversity within each so-called sex. Forcing that diversity into just two categories doesn't do it justice.

So, we've got three challenges to the sex binary: intersex conditions, hermaphrodites, and within-sex variation. For anyone who thinks that the female–male distinction is an unassailable fact of nature, all of this should make their heads explode.

Or should it? Time to stress-test the arguments. First question: Do intersex individuals undermine the female–male distinction? First answer: No. On the contrary, it's only possible to even *describe* intersex conditions if we *assume* the female–male distinction. Intersex conditions are, after all, defined as involving a mixture of female- and male-typical attributes. To be fair, these conditions do show that not every *individual* can easily be categorized as female or male. The vast majority can – 99.98% in our species, according to one estimate – but not everyone.[6] Still, intersex conditions don't undermine the claim that there are only two sexes. Why not? Because intersex individuals don't produce a third type of gamete, and thus aren't a third sex (or a fourth or a fifth sex).

What about hermaphroditic species? Do they undermine the female–male distinction? They don't. As with intersex conditions, rather than upending the distinction, the very concept of hermaphroditism assumes it. Simultaneous hermaphrodites are defined as producing both *female* and *male* gametes, whereas sequential hermaphrodites are defined as transitioning from *female* to *male* or vice versa. We couldn't even describe either group without the female–male distinction. Certainly, simultaneous hermaphrodites again undermine the idea that every individual must be *either* female or male; some are both at once. And certainly, *sequential* hermaphrodites undermine the idea that sex is always a stable property of an individual; it is in most species, but not in all. Importantly, though, as with intersex conditions, neither form of hermaphroditism challenges the female–male distinction, or the idea that there are only two sexes.

Final question: Does within-sex variation topple the sex binary? Consider first the bluegill sunfish and orangutans. Should we say that species like these have more than two sexes, as opposed to just having several types of one or the other? You've probably guessed my answer: Although these species have more than two morphs, all are either female or male because all produce either eggs or sperm. But are scientists just arbitrarily elevating the importance of eggs and sperm by insisting on this binary division? They're not. The division captures something biologically crucial, which is that you need one of each type – a female and a male – to make a new bluegill sunfish or orangutan. It can be any type of male, but you need one of them plus a female to do the job. Needless to say, the same applies to species like our own that have only two morphs. That's why extensive within-sex variation doesn't imply that sex is a spectrum rather than a binary. *Sex-linked traits* like masculinity and femininity are clearly spectrums; I don't think anyone could deny that. Sex itself, however, is not.

The gamete definition of sex is one of the great intellectual accomplishments of our species. It isolates a simple but important regularity in nature that's enabled scientists to explain much of what we see in the living world. Working with this definition, scientists have figured out why the sexes evolved in the first place; why there are two of them rather than three, seven, or 37; and why in most species, there are equal numbers of each sex.[7] More relevant for our purposes, and as I'll explain later, scientists armed with this definition have also figured out why certain sex differences are more common than others across the living world. Rejecting the gamete definition of sex would mean casually throwing away more than a century's worth of rigorous science. We should insist on much stronger arguments than those we've been offered so far before contemplating such a rash move.

Why I'm Not a Fan of Gender

There's one more terminological issue to deal with before we get to the main event. That issue is gender. Many social scientists draw a distinction between *sex* and *gender* where, roughly speaking, sex refers to biological aspects of female and male, and gender refers to social aspects. The sex–gender distinction has become hugely popular in recent years, and many consider it indispensable. Personally, I'm not a fan. More precisely, I'm not a fan of the concept of *gender*, which I think confuses more than it enlightens.

There are several reasons for this. The first is that the term has multiple meanings. Sometimes gender refers to female–male differences that are (supposedly) shaped by nurture rather than nature; sometimes it refers to masculinity and femininity; sometimes it refers to psychological profiles that are more common in one sex than the other; sometimes it refers to widely held stereotypes of the sexes; sometimes it refers to the roles that society provides for females and males; sometimes it refers to people's gender identity (their sense of themselves as a boy or a girl or a man or a woman); and sometimes it's just a polite synonym for sex: a term that makes it clear that you're talking about biological sex rather than the fun kind of sex.[8] The profusion of partially overlapping meanings makes it difficult to know what people using the term are actually talking about. It's like trying to juggle jelly.

A second reason I prefer not to partake of gender is that, even if we could agree on a definition, most of those on offer are profoundly flawed. Take, for example, the idea that gender refers to female–male differences due to nurture rather than nature. An initial problem is that this is invariably assumed rather than demonstrated; indeed, describing a female–male difference as a gender difference often seems to be a way to settle the nature–nurture issue by definitional stipulation rather than arguments and evidence. A deeper problem, however, is that the gender-is-nurture approach assumes a radical dichotomy between nature and nurture, such that differences between the sexes can be neatly divided into those due solely to one and those due solely to the other. As we'll see in later chapters, this assumption is almost always false; most are due to both. As such, if we cling to the 'sex-is-nature/gender-is-nurture' definition, we'll have to say that most female–male differences are part sex difference and part gender difference. That's an awkward way to construe things. A much better way, in my view, is to describe all the differences as sex differences – that is, average differences between biological females and biological males – but with no implication that these differences come from nature, nurture, or a blend of the two. The nature–nurture question can then be dealt with separately.

Other definitions of gender face equally serious problems. Consider, for example, the idea that gender refers to psychological profiles loosely linked to sex: Men tend to be stoic and assertive, for instance, whereas women tend to be caring and emotional. This definition is assumed by people who argue that there are multiple distinct genders, rather than just the two vanilla options of *man* and *woman*. Again, this doesn't strike me as a useful way to construe things. The problem is that it involves imposing categories – even if more than just two – on what is actually continuous psychological variation. No two human beings have exactly the same psychological profiles, so the logical endpoint of this approach is that there are as many genders as there are human beings – and we're really just talking about personality.

I could go on, but I think I've said enough. The bottom line is that, based on problems like these, I usually avoid the term 'gender', except when it's part of a widely used phrase like 'the gender pay gap'. I'm not too zealous about this; as long as we know what we're talking about, the words we use don't matter. In general, though, sex is better.

Understanding Sex Differences

We've taken our first step toward solving the mystery of sex differences: We've worked out what sex is. Now, we need to turn our attention to the second part of the phrase: the differences. What exactly does it mean to say that men and women differ from each other?

This is a much harder question than it first appears to be. The main reason it's hard is that people are poor intuitive statisticians, and make a pastime of misunderstanding claims about sex differences. Two misunderstandings are particularly common. I call them *polarizing the differences* and *projecting the average onto the majority*. The aim of this section is to cure my beloved readers of these terrible, debilitating maladies.

To guide the discussion, we'll focus on a fairly uncontroversial sex difference: the fact that, on average, men are more aggressive than women. On hearing a statement like this, many imagine an aggressive man and a non-aggressive woman, and assume that the claim is that most men and most women are like that. People might not *accept* this claim, but that's what they think the claim is.

But it's not! It's not a *complete* misunderstanding; it's closer to the truth than the opposite claim would be: that most *women* are aggressive while most men are not. However, it's still far enough away from the truth to represent a fundamental error.

What, then, *does* it mean to say that, on average, men are more aggressive? Let's start by spelling out some of the things that it doesn't mean. One thing it doesn't mean is that all men are aggressive, whereas all women are non-aggressive. That would be like saying that, because on average men are taller than women, all men are tall, whereas all women are short. Actually, it's worse than that; it'd be like saying that all men are tall whereas no woman has any height at all.

At the same time, though, the statement also doesn't mean that *most* men are aggressive, whereas most *women* are non-aggressive, but that of course there are plenty of exceptions. *That* would be like saying that most men are tall, whereas most women are short, but that there are of course exceptions to that. In both cases, we'd be making the first of our two major errors: polarizing the sex difference. Most men are *not* tall, and most women are not short. Most members of both sexes are somewhere in between. Ditto aggression.

So, let's move away from the poles, and ask ourselves our question again: What does it mean to say that, on average, men are more aggressive than women? At this point, many would suggest that it means that most men exhibit roughly the average level of aggression for men, while most *women* exhibit roughly the average level for women.

This is definitely an improvement on our first attempt. Nonetheless, it exemplifies our second major error: projecting the average onto the majority. The main problem with the idea that most people exhibit the average level of aggression for their sex is that most people . . . *don't* exhibit the average level of aggression for their sex! Most people are not average. This might sound like a contradiction; we often assume that 'average' means 'typical'. But it doesn't. Statistically speaking, the average is just a measure of the central tendency of a broad distribution. Most people are significantly above or below the average. A simple way to make this point is to ask people to imagine what would happen if everyone were issued with the average-sized shoes for their sex. Would most people end up with shoes that fit well, and only a minority with shoes that didn't? No, it'd be the opposite: Most people would end up with shoes that *didn't* fit, and only a minority with shoes that did.

Third time lucky: What does it mean to say that, on average, men are more aggressive than women? This is one of those situations where a picture's worth a thousand words. What it means is this . . .

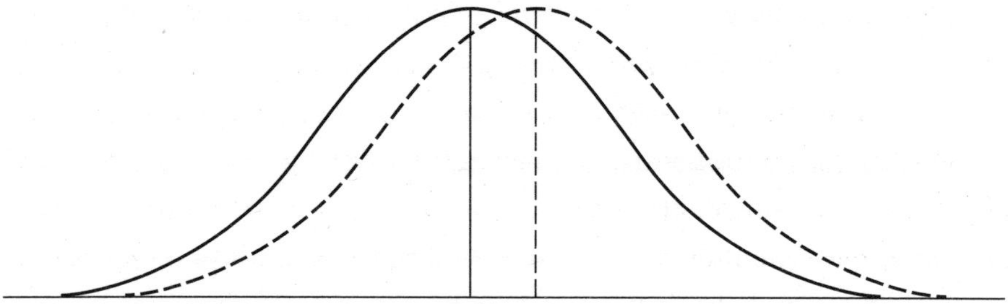

Figure 1 The single most important graph for understanding human sex differences: overlapping normal distributions. The vertical lines indicate the mean for each sex.

If you want to understand sex differences, the first thing you need to do is burn this image into your brain. The horizontal axis (or *x*-axis) represents scores on a given trait: in our example, aggression. The vertical axis (or *y*-axis) represents the number of people with a given score. The distribution on the left represents women; the one on the right represents men. Converting the figure into words – I'll try to keep it to fewer than a thousand – here's what it means to say that men are more aggressive than women:

> Men and women can be found at almost every level of aggression. Few people exhibit extremely high levels of aggression, but among the minority who do, more are men than women. Conversely, few exhibit Gandhi-like levels of pacifism, but among the minority who do, more are women than men. Most people – most men *and* most women – fall somewhere in between: not particularly aggressive but also not particularly Gandhi-like. At the same time, the sexes are not identical: The distribution for men is shifted somewhat to the right of that for women, such that the average level of aggression – not the *typical* level but the centre of the distribution – is somewhat higher for men. And of course, all of this applies in reverse for traits where women score higher.

If this isn't what springs to mind when you hear a claim about a sex difference – if you instead picture an archetypal man and an archetypal woman, and assume that that's what most men and women are like – you've misunderstood the claim. I won't hold it against you; we all find it easier to think in terms of archetypes than to think statistically. Still, it is worth getting into the habit of replacing those little pictures in your head with the overlapping distributions above. Doing so will help you to avoid polarizing the sex differences or projecting the average onto the majority. Importantly, it will also help you to see how average differences between the sexes can coexist with individual differences within each sex.[9]

And if that weren't enough, it'll even help you to avoid a common fallacy that psychologist Diane Halpern named the *'I know a person who . . .' fallacy*.[10] This refers to the fact that, whenever someone suggests that the sexes differ in some way, certain people will immediately furrow their brows and point to supposed exceptions. For example, in response to the claim that men are more aggressive than women, some will say 'But I know plenty of women who are aggressive, and plenty of men who aren't. This is junk science, fake news, and an affront to human dignity!' Rather than refuting the original claim, however, the response shows only that the person misunderstood it. It's the equivalent of saying, in response to the claim that the average family has 2.4 children, 'Hang on, I know plenty of families that have one child, or two, or even three, but I don't know a single family that has 2.4!' In both cases, the claim is about averages rather than archetypes, but the person is interpreting it as a claim about archetypes. The fact that some women are aggressive, and that some men are not, is in no way inconsistent with the claim that, *on average*, men are more aggressive than women.

To be clear, my point is *not* that there are exceptions to the rule. Aggressive women and non-aggressive men are *not* exceptions to the rule, because the rule is not that men are aggressive whereas women are not. The rule is the overlapping distributions depicted in Figure 1 – and those distributions *include* aggressive women and non-aggressive men.

In saying this, am I committing the scientific sin of making my claim unfalsifiable? I'm not. Certainly, you can't falsify it by pointing to any one individual. But the claim was never about individuals in the first place.

It was about the distribution of scores for each sex. If research showed that those distributions were different from the ones in Figure 1 – if they overlapped completely, for instance, or the differences went the other way – then the claim would be falsified as surely as the theory that the Earth is flat. Until that day comes, however, individuals at the tails of the distribution don't falsify anything, because they're part of what's being claimed.

How Big Are Human Sex Differences?

Hopefully, you've now been cured of the twin maladies of polarizing sex differences and projecting the average onto the majority. As you take some time to convalesce, let me add another wrinkle to the story. This is the fact that sex differences are not all created equal, but come in all sorts of shapes and sizes. Some are so large that only an intellectual could deny them; some are too small to see with the naked eye; most fall somewhere in between. We need a way to keep this in our sights.

In statistics, there's a standard metric for indexing the size of the differences between groups. It's called Cohen's *d*.[11] In the simplest case, Cohen's *d* is a measure of the distance between the average scores for any two groups, expressed in standard deviation units. (If you've forgotten your high school maths, the standard deviation is a statistic that tells us how spread out a set of scores is around the average.) According to a widely used convention, a *d* value of 0.2 is a small effect, a *d* value of 0.5 is a medium effect, and a *d* value of 0.8 is a large effect. One could quibble about the appropriateness of these labels; indeed, I've done so in several papers.[12] However, rather than worrying about semantics, let's see if we can get an intuitive grasp of the meaning of any Cohen's *d* effect size.

The most useful way I've found to do this is to imagine picking pairs of people at random, one man and one woman, and asking: How often would the man score higher than the woman on a given trait, and how often would the woman score higher than the man? Here's the answer for Cohen's small, medium, and large effect sizes. We'll assume, for the sake of argument, that the average score for men is higher than that for women, but it works the same way in reverse if the average for women is higher.

- For an effect size of $d = 0.2$ (a small effect size), the man would score higher than the woman in 55.6% of randomly chosen pairs. This might sound like a lot but bear in mind that if there were *no* sex difference, the man would score higher in 50% of pairs.
- For an effect size of $d = 0.5$ (a medium effect size), the man would score higher than the woman in 63.8% of pairs.
- For an effect size of $d = 0.8$ (a large effect size), the man would score higher than the woman in 71.4% of pairs.[13]

Returning to our earlier example, if we use this system for face-to-face aggression, the man would be more aggressive than the woman in roughly two out of every three pairs ($d \approx 0.5$).[14] If you had to bet on who'd be more aggressive, your best bet would be the man. But it wouldn't be a *good* bet. You wouldn't want to put your life savings on it; after all, around a third of the time, the woman would be more aggressive. Sure, that's a minority of the time. But it's not a trivial minority. It leaves you with only a 67% chance of winning, which is closer to 50:50 (a coin flip) than to 100:0 (a sure thing).[15]

Another way to get an intuitive grasp of the effect size for any psychological sex difference is to compare it to a more concrete, less abstract difference: the difference in human height. This is a sex difference that we can see with our own two eyes, and that we're all intimately familiar with. As such, it provides a useful yardstick for grasping the magnitude of differences that we *can't* see with our own two eyes, or that are less familiar to us. So, how large is the sex difference in height?

The answer is that, although it's impossible to miss, it's not gargantuan; it's not as if men *tower* over women in the way that male gorillas tower over female gorillas. Perhaps, then, we might guess that the human height difference would be classed as a medium difference using Cohen's standard labels. As it turns out, however, it's much larger than that. The exact value varies from study to study, but one large international survey reported an effect size of $d = 1.63$.[16] This means that the effect size for the unmissable-but-relatively-modest sex difference in height is around twice as large as the effect size customarily designated large: $d = 0.8$. That's one reason I'm sceptical of Cohen's labels.[17] In any case, by comparing the effect size of any given psychological sex difference to that of the sex difference in height, we can get a rough sense of its relative magnitude.

We've now got three tools for understanding the size of any human sex difference: Cohen's *d*, randomly plucked pairs of men and women, and the comparison with the sex difference in height. With these tools in hand, let's now revisit some of the standard-issue sex differences, and see how they measure up.

The first point to make is that some sex differences are genuinely enormous: much larger than the sex difference in height, let alone Cohen's so-called large effect. Almost all of these, however, are physical differences rather than psychological ones. One example is the sex difference in upper-body strength, which has an effect size of between $d = 2$ and $d = 3$.[18] Another is the sex difference in voice pitch, which has an effect size of around $d = 4$.[19] (Curiously, the sex difference in voice pitch is larger in humans than in any other ape, including those that are much more dimorphic than us for size.) These physical sex differences border on Mars-and-Venus territory; in almost every randomly chosen pair, men would score higher than women on upper-body strength, whereas women would score higher on voice pitch. The only *psychological* sex difference that's even in the same ballpark is the sex difference in which sex one is primarily attracted to.

Lowering the bar a little, we find a handful of psychological sex differences that are similar in size to the human height difference – in other words, that have *d* values between 1 and 2. One of these, surprisingly, is the sex difference in toy preferences.[20] Another – also surprisingly – is the sex difference in occupational interests.[21] The reason these differences are surprising is that they're among the largest and most reliable sex differences on record, yet both relate to phenomena that are evolutionarily novel. For most of human history, we didn't have anything like modern toys or occupations. It's therefore not at all clear why we have such robust female–male differences in these domains.

Moving further down the scale, we find various sex differences with so-called large effect sizes: that is, effect sizes of around d = 0.8. These include the sex difference in interest in casual sex and the sex difference in rough-and-tumble play in childhood.[22] Both are substantial: They're easily spotted in day-to-day life, and their reality is hard to deny. At the same time, though, it's worth reiterating that differences of this magnitude are only around half the size of the relatively modest sex difference in height. They're statistical differences, rather than Mars-and-Venus ones. Granted, they're among the largest sex differences found in our species. But this might just reflect the fact that we're a relatively monomorphic animal.[23]

Consistent with this idea, a large majority of sex differences are even smaller than those discussed so far. Sex differences in sex drive and interest in sexual variety, for instance, are medium differences by Cohen's standard. So are sex differences in aggression, risk-taking, and most spatial abilities. Sex differences in emotions and personality tend to be small-to-medium. And sex differences in verbal ability and self-esteem are small.[24]

In short, human sex differences vary a lot in size, but most are a whisper rather than a shout. See the Appendix for an overview of effect sizes for the standard-issue sex differences.

How Sex Differences Can Be Large Even When They're Small

Having argued that sex differences in our species are generally modest, let's now balance things out by looking at four ways in which, paradoxically, even small sex differences can have important societal impacts.

1. SEX DIFFERENCES ARE OFTEN LARGER AT THE EXTREMES

For normally distributed data (like the data in Figure 1), even small differences in the average scores of any two groups are associated with large differences among the minority at either extreme.[25] I call this the *tail-of-the-distribution effect*. A good example is the sex difference in height. At the mean, as mentioned, this difference isn't particularly big. If we see a woman who's the average height for men, we don't faint from shock. However, if we look at the tallest people in the world – people who are, say, two metres tall or above – we find that virtually all of them are men. Of course, very few men attain those lofty heights. But thousands more men do than women.

And what holds in the physical realm also holds in the mental. One example concerns aggression. As we've seen, the average sex difference in low-level aggression is real but relatively modest. However, when we turn our attention to the extremes – to severe violence or homicide, for

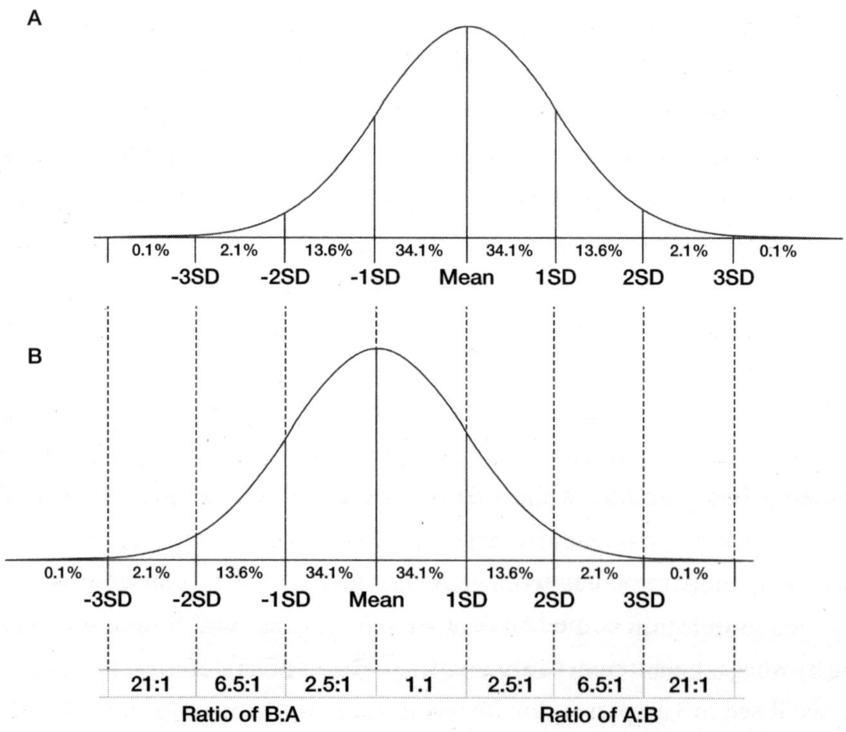

Figure 2 Even small differences at the mean are associated with large differences at the tails of the distribution.

instance – we find that men vastly outnumber women as the perpetrators.

Another example concerns verbal ability. At the mean, the sex difference in this trait is barely perceptible.[26] At the extremes, however, many more girls than boys are at the top of the class for reading and writing, and many more boys than girls at the bottom.[27]

Like overlapping normal distributions, the tail-of-the-distribution effect is crucial information for anyone who wants to understand sex differences. And it raises three important points. The first is that if we use data from the extremes as a barometer of the size of a sex difference in the general population, we'll end up with an exaggerated view of its magnitude. People sometimes look at the gender gap in homicide, for instance, and conclude that men are vastly more aggressive than women. But although many more men than women kill someone, most men would never dream of it. And if we look at less extreme, more common forms of aggression, we find that the sex differences are much more modest.[28]

The second point is that the tail-of-the-distribution effect may contribute to misleading stereotypes of the sexes. Because extreme cases grab our attention so forcefully, they may sometimes provide the templates for our views of men and women in general. The problem with this is that these templates are based on the attention-grabbing exceptions rather than the everyday rule, and thus they're caricatures rather than faithful portraits.

The third point is that although sex differences are usually modest at the mean, they're still critical in explaining important sociological phenomena. For example, while average sex differences in aggression and risk-taking aren't particularly large, they go a long way toward explaining why many more men than women are criminals.[29] The explanation is that the men in question come from the extreme of the distribution for these traits, where the differences are greatly magnified. And it's not just crime. As we'll see in Chapter 9, for instance, the tail-of-the-distribution effect also helps explain sex differences in mental health. Women are somewhat more prone to sadness and fear than men; at the extreme, many more women than men are diagnosed with depression and anxiety disorders.

Similarly, boys are somewhat more active and less attentive than girls; at the extreme, many more boys than girls are diagnosed with ADHD. In these and other cases, small differences in common traits explain large differences in uncommon outcomes.

2. THE SEXES SOMETIMES DIFFER IN HOW VARIABLE THEY ARE

There's another reason that sex differences can sometimes be larger at the extremes than the mean. For some traits, one sex is more *variable* than the other – that is, the peak of the distribution is slightly lower for that sex, while the tails stretch out slightly further on either side. Most often, males are more variable, an observation that goes by the name the *greater-male-variability hypothesis*. What this implies is that even if the average scores for a trait are identical for both sexes, somewhat more men than women will be found at both extremes, while somewhat fewer men will be found in the centre (although to be clear, most will still be found in the centre; it's a subtle effect).

Greater male variability has been documented for a wide range of traits, including height, running speed, various brain parameters, daily energy expenditure, grades, aggression, risk-taking, some mate preferences, some personality traits, some occupational preferences, specific cognitive abilities such as verbal, maths, and spatial ability, and even general cognitive ability or intelligence.[30]

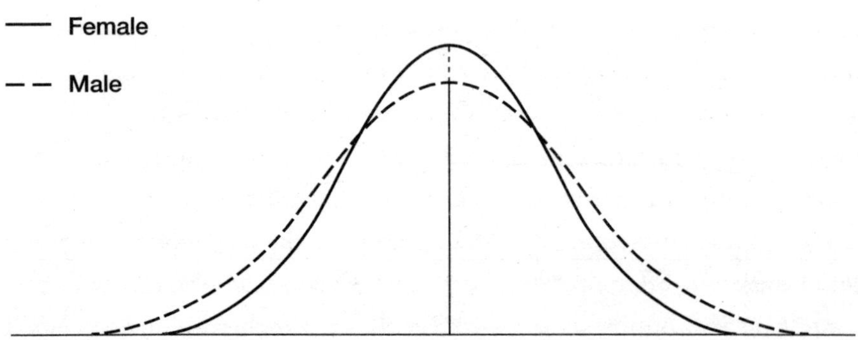

Figure 3 A common sex difference in humans and other animals: For a range of traits, males are more variable than females.

The greater-male-variability hypothesis is controversial, and the subject of vigorous debate. Enemies of the hypothesis point out that variability sex differences are often trivially small, and that some studies don't even find them.[31] They also point out that, for some traits, women are more variable than men. (Curiously, greater *female* variability often centres on traits related to sexuality, including orgasm frequency, sex drive, and sexual enjoyment.)[32] Still, the hypothesis has enough research behind it to justify taking it seriously. And to the extent that either sex exhibits greater variability, this may be an additional contributor to larger sex differences at the extremes than in the general population.

3. SEX DIFFERENCES ARE OFTEN LARGER IN EARLY ADULTHOOD

Many sex differences are larger in early adulthood than at any other time of life: They grow in the years following puberty, then start shrinking from the mid-to-late twenties. This is the case, for instance, for sex differences in accidental death, aggression, alcohol consumption,

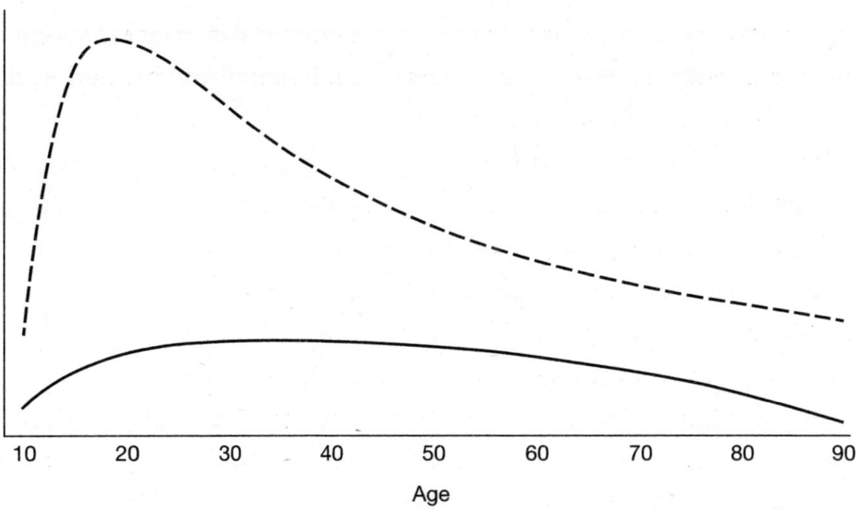

Figure 4 Sex differences across the lifespan. Each line represents one sex. Many sex differences grow larger after puberty, then shrink again later in life.

anxiety disorders, crime, depression, disgust sensitivity, fireworks-related hospitalizations, homicide rates, interest in casual sex, risk-taking, road deaths, sexual behaviour, and spatial ability.[33] Not all sex differences follow this trajectory, but it is a pervasive trend.

4. SMALL SEX DIFFERENCES IN INDIVIDUAL TRAITS CAN ADD UP TO LARGE DIFFERENCES IN PSYCHOLOGICAL PROFILES

Although sex differences in most traits are modest, when we consider sets of related traits together, the resulting 'multivariate' differences are markedly larger.[34] Once again, physical traits are the best on-ramp for understanding this idea. Consider, for instance, men's and women's faces. For any given facial attribute – the size of the eyes, the width of the nose, the fullness and shape of the lips – the sexes don't differ enormously, and we'd struggle to identify a person's sex from this one piece of information alone. However, when we consider all these traits simultaneously – as we do automatically when we encounter faces in everyday life – the overall *multivariate* sex difference in facial appearance is huge, and we can almost always tell a man's face from a woman's.

According to evolutionary psychologist Marco Del Giudice, the same is true of psychological sex differences. For example, sex differences in individual personality traits are fairly small. Sex differences in overall personality *profiles*, on the other hand, are anything but. Indeed, they may come close to Mars-and-Venus differences; one study found a multivariate effect size for the personality sex difference of 2.71.[35] As the psychologist Paul Irwing put it, when it comes to personality profiles, men and women are virtually different species.[36]

The concept of multivariate sex differences provides an answer to one of the most controversial questions in psychology: Do men and women have different brains? The answer is yes . . . and no. The neuroscientist Kevin Mitchell put it well when he observed that men and women don't have different brains in the way they have different genitals, but they *do* have different brains in the way they have different faces.[37] In other words, men's and women's brains aren't categorically different, and for any specific brain attribute, the differences are generally small. However, these small differences add up to a relatively large difference in men's and women's multivariate brain profiles. The proof in this pudding is that algorithms fed masses of brain data can distinguish female from male brains with close to perfect accuracy – around the same level of accuracy, in fact, that people can distinguish female from male faces.[38]

Moving On

A huge body of research shows that there are reliable sex differences in various psychological traits.[39] Unfortunately, another huge body of research shows that human beings have a remarkable talent for misunderstanding claims about sex differences. The muddled interpretation of some of the differences we've discussed in this chapter would be that women are constantly worrying, have low self-esteem, and can't park a car without crashing it, whereas men are violent, sex-crazed delinquents with the language abilities of chimpanzees but the spatial abilities of Albert Einstein. If you catch yourself thinking along these lines, reread the section on Understanding Sex Differences. Once you've done that, we're ready for the next stage of the operation: trying to figure out where the differences come from.

3

Born and Bred

The Nature and/or Nurture of Human Sex Differences

Five Positions on the Nature–Nurture Issue

The first sentence most people hear when they enter the world is 'It's a boy!' or 'It's a girl!' It doesn't mean a lot to them at the time, but those three simple words foreshadow much of what life has in store for them. How much of what's in store, though, is due to society channelling its members into pink and blue gender roles, and how much to the evolved nature of our species?

In this chapter, we'll throw ourselves into the ongoing, sometimes heated debate about the nature and nurture of psychological sex differences. Simplifying recklessly, there are five main positions we can take for any given difference.

1. **The Nature-Only Position** (also known as *biological determinism*). The sex difference in question is innate. It doesn't matter how you raise your kids, what educational interventions you give them, or what role models you expose them to. Short of brain surgery, the difference is as inevitable as the sun coming up in the morning.
2. **The Mainly-Nature Position.** The sex difference emerges from a complex, little-understood interaction between nature and nurture, but nature is the dominant player in the process. Although nurture can push things around a little, the difference is likely to persist in all or almost all cultures.

3. **The Nature-and-Nurture-as-Equal-Partners Position.** Not only do nature and nurture both help shape the sex difference in question, they're about equally important in doing so.
4. **The Mainly-Nurture Position.** Nature and nurture are both involved in shaping the sex difference, but nurture has the upper hand. Culture often amplifies an initially trivial inborn difference, but it could just as well shrink or eliminate it.
5. **The Nurture-Only Position** (also known as *environmental determinism*). The sex difference is due entirely to learning, socialization, and culture. These forces could just as easily have created no sex difference, or even the opposite of the difference we see today.

The first thing to emphasize is that we shouldn't think of these positions as five overarching theories of all sex differences, but rather as a toolkit of five possible explanations for any specific difference we encounter. Each position might apply to some differences but not to others. The sex difference in which sex one is primarily attracted to, for instance, is presumably a Nature-Only difference or something close to it; the sex difference in people's names within a culture is presumably a *Nurture*-Only difference. For most other female–male differences, things are much less clear. Still, it doesn't seem unreasonable to think that each of the five positions might apply to at least some familiar sex differences.

But although the positions are not overarching theories of all psychological differences, people do often favour one or another. Putting aside sexual orientation, I'd argue that no one favours the Nature-Only position anymore, if anyone ever really did. However, plenty of people lean toward each of the other positions. I probably don't need to spell it out at this point, but I tend to favour positions two or three for most of the standard-issue sex differences. As such, my aim in this book will be to show not only that nature is involved in shaping these differences, but also that the contribution of nature is substantial – more substantial, in many cases, than that of nurture.

Now, some would object to the implication that significant numbers of people lean toward position five. In their view, the Nurture-Only position is a straw man, just as in my view, the Nature-Only position is. I've encountered this objection many times when arguing that a given sex difference isn't due solely to nurture. In fact, I've encountered it so many times that I've got three stock responses to the complaint.

My first is: 'Great – we agree that the difference is partly innate!' Strangely, my interlocutors aren't always comfortable with this implication when it's explicitly pointed out like this.

My second response is that, even if it really *were* just a straw man, and even if everyone really *did* agree that nature and nurture are co-conspirators in shaping most sex differences, we should still make the case for this position, rather than simply accepting it without arguments or evidence. After all, maybe everyone's wrong, and the Nurture-Only position is true in most cases! (Spoiler alert: It's not. But we shouldn't just take this on faith.)

My third and final response is that the Nurture-Only position is *not* just a straw man; it's made of flesh and blood. To start with, some scholars and activists have openly disavowed any role for nature in shaping human sex differences.[1] In addition – and more insidiously – many act *as if* they hold the Nurture-Only view, but without actually coming out and endorsing it. Some automatically assume an environmental origin for any sex difference they come across, without even contemplating the possibility of an innate contribution. Some argue that cross-cultural variation in men's and women's behaviour proves that evolutionary explanations are false: an argument that tacitly assumes that the only options are the Nature-Only and Nurture-Only positions, and that the Nurture-Only position has won. Some give lip service to the idea that nature and nurture are both involved in shaping most sex differences, but then carry on talking as if only nurture is, while rejecting any claims about specific evolved differences – differences in sexual inclinations, competitiveness, and occupational interests, for example: the stuff that people hate. And some try to short-circuit the discussion altogether by arguing that the nature–nurture distinction is a false dichotomy, and that it's impossible to separate one from the other. Curiously, those adopting this final tactic – the nuclear option, I call it – only ever do so in response to claims that *nature* contributes to a difference, never that nurture does, and they don't seem to notice that if the argument undermines nature explanations, it equally undermines nurture ones. What all of this shows is that the Nurture-Only position is more than a mere straw man, in practice if not always in principle. And that's another reason – the most important reason – that it's worth thinking through the arguments for and against it.

The Nature of Nurture

> One is not born, but rather becomes, a woman.
>
> Simone de Beauvoir (1949/1953), p.267

> The key biological fact is that boys and girls have different genitalia, and it is this biological difference that leads adults to interact differently with different babies whom we conveniently color-code in pink or blue to make it unnecessary to go peering into their diapers for information about gender.
>
> Anne Fausto-Sterling (1992), pp 152–3

We'll start with a survey of the sociocultural explanations for sex differences. The basic idea underpinning all such explanations is that societies have templates for what the sexes are like – and for what they *should* be like – and that, in various ways, we act to make these templates a reality. Psychologists have a well-stocked arsenal of theories to describe how this process takes place: reward and punishment, imitation, socialization, self-socialization, and the like. These theories are not mutually exclusive, and indeed it might be useful to try to knit them together into an overarching theory of gender-role socialization. Let's give it a whirl.

The process begins in the home. From day one, parents treat their sons and daughters differently. They see their sons as stronger and more robust, and encourage them to be active and independent. They see their daughters as gentler and more nurturing, and assign them more chores involving childcare. They give boys balls, building blocks, and toy cars; they give girls dolls, toy kitchen utensils, and fashion accessories. Gender-typical behaviour earns praise; gender-atypical behaviour earns criticism. Like compound interest, even subtle nudges soon add up. Little by little, through their actions and omissions, their appreciative smiles or furrowed brows, parents begin moulding unisex preschoolers into chronically gendered beings.

Others soon take the baton. As children's social worlds expand, they encounter a wider and wider range of people, each of whom is a potential vector for gender-role socialization. This includes siblings, extended family, teachers and – most importantly – other kids. Children quickly learn what's acceptable for their sex in their peer group and the wider culture. Boys shouldn't show pain and should keep a lid on their emotions, other perhaps than anger. Whatever they do, though, they shouldn't cry – not without extremely good reason. Girls, on the other hand, should be kind and caring, and shouldn't be too assertive or competitive – leave that to the dry-eyed boys. These aren't just gentle recommendations. Kids soon learn that there's a price to be paid for breaking the gender rules. Boys in particular get it in the neck if they do: if they play with dolls, for instance, or wear pink. But both sexes, although born free, are everywhere in gender chains.

The mechanisms described so far begin shaping sex differences before children even grasp that they're boys or girls. As soon as they *do* grasp this, however, the process goes into overdrive. According to *social learning theory*, children latch onto same-sex role models, and immediately start imitating and emulating them.[2] Our first such role model is often our same-sex parent, but others include same-sex siblings, teachers, and peers. In the modern world, they also include virtual role models, in the form of same-sex characters in fairy stories, books, TV shows, and movies. Often, these virtual role models embody extreme stereotypes of the sexes, or did, at least, until recently: Boys are adventurous rogues, girls their cautious, crying sidekicks; men are breadwinners and heroes, women homemakers and damsels in distress. Whatever we see in the home, the community, and the media comes to seem as natural as breathing, and thus we replicate it later in our lives. In this way, gender roles become self-sustaining, like a virus that hijacks a cell and forces it to pump out replicas of itself. In effect, we're all actors acting out a script, who don't even realize we're in a play.

But it's not just imitation and vicarious learning that shape our gendered performance. According to cognitive-developmental approaches to sex differences, as soon as children come to classify themselves as female or male, they start striving to conform their behaviour to their mental template of their sex. As a result, gender-role-consistent behaviour becomes inherently rewarding, rather than having to be rewarded by outside parties.[3] Admittedly, it can take children a while to get their gender templates straight. One of the cutest passages I've ever read in a scientific paper was a quote from a four-year-old girl who, while showing her aunt a picture she'd drawn of a group of children, confidently explained that 'The ones with eyelashes are girls; boys don't have eyelashes.'[4] Still, whether the templates are accurate or not, the minute they coalesce in children's minds, they start exerting a powerful gravitational pull on their behaviour. Failure to toe the gender line is seen not as a curious statistical anomaly, but as a source of shame or a moral infraction. The upshot is that people effectively model themselves on stereotypes of their sex.

Sex stereotypes can also act as self-fulfilling prophecies. For example, if parents and teachers assume that maths and science are for boys, whereas reading and writing are for girls, they may fail to notice or nurture kids' talents in domains that clash with their expectations. Meanwhile, if boys come to believe that they won't be good with babies, or girls that they won't be good with numbers, they may devote less time and effort to these activities, guaranteeing in the process that they *won't* be good at them. And even if they think they *could* be good, kids don't want to seem weird, especially in the teen years, so they often limit their daily activities and life ambitions to those considered normal for their sex.

In these ways and others, subtle and not-so-subtle, the world steers boys and girls, men and women, into the restrictive gender moulds of their society. Parents do it; teachers do it; friends do it; you do it. Not only that, but people also steer themselves into these gender moulds. Sometimes, they just conform outwardly: A boy who would never dream of playing with a doll at kindergarten might do so when he's safely at home, away from the judgemental eyes of his peers; a woman who's ultra-assertive in the office might play up her femininity on a date.[5] (Ironically, in doing this, these individuals become gender-typical role models for others, despite their own gender atypicality.) But although sex-related behaviour is sometimes a mask or a social tool, often social pressures create genuine differences in the minds of men and women. And although many of these pressures have weakened in recent decades, fossil traces of the old ways persist. When it comes to gender socialization, the present is a watered-down version of the past, not a gender-neutral utopia.[6]

Is this all just evidence-free speculation? It's not, say the champions of the approach. If socialization had no impact, why would parents everywhere bother trying to socialize their children? If boys naturally cried less than girls, why would parents and peers in traditional cultures need to pressure them *not* to cry? Men's and women's behaviour and roles differ immensely across cultures and times. What are the chances that we just happen to have been born into the first society in the history of the world where existing sex differences reflect the natural order of things, undistorted by discrimination and socialization? 'Slim' would be understating it. And we know that it's all too easy to mistake nurture for nature. If you gave men and women in Saudi Arabia a driving test before 2018, you might conclude that women were constitutionally unable to drive. But you'd be wrong; Saudi women couldn't drive because they were forbidden to learn how to do so. Likewise, if you gave boys and girls in the Taliban's Afghanistan a test of academic ability, you might assume that girls were naturally less intellectually able than boys. Again, though, you'd be wrong; girls were just forbidden from going to school, which impedes the development of the mind just as surely as foot binding impedes the development of the foot. To assume that today's sex differences reflect our true nature isn't just unrealistic, it's dangerous, entrenching inequalities between the sexes. We can and must do better.

Four Cracks in the Nurture Edifice

I don't think any reasonable person could deny that the environment helps shape sex differences. That doesn't necessarily mean, however, that our current crop of sociocultural theories does a good job of explaining how. Certainly, the theories seem plausible. But so do lots of ideas that turn out to be false. Sure enough, when we start digging into the details, we find that many sociocultural explanations suffer one of four main defects.

1. PHANTOM CAUSES

In some cases, sociocultural explanations point to causal factors that don't exist, or that are the reverse of what the explanations claim. For example, contrary to the idea that parental socialization is a major contributor to sex differences, several large meta-analyses – that is, studies that aggregate the results of other studies – suggest that, in important ways, modern Western parents don't treat their daughters and sons particularly differently.[7] Among other things, parents are just as likely to encourage independence and achievement in daughters as sons, and are no more restrictive of daughters. Moreover, when parents and others *do* treat boys and girls differently, it's often in the opposite direction to that presupposed by the sociocultural theories. Rather than discouraging aggression in girls more than boys, for instance, parents spend more time discouraging it in boys. Why? Because boys engage in more of it![8]

2. ON CHICKENS AND EGGS

Sometimes, the sociocultural theories get their facts straight, but face a chicken-and-egg problem in explaining them. Are boys and girls different because people treat them differently, or do people treat them differently because they're different? Do women cry more than men because they've seen more movies in which women cry, or do movies feature more women who cry because most movies are set in this universe, and in this universe, women tend to cry more? Do stereotypes of the sexes cause sex differences, or do sex differences cause stereotypes of the sexes? Alternatively, does the causal arrow point in both directions in each of these cases?

These are all legitimate possibilities. Most of the time, however, psychologists assume a single direction of causation, and put all their eggs in that one basket. For some reason, almost invariably, they seem to choose the least plausible or least important direction to focus on. To give one example, psychologists often attribute huge causal power to stereotypes, when the best available evidence suggests that, although stereotypes *can* function as self-fulfilling prophecies, the effects are generally modest, and stereotypes *reflect* reality more than they shape it.[9] It's hard to dodge the conclusion that psychology often describes the world the way psychologists would like it to be, rather than the way it is.

3. THE SECOND LAW OF BEHAVIOUR GENETICS

Even to the extent that people treat the sexes differently over and above any pre-existing differences between them, we still need to ask how much impact this has. If you treat a dog like a cat, it'll still act like a dog. Maybe it's the same with boys and girls.

Consistent with this suggestion, we now know that the source of socialization that many consider the most important – the family home – has surprisingly little effect on how people turn out. The evidence for this comes from twin and adoption studies, with two findings in particular leaving little room for doubt. The first is that identical twins raised together are often no more similar than those raised apart. The second is that unrelated individuals adopted into the same home are often no more similar than randomly chosen non-relatives. Apparently, sharing a family home doesn't make people much more similar than they'd otherwise be, at least by the time they're adults. Identical twins *are* more similar than other siblings, who in turn are more similar than non-relatives. However, the similarity is due largely to shared genes rather than shared environment.

It might sound like I'm saying that genes are all that matters, but I'm not; identical twins aren't literally identical. What I am saying, though – or rather, what the evidence shows – is that whatever the environmental variables shaping us are, the things people share if they grow up together aren't significant contributors. Awkwardly, these include many variables that folk psychology and even many psychologists assume are hugely influential, including whether the parents are married or divorced, their socioeconomic status, their parenting philosophy, and so on. Of course, childhood abuse and neglect almost certainly have an impact. Within the normal range, however, the family home makes hardly any difference.

Whenever I lecture on this topic, I ask my students to raise their hands if they're surprised by the finding. Every hand goes up – including my own. I've known about this for a long time now, but it still surprises me. The finding is known as the *Second Law of Behaviour Genetics*.[10] It's earned the title 'law' by being replicated in multiple studies over multiple decades.[11] And it's an existential threat to many traditional theories in psychology – including any theory that suggests that parents or the family home are important players in the creation of sex differences.

4. THE GENDER-EQUALITY PARADOX

Fourth and finally, in some cases, sociocultural theories don't just predict mountains that turn out to be molehills, they predict the reverse of what we actually find.

The best example is a counterintuitive phenomenon known as the *gender-equality paradox*.[12] This refers to the fact that, for many traits, sex differences are larger, rather than smaller, in more gender-equal nations – the exact opposite of what we'd expect if the differences were due to rigid sex roles, gender inequality, or patriarchy.[13] Among the traits where we find a gender-equality paradox are attitudes to same-sex sexual orientation, the Big Five personality traits, competitiveness, crying, depression, the fields people choose to study, gender gaps in the caring professions, gender gaps in STEM fields, interest in people vs things, interest in STEM subjects at school, meat eating, mental illness, moral judgements, narcissism, negative emotions, occupational interests, patience, reading ability, risk-taking, self-confidence, self-esteem, spatial ability, subjective well-being, suicide, trust, values, and violence.[14]

Importantly, the gender-equality paradox is found not only in answers to self-report surveys but also in objectively measurable traits such as height, weight, blood pressure, life expectancy, and some tests of cognitive ability.[15] This suggests that the pattern is not just a product of cross-cultural differences in how people respond to surveys. It seems to be a genuine phenomenon.

To be clear, not all sex differences are larger in more gender-equal nations. The sex difference in the desire for good looks in a mate is apparently unrelated to gender equality, and sex differences in interest in casual sex, intimate partner violence, and maths performance are *smaller* in more gender-equal nations, just as we might originally have expected.[16] Nonetheless, the gender-equality paradox is surprisingly pervasive.

What explains it? My best guess – and it *is* just a guess at this stage – is that in enriched and relatively unconstrained environments, natural differences between individuals, and average differences between the sexes, have more opportunity to flower and grow. When people have plenty of food and low levels of disease, for instance, not only does everyone get taller, but the sex difference in height expands. Likewise, when people have more scope to follow their hearts and nurture their own individuality, average *psychological* sex differences expand as well.[17]

Although the phenomenon has come to be called the *gender-equality paradox*, it's probably not gender equality per se that produces it. Instead, it's any societal-level variable that increases people's ability to act on their preferences and cultivate their strengths, including not only gender equality but also wealth, health, education, and individualism.[18]

Whether or not this explanation is correct, the gender-equality paradox shows us that although culture matters enormously when it comes to sex differences, its effect often goes in the opposite direction to what traditional sociocultural explanations predict. We're therefore in the strange position where we know that the environment plays a critical role, but we have far less idea *how* it does than we usually think. One possible reason for this is that the traditional explanations leave out a crucial ingredient: nature.

Six Lines of Evidence That Nature Plays a Role

The standard sociocultural explanations for sex differences are flawed in various ways. That doesn't mean, however, that the differences necessarily have an innate basis. It could just be that we need better sociocultural theories. How, then, can we know whether nature plays a role?

A common reaction to this question is to say that we *can't* know, because there's never been a society in which the sexes have been treated identically. The implicit assumption is that treating the sexes identically is the only way to establish whether there's an innate contribution. Not true! At least six lines of evidence can help us settle the issue in the absence of identical treatment.

Before getting to that, though, I should highlight something that many will find surprising, namely that brain evidence isn't one of the six. People commonly assume that tracing a psychological sex difference to a brain difference constitutes unambiguous evidence for its innateness. It doesn't. The reason is simple: The brain isn't shaped only by nature; it's shaped by nurture as well. This means that, as a general rule, sex differences in the brain are silent witnesses to their own causes, telling us nothing about the nature–nurture issue. Certainly, some differences appear before birth, ruling out socialization as a cause.[19] But even then, the implications are far from straightforward. That's because differences in the brain don't necessarily imply differences in the mind or behaviour. Intelligence, for example, is instantiated in somewhat different ways in men's brains than in women's, and yet men's and women's average intelligence is the same.[20] For both these reasons, leaping from 'brain sex difference' to 'innate psychological sex difference' is a risky game. And it's not one we need to play. There's plenty of other evidence.

1. DEVELOPMENTAL TRAJECTORY

The first line of evidence concerns the developmental trajectory of the sex difference under investigation. To start with, many female–male differences appear in a rudimentary form remarkably early in life. Examples include not only sex differences in physical traits like size, strength, and body fat percentage, but also differences in behavioural traits such as activity levels, aggression, and play patterns. In all such cases, the differences appear long before children are exposed to TV, movies, or media, and long before they even know their own sex.[21]

Of course, presence in early life doesn't *necessarily* mean that a sex difference has an innate basis; perhaps kids are just highly sensitive to gender-related social influences that most of us can't see. But early appearance does paint the Nurture-Only perspective into a tighter corner, and in the process, adds more weight to the scales on the nature side of the nature–nurture equation.

Needless to say, not all psychological sex differences are found in early childhood; many appear further down the line. Even then, though, we can't assume that the differences are products of nurture alone – after all, we're not born with teeth or beards, but that doesn't mean we're socialized to have them. Rather than being pure products of nurture, many later-appearing psychological sex differences could be part of the evolved maturation process of our species. This is most plausible for differences that emerge in the wake of puberty. As Darwin pointed out, many sex differences, in our species and others, stage their first appearance at puberty or become more prominent at that time.[22] Indeed, that's part of the *definition* of 'puberty'. This pattern is impossible to miss for many physical sex differences in humans, including those in height, strength, and athletic prowess. As we saw in Chapter 2, however, it's also true of many *psychological* sex differences, including differences in sexual inclinations, aggression, and risk-taking.[23]

As with appearance in early childhood, appearance at puberty isn't conclusive proof of an innate contribution. Aside from anything else, the world often starts treating people differently at that time of life: If you're a young woman, men start hitting on you; if you're a young man, people start becoming wary of you. Still, appearance at puberty does increase the plausibility of an innate contribution, especially when combined with other evidence.

2. STABILITY OVER TIME

A second line of evidence for an innate contribution is stability over time. With more than a century of research behind us, scientists can now point to various sex differences that have persisted over many decades or generations. For example, sex differences in mate preferences and sex differences in occupational interests persisted in the United States right across the twentieth century.[24] This is especially noteworthy given that that century saw several social movements that, based on a Nurture-Only or Mainly-Nurture view, we'd expect to have obliterated or at least shrunk the differences. At the top of the list are the sexual revolution and second-wave feminism.

Like appearance at birth or puberty, persistence over time isn't unassailable evidence for an innate foundation; it could just reflect cultural inertia. But how likely is that? Many aspects of culture change rapidly; the world adopted smartphones in a matter of years, for instance, and fashions change in the blink of an eye. If sex differences were just down to culture, why would so many be so uniquely resistant to efforts to reform them? Without a good answer to that question, persistence over time must be counted as further evidence for a significant contribution of nature.

3. RESISTANCE TO SOCIAL PRESSURE

A third line of evidence for an innate contribution is that, just as children's love of chocolate and sweets persists even in the face of parental efforts to foist healthier options on them, so too sex differences often persist even in the face of social pressure in the opposite direction. In other words, sex differences often appear *despite* culture, not because of it.

The most striking examples are children who, for one reason or another, were raised as members of the other sex. Such cases are, in effect, natural experiments pitting nature and nurture against each other. Consider, for instance, the story of David Reimer. David was one of a pair of identical twins. At seven months of age, his penis was destroyed during a botched medical circumcision. His distraught parents eventually found their way to the office of John Money, a famous sexologist at Johns Hopkins University. Money persuaded them that David should be transformed into a girl, both medically and socially. The medical transformation involved two parts. First, David was surgically castrated and given an artificial vagina. Second, at age twelve, he started taking hormones to mimic female puberty and stimulate the development of breasts and other features of an adult woman's body. The *social* transformation involved raising David as a girl. To that end, he was given a girl's name, encouraged to engage in stereotypically girlish activities, and never told he'd once been a boy. Money's theory was that, as long as this gender-role socialization began before the age of two, David would be psychologically indistinguishable from any (other) girl.

For many years, this was exactly the outcome that Money reported, and that social scientists gleefully repeated in their classrooms and textbooks: David was a typical feminine girl, while his identical twin brother was a typical rough-and-tumble boy.[25] It seemed like a slam dunk for the view that gender is largely a matter of socialization.

But as you've probably guessed, it wasn't. After Money mysteriously went silent on the topic, a sceptical rival scientist named Milton Diamond tracked David down and discovered what had really happened. David had never been comfortable as a girl. As a preschooler, he'd ripped off his dresses and refused to play with dolls, preferring toy guns and other stereotypically male toys instead. At school, he'd gotten into fist fights and been nicknamed the cavewoman for his male-typical behaviour and gait.

Given a skipping rope, David would tie up his schoolmates or whip them, rather than jumping rope like the girls. Finally, at age fourteen, when he'd started credibly threatening suicide, his parents had told him everything. He'd immediately started living as a male, and soon afterward, had his breasts removed and an artificial penis constructed. Later, he'd married a woman, and started working in a slaughterhouse: a male-typical occupation.[26] The sad end to this sad story is that at age 39, David took his own life after his wife left him.

This is just one case, and some commentators question how much it can tell us. But other cases lean in the same direction.[27] And the conclusion they all lean toward is that, when nature and nurture are pitted against each other, nature often wins. Boys will be boys, and girls will be girls, even when you subject them to the most extreme environmental manipulation imaginable: raising them as a member of the other sex 24/7 for more than a decade.

4. HORMONAL EVIDENCE

Many of the standard-issue sex differences have been linked, at least tentatively, to hormones such as testosterone and estrogen. Contrary to popular belief, the links between people's current hormone levels and sex-typical behaviour are weak: People with higher testosterone aren't necessarily more aggressive or competitive, for example. In contrast, the links between *prenatal* hormone levels and sex-typical behaviour are often fairly strong.

One line of evidence for the role of prenatal hormones comes from individuals with *DSDs* – that is, disorders (or differences) of sexual development. The most famous of the DSDs is *congenital adrenal hyperplasia*, also known as *CAH*. Individuals with CAH are exposed to high levels of androgens in the womb. For males, this makes little difference, as males are normally exposed to high prenatal androgen levels. For females, however, it's a game-changer. The surplus androgens partially masculinize females' bodies – and, it seems, their minds. As children, girls with CAH tend to be less interested in dolls and other female-typical toys, and more interested in so-called boys' toys.[28] They're also less interested in babies or having children, and often have more male-typical interests and career aspirations. As adults, women with CAH are more likely to be sexually attracted to other women and often end up in male-typical jobs.[29] Their gender-atypical behaviour doesn't seem to be a result of being socialized to be more masculine. On the contrary, some evidence suggests that CAH girls act in male-typical ways even when their parents encourage them to act more like stereotypical girls.[30] In other words, prenatal hormones sometimes trump postnatal socialization.

Alongside natural experiments like the DSDs, scientists have undertaken various 'unnatural' experiments – that is, lab studies investigating the roles of prenatal and pubertal hormones in shaping sex-related behaviour. Obviously, we can't do research like this on humans. For that reason, the lab studies have focused on nonhuman mammals, from rats to guinea pigs to macaques. One line of research shows that when males are starved of androgens in early life, they exhibit female-typical behaviour: As youngsters, they engage in less rough-and-tumble play, and as adults they're less aggressive. Another line of research shows that when females are given megadoses of androgens, they exhibit *male*-typical behaviour: As adults, they mount other females sexually, and are less parentally inclined.[31]

A more detailed account of the process is given by the *organizational–activational hypothesis*. The basic idea is that to build an animal wired for male-typical behaviour, you need prenatal androgen exposure to set up the brain areas associated with that behaviour, followed by a second round of androgen exposure at puberty to activate the areas in question. Conversely, to build an animal wired for *female*-typical behaviour, you need an *absence* of androgen exposure during early development to set up the relevant brain areas, followed by exposure to female-typical sex hormones at puberty to activate them.[32] No doubt, the reality is much more complicated than this. For many traits, though, this two-step model seems like a reasonable first approximation.

5. CROSS-CULTURAL EVIDENCE

Contrary to the common claim that sex differences vary capriciously from culture to culture, many seem to show no respect at all for cultural boundaries. In every known society, for instance, men are larger and stronger than women, women hit puberty earlier, men are more interested in casual sex and sexual variety, men engage in more face-to-face aggression, and women are more involved in childcare.[33] Conversely, despite strenuous efforts spanning many decades, social scientists have yet to document even a single society where women watch more porn than men or are the main consumers of prostitutes, or where more women than men die in car crashes or end up behind bars.

To be clear, sex differences often interact with cultural factors in complex and unexpected ways. My favourite example is that although absolute levels of most traits vary a great deal across cultures and times, *sex differences* in those traits often stubbornly persist. Average height, for instance, increased substantially across the twentieth century, such that the average woman in 1999 was taller than the average man in 1900. Despite that, the sex difference in height was preserved throughout the process.[34]

This might not seem too surprising; few doubt that the sex difference in height is largely innate. But the same pattern is also found in the realm of mind and behaviour. For example, absolute levels of interest in sexual variety differ considerably across cultures, such that women in some cultures report desiring more lifetime sexual partners than men in others. Despite this cross-cultural variation, however, the sex difference in desired number of partners remains intact in every culture.[35] Likewise, levels of crying vary a lot across nations, such that men in some nations cry more than women in others. Still, within each nation, women cry more than men.[36] What maintains these differences in the face of the apparent cultural plasticity of the traits in question? Not sure! But it is a common trend. Apparently, it's easier to change the absolute levels of many traits than to eradicate average differences between the sexes.

The cross-cultural record is not always easy to interpret. As with other lines of evidence, universality is not a fail-safe indicator of innateness; if it were, we'd have to conclude that wearing jeans, eating pizza, and doomscrolling are innate to *Homo sapiens*. At the same time, though, the *absence* of universality isn't a fail-safe indicator of the *absence* of innateness. In principle, we could eliminate or even reverse the sex difference in height; all we'd need to do would be starve all the boys or force feed the girls growth hormones. Does this imply that the height difference we usually see is entirely due to culture? Clearly not. As with most evidence, cross-cultural differences and similarities are ambiguous to some degree.

Nonetheless, universality should generally nudge the dial toward an innate contribution. Cultures differ in almost every imaginable way: in their cuisines, their religions, their languages, fashions, and fads. If sex differences were purely or even largely a product of cultural conditioning, why would we find the same cluster of differences in all or most cultures? Until we've got a plausible answer to that question, cross-cultural universality is easier to square with the idea that there's a significant innate component than with a Nurture-Only explanation.[37]

6. CROSS-SPECIES EVIDENCE

Our sixth and final line of evidence is that many of the standard-issue sex differences are found as well in other animals. In most mammals, for instance, and in many non-mammalian species, males are more interested than females in seeking multiple mates, females are choosier about their mates, males are more likely to get into scraps and scrapes, and females are more parental.[38] The differences are larger in most other mammals than in humans.[39] Still, the similarity is unmistakable, and it shifts the balance of probabilities toward the assumption that the differences we see in our species have an evolutionary origin.

Of course, there's a ton of variation in female and male behaviour across the animal kingdom, and some critics of the evolutionary approach have argued that its advocates cherry pick species that happen to mirror their preferred social arrangements. From this perspective, any resemblance to other species, living or dead, is purely coincidental. I think it's fair to say that people do sometimes cite the animal literature selectively. It's also fair to say, however, that this happens on both sides of the political aisle. On the one hand, gender-role traditionalists – who often steer clear of evolutionary theory – find role models in the patriarchal protectiveness of silverback gorillas. On the other hand, gender-role progressives – who usually deny that other animals can tell us anything about our own species – suddenly change their tune when they hear about female-dominated hyenas, sexually liberated bonobos, sex-role-reversed jacanas, all-female 'lesbian' lizards, female albatrosses that form same-sex pair bonds, and clownfish that change sex from male to female. Both sides are prone to cherry picking, so we should always be cautious when comparing humans to other animals.

To be fair, though, the evolutionary argument is not simply 'Hey, here's a species that has a sex difference vaguely reminiscent of one found in humans; therefore, the human sex difference is innate.' The argument is that in other species *subject to the same selection pressures as us* – selection pressures we'll explore in more detail in the next chapter – we tend to find the same *cluster* of sex differences typically found in humans. When we find this cluster in other species, we don't hesitate to explain it in evolutionary terms. No one would argue, for instance, that female and male raccoons act differently because they're rewarded for behaviour consistent with arbitrary raccoon gender roles, or because as soon as baby raccoons learn to label themselves as female or male, they start striving to conform their behaviour to widely held raccoon stereotypes of their sex. Sure, raccoons aren't humans, and humans aren't raccoons. But given that the gaps clearly have an evolutionary genesis in other species, it would be extremely odd if in one peculiar primate, the exact same gaps had an entirely different explanation: learning, socialization, and culture. Why would natural selection wipe the slate clean of these sex differences in our species alone, only for us to then reinvent the same set of sex differences in every society on record?

When Many Paths Lead to Rome

So, there we have it: six lines of evidence for an innate contribution to any given human sex difference. As I've tried to make clear, none of these lines of evidence is beyond dispute. Hormone studies often have small samples of participants, which increases the risk of both false positives and false negatives. Most experiments on the effects of hormones have been done on other animals, and other animals are . . . well, they're just that; they're other animals, so the findings might not apply to us. Cross-cultural universality *could* reveal inborn psychological sex differences, but as we'll discuss later, it could just be an indirect effect of inborn *physical* differences.[40] And so on. The question is, then: Are we condemned to eternal agnosticism about innate contributions to human sex differences?

The answer is no. First, it's worth mentioning that if imperfect evidence ruled out drawing tentative conclusions, this would be just as fatal to sociocultural explanations as to evolutionary ones; after all, the evidence for the sociocultural explanations is also imperfect. Fortunately, though, it's not fatal to either side, because science always involves doing the best we can with the imperfect evidence we've got.

Second, when multiple lines of imperfect evidence all point in the same direction, we can be almost as confident in our conclusions as we would be if we had a single line of perfect evidence. As psychologists Douglas Kenrick and Richard Keefe put it,

> The deaf woman, the blind man, the emotionally distraught spouse of the murder victim, and the dimwitted child are all, in themselves, dubitable sources of evidence. Nevertheless, if from each of their fuzzy vantage points, they all agree that the butler did it, we should suspect that the butler did indeed do it.[41]

To maintain a Nurture-Only view of human sex differences in the face of multiple, converging lines of evidence to the contrary requires multiple alternative explanations for the data: The hormonal evidence is unreliable because X; the cross-cultural evidence is unreliable because Y; the cross-species evidence is unreliable because Z. Not only is this unparsimonious, but it raises a new and awkward question: Why do these supposedly unreliable lines of evidence all point in the same direction

– the direction we'd expect if there were a significant innate contribution? If, on the other hand, we simply accept that there *is* a significant innate contribution, we explain all the evidence in one fell swoop, while also dissolving the residual coincidence.

The Nurture-Only position on psychological sex differences is an inherently extreme position – exactly as extreme as the Nature-Only position. It's put up a good fight over the years, but it's now straining under the weight of the evidence. I'd argue, in fact, that it's already dead, but that some haven't yet come to grips with its passing. But we can't wait forever for the stragglers to catch up. We need to keep pressing on. For we've now arrived at the doorstep of a certain Mr Charles Darwin, the originator of one of the greatest ideas in the history of human thought: evolutionary theory.

4

Nature's Blueprint

The Evolution of Human Sex Differences

Evolving Adam and Eve

I hope I've made a convincing preliminary case that the standard-issue sex differences are not just products of nurture, but that nature contributes as well. Even accepting this, though, we've still got a long way to go. Solving a scientific mystery is like cutting the head off a hydra: Two more instantly appear in its place. The nature–nurture question is no exception. The moment we're persuaded that there's an innate contribution to many human sex differences, we immediately want to ask: Why? How did we end up with genes in our genomes that cause female minds to develop somewhat differently than male minds?

To jump the gun a bit, the basic idea is that we have these genes today because, in our ancestral past, they nudged people to behave in ways that, on average, led them to have more children than their neighbours. Importantly, the best way to have more children sometimes differed for men and women. This is mainly because, in our species as in most, males can potentially have a higher number of offspring than females.

As I mentioned in Chapter 1, this is the idea that really clicked for me when I first encountered evolutionary psychology on my honeymoon. In this chapter, I'll see if I can get it to click for you too. It would probably be best, however, if we could start with a clean slate, because there are many misconceptions in circulation about the evolutionary explanation for sex differences. So, to try to do a factory reset on your ideas on this topic, let me first spell out what I'm *not* going to argue in this chapter.

WHAT I'M NOT GOING TO ARGUE

I'm not going to argue that sex differences are a result of sperm being cheaper than eggs. I'm not going to argue that sex differences trace back to differences in parental investment – not exactly, anyway. I'm not going to argue that, across the animal kingdom, males are violent sex maniacs and deadbeat dads, whereas females are chaste pacifists, doting on the kids while the males do all the interesting stuff. And I'm not going to argue that humans are a highly dimorphic species, with males alone competing for mates and females alone choosing from among the mates on offer. All of these ideas are out of date . . . or were never really *in* date in the first place. It's time to pull the conversation out of the past.

With that in mind, this chapter has two main goals. The first is to explore the main theories in evolutionary biology explaining sex differences across the living world. The second is to look at how these theories apply to one primate species in particular – us – and why they predict much more modest sex differences in our species than we find in many others. The first part of the chapter will annoy gender-role progressives with their beta bias and penchant for Nurture-Only explanations. The second part will annoy gender-role traditionalists with their *alpha* bias and preference for clearly demarcated roles for men and women. Let the annoyance commence!

Introducing Sexual Selection

How do evolutionary biologists explain sex differences? The short answer is that it's a long story, and the best way to tell a long story is to start at the beginning. So, let's wind back the clock to the late nineteenth century, and kick off our exploration with the man who, more than anyone else, set this whole endeavour in motion. I'm sure you know who I mean, but just in case you slept through high school biology, the man in question is none other than Charles Darwin. Darwin wasn't the first person to notice that female and male animals differed, but he was the first to provide a cogent explanation for this fact. To get our heads round his explanation, we should first get clear on what he was trying to explain. To that end, here's a quick run-down of six major sex differences in the animal world that particularly stood out to Darwin, and which inspired some of his greatest work.

1. **Ornamentation**. In many species, males are more ornamented than females. Birds are the overachievers in this category. If you thumb your way through a coffee-table book about birds of the world, you'll find an endless parade of brightly coloured feathers, extravagant head crests, and ridiculously oversized tails. But although birds take this trend to its extreme, male ornamentation is found in other groups as well – including in our own group, the primates. Examples include the comically large nose of the male proboscis monkey, the dark red 'trousers' of the male red-shanked douc, and the bright red face of the male uakari monkey.
2. **Choosiness**. Females tend to be choosier than males about their sexual partners, and more often say no to potential suitors. Males, on the other hand, are more inclusive when it comes to selecting partners, and keener to 'jump into bed' with any available stranger. Female choosiness is especially interesting given that, in many species, the females are drabber and less ornamented than the males. You might not think that a drab individual could afford to be super-picky, but they can – mainly because the males are hardly picky at all.
3. **Weaponry**. Across the animal kingdom, males are often built for combat. To start with, males in many species have built-in weapons systems. Among deer, for instance, males have multi-pronged antlers; among peacocks, males have vicious leg spurs; and among primates, males have oversized canine teeth. Males also tend to be better

armoured than females against the built-in weaponry of other males. Examples include the lion's mane, which helps protect his regal neck from the fangs of same-sex challengers, and the thickened skull of the male bighorn sheep, which helps him survive his extended headbutting battles with his thick-skulled male rivals. And not only are males equipped with weaponry and armour, they're equipped with a temperament matched for their use: They're typically more belligerent and prone to violence than females, especially in their dealings with other males.

4. **Sexual Size Dimorphism**. Another common trend is that, in many species, the sexes differ in size. People tend to assume that this means males are larger, presumably because that's what we find in our own species. Most of the time, however, it's the opposite: Males are the midgets, and *females* the larger sex. This is the case with many insects and most spiders, as well as most fish, many frogs, and most birds of prey. It's also the case with blue whales, which has the interesting implication that the largest individual animal on the planet is probably a female. But although females are *normally* the larger sex, in some species, the tables are turned, and males take the title. We see this, for example, in many reptiles, many birds, and many mammals.[1]
5. **Mating Effort**. As a general rule, males devote more time and energy to seeking out and wooing mates. To use the modern technical terminology, males put forward more *mating effort*. This is true not only at the behavioural level, but at the level of physiology as well. In most species, males produce vastly more sperm than females produce eggs, not just in terms of raw numbers but also in terms of volume. Just imagine how many bathtubs full of sperm the average human male produces in his lifetime. In contrast, human females don't produce even a single bathtub full of eggs; all the eggs they'll ever produce were inside them before they were born. (This implies, incidentally, that a little part of you – the egg you grew from – was inside your grandmother while she was pregnant with your mother.)

The same asymmetry is also found in plants: Many flowering plants release copious amounts of pollen during their 'breeding season', hoping to make the acquaintance of the much less numerous eggs. Whenever you have hay fever, you're inhaling evidence of a general principle in nature, namely that males put forward more mating effort.

6. **Parental Effort.** Finally, whereas males usually put forward more mating effort, females usually put forward more *parental effort* – that is, they devote more time and energy to bearing and rearing the young. Most obviously, females tend to do more hands-on parental care. Again, though, the sex difference isn't just found at the behavioural level; it's etched into female anatomy. Among mammals, for instance, females alone have the 'equipment' for incubating offspring within their bodies, and for nourishing them when they arrive in the world.

Like I say, differences like these had been spotted long before Darwin, but it was Darwin who took the first real steps toward explaining them. This he did in his second masterpiece, the 1871 book *The Descent of Man, and Selection in Relation to Sex*.[2] Darwin's explanation was a process he called *sexual selection*.

Sexual selection is sometimes defined as selection related to reproduction rather than survival. But this would imply that everything from placentas to parental care comes within the ambit of sexual selection. It's too broad. A better definition is that sexual selection is selection related to obtaining mates and achieving fertilizations.[3] Darwin saw sexual selection as a process distinct from natural selection; most biologists today, however, see it as a *subtype* of natural selection. Either way, it's an extremely important selective force in nature, helping to sculpt every sexually reproducing species.

In Darwin's original formulation, sexual selection comes in two main flavours, the twin pillars of his revolutionary theory. These are *intersexual selection* and *intrasexual selection*. Intersexual selection is selection for traits that increase one's chances of being chosen as a mate by members of the other sex. *Intra*sexual selection is selection for traits that increase one's chances of beating members of one's *own* sex in conflict over mates. These processes are often referred to as *female mate choice* and *male–male competition*, respectively. As we'll soon see, these terms are somewhat misleading; there's also plenty of *male* mate choice and *female–female* competition in nature. Moreover, as we'll also soon see, intersexual and intrasexual selection aren't the only varieties of sexual selection. Still, they are particularly important ones, which account for many of the sex differences outlined above. Our next assignment, then, is to explore them both in detail.

Choosing a Mate

We'll start with intersexual selection. This was Darwin's explanation for the ornamentation found in the males of many species. One ornament that particularly haunted the great scientist was the extravagant tail of the peacock. In a letter to the American botanist Asa Gray, Darwin wrote that 'The sight of a peacock's tail, whenever I gaze at it, makes me sick!'[4] The reason for the tail-induced nausea is that, at first glance, the peacock's tail seems to overturn his theory of natural selection. The core of that theory, after all, is the idea that selection favours useful traits: traits that help their owners to survive and thrive in the world. Apparently, though, the peacock's tail didn't get the memo. Rather than being useful, the tail seems a pointless extravagance. In fact, it's worse than pointless; it's an albatross round the peacock's neck. Instead of boosting the bird's chances of survival, it boosts its chances of meeting an untimely end. For one thing, the tail is conspicuous, which means that it readily attracts the attention of tigers and other hungry predators. For another, it's heavy and unwieldy, which means that, having attracted those predators, it makes it harder for the peacock to escape. How could selection have favoured a ticking time bomb like the peacock's tail?

The answer, Darwin eventually concluded, is that although the peacock's tail doesn't help him survive, it does help him do something else that, in evolutionary terms, is much more important: It helps him get a date. Peahens prefer well-endowed males – males with larger, prettier, more colourful tails. As a result, males with tails meeting this description have more offspring than their less well-endowed compatriots, and the average male tail evolves over the generations to be larger, prettier, and more colourful. In effect, the females redesigned the males with their sexual tastes and choices.

Intersexual selection provides an elegant explanation for the peacock's crazy tail. In doing so, however, it leads us down the rabbit hole to another perplexing mystery: Why did peahens evolve a preference for such a costly, survival-harming contraption to begin with? On the surface, it would seem a terrible move in the Darwinian game of life. After all, the sons of females with such a preference would have a good chance of inheriting their father's tail, and all the baggage that comes along with it. Wouldn't this harm rather than boost the female's reproductive success?

Evolutionary biologists have come up with several theories aiming to solve this mystery.[5] The main ones are *runaway sexual selection* and the *indicator approach*. Runaway sexual selection happens when a female sexual preference for a male trait sets in motion a feedback loop wherein the trait gets more and more extreme, while the preference gets more and more common. Initially, the female preference may target a trait linked to greater survival. Perhaps, for instance, male peacocks with larger-than-average tails were more agile, and thus better at dodging predators. Any female with a preference for males with larger-than-average tails would therefore have offspring with a better-than-average chance of living to a ripe old age. Both the larger tails and the *preference* for larger tails would be selected. And because the genes for these two traits would tend to end up in the same genomes (those of the offspring of parents possessing the traits), selection for larger tails would simultaneously be selection for the larger-tail preference, and vice versa, speeding up the process. As the preference got increasingly common, selection for larger tails would get increasingly strong, resulting in accelerating evolutionary change. Before too long, males' tails would be so large they'd be a burden to their owners. The early survival benefit of the larger tails would shrink and then reverse. But larger-than-average tails could still be selected for a time, because by this point, the preference for larger tails was so widespread that the mating benefits of sporting such a tail would more than make up for the hit to survival. Meanwhile, any female that preferred shorter-tailed, longer-lived males would produce sons that no female wanted to mate with. Thus, a trait that initially conferred a survival benefit on its owners would be favoured in a form harmful to survival, purely because the preference for that trait was now fashionable among the females.

Of course, this process couldn't continue forever; peacocks couldn't evolve tails as large as buildings or planets. Instead, runaway sexual selection would grind to a gradual halt as the survival costs of having a ludicrously large tail started matching the reproductive *benefits* of making females go weak at the knees.[6]

The second approach to explaining extravagant ornamentation is the indicator approach. According to this family of theories, ornaments like the peacock's tail signal something good about their owners: something that would make them suitable mates. Obvious candidates include health, fertility, and the ability to obtain sufficient resources to grow the ornament in the first place. Attributes such as these may be directly beneficial to females seeking a mate: A male's health, for instance, suggests an absence of diseases that he might pass on to her and her offspring, while the ability to obtain resources suggests – at least in biparental species – the capacity to invest in the young. At the same time, these attributes might also have *indirect*, genetic benefits. Like virtually all traits, health, fertility, and competence are shaped in part by genes. As such, ornaments that showcase these traits signal to the world that their owners must have *good* genes – in other words, that they must have relatively few deleterious mutations, and genes that make them relatively immune to the local parasites and pathogens.[7] This is welcome news for any prospective parent. Individuals can pass on only half their genes to each offspring. To give those genes a fighting chance of surviving in the gene pool, you need to make sure they'll be in good company. A preference for mates with traits suggestive of good genes would be an effective way to achieve that goal.

Regardless of what indicators indicate, however, one thing is clear: Not just any trait will do. Like money, indicators are only useful to the extent that they can't be easily faked. What, then, makes an indicator *hard* to fake? One suggestion is that indicators tend to be traits that are difficult to grow successfully, such that only the fittest individuals can accomplish the feat. Symmetrical antlers, tails, and faces are all plausible candidates. A competing suggestion, from the evolutionary biologist Amotz Zahavi, is that indicators are active impediments to their owners, even after they're grown. That, argues Zahavi, is how they signal fitness: Any individual that can survive and flourish despite having to lug them around must be an extremely fit specimen.[8] My sense is that the hard-to-grow explanation has more support than the active-impediment alternative. In any case, though, it's safe to assume that the only indicators that stick around in a species are those that can't be easily forged.

One last question: Why don't both sexes inherit ornaments like the peacock's tail, rather than only the males? Well, initially, perhaps they did. Traits selected for their effects in one sex do sometimes appear in the other, a phenomenon known as *genetic correlation*. But genetic correlations tend not to last long. For peahens, large tails carry all the costs borne by males, but none of the benefits. This creates a selection pressure for genes that produce the large tails in males only, or that stifle their development in females. Before too long, the tails would appear only in the male of the species, at least in their most extreme form. Ditto the many other male ornaments we see dotted round the animal kingdom.

Beating Up the Competition

Let's now turn to our second mode of sexual selection, *intrasexual selection*. This was Darwin's explanation for another set of sex differences that, although they weren't quite as nauseating as the peacock's tail, didn't seem to make sense in terms of gender-neutral selection for survival. The classic example is the deer's antlers. At first, you might suspect that antlers are a perfectly unexceptional survival device. Perhaps they help their owners fight off predators, for instance, or perhaps they help them dig up food. But if that were the case, we'd expect to find antlers on female heads as well as male ones. Most of the time, we don't. Females either have no antlers, or their antlers are faint echoes of those of the males. Something else must be going on.

That something, said Darwin, is intrasexual selection: selection for traits that help members of one sex – usually the males – defeat same-sex rivals in combat over mates. Intrasexual selection quickly resolves the mystery of the deer's antlers. During the mating season, male deer attempt to monopolize harems of females. As soon as any male achieves this goal, other males start trying to take the harem off his hooves. Males that can fight off these would-be usurpers, and keep control of a harem, end up siring more offspring, and thus pass on to their sons any traits that helped them do it. Antlers are part of that package. When two male deer meet and lock horns, males with larger, sturdier antlers have a better chance of prevailing. For that reason, antlers evolve over evolutionary time to be larger and sturdier. No less than the peacock's tail, their ultimate function is to acquire mates.

Intrasexual selection explains not only built-in weaponry but also greater male strength and aggressiveness. The recipe for these traits is the same as that for antlers: Stronger, more aggressive males typically win more fights and gain more mates, and thus males evolve over the generations to be stronger and more aggressive.

Importantly, there's a dose-response relationship in all of this: The greater the number of females that males in a species can monopolize, the stronger the selection pressures for male weaponry, strength, and belligerence, and thus the larger the sex differences in these traits.

Male–male competition and female choice often favour different traits. Sometimes, however, they put aside their differences and favour the same trait simultaneously.[9] This leads to the evolution of male attributes that are at once sexually attractive to females and scary to other males. Examples include the songs of territorial male songbirds, the antlers and low-pitched bellows of male red deer, the multicoloured facial 'war paint' of male mandrills – and perhaps the deep voices and muscular upper bodies of male humans.

Sizing Up the Sexes

Things get a bit more complicated when we turn to average sex differences in size. I mentioned earlier that, in most species, females are larger than males. According to Darwin, the main reason for this is that larger females can produce more eggs.[10] Largeness isn't usually as advantageous to males, so males tend to be smaller. Sometimes, in fact, they're tiny compared to their female counterparts. For example, male green spoonworms are around 200,000 times smaller than the females, which as the evolutionary biologist Olivia Judson remarked, is equivalent to a human male being as big as the eraser on the end of a pencil.[11]

But although females are larger in most species, in a minority, *males* are – a pattern that would seem decidedly odd to a scientifically minded green spoonworm. What the spoonworm would eventually figure out is that greater male size, on the rare occasions it's found, is usually a product of the same selective process that brought us the deer's antlers and grumpy demeanour: intrasexual selection. In many species, being larger gives males an advantage in fights with same-sex rivals. Winning more fights means siring more offspring, and thus the average male size in these species increases. Sometimes, it even increases to the point where males become the larger sex.

Selection for fighting ability doesn't *always* favour larger males. For species that fight in midair or underwater – including many birds, bats, and marine mammals – it's sometimes better to be smaller and thus more agile in this three-dimensional fighting space. Still, for species that fight in *two* dimensions, being bigger often gives you the upper hand. This is true, for instance, for gorillas, red deer, and elephant seals. And it's also true for us. That's why we have weight classes in boxing: They're not to protect the big guys from the little guys; they're to protect the little guys from the big.

Various lines of evidence support the claim that greater male size is primarily about male–male combat. The most obvious is that, when males in a species are larger, they also tend to fight more and have more built-in weaponry. To really ram the point home, however, let me outline my two favourite, more offbeat lines of evidence.

The first concerns the group of species we met in Chapter 2 for which sex is determined not by sex chromosomes but rather by the temperature of the egg. In some such species, warmer eggs develop into females and cooler ones into males, whereas in others, it's the other way around. What determines which way it goes? The answer lies in the fact that warmer temperatures prior to hatching presage better conditions and more food in the coming months, which means that both sexes can potentially grow larger. The question then is: Which sex is more advantaged by greater size? In species where males *don't* fight over females – including, for example, most turtles – being larger isn't especially advantageous to males. But it *is* advantageous to females because larger females can lay more eggs. Thus, in these species, warmer eggs tend to develop into females, whereas cooler ones develop into males. In contrast, in species where males *do* fight over females – including snapping turtles, crocodiles, and alligators – being larger is often more advantageous to males. Sure enough, in *these* species, warmer eggs tend to develop into *males* and cooler ones into females.[12] It all fits perfectly.

My second offbeat line of evidence concerns another group of species we met in Chapter 2: the sequential hermaphrodites like Nemo that change sex during the course of their lifetimes. Clownfish change from males to females, but other sequential hermaphrodites, such as bluehead wrasse, change from females to males. What determines the direction of travel? The rule of thumb seems to be: Start out as the sex that does better when it's small, then when you're older and larger, switch to the sex that does better when it's big. Here's how the rule plays out. In sequential-hermaphroditic species where we *don't* find male–male combat, individuals tend to start out as males then turn into females when they're older and larger, because larger females can produce more eggs. Conversely, in species where we *do* find extensive male–male combat, individuals tend to start out as *females* then turn into *males* when they're older and larger, because of the fighting advantage conferred by greater size.[13] An interesting implication of this is that if deer, gorillas, or humans were sequential hermaphrodites, they'd change from females to males, whereas if eagles, frogs, or sharks were, most would make the opposite journey.

As with other products of sexual selection, we find a dose-response relationship for intrasexual conflict and sexual size dimorphism. Consider, for instance, gorillas and gibbons: two species that bookend the range of size dimorphism found among the apes. Gorillas are polygynous; successful males monopolize harems of females, leaving many roaming bachelors with none. This creates a strong selection pressure for traits that help males assemble a harem and fight off envious rivals. As a result, male gorillas are more than twice the size of females. Gibbons, on the other hand, are largely monogamous; male gibbons tend to have just one mate, which means that there's someone for almost everyone, and male–male competition is greatly reduced. For that reason, male gibbons are only a little larger than their female consorts. The general rule is that, in various families of animals, from primates to seals to ungulates, the greater the number of females that males in a species can monopolize, the more intense the conflict between the males, and the more size dimorphic the species tends to be.[14]

Sexual Selection 2.0

Darwin's theory of sexual selection was a great leap forward in our understanding of female–male differences. Still, as we'd expect in any science, it was really only the first draft of the theory. Following Darwin's pioneering efforts, evolutionary biologists built on and refined sexual selection in many important ways. To start familiarizing ourselves with the new and improved version of the theory – what we might call *Sexual Selection 2.0* – here are two friendly amendments to Darwin's original proposal.

FRIENDLY AMENDMENT #1: IT'S NOT JUST ABOUT FEMALE CHOICE AND MALE–MALE CONFLICT

Evolutionary scientists have traditionally put a strong emphasis on female mate choice and male–male conflict over mates. But although there's a lot of both in the animal kingdom, there's also plenty of *male* mate choice and *female–female* conflict over mates – including, you might have noticed, in our own species. The strong emphasis on female choice and male–male conflict may be an example of the alpha bias discussed in Chapter 1: that is, the tendency to read Mars-and-Venus sex differences into what are actually modest statistical discrepancies. Because of this bias, scientists may have overlooked and underestimated male choosiness and conflict between females.[15]

Unfortunately, however, human beings seem to be constitutionally unable to spot an error without overcompensating and making the opposite error in its place. As such, in certain circles, people substitute the alpha bias for the delta bias, and strongly emphasize anything that goes against traditional sex differences: choosy males, violent females, male parental care, and the like. The danger in shining too bright a spotlight on the exceptions is that the general trends are obscured, giving a false impression that anything goes in nature, and that everything is as common as everything else. Certainly, we shouldn't exaggerate the ubiquity of female mate choice or male–male conflict. But we also shouldn't lose sight of the fact that these tendencies are more common than their opposites.[16] They're Coke compared to Pepsi.

FRIENDLY AMENDMENT #2: IT'S NOT JUST ABOUT INTERSEXUAL AND INTRASEXUAL SELECTION

Mate choice and same-sex conflict are crucial components of sexual selection. They don't, however, exhaust sexual selection's repertoire.

Another category of sexual selection – one even uglier than same-sex conflict, unfortunately – is sexual coercion.[17] Almost always, this means male coercion of females. Although males seeking a mate will often sweeten the deal with gifts of food, protection, or help with the kids, sometimes they'll renounce the carrot in favour of the stick, and resort to harassment, force, or threats of force to obtain sex from unwilling females.[18] Such behaviour has been documented in various mammals, including chimps, orangutans, and dolphins. It's also been documented in more remotely related species, from ducks to guppies to bedbugs. Indeed, in scorpion flies, males even have an organ whose sole function is to hold females in place while forcibly copulating with them.[19]

Regardless of the species, though, as soon as one sex evolves to coerce the other, the other sex evolves counteradaptations. Thus, a common pattern in nature – including in our own group, the primates – is that while males evolve to try to control females, females evolve to resist male control: They fight, they flee, they form alliances with fellow females.[20]

The Ultimate Origins of Sex Differences

I mentioned at the start of the chapter that solving a scientific mystery is like cutting the head off a hydra: As soon as you do it, two more appear in its place. Well, we've just come to another example – or more precisely, to two of them. You might assume that having explained the peacock's tail in terms of female choice, and the deer's antlers in terms of male–male combat, we'd now have two fewer questions to answer than we did before. But even as these two recede from view, four new ones step in to replace them. Why is it more often females that exert mate choice? Why is it more often males that sport ostentatious ornaments and fight to accumulate mates? Why not the reverse or equal numbers of both? Come to think of it, why are there any sex differences at all in mate choice or same-sex combat?

These are tough questions, and biologists still debate the finer points of their answers. In my view, though, the big-picture explanation is largely in place, and constitutes one of the great breakthroughs in the history of science. To outline this breakthrough, I suggest we work our way through a series of hypotheses about the ultimate origins of sex differences, which roughly recapitulates the development of scientists' thinking in this area. To get the ball rolling, we'll turn the clock back to 1948.

HYPOTHESIS #1: IT'S ALL ABOUT EGGS AND SPERM

Our first hypothesis traces back to the seminal work of geneticist A.J. Bateman.[21] In a famous series of experiments, Bateman put groups of fruit flies into jars, observed who mated with whom, then looked at the connection between the number of mates each fly had and the number of subsequent offspring. For both sexes, moving from zero mates to one obviously made a big difference – all the difference in the world, in fact, as it meant moving from zero offspring to more than zero. Beyond that, however, the story diverged profoundly for males and females. For males, each additional mate increased their tally of offspring in a simple linear way: Two mates meant twice as many offspring as one, and three mates meant three times as many. For females, in contrast, additional mates *didn't* increase their offspring tally. From a Darwinian perspective, it was a waste of time and effort.

Bateman argued that this ultimately traces back to *anisogamy*: the fact that eggs are larger than sperm and thus less numerous. As a result of this sexual asymmetry, a female's entire stash of eggs can be fertilized by just one male, after which further romantic dalliances would be reproductively pointless for her. The male, on the other hand, would still have plenty of sperm left over, and each new dalliance for *him* would represent a further stash of eggs that he could convert into his own offspring, each a bearer of half his genes. The upshot, argued Bateman, is that males throughout the animal kingdom have evolved to seek multiple mates, whether through fighting, showing off, or whatever, whereas females have evolved to prioritize quality over quantity.

Bateman's fruit fly experiments were flawed in various ways.[22] Nonetheless, the idea that having multiple mates can boost male fitness more than female fitness has an intuitive appeal, and subsequent, higher-quality research has confirmed that it's usually true. Bateman was definitely on to something.

At the same time, though, it soon became apparent that not all species fit the Bateman mould. It's simply not the case that males only ever seek multiple sexual conquests, whereas females only ever seek Mr Right. Two groups of species in particular buck the Bateman trend.

The first are what are called *sexually monomorphic species*. These are species where females and males are virtually identical in every trait other than their primary sex organs. Monomorphic species include our fellow apes the gibbons, various New World monkeys, and a large majority of birds. Shown a photo of a female and a male from any of these species, it's nearly impossible to say which is which. You might as well throw a coin.

The second group of trend-buckers are the *sex-role-reversed species*. These are species where all the usual sex differences are flipped into reverse. A good example is the pipefish, a close relative of the seahorse. In many pipefish species, females are more brightly coloured than males, and pushier about soliciting mates: the opposite of the traditional pattern.[23] Sex-role reversal is also found in some shorebirds and wading birds. For instance, among Wilson's phalaropes, females compete vigorously for sexual access to males, rather than the other way around. As one observer noted, 'it is common to see solitary males swimming nervously along the edges of grassy ponds pursued by several females'.[24] Other sex-role-reversed birds include jacanas and spotted sandpipers, among whom females are larger and more aggressive, and compete among themselves to assemble harems of the timid little males. My female students always seem to love hearing about the sex-role-reversed species. Finally, guys get a taste of their own medicine!

I'll come back to these evolutionary anomalies soon. The crucial point for now is that in every monomorphic and sex-role-reversed species, eggs are more expensive than sperm, and yet the Bateman sex differences are absent. This tells us that sex differences can't just be about eggs and sperm. We need a bigger theory.

HYPOTHESIS #2: IT'S ALL ABOUT PARENTAL INVESTMENT

The next big breakthrough came from one of the giants of twentieth-century evolutionary biology: Robert Trivers.[25] Trivers argued in 1972 – as a graduate student, no less – that the ultimate source of sex differences is not anisogamy, but rather *parental investment*. He defined parental investment as any contribution that a parent makes to a particular offspring that forecloses the option of contributing to other offspring. Part of parental investment is the egg or sperm that launches each new individual – and in fact, for many species, the egg or sperm is the start, middle, and end of parental investment. In some lineages, however, it's such a minuscule part of overall investment that it barely makes a dent. It's swamped by other contributions, such as gestation, incubation, feeding, protection, and transportation.[26] As every human parent knows, the list is long.

The core of Trivers's theory is the idea that, in species where the sexes differ in how much they invest in each offspring, the sex that invests more will evolve to be choosier about its mates, while the sex that invests less will evolve to compete for mates more fervently.

To understand the logic of Trivers's hypothesis, we can start by asking: What would be the best way for an individual to boost the number of surviving offspring they produce? Two main options suggest themselves. One is to be highly selective about your mates, choosing only those with the most resources, the best health, or the best genes. The other is to aim at *quantity* of mates rather than quality. Which of these approaches is better?

Well, it depends how much you invest in each offspring. If you invest a lot, then aiming at quantity rather than quality would probably be a fool's errand. That's because, like Bateman's female fruit flies, you'll quickly reach the point where further mates won't increase your offspring headcount. A better bet would be to prioritize quality over quantity – that is, to be pickier about your partners.

But what if you instead invest little in each offspring? *Then* your best bet might be to seek as many mates as possible. Because you invest so little, you could potentially have offspring with more than one high investor – or maybe more than two, or three, or four. Of course, this is the best bet not just for you but for every other low investor as well, and if some low investors have more than their 'fair share' of offspring, others must have less. This introduces a new element into the game: same-sex competition. Low investors evolve to compete among themselves for access to high investors, either with traits that meet the high investors' exacting standards, or by fighting each other for access to the high investors: the peacock approach or the deer approach, respectively.

The net result of these selection pressures is that, where there's a sex difference in parental investment, the higher-investing sex evolves to be choosier about its mates, whereas the lower-investing sex evolves to compete for mates more vigorously. In most species, females are the higher-investing sex and males the lower-investing sex, so females evolve to be choosier and males to be more competitive. But it doesn't always go that way. According to Trivers, when males invest as much in offspring as females, the sexes don't particularly differ in choosiness, competitiveness, ornamentation, or weaponry. And when males invest *more* than females, we find the mirror image of the usual differences.

As you might have noticed, this immediately suggests an explanation for the evolutionary anomalies that led us to reject the Bateman hypothesis: the monomorphic and sex-role-reversed species. Sure enough, the evidence lines up nicely with the explanation.

First, in the monomorphic species, the sexes typically invest roughly equally in each offspring. In most birds, for instance, females and males form pair bonds, and both help take care of the young. As a result, sex differences in these species are muted, just as parental investment theory would predict.

Second, in the sex-role-reversed species, the males typically invest *more* in each offspring than the females. For example, in pipefish (as among seahorses), the females lay their eggs into the males' kangaroo-style brood pouch using a penis-like structure called an *ovipositor*, after which the males nourish the developing embryos via a structure akin to the mammalian placenta. This means that, in many pipefish species, males invest more in each offspring. For that reason, males in these species evolved to be choosier about their mates, while females evolved to be more ornamented and sexually pushy. Similarly, among jacanas, harem-holding females lay a clutch of eggs with each of the males in their harem, then leave them to raise the kids on their own. That's why male jacanas evolved to be choosier, while females evolved to be more ornamented, more aggressive, and larger.

One of the great virtues of Trivers's theory, then, is that it effortlessly explains exceptions to the rule like the monomorphic and sex-role-reversed species. In fact, though these species are exceptions to *Bateman's* rule, they're *not* exceptions to Trivers's. They're powerful confirmation of it.

With the concept of parental investment, Trivers took us many steps closer to a complete explanation for evolved sex differences. You can almost feel the puzzle pieces falling into place. But is parental investment the end of the line when it comes to explaining differences between the sexes? It's not. As we'll see in the next section, in some species, females invest considerably more in each offspring than males, yet the species shows little in the way of sex differences. Meanwhile, in other species, males invest as much or even more than females, yet the sexes differ in all the usual ways. We've still got some work left to do.

HYPOTHESIS #3: IT'S ALL ABOUT REPRODUCTIVE VARIABILITY

The next step is a little trickier, and my framing of the issues here a little idiosyncratic. As I see it, the best way to understand the evolution of sex differences is to focus not on eggs vs sperm or on parental investment, but rather on *reproductive variability* – that is, the extent to which individuals differ from one another in the number of offspring they produce. Importantly, levels of reproductive variability often differ between the sexes. The *average* number of offspring for each sex has to be roughly equal, at least as long as the adult sex ratio is roughly equal.

The *variance*, however, can be greater for one sex or the other. Most often, the variance is greater for males: The male distribution is flatter and stretches out further on either side of the average. This means that, in most species, more males than females have no offspring at all, but also that more males than females have a very high number of offspring – many more, often, than even the most reproductively prolific female. In other words, males have a higher *potential reproductive rate* or *maximum offspring number*.[27]

To be clear, Bateman and Trivers were both well aware of the importance of sex differences in reproductive variability. Indeed, we might say their theories were attempts to explain those differences, with parental investment coming closest. As we'll see, though, parental investment isn't the only contributor; various other factors play a role. This makes it conceptually messy to focus on the *causes* of sex differences in reproductive variability as the primary locus of our explanation for sex differences in general. In my view, we should take a step back and focus instead on reproductive variability itself. Doing so not only makes the explanation less cumbersome, it provides, I think, the clearest understanding of how most female–male differences evolve.

So, how does the reproductive variability explanation work? The key is the sex difference in the maximum number of offspring one can produce. For both sexes, any trait that shunts an individual toward the maximum number for their sex has a good chance of being selected – and the further it shunts them, the greater the chance. However, because more males than females have a very high number of offspring, selection for such traits is stronger for males. Moreover, the traits that enable males to reach the reproductive heights for their sex often differ from those that do it for females. They differ for the same reason that males often have a higher maximum offspring number in the first place, namely that males can have offspring with more females than females can have with males. Consequently, pursuing multiple mates often pays greater reproductive dividends for males than females, and males evolve to do more of it.

The most obvious way this happens is that males evolve a stronger *desire* for multiple mates. Just as hunger pushes animals to eat and thirst to drink, the desire for multiple mates pushes males to try to spread their seed. Desiring alone, however, is never enough; as we've seen, every male might *want* an above-average number of sexual partners, but the laws of logic dictate that not every male can have this. As such, any trait that helps a male beat the odds and have multiple partners is likely to be selected. Depending on the species, this can include traits that enhance males' ability to attract females, traits that enhance males' ability to beat up rival males, traits that enable males to coerce unwilling females, or some combination of these options.

Just as Trivers explained phenomena that Bateman couldn't, reproductive variability explains phenomena that Trivers couldn't. To begin with, in some species, we find significant sex differences in parental investment but low levels of sexual dimorphism. This can happen, for instance, in species where females are widely dispersed, and thus males can't monopolize multiple females. As a result, even if males invest little in their young, the sexes have similar levels of reproductive variability and aren't especially dimorphic.[28] We see this, for example, in gibbons and in some solitary deer and antelopes.

Conversely, in some species, we find high male parental investment but also high levels of traditional dimorphism. In many territorial fish, for instance, females lay their eggs in the male's territory, then abandon them with the male, who takes on the remaining duties of childcare: guarding the eggs, fanning them to keep them oxygenated, clearing up waste, and so on. Despite the heavy paternal burden, however, these species exhibit most of the usual sex differences: Males are more aggressive and inclined to seek multiple mates; females are choosier about who they mate with. To be fair, this isn't *necessarily* inconsistent with a parental-investment account. As mentioned, Trivers defined parental investment as any investment in one offspring that limits the ability to invest in others. With territorial male fish, it's not much harder to guard a hundred tiny eggs than to guard fifty. Thus, although males invest a lot of time and energy into caring for offspring, male investment *per offspring* is low – perhaps lower than *female* investment per offspring.[29] Let's assume, though, as seems plausible, that males *do* invest more per offspring. This would challenge the parental-investment explanation for sex differences in territorial fish, but it *wouldn't* challenge the reproductive-variability explanation. That's because males in these species can invest heavily in offspring without foreclosing the option of acquiring additional mates. And because males can care for many clutches of eggs at once, successful males can have many more offspring than any female.[30] In other words, males have greater reproductive variability. Everything else follows from that.

Again, the main reason that, in most species, males have greater reproductive variability is that, in most species, males invest less in each offspring. But that's not the only reason, and in the final analysis, sex differences come down to reproductive variability, rather than parental investment.

In my view, reproductive variability explains most of what we want to explain about the evolutionary origins of sex differences. Full disclosure, though: Some biologists argue that we should frame things instead in terms of the sex ratio of reproductively ready individuals, or that other variables – including the adult sex ratio – should be considered independent contributors to evolved differences between the sexes.[31] For our purposes, however, reproductive variability has sufficient explanatory power, and is sufficiently intuitively graspable, to serve as a useful working hypothesis.

The Evolution of Mutual Mate Choice

We've now got a comprehensive theory of the evolution of sex differences in the animal kingdom. Time for the question you've been waiting for: How do humans fit into this framework? In many ways, as you've no doubt already noticed, our species fits the same mould as most other animals, and particularly other mammals. For a start, the minimum biological contribution required to make a new human being is larger for women than men. Women's minimum is a nine-month pregnancy and – until recently – several years of breastfeeding. *Men's* minimum is notably more modest: in principle, as little as a single sex act. The philosopher and psychologist Cordelia Fine captured the asymmetry like this:

> As we all know, the two parents of every human baby are owed grossly unequal debts for the miracle of life. According to my rough calculations, the mother is due more or less a lifetime of unwavering gratitude in return for the donation of a nice plump egg, forty weeks or so full bed and board *in utero*, many hours of labour, and several months of breast-feeding. But for the father, who by the time of birth may have supplied nothing more than a single sperm, a quick appreciative nod might well seem sufficient.[32]

(Note that Fine isn't a fan of the evolutionary approach to sex differences, and that the passage above comes from a book critiquing it. But she's a great writer, and I love the passage!)

As a result of the sex difference in minimum parental investment, men can potentially have many more offspring than women. Of course, the fact that men can do this in principle doesn't necessarily mean any do. But sociological, anthropological, and genetic evidence indicates that, in virtually every society, men's reproductive output is more variable than women's, with more men than women having many offspring and more men than women having none.[33] And just as we'd expect in such a species, humans exhibit most of the sex differences found in our nonhuman kin: Women are often more selective about their sexual partners, men are often more aggressive, and so on – the usual list. At first glance, then, we seem to be typical mammals with typical mammalian sex differences.

But it's time for a twist in the plot. Humans, you see, turn out to be anything but typical. As I argued in a 2013 paper in *Psychological Inquiry*, co-authored with my then-PhD student Andrew Thomas, there are two main ways we can construe humans' evolved sexual psychology.[34] The first we dubbed the *males-compete/females-choose* (or *MCFC*) model.

According to this model, humans are a highly dimorphic species, in which males compete for mates, and females choose from among the males on offer. The second model we called the *mutual-mate-choice* (or *MMC*) model. According to *this* model, humans are a relatively *monomorphic* species: a species in which both sexes are choosy about their long-term mates, and both compete among themselves for the most desirable mates in their league. As you've probably guessed, we argued that the latter is a better fit for our species.

Certainly, women are often choosier than men, and certainly, men often compete in more extreme and risky ways. However, these are differences of degree rather than kind, and compared to most other mammals, sex differences in our species are modest. Rather than being highly dimorphic critters like gorillas or red deer, humans are somewhat monomorphic ones, like gibbons or grebes. Here's our five-step explanation for how we came to be this way.

1. MAKING A NEW HUMAN IS COSTLY

The first step is the observation that, because of our big, clever brains, human offspring require much more parental input than the average baby chipmunk or water buffalo. There are two main reasons for this.

Reason number one is that our offspring are entirely dependent at birth. This traces back to the fact that humans are bipedal: We habitually walk on two legs. Because of this evolutionary quirk, we have narrow pelvises, which serve as platforms for the top halves of our bodies. But because our pelvises are narrow, women's birth canals are narrow too. That was fine when we first evolved our bipedal ways, as our brains weren't particularly big back then – no bigger than the average chimpanzee brain. But as soon as we started evolving bigger brains, the narrow birth canals started causing serious problems for our female ancestors: problems roughly akin to pushing a bowling ball through an exhaust pipe.

The solution that natural selection hit on was for women to give birth early, when the fetus's head was still relatively small. Of course, 'relatively' is the operative word here; giving birth is still not a walk in the park for the average woman. Nonetheless, scaling back the size of our newborns' heads even a little meant giving birth to babies that are, in effect, premature. If our young were born at the same developmental stage as the average primate, our pregnancies would last for nearly two years – a horrifying prospect, I've been told, for many women.[35]

The second reason that our young are so costly is that humans have an extended childhood. In our species and many others, childhood is an apprenticeship for adulthood: a time when the young acquire the knowledge and skills required for life as an adult. However, because of our big brains and extreme behavioural flexibility, this apprenticeship is a particularly long one for us. It can take up to two decades for a child to reach full nutritional independence in a traditional, non-state society – a horrifying prospect, I've been told, for prospective parents of both sexes.[36] (Kidding.)

These difficulties are compounded by the fact that, despite the extreme and extended dependence of our young, women have a shorter *interbirth interval* than most other female apes: The gap between one offspring and the next tends to be briefer for us. Admittedly, compared to most other animals, we're slow-motion breeders. Compared to most other *apes*, however, we pump out sprogs like confetti from a confetti cannon. As a result, mothers often have more than one dependent offspring at a time.

2. THE COSTLINESS OF OUR OFFSPRING LED TO THE EVOLUTION OF ALLOMATERNAL CARE

The exorbitant price tag placed on human offspring, along with women's short interbirth interval, had an important consequence: Unlike most female apes, women can't do it alone.[37] Mothers need a spare pair of hands – or better yet, a whole village of them. We can surmise, therefore, that the evolution of smart, big-brained offspring went hand in hand with the evolution of various forms of *allomaternal care*: that is, care from individuals other than the mother.

In our species, allomaternal care comes from a variety of sources, including grandparents (especially maternal grandmothers), older siblings (especially sisters), and assorted other relatives.[38] Often, though, it comes from the father.[39] Fathers are rarely the only allomaternal investors, but they are usually important ones. This makes perfect evolutionary sense: Aside from the occasional adult sibling, fathers are the only adults in the world who are as closely related to a woman's offspring as she is.

What psychological mechanisms did natural selection build into our heads to facilitate biparental care? Two in particular stand out. The first is a tendency to form pair bonds. The glue that binds human pair bonds together is romantic love. Men and women everywhere have a built-in capacity to fall in love – sometimes for months, sometimes for years, sometimes even for life. Romantic love has several functions. One is to keep the couple in each other's orbit for long enough for the woman to get pregnant. Another, though, is to provide a setting for dual-parent care of the young, especially during the early, difficult years.[40] Needless to say, things don't always work out this way; women are sometimes left 'holding the baby'. Still, the capacity to fall in love for years rather than mere months most likely evolved to facilitate biparental care of shared offspring.[41]

The second piece of mental hardware designed to generate biparental care is the capacity for fathers, rather than only mothers, to 'fall in love' with their offspring. Just as women have a maternal instinct, so too men have a paternal one. More precisely, both sexes have essentially the same *parental* instinct; natural selection just 'decided' to start installing it in male brains as well as female brains.

This isn't to suggest, by the way, that the natural human mating system is a 1950s-style nuclear family or till-death-do-us-part monogamy. Humans engage in every imaginable permutation of sexual and child-rearing behaviour, and plenty of unimaginable ones as well. Our repertoire includes everything from lifelong monogamy to serial monogamy to polygamy and casual sex. But pair bonding does seem to be our *primary* reproductive arrangement, if only in the sense that it's our most common one. And it's not just common in the West, where polygamous marriage is outlawed. Even in societies where men are permitted to take multiple wives, pair bonds are almost always the most common relationship type.[42] Plausibly, this is because pair bonds provide a suitable platform for two-parent care of the young.

3. PATERNAL CARE COEVOLVED WITH MUTUAL COURTSHIP

As soon as men started falling in love and helping foot the bill for their offspring, the selective forces acting on our species shifted dramatically. The falling and the helping lowered the number of offspring that most men could realistically sire. And that, in turn, ushered in two major changes in the nature of human courtship.

The first was that men evolved to be choosier about their mates, at least when it came to long-term, committed relationships. They evolved to be choosier for the same reason that women had: because they were investing more in each offspring, and thus each offspring counted for more.

But it wasn't just men who rewrote the script. As males evolved to invest more in offspring, females evolved to compete for the best investors. They hadn't particularly needed to before; when a man's contribution to the baby-making process is just a bouquet of flowers and a sperm donation, he can pair up with every woman who wants him, and women have little reason to risk competing to be first in line. However, as soon as men started investing significant time and effort in their young, male investment became a scarce commodity, and competing for it was suddenly worth the risk.

Long story short, pair bonding and paternal care coevolved with mutual mate choice. Rather than females alone being picky and males alone competing for mates, both sexes started doing both.

4. BOTH SEXES HAVE THEIR EQUIVALENTS OF THE PEACOCK'S TAIL AND THE DEER'S ANTLERS

As a result of the two-way sexual selection process that now typified our species, both sexes put the other under selection for the traits they most wanted in a mate. This then led to the evolution of sexual ornamentation in both sexes. The clearest examples are physical traits that appear at puberty, and which heterosexual members of both sexes find attractive in the other. These include breasts and the hourglass figure in women, and the V-shaped torso in men. Such traits are human equivalents of the peacock's tail, but with one important difference: Unlike peacocks, both sexes have them.[43]

It's not just about the physical, though. As evolutionary psychologist Geoffrey Miller argued, both sexes also have various *psychological* peacock's tails: traits like humour, generosity, and creative intelligence that evolved, at least in part, to attract mates.[44]

In case you're finding it hard to swallow the idea that both sexes could have peacock's tails, bear in mind that the same thing is found in other species. In many pair-bonding birds, for instance, both sexes have colourful feathers and elaborate mating dances; in cotton-top tamarins, both sexes have cute little matching mohawks; and in some pterosaurs and dinosaurs, both sexes seem to have had ornamental head crests.[45]

As well as our his-and-hers peacock's tails, both sexes in our species have their equivalents of the deer's antlers. For men, these include many of the same physical features that women find alluring, including strength, muscularity, and deep voices. Such traits appear to be peacock's tails and deer's antlers all wrapped up in one.[46] *Women's* antlers, in contrast, tend to be subtler and less intrusive. Although women less often engage in physical combat, they easily match men when it comes to psychological warfare.[47] To the extent that this boosted women's odds of outmanoeuvring rival females and winning a preferred mate, the tendency is a product of the same selective force that brought us male muscularity, male aggression, and the deer's gigantic antlers: intrasexual selection.

5. PAIR BONDING AND BIPARENTAL CARE LED TO REDUCED DIMORPHISM

The final step in our theory is that as men and women started joining forces to care for the young, the overall level of sexual dimorphism in our species dropped. Although the sex difference in *minimum* parental investment remained large, the sex difference in the *typical* level of investment was now notably smaller. As such, the maximum number of offspring that most men could produce fell, bringing it closer to the number for women. And that, in turn, led to a proportionate reduction in the level of dimorphism in our line.

Consistent with this analysis, and as we saw in Chapter 2, most psychological sex differences in our species are less than half the size of the relatively modest sex difference in height. More than that, most are smaller than the size difference in *gibbons*. This comparison is important, because gibbons are the archetypal example of a monomorphic primate.[48] The only place where human sex differences even approach Mars-and-Venus levels is among the minority at the extremes of the distribution.

At this point, a sceptic might argue that my framing underestimates the level of reproductive skew in our species. Throughout human history, males at the top have always had many more mates and offspring than those on the lower rungs. The history books are littered with despotic leaders who seemed to make it their life's mission to populate the world with their progeny: Genghis Khan, Niall of the Nine Hostages, Ismail the Bloodthirsty, and many others.[49] The problem with this argument, however, is that everyone who's read even a little on this topic is familiar with all of these names – and the fact that we're all familiar with the *same* set of names suggests that these cases are rare exceptions. To treat them as illustrative of the kind of selection pressures typically acting on our species is equivalent to going to a circus sideshow and generalizing from the performers there to the entirety of humankind. When we look at aggregate data rather than anecdotes, we find that although reproductive variability is greater among men than women, the variability sex difference in our species is at the lower end of the range for mammals.[50]

Not only that, but the fossil record testifies to the fact that, as our species evolved its watermelon heads and superior cognitive firepower, we also evolved lower levels of sexual dimorphism. Our long-lost ancestors the australopithecines were considerably more dimorphic than we are. Tracing a path from them to us, we find that as our brains got bigger, the level of sexual size dimorphism in our lineage got smaller. This is particularly telling given that, during the same period, our overall body size increased, and larger species tend to be *more* dimorphic, not less. Thus, the fact that dimorphism shrank as our brains grew bigger is even more significant than we might initially have supposed.

Having said all this, it's worth remembering that, despite the shrinkage, many important sex differences remain, and an evolutionary perspective provides a beautiful, deeply satisfying explanation for that fact. With the broad outline of that explanation now in place, our next task will be to zoom in on the details of some of the most important differences. We'll start at ground zero, with the process that put us all here in the first place: sex.

5

Sex on the Brain

Men and Women in the Bedroom

Getting a Camel Through the Eye of a Needle in a Haystack

Perhaps you've heard the rumours, but men and women aren't always on the same page when it comes to sex and love. This is nicely illustrated by the story of a young woman who, tired of receiving unsolicited dick pics from every Tom, Richard, and Harry, decided to return fire with her own 'crotch shot'. To her surprise, the recipients didn't react the way she had. Rather than being shocked or chastened, they were over the moon.[1] The behaviour of the woman in this scenario, and that of the men who sent the dick pics to begin with, exemplifies what psychologists call *failures of cross-sex mindreading*. Why are such mindreading mishaps so common?

After many years of studying and seeking an answer, I've hit upon a radical new theory that, in my view, lays this age-old mystery to rest: Men and women are different.

Wait a minute, you might protest; didn't you just finish arguing that men and women *aren't* particularly different? Well, I did. Sex differences in humans are generally modest. However, when it comes to sexual psychology, the gaps are notably larger. In fact, it's in the realm of sexuality that we find the single largest psychological sex difference ever documented in our species. (See if you can guess what it is; I'll come back to it soon.)

Certainly, most sex differences in sexuality aren't like night and day. But they are big enough to matter. That's why the shelves of most bookstores are groaning under the weight of books about navigating sex and relationships. In this chapter, we'll explore the evolutionary origins of some of the sex differences that turn these tomes into bestsellers.

Sex Differences in Sexual Psychology

To kick things off, let's survey some well-established sex differences in sexual psychology, while strictly adhering to our policy of avoiding exaggerating or minimizing the differences.

1. THE LARGEST PSYCHOLOGICAL SEX DIFFERENCE

I asked you a moment ago to guess the largest psychological sex difference in our species. Did you take a guess? The answer is – drum roll – the sex difference in which sex one is primarily attracted to. Most men are primarily attracted to women; most women are primarily attracted to men.

If you guessed wrong, don't feel bad; even scientists tend to overlook this difference, despite its magnitude and obvious evolutionary rationale. Case in point: In an otherwise excellent review paper on evolved human sex differences, the psychologist John Archer neglected to even mention this one.[2] What explains our blindness to the difference? Perhaps the fact that we're all so familiar with it that we barely notice it's there.

Familiar or not, though, omitting it from the discussion of sex differences is like omitting the sun from a list of bodies that make up the solar system, and mentioning only the planets and moons: It's not a trivial mistake.

2. SEX DIFFERENCES IN SEX DRIVE

With the sun duly noted, we can now turn to some of the sexual planets and moons. The first is a Jupiter-sized sex difference: On average, men have a higher sex drive than women.[3] A recent meta-analysis synthesized the results of 211 studies on this topic – in case the first 111 weren't convincing enough – and confirmed that the sex difference is robust and replicable.[4] Men think about sex more; they dream about sex more; they masturbate more; they more frequently experience sexual desire; they spend more money and take more risks to get sex; they're less happy with involuntary celibacy; and at the extremes, they're over-represented among people exhibiting hypersexuality.

Is it just that it's more socially acceptable for men to admit to such things? Apparently not: Statistically controlling for reporting bias only shrinks the gap a little.[5] The sex difference appears to be real.

It's also something of a sensitive subject, however, so it's worth revisiting our earlier cautions about the nature of human sex differences. First, to say that, on average, men have a higher sex drive than women isn't to say that women are uninterested in sex. That would be like concluding that because, on average, men have larger feet than women, women don't have feet. Likewise, to say that, on average, men have a higher sex drive than women isn't to say that most women have a *low* sex drive. *That* would be like concluding that because, on average, men are taller than women, most women are three feet tall.

As usual, the reality is individual variation within each sex and overlap between the sexes. Some women have a low sex drive; some have a high sex drive; most fall somewhere in between – just like men. And although the male *average* is higher, plenty of women have a higher sex drive than plenty of men. The sex difference is only substantial among the minority at the extremes of the distribution. As the sex therapist Marty Klein observed, if you knew that a person behind a screen was six-foot-six, you could guess that that person was almost certainly a man. However, if you knew that the person was *five*-foot-six, you couldn't hazard a confident guess. By the same token, says Klein, if you knew that a person was hypersexual, you could guess that that person was probably a man – but if you knew that the person wanted sex a few times a week, you wouldn't have a clue.

3. SEX DIFFERENCES IN INTEREST IN CASUAL SEX AND SEXUAL VARIETY

Not only do the sexes differ in sex drive, but they differ in some of the sexual activities that most entice them. On average, men are more interested than women in casual, no-strings-attached sex, and more willing to engage in sex in the absence of a close relationship.[6] Men are more willing to consent to sex with someone they've known for only a short time, and less likely to regret it later.[7] Men report wanting more sexual partners than women over the next month, the next year, the next twenty years, and the course of the rest of their lives.[8] Men are more likely to cheat on a partner – a particularly revealing finding given that women have more sexual offers and thus more opportunities to cheat.[9] And among those people who do cheat on a partner, the men are more likely than the women to do so just for fun and despite being happy in their relationship.[10] These generalizations aren't based on merely a study or two or three; they're among the best-replicated findings in psychology.[11]

One criticism of the research on this topic is that much of it involves self-report surveys, and may therefore be less than accurate. People sometimes bend the truth in socially desirable directions, and even when they tell the truth as they see it, people's self-assessments are sometimes misguided. Until we can give research participants truth serum and papal infallibility, we can't rest our case on self-report studies alone. We also need to look at real-world behaviour.

Unfortunately, that's easier said than done. For one thing, there are privacy issues, and the pesky fact that scientists can't just go round peeking into people's bedroom windows. Even if they could, though, it takes two to tango, so people's real-world sexual behaviour doesn't always reflect their true desires.

One way to get around these roadblocks is to look at the subset of people who can most reliably get what they want on the mating market. This includes, to begin with, gay men and lesbians. As the anthropologist Donald Symons observed, when it comes to sex and love, gay men and lesbians don't have to compromise with the typical desires of the other sex, for the simple reason that they're not sexually or romantically interested in the other sex.[12] As such, their behaviour more reliably reveals what they genuinely want. Sure enough, when we look at the behaviour of gay men and lesbians, we see the sex difference in casual sex laid bare. On one side of the ledger, gay men tend to rack up many more sexual partners than straight men, and gay-male culture often places a premium on casual sex. The only place in Straightsville where such a situation is common is in the imaginations of frustrated straight men.[13] On the other side, lesbians tend to have *fewer* sexual partners than straight women, despite the fact that lesbians don't have to worry about accidental pregnancies or the fact that their preferred sexual partners are almost always larger, stronger, and more prone to violence than them.

A second group of people who can reliably get what they want on the mating market are individuals with absolute power. As the anthropologist Laura Betzig documented, in every one of the world's early civilizations, despotic male leaders assembled large harems of fertile young women. Despotic *female* leaders, in contrast, didn't assemble even *small* harems of fertile young men.[14] To be fair, despots presumably come from the extreme of the distribution for male-linked traits such as dominance, aggression, and polygamous desire, and as we know, sex differences are magnified at the extremes: the tail-of-the-distribution effect. Still, despotic leaders presumably exhibit an exaggerated version of a common sex difference – one found in a less pronounced form among the majority in the middle.[15]

Another line of evidence for female–male differences in sexual behaviour is a famous study from the how-the-hell-did-they-get-ethical-approval-for-*that*? file.[16] To settle a bet, Russell Clark and Elaine Hatfield had research assistants go undercover and approach members of the other sex on a busy US campus. 'Hi', the assistants would say, 'I've been noticing you around town lately, and I find you very attractive.' After this bold icebreaker, the undercover agents made one of the following requests: (1) 'Would you go out with me tonight?'; (2) 'Would you come over to my apartment tonight?'; or (3) 'Would you go to bed with me tonight?'

For the first question – the go-out-with-me question – there was no sex difference, though later research suggests that men are typically more willing than women to say yes to that request. For the second question, however – the come-over-to-my-apartment question – a large sex difference emerged: 69% of men said yes, whereas only 6% of women did. But you ain't seen nothing yet. For the third question – the go-to-bed-with-me question – the results were close to a Mars-and-Venus sex difference: 75% of men answered in the affirmative, whereas *0*% of women did. Furthermore, among the 25% of men who declined the invitation, many politely explained that they were busy, and asked whether they could reschedule the sex for later. Not even one of the women did that.

The Clark and Hatfield study has been rerun many times over the last half century, and the same pattern is always found.[17] It's found when the proposer is average in the looks department, and when the proposer is highly attractive.[18] It's found in the somewhat sexually conservative United States, and in the most sexually liberal nations in the world.[19] And it's even found in nightclubs, where such offers might not be so unusual, and alcohol lowers everyone's inhibitions.[20] The exact numbers vary from study to study, but the general trend is clear.

What's less clear is how to interpret it. Although 0% of women said yes to the would-you-go-to-bed-with-me offer, no one would argue, I assume, that 0% of women are ever interested in casual sex. The explanation is presumably that the experiment didn't just measure willingness to engage in casual sex; it measured willingness to engage in casual sex *with a total and complete stranger*. That's a very different proposition for women than for men. Aside from anything else, a woman consenting to be alone with a male stranger is taking a bigger physical risk than a man consenting to be alone with a *female* stranger. As Cordelia Fine suggested, 'what this study is *actually* primarily showing is women's lack of interest in being murdered, raped, [or] robbed'.[21] It's a fair point. At the same time, however, the sex difference couldn't *just* be about physical risk. If it were, there'd be no difference in response rates between the 'apartment' condition and the 'bed' condition. Moreover, if risk were the only relevant variable, lesbians would presumably have more casual sex than straight women, while gay men would presumably have *less* casual sex than straight men. As we've seen, it's the other way round in both cases. The greater riskiness of the situation for straight women presumably enlarges the sex difference, but it doesn't explain it in full. One nice feature of this interpretation is that it allows us to reconcile the Mars-and-Venus sex differences observed in the Clark and Hatfield studies with the more modest, statistical sex differences found with questionnaires.[22]

A further line of real-world evidence for the differences comes from consumer behaviour. The best-known findings here are that men consume more pornography than women, whereas women consume more romance novels than men.[23] Needless to say, these consumption patterns map on to the sex differences under discussion: Pornography invariably focuses on no-strings-attached sex with a parade of anonymous partners; romance novels focus on the formation of romantic bonds with just one person – a person who's not only exceptionally good looking but also has a personality and even a name. When it comes to porn and romance novels, both sexes are typically mystified by the recreational pursuits of the other. As Catherine Salmon and Donald Symons observed, 'To encounter erotica designed to appeal to the other sex is to gaze into the psychological abyss that separates the sexes.'[24]

And erotica's just the beginning. A similar abyss can be found in the self-help section of any bookstore. The best-selling book *The Game*, for instance, teaches men how to pick up women for casual sex, whereas the best-selling book *The Rules* teaches women how to snag a husband.[25] Meanwhile, in the online dating world, the abyss is magnified a hundredfold. Consider, for example, the website Ashley Madison, which caters to married people seeking affairs. After hackers leaked the website's user data in 2015, it was revealed that more than 99% of the 'women' on the site were actually fake accounts designed to keep the male customers hopeful and coughing up their fees. An analysis of *real* accounts found that, at its peak, Ashley Madison had 20 million active male users, but only 1492 active female ones. This difference is particularly astonishing given that men had to pay to use the website, whereas women were automatically given a free lifetime membership.[26]

A final sex-related sex difference is that men are usually more interested than women in what psychologists call *visual sexual stimuli*.[27] This is presumably part of the reason that men are more avid consumers of pornography, and part of the reason that many men think that women will be pleased or even honoured to receive photos of their penises. And in case you're wondering, it's not just that men are more willing to *report* an interest in visual sexual stimuli, but that women are secretly just as interested: Behavioural experiments show that men are more distracted than women by erotic images, and brain scans show that men's brains respond more strongly to them.[28] Once again, the difference is real.

4. THE BATTLE OF THE SEXES

Sex differences in sex drive, interest in casual sex, and interest in sexual variety strongly shape the dynamics of heterosexual relationships. For starters, men tend to be more proactive in the mating game: Traditionally, men asked women to dance, asked women on dates, and proposed to women; in modern times, men message women on dating apps much more than women message men. Men are more likely than women to assume that someone is sexually interested in them when they're not: a tendency known as the *sexual over-perception bias*.[29] Men objectify women more than women objectify men, a situation that neither sex seems especially happy with: Women want less of it; men want more. When adoring fans pursue male rock stars, they're called groupies and seen as a perk of the job; when men try to act like groupies of female stars, they're called stalkers and seen as a matter for the police. Women can generally obtain a more attractive partner if they offer sex without commitment: A hundred women can sleep with a rock star or sports star, but only one or a few can have a relationship with him. In contrast, *men* can generally obtain a more attractive partner if they offer commitment as well as sex: Plenty of men who have little trouble finding a long-term mate would die virgins if they took the would-you-go-to-bed-with-me approach to romance.[30]

Another important tendency, first described by Donald Symons, is that sex is often tacitly seen as something that women give to men, rather than men to women. This is the case even when the woman instigates the sex and enjoys it as much as the man.[31] The implicit notion of sex as a female service manifests in various ways. During courtship, men give women gifts more than the reverse, despite the fact that women are usually the bigger gift-givers.[32] Most prostitutes are women; most clients are men – and although male prostitutes do exist, their customers tend to be men as well.[33] In many traditional societies, men pay for their wives – literally – and insist on a refund or replacement if they're unhappy with their 'purchase'.[34] And in modern societies, we find many websites for men seeking mail-order brides, but none for women seeking mail-order grooms.[35]

All of this is exactly as we'd expect if sex differences in sexual leanings are real, and not just figments of our stereotype-soaked imaginations.

The Nature and Nurture of Sex Differences in Sexual Psychology

At this point in proceedings, denying the existence of sex differences in sexual psychology requires Cartesian or Humean levels of scepticism. So, let's move on to the next question: Where did these differences come from?

The immediate answer for many is culture. Young men are encouraged to sow their wild oats; young *women* are encouraged to save themselves for the one – or at least not to let their 'body count' get too high. Women are typically judged harshly for casual sex or cheating on a partner; men are more often given a pass or a slap on the back: the traditional sexual double standard. For men, each new sexual conquest is another notch on the bedpost; for women, it's another mark against their good name. We know that cultural factors like these matter, because we know that women's willingness to engage in casual sex varies across cultures and times. Who could deny that social factors play a powerful role in shaping sex differences in sexual behaviour?

Of course, even accepting that social factors are involved, we'd still want to know where they came from, and why they point in the direction they do. Why aren't *women* encouraged to sow their wild oats, and *men* to save themselves for the one? These are reasonable questions, but it's easy enough for sociocultural theorists to cobble together an answer. The most obvious answer would be that it's a result of what we might call the *two Ps of human reproduction.*

The first P is pregnancy. Because women rather than men get pregnant, sex has always been a higher-stakes game for women than men, and women have always been more reticent about it. Not only that, but women's families have been more reticent on their behalf: Parents have been more concerned about their daughters' sexual activities than their sons', and siblings more concerned about their sisters' sexual activities than their brothers'. We needn't assume that any of this is instinctive; all we need assume is that people are aware of the connection between sex and pregnancy, and act accordingly.

The second P is paternity. Throughout history, men have been less willing than women to marry a promiscuous partner. This is partly because men have often had more power in such matters. But it's also partly because a woman's sexual adventures might mean that her husband ends up raising someone else's child, whereas a man's won't mean that for his wife. Men's stronger preference for a chaste partner is another reason that parents have tried to keep their daughters 'pure'. How else could they marry them off to a wealthy, high-status suitor?

As a result of the two Ps, people have generally been more restrictive of women's sexual behaviour than men's. This has then become enshrined in the norms, the moral systems, and the laws of many cultures, reinforcing the original tendency.

One line of evidence for the sociocultural explanation comes from a third P: the pill. The arrival of oral contraception in the 1960s, along with other reliable forms of birth control, radically altered the sexual landscape. Women could suddenly avoid getting pregnant without having to act like nuns. And just as we'd expect based on a sociocultural account, casual sex soon became more common for women, and less of a moral taboo.

That, then, is my best crack at a sociocultural explanation for sex differences in sexual behaviour. What should we make of it? First of all, let's agree that pregnancy, paternity, and the pill clearly play a role in shaping the differences. This immediately rules out the Nature-Only position. As we saw in Chapter 3, however, the Nature-Only position is held by approximately no one, and the *Nurture*-Only position is not the only alternative. Another is that sociocultural and innate factors work together to shape the relevant differences. Do we have any reason, though, to favour this view over the Nurture-Only hypothesis?

We do. In fact, we have many. First, sex differences in sexual inclinations are remarkably stubborn. As mentioned, sociocultural theorists point to the cultural impact of the pill as evidence for the malleability of human sexuality. But it could equally well be spun as evidence for the *limits* of that malleability. More than half a century after the pill first appeared, and contrary to the predictions of many, the casual-sex gender gap is still going strong. It might have shrunk a bit, sure. But it's still one of the largest effects in psychology.

Now, one could argue that this is because social pressures that predate the pill persist to some degree. I don't see why, on a Nurture-Only account, those pressures would be so resistant to change, but I concede that it's possible in principle. If we're going to go down that road, however, we need to acknowledge that the relevant social pressures are much messier and more contradictory than the sociocultural explanations allow. Indeed, they often push *against* sexuality sex differences, rather than toward them. For example, rather than being uniformly encouraged, men's stronger taste for casual sex has persisted even in the face of concerted efforts to stifle it, from threats of eternal damnation to the glorification of marriage and monogamy to the stigmatization of promiscuity as the product of repressed homosexuality.[36] At the same time, women's greater *reticence* about casual sex has persisted even in the face of social pressures aimed at overcoming it. These include, first and foremost, pressure from men trying to persuade women to engage in casual sex specifically with them. And they also include the efforts of some feminists and opinion leaders to persuade women that they can and should engage in casual sex just as freely as men do given half a chance – as seen, for instance, in articles such as '5 Fantastic Ways to Engage in Feminist Hookup Culture' and 'How to Bio-Hack Your Brain to Have Sex Without Getting Emotionally Attached'.[37] At a minimum, we'd have to acknowledge that society doesn't give a consistent, monolithic message to either sex. It gives both sexes mixed messages about casual sex and everything else – not because society is hypocritical or confused, but because society isn't one person; it's lots of different people with different views and agendas. Yet through all the messaging messiness, the same basic sex differences persist.

More than that, they persist wherever in the world we look. Sex differences in sexual leanings have been documented in nations and cultures from every corner of the globe.[38] They've been documented in sexually liberal nations, sexually conservative nations, and everything in between.[39] They've been documented in wealthy nations and poor nations, capitalist nations and socialist nations. And they've been documented in every ethnic group and religious community ever surveyed.[40] Granted, the size of the gaps varies from place to place and from culture to culture. However, despite more than a century of careful research, scientists have yet to find a single culture where women are more interested than men in casual sex or sexual variety, where most prostitutes are men and most clients are women, or where women are the main connoisseurs of pornography. This isn't what we'd expect if the differences were purely cultural. There'd be more variation.

On top of all that, the sex differences we see in humans aren't unique to us; they're also found in many other species. I'll give you five examples. First, across the animal kingdom, males are more likely than females to try to initiate sex. For instance, among hedgehogs, males try their luck while females say yay or nay – usually nay. As one author noted, 'Hedgehog courtship is an understandably cautious process, for the male in particular. This is a species where no really does mean no.'[41] Second, males are often more sexually driven; among nonhuman primates, for example, as among human primates, males masturbate more than females.[42] Third, males are less easily diverted from sex. The sexologist Alfred Kinsey once wrote that 'Cheese crumbs spread before a pair of copulating rats will distract the female, but not the male', and one recent study on fruit flies found that when males are about to mate, they'll often be so focused on the task at hand that they'll fail to spot an approaching predator: a phenomenon known as *love blindness*.[43] Fourth, males are more likely to 'pay' for sex: Male baboons, for instance, form special friendships with females, and protect them and their offspring in exchange for sexual access.[44] And fifth, males in many species are more responsive than females to visual sexual stimuli. In a fascinating paper titled 'Monkeys Pay Per View', male rhesus macaques were given the choice of drinking some juice or viewing pictures of females' hindquarters. They more often opted for the latter, showing similar priorities to another male primate I can think of.[45]

Here's the bottom line. If sex differences in sexual inclinations in humans were purely down to culture, it would be a bizarre coincidence if cultures all over the world had replicated most of the differences we see in other animals. What are the odds?

The Evolution of Sex Differences in Sexual Psychology: It's Not (Just) What You Think

To say that there's an innate contribution is, of course, to say nothing about how it came about. Why did natural selection 'decide' to give men and women somewhat different, somewhat incompatible desires? If a god were behind it, we might suspect that he was playing a cruel joke on us or trying to make the soap opera of human life more entertaining for himself. With natural selection as the architect, however, no such explanation is available. Somehow, male-typical sexual leanings must have been adaptive for our male ancestors, whereas female-typical sexual leanings must have been adaptive for our female ones. The only real question is why.

Now, you might think you know the answer already. I touched on it in Chapter 4, and in any case, the basics are quite well understood these days. But not so fast. As with sexual selection, the evolutionary explanation for sex differences in sexual inclinations is long overdue for an overhaul. The aim of this section is to sketch out a new and improved version of the explanation. We'll start with the standard story, then gradually thicken the plot.

The standard story goes like this. As a result of sex differences in reproductive physiology, men can potentially have many more offspring than women. A man who has, say, five sexual partners in a year could end up with five new offspring; in contrast, a *woman* who has five sexual partners in a year would probably end up with no more offspring than she would if she'd just had one.

This created very different selection pressures for our male vs our female ancestors. Men who sought multiple partners typically had more offspring than men with less wide-ranging interests, and the genes underpinning that tendency became increasingly common in the human gene pool. Men evolved a higher sex drive, a greater hunger for casual sex, a stronger desire for sexual variety, and a capacity to be quickly aroused by sexual stimuli (which for most of our evolution meant flesh-and-blood women rather than porn).

Meanwhile, ancestral women couldn't greatly increase their reproductive output by mating with every available man, so instead evolved to prioritize quality over quantity. To that end, they evolved a *lower* sex drive than men, less interest in casual sex, less interest in sexual variety, and a weaker response to visual sexual stimuli. Perhaps more accurately, women evolved to be more *selective* in these domains. Thus, rather than evolving a *lower* sex drive, women may have evolved a more *selective* sex drive: one that isn't automatically set to full volume but rises or falls based on the suitability of circumstances and potential partners. Similarly, rather than evolving a *lower* desire for casual sex, women may have evolved to be choosier about their casual sex partners. Regardless of the details, however, the key point is that, according to the standard story, differences in maximum offspring number led in a straightforward way to profound differences in men's and women's sexual psychologies.

This story isn't wrong exactly, but it is incomplete – and it's incomplete in a way that leaves it vulnerable to premature dismissal by its critics. The main problem with the standard story is that females in many species seek multiple mates almost as fervently as males. We don't have to look far from home to find examples: Our two closest living relatives – the chimpanzees and bonobos – both exhibit this pattern, even though females in these species invest heavily in the young, whereas males invest barely at all. And although humans aren't chimps or bonobos, we are somewhat anomalous by the lights of the standard story. As we've seen, the casual-sex gender gap in our species isn't huge. Plenty of women engage in casual sex, and don't seem to be going against their instincts when they do so. Most of the time, they do it because they want to. Conversely, plenty of men aren't especially interested in casual sex; they see the theoretical appeal of sleeping around like a rock star, but they don't find the fantasy alluring enough to devote significant time or effort to achieving it, and thus have less casual sex than they could. The standard story seems to predict a Mars-and-Venus sex difference, but the reality is much more Earthbound.

The solution is that the standard story needs several more layers of complexity to account for the sexual diversity we see in nature – and in our own species. In its simple form, the story fixates on just one variable: the sex difference in maximum offspring number. But maximum offspring number is only one factor among many shaping the mate-seeking gender gap. As we'll soon see, others include infanticide risk, the risk of sexually transmitted infections, and the need for paternal care.

At first glance, this might suggest an easy fix: Append these other variables to the standard story. In my view, however, we need to go further, and rethink how we frame the whole issue. I came to this view after many years of teaching these ideas to undergraduate students in my evolutionary psychology class. Initially, I'd start with the sex difference in maximum offspring number, then qualify the explanation by introducing the other variables. What I began to notice, though, was that no matter how strongly I emphasized the other variables, maximum offspring number remained the centre of gravity for most people's understanding of the evolutionary account.

So, I began casting around for another way to formulate the explanation. Here's what I came up with. Instead of starting with maximum offspring number then qualifying the explanation, I decided it would be better to first zoom out and take in the big picture. The big picture is that in every species, both sexes are subject to selection pressures for more mate seeking, and both are subject to selection pressures for less. Crucially, the strength of these selection pressures often differs for each sex. The final sex difference in a species – or the lack thereof – is the net outcome of these multiple, countervailing selection pressures.

To be clear, the sex difference in maximum offspring number *is* an important contributor. But it's not the only one, and we need to put the others on an equal footing with it if we want to understand sex differences in mate seeking across species.

Let's look, then, at some of the other contributors. We'll start with selection pressures pushing *up* the level of mate seeking in females. One of the most important is infanticide by males. In many species, including gorillas, langur monkeys, lions, hippos, horses, zebras, and mice, when a male first takes over the group or territory, he immediately starts killing all the youngsters.[46] Why would he do such a terrible thing? Simple: Those youngsters were sired by the previous male, and thus do nothing to boost *his* fitness. Furthermore, as long as the females are still caring for the last male's offspring, they won't be ready to have more: his. By going full King Herod on the existing young, he can bring forward the date when the females *will* be ready. Sure enough, soon after he does the evil deed, most females mate with their children's murderer. They apparently feel no resentment toward him and no desire for revenge. This is a stark example of how, in important ways, our minds are profoundly different from those of even our closest living relatives. And it's also a useful reminder that selection favours traits that boost individual fitness, rather than those that benefit the group or the species.[47]

But although male infanticide is good for the *male's* fitness, it's anything but good for the female's. For that reason, females have evolved various counteradaptations against infanticidal males. According to

Sarah Hrdy's *seeds-of-confusion theory*, promiscuous mating is one such counteradaptation.[48] The starting point for Hrdy's theory is the idea that in species with male infanticide, males have evolved to be tolerant of the offspring of females they previously mated with, because those offspring could potentially be theirs. This means that, by mating with multiple males, females can ensure that multiple males will be tolerant of their offspring (which is a polite way of saying 'won't kill them'). In effect, paternity is distributed probabilistically among the females' prior lovers. A common observation in evolutionary biology is that when males can't be certain that they're the father, they're less likely to invest in the young. Promiscuous species flip this on its head: When males can't be certain that they're *not* the father, they're less likely to *harm* the young. The upshot is that, in many species, the risk of infanticide by males ratchets up the average level of mate seeking in females, shrinking the usual promiscuity gender gap.

But infanticide isn't the only factor selecting for greater female promiscuity, and some of the others may be more relevant to our own species. Casual mates may provide resources or protection.[49] Casual sexual relationships may be a way to take a male for a test drive or switch from a current partner to a new one – after all, casual relationships can put you on a slippery slope to non-casual, committed ones.[50] More controversially, extra-pair mating may sometimes be a best-of-both-worlds strategy for females: obtain genes from the male with the best genes; obtain investment from the male most willing and able to invest.[51]

As always, the claim isn't that people are thinking about such things when deciding how to conduct their sex lives, any more than any other animal is. Instead, the claim is that natural selection calibrated our preferences and motivations in such a way that we often end up acting *as if* we're thinking about them, even though we're usually not.

While some selection pressures favour greater promiscuity, others favour less. One example of the latter for both sexes is the risk of sexually transmitted infections (STIs). For viruses, sex is a royal road from one host to another, and many viruses have evolved to specialize in this mode of transmission. Contracting an STI could put an end to an individual's philandering or maybe even their life. This risk may have dialled down promiscuous inclinations in both sexes, at least to some degree.

Other selection pressures may have done this in males only. An important example in our own species is the need for paternal care. In ancestral times, men's fitness may often have been boosted more by helping care for their offspring than by constantly pursuing new mates. Indeed, if this *weren't* the case, our paternal tendencies would presumably never have evolved. Part of the reason that caring for the young was often better for men's fitness is that, for most of our evolutionary history, opportunities for impregnating and abandoning women were few and far between.[52] Until recently, humans lived exclusively in fairly small, fairly close-knit communities, so novel mating opportunities were nowhere near as abundant as they are for modern city slickers glued to their dating apps. Moreover, a man trying to pursue a love-'em-and-leave-'em strategy might often have faced pressure from the woman's relatives and friends to 'do the right thing' – or he might have incurred their wrath, leading to violence, ostracism, or worse. For all these reasons, selection may have scaled back the strength of men's desire for casual sex and sexual variety.

It's unlikely, though, that it would have eliminated the desire altogether, or eliminated the sex differences in this arena. That's because even a single extra-pair liaison could greatly boost a man's reproductive output in a way that it couldn't for a woman's. A man with two children with his official partner, for instance, could increase his offspring headcount by a whopping 50% with just a single one-night stand or brief affair. Sure, in earlier times, the resulting child may have been less likely to survive without input from the father. But even a small chance is better than none. And if the woman had a husband – as most probably did in our evolutionary past – the child might have been unknowingly raised by him. In effect, the adulterous man would have parasitized the parental instincts of his affair partner's husband, just as cuckoo birds parasitize the parental instincts of the reed warblers in whose nests they sneakily lay their eggs.

In short, sex differences in sexual behaviour aren't just about the gender gap in maximum offspring number. Other variables come into play as well, and must be added to our theory of the evolution of these fundamental differences. The resulting expanded theory explains many of the apparent anomalies that led critics to dismiss the evolutionary approach. Most notably, it explains the fact that, although there *are* average sex differences in sexual behaviour in our species, they're nowhere near as large as we'd expect if maximum offspring number were the only relevant variable.

An Excuse for Male Misbehaviour?

Some worry that evolutionary explanations for sex differences in sexual inclinations justify male misconduct: philandering, infidelity, sexual coercion, and the like. If bad behaviour can be explained in evolutionary terms, goes the argument, then people can't be blamed for it. Some even hint that this is the real purpose of the explanations: to let men off the hook.

The first thing to say about this is that the evolutionary approach doesn't just explain *male* misbehaviour; it explains plenty of female misbehaviour as well, including, for instance, female infidelity. As such, if evolutionary explanations let men off the hook, they also do the same for women.

The second thing to say is that, even if they really did do this, we'd still have to ask whether *non*-evolutionary explanations do anything different. And the answer, as far as I'm concerned, is that they don't. If one type of causal explanation exonerates people, so does every other.

The third thing to say, though, is that there's no reason at all to think that any does. To explain bad behaviour is not to excuse it. If it were, we'd have to excuse all bad behaviour immediately, because all bad behaviour must have *some* explanation, even if we don't yet know what it is. Such a policy, however, would make less than zero sense. The purpose of holding people responsible is to incentivize good behaviour, disincentivize bad, and protect the rest of society. Why assume that we can only do this if people's behaviour is inexplicable? We should hold people responsible regardless of the ultimate origins of their behaviour – not because people are the uncaused causes of their actions, but because it's the only way to maintain a functioning society.[53]

Nature's Rainbow

Let's wrap up the chapter by exploring the question I'm most often asked when I give talks on the evolution of sexual behaviour: Why are some people exclusively attracted to members of their own sex?

Heterosexuality is no mystery in evolutionary terms. Its primary function is clearly about making new life, and secondary functions – such as galvanizing the bond between potential parents – are just as clearly linked to the primary function. As soon as we put on our Darwinian goggles, however, *homo*sexuality starts to seem mysterious. The mystery is *not* that individuals sometimes engage in sexual activity with members of the same sex; the occasional same-sex dalliance is unlikely to have much impact on the number of children one has in one's lifetime. The mystery is that a non-trivial number of people *never* want to have sex with members of the *other* sex. Individuals with such a profile might occasionally have children, especially in societies with strong social pressure to marry and have a family. More than likely, though, they'll have fewer children than people with a heterosexual (or at least a bisexual) orientation. This is especially true of men, because of men's higher maximum offspring number.

How, then, does homosexuality persist? To the extent that it's genetic, why hasn't selection removed the genes contributing to its development from the gene pool? To the extent that it has non-genetic causes, why hasn't selection made the development of heterosexuality more robust to perturbations?

Before exploring the best modern answers to these questions, let's consider some of the traditional ones.

IS SAME-SEX SEXUAL ORIENTATION A CHOICE?

No. Many gender-role traditionalists have taken this view, but it's simply not credible. Same-sex sexual *behaviour* is a choice, as is heterosexual behaviour and virtually all behaviour other than reflexes. Same-sex sexual *orientation*, on the other hand, is not.[54] If it were, we might expect gay people to remember choosing to be gay – and, for that matter, straight people to remember choosing to be straight. No one has such a memory, however, because no one makes such a choice. In any case, who'd choose to be part of a persecuted minority? On the contrary, many gay people remember trying to choose *not* to be gay as they became aware of their same-sex longings, only to learn the hard way that you can't just decide which stimuli cause you to become sexually aroused.

IS SAME-SEX SEXUAL ORIENTATION A RESULT OF EARLY SEXUAL EXPERIENCES OR SEDUCTION BY OLDER SAME-SEX INDIVIDUALS?

No. Among the Simbari of Papua New Guinea, younger boys traditionally performed fellatio on older ones. Somewhere along the line, the younger boys moved up the ranks and switched roles: The fellator became the fallatee.[55] If any childhood experience was going to create a same-sex sexual orientation, it'd be this one. But it doesn't. The vast majority of Simbari boys grow up to be fully heterosexual, with only a small number continuing to have sex with other males – exactly what we see everywhere else.[56] Apparently, early same-sex sexual experience makes absolutely no difference.

IS SAME-SEX SEXUAL ORIENTATION A RESULT OF EARLY-LIFE SOCIAL INFLUENCES?

No. Siblings who grow up in the same household are no more likely to develop a same-sex sexual orientation than siblings who grow up apart: an example of the Second Law of Behaviour Genetics discussed in Chapter 3.[57] Furthermore, boys raised as girls – including David Reimer, who we also discussed in Chapter 3 – are usually still attracted to women. Gay men and lesbians generally experience social pressure to conform to the norms for their sex, including in their choice of sexual partners. Most of their same-sex role models are straight. Nonetheless, they are what they are.

So, we've got a clear idea of where same-sex sexual orientation *doesn't* come from. What do we know about where it does?

The first thing we need to ask is whether genes are involved in shaping same-sex sexual orientation. And the answer is that they definitely are. Twin studies show that if you've got an identical twin who's gay, you're more likely to be gay yourself, even if you and your twin were raised in separate homes.[58] The implication is that same-sex sexual orientation has a genetic component. This isn't to say, as people used to, that there's a 'gay gene'. As with all complex traits, sexual orientation is the product of a large symphony of genes, rather than just one or a few.[59] It's also not to say that sexual orientation is down to genes alone. The heritability of same-sex sexual orientation – that is, the extent to which individual differences in orientation are due to genetic differences – is actually surprisingly low: well below 50%. It's one of the few traits where people *over*estimate heritability rather than underestimate it.[60]

Still, genes are part of the explanation. Our next question, therefore, is this: How do these genes remain in the gene pool? Why aren't they selected out?

Many people's first thought is that there must be some adaptive advantage to same-sex sexual orientation. The best-known idea in this vein comes from evolutionary biologist E.O. Wilson, who argued that it's a product of *kin selection*.[61] Kin selection is a subtype of natural selection in which traits are selected not because they boost their *owners'* reproductive success, but because they boost the reproductive success of their owners' close relatives.[62] The classic examples are non-reproductive worker insects in eusocial ants, bees, and wasps. Instead of having offspring of their own, workers help their mothers to have offspring, thus passing on their genes indirectly through them. According to Wilson, gay men and lesbians are functionally equivalent to non-reproductive worker insects. Freed from the burdens of parenting, they can devote their time and energy to caring for nephews and nieces, many of whom will go on to have kids of their own. In this way, genes associated with same-sex sexual orientation can keep themselves afloat in the gene pool.

Even before we look at the evidence, Wilson's hypothesis seems like a non-starter. Worker ants, bees, and wasps don't go around having sex with each other, and it would be very strange if they did: It would distract them from the task of helping raise a brood of siblings.[63] Workers in eusocial species aren't gay; they're asexual celibate monks. If humans had a non-reproductive caste, they'd presumably be the same.

Consistent with these theoretical musings, most research exploring the issue finds no evidence that gay people are any more likely than straights to care for their nephews and nieces.[64] To be fair, a few studies *have* documented such a tendency, including among the Fa'afafine of Samoa.[65] However, such findings are the exception rather than the rule. There are two main ways to interpret this. The first is that gay men and lesbians have an evolved tendency to invest heavily in nephews and nieces, but the surrounding culture has suppressed this tendency in almost every society on Earth. The second is that gay men and lesbians *don't* have an evolved tendency to invest heavily in nephews and nieces, but that culture has *created* this tendency in a handful of societies. To my mind, the latter is much more plausible. It avoids the implication that natural selection favoured a tendency so weak that it's suppressed in almost every culture, and it dissolves what would otherwise be an inexplicable coincidence: the fact that almost every culture has ended up suppressing that very tendency. Why would they do this? Come to think of it, *how* would they do this? If there's a near-universal social norm that childless people should resist the urge to invest more in their nephews and nieces, it's news to me. Why have sociologists and anthropologists never noticed it?

So, that's the first mark against the kin-selection explanation for same-sex sexual orientation: Gay men and lesbians don't typically invest more in their nephews and nieces. Even if they did, though, the kin-selection explanation would still face a major hurdle: Do they invest enough? Wilson's theory proposes that people with a same-sex sexual orientation are good aunts and uncles. But they'd have to be *unbelievably* good aunts and uncles to compensate for forgoing having kids of their own. Because their nephews and nieces are only half as related to them as their own children would be, for every child they could have had if they were straight, they'd have to help their siblings to have two extra children just to break even.[66] This seems like an impossibly high bar.

Let's shift, then, to some of the non-adaptationist explanations for the persistence of genes linked to homosexuality. One popular theory is that when genes linked to *male* homosexuality are found in women, those women have higher than average fertility, thereby matching the reproductive costs that the genes inflict on men.[67] In effect, the relevant genes are genes for female fertility, rather than for male homosexuality.

Some argue that this proposal again imposes too high a bar: If a gay man has zero kids when he'd otherwise have two, his sister would have to have two more kids than the average to balance out the costs. But this assumes that every man with the relevant genes will be gay. If, on the other hand, those genes just raise his *chances* of being gay, while more consistently boosting women's fertility, the maths could potentially work.

This loophole – the idea that the relevant genes don't always result in same-sex sexual orientation – opens the door to another, perhaps more plausible version of the theory. This is the idea that men who have genes predisposing them to same-sex sexual orientation, but who happen not to develop it, may be especially attractive to women. As a result, they may have more sexual partners and more children than other men, which compensates for their somewhat elevated chance of developing a same-sex sexual orientation.[68]

All these theories are just as applicable to other species as to our own. They therefore leave an important data point unexplained: the fact that, while we find same-sex sexual orientation in a significant minority of human beings, we don't find it in most other species. Certainly, same-sex sexual *behaviour* is found in many species, from bonobos to dolphins to giraffes. But exclusive same-sex sexual *orientation* is rare. As far as we know, the only nonhuman species where it's as common as it is in humans is domesticated bighorn sheep. If we could find a theory that could explain why we're such an outlier in this respect, that'd be a strong point in its favour.

Unfortunately, we don't yet have such a theory. We do, however, have several theories – for male homosexuality alone, alas – that even if they don't apply uniquely to humans, apply less widely than all the rest. One is the idea that male homosexuality is a side effect of selection for male parental care, which in our species includes female-linked traits such as empathy: If males get a small dose of the relevant feminizing genes, they become heterosexual doting fathers; if they get a large dose, they become gay.[69]

A second theory is that male homosexuality is a product of 'self-domestication' in our species: that is, selection against hot-headed aggression, comparable to the process we put our domesticated animals through to make them less belligerent.[70] Again, a modest dose of the relevant genes results in cool-headed heterosexuality, but a large dose results in same-sex sexual orientation.

At this stage, we don't know for sure what keeps genes predisposing people to same-sex sexual orientation in the gene pool. Still, we've come up with enough plausible theories that it no longer seems like an insoluble mystery. It's only a matter of time before we solve it.

Even when we do, though, we still won't have wrapped up the case. Although being gay isn't a choice or a product of social influences, it's only partially heritable. Genes, it seems, are mere bit players in the story of sexual orientation. What are some of the non-genetic contributors?

By far the most important is prenatal hormonal exposure.[71] Two lines of evidence seal the deal for this conclusion. First, scientists have managed to create a same-sex sexual orientation in various nonhuman mammals by castrating males early in life, thereby cutting off their testosterone supply, or by giving females megadoses of androgens in the womb and again at puberty.[72] Second, disorders of sexual development reveal the same pattern in humans. Women with congenital adrenal hyperplasia, who were exposed to high levels of androgens in the womb, are more likely to be attracted to other women, either as lesbians or bisexuals – and the greater the level of exposure, the more likely this becomes.[73] Similarly, some evidence suggests that males exposed to *low* levels of androgens in the womb are more likely to end up gay. Complicating the picture, males exposed to very *high* levels of androgens may also be more likely to end up gay, a pattern some research suggests is found in mice as well as men.[74] Either way, prenatal hormones appear to be an important non-genetic contributor to the development of same-sex sexual orientation.

Another non-genetic contributor is birth order. The original claim here was that the more older brothers a man has, the more likely it is he'll be gay, with no such effect of older sisters and no effect of birth order in women.[75] This came to be known as the *fraternal birth order effect*. More recent research suggests, however, that later-borns of both sexes are more likely to develop a same-sex sexual orientation, and that this is the case regardless of whether their older siblings are brothers or sisters.[76]

You might wonder whether this is a social effect of some kind – a side effect of growing up with older siblings. But there's reasonable evidence that the pattern appears even when people grow up *without* their older siblings.[77] This suggests a prenatal rather than a social origin. Somehow, the mother's previous pregnancies change the prenatal environment in ways that slightly elevate the chances of a same-sex sexual orientation.

What's the birth order effect *for*, evolutionarily speaking? It's not for anything! Instead, it's an example of the fact that development doesn't always go according to 'plan' (and notice that 'plan' is in inverted commas, as natural selection doesn't literally plan anything).

To sum up, same-sex sexual orientation isn't an adaptation, and it isn't primarily genetic. But that doesn't mean it's due to social factors. Rather, it has the curious distinction of being *biological* but largely non-genetic. Genes are certainly part of the picture, although it's still not clear how the relevant genes continue to find a home in the gene pool. The main cause of same-sex sexual orientation, however, is atypical prenatal hormones. The same likely holds for transgender identity, though there's much less research on that.

One last thing: We should resist the urge to draw any moral lessons from these conclusions. A lot of people want to argue that 'Homosexuality is natural; therefore, homosexuality is OK.' I agree that it's OK, and I agree that it's natural, but I don't agree that it's OK *because* it's natural. To argue that way would be to commit the naturalistic fallacy: the idea that what's natural is necessarily good. A better approach would be to argue that homosexuality is OK regardless of its causes. Consenting adults don't need a biological justification – or any kind of justification – for who they are or who they love.

6
Sex, Love, and Rock ‘n’ Roll

Dating, Mating, Deviating

Women writing men: He was a billionaire from old money, but somehow it hadn’t ruined him. He was kind and giving, tall, handsome, his penis was the perfect size. He had dated other women, but only you had ever truly captivated him, also he was a werewolf.

Ricky Tarr on Twitter/X

Male writers writing female characters: Cassandra woke up to the rays of the sun streaming through the slats on her blinds, cascading over her naked chest. She stretched, her breasts lifting with her arms as she greeted the sun. She rolled out of bed and put on a shirt, her nipples prominently showing through the thin fabric. She breasted boobily to the stairs, and titted downwards.

scottbaiowulf on Tumblr

Looking for Love

One of the most important decisions in the life of any animal, whether parrotfish, porcupine, or person, is who they ought to mate with. If you rarely encounter members of your own species – if you’re an anglerfish or a trapdoor spider, for instance – the answer might be ‘Anyone you possibly can.’ That might also be the answer if you encounter members of your own species often, but invest little in each offspring you produce. Might as well go for broke.

In contrast, if potential mates are as common as McDonald's *and* you invest a great deal in each offspring, mating with anyone you possibly can is no longer the optimal strategy. You should try a different approach: You should be selective about your mates. You should become, in a word, *choosy*. You shouldn't be *too* choosy; if you're holding out for an angel, you'll go to the grave without any progeny, and your I'm-too-good-for-anyone genes will go there with you. But you should be as choosy as you reasonably can be.

What, though, should you be choosy about? What makes one bachelor or bachelorette a better catch than another? We touched on this in Chapter 4. For peacocks, it's having the largest, healthiest tail; for proboscis monkeys, it's having the largest, longest nose. But what about us? We've long since lost our tails, and we don't seem especially focused on noses. So, what do we look for in a mate?

Before jumping in, a warning. The research on human mate preferences has always been hyper-focused on differences between the sexes, with similarities often falling between the cracks. This is partly because the differences are more theoretically interesting, affording a critical test of evolutionary hypotheses. And it's partly because the differences are more interesting, full stop: They're sexier than the similarities. For both reasons, my discussion in this chapter will follow the general trend and put a microscope to the differences. It's important to stress, however, that in many ways, men and women want exactly the same things in a mate. Both want someone who's kind, smart, funny, dependable, healthy, and emotionally stable. Both want someone who loves them and who desires them sexually. And both tend *not* to want a commitment-phobic player for whom cheating is as easy as falling off a diet.[1] We need to keep this in mind as we explore differences between the sexes, because if the similarities drop off the radar, we'll end up with a distorted picture of our evolved psychology.[2]

OK, enough with the boring warnings. Let's get to the interesting stuff: sex differences in human mate preferences. Our focus in this chapter will be differences in overall choosiness, and in the desire for looks, age, wealth, and status in a mate. A common understanding of these differences is that women are choosier than men, that men put more weight than women on a mate's looks and youthfulness, and that women put more weight than men on a mate's status and wealth. This is a reasonable first approximation, but as we'll see, it needs some quite substantial tweaks.

Women Are Choosier than Men About Their Mates . . . But Not Always

> Woman is the dominant sex. Men have to do all sorts of stuff to prove that they are worthy of woman's attention.
>
> –Camille Paglia (attributed)

An initial sex difference concerns overall sexual choosiness. The evolutionary rationale for this difference is straightforward. Both sexes evolve to be choosy in proportion to their level of parental investment. If females and males in a species invest equally in the young, the sexes evolve to be equally choosy. Conversely, if one sex invests more than the other, the higher-investing sex evolves to be choosier than the lower-investing sex. As we know from Chapter 4, in most species, females invest more than males in each offspring. Ergo, females in most species are choosier about their mates.

Even a cursory glance at the living world confirms the accuracy of this claim. A common trend among animals is that males do everything within their power to impress females, only for the females to remain entirely *un*impressed, nine times out of ten. A nice example concerns the greater superb bird of paradise. Males in this species perform one of the most elaborate and bizarre courtship dances known to modern science; google it if you want to feel insecure about your own dance moves. Despite the male's strenuous efforts, however, females typically reject several dozen suitors before finally consenting to mate. The funny thing is that because females evolved to be so super-choosy about the males' displays, we humans are probably more impressed by the superb male's dance than is the average female of his own species. Ditto the peacock's tail and every other nonhuman mating display.

Greater female choosiness doesn't just explain males' desperate attempts to wow the ladies; it explains all sorts of otherwise mysterious behaviour found across the animal world. In some frog species, females fake their own deaths to escape unwanted male attention; males, on the other hand, never fake theirs to escape female attention.[3] In some spiders, females attempt to eat any male that tries their luck with them, thus filtering out suitors that don't have the skills to avoid becoming dinner.[4] And in some octopus species, females throw shells and other objects at amorous males who they don't feel measure up.[5] Even apparent exceptions to the choosy-female rule generally turn out not to be. We saw in the last chapter that female chimps and bonobos are highly promiscuous, commonly mating with every adult male in the group. Importantly, though, underneath this stereotypically male behaviour is a strong undercurrent of stereotypically female choosiness. The females' sexual adventurousness, you see, is largely confined to the period leading up to estrous – that is, the period before they're fertile. As soon as estrous kicks in, the females become much more socially conservative, reserving their sexual favours for the highest status males.

And we're still only scratching the surface! Female choosiness isn't just a behavioural phenomenon; it's often stamped into female anatomy and physiology. Some female ducks, for instance, have corkscrew vaginas that spiral in the opposite direction to the males' corkscrew penises, helping them to avoid fertilization by rapist males.[6] In some species, including some rodents and sea urchins, eggs are choosy about which sperm they allow to fertilize them.[7] And in some plants, female reproductive organs are choosy about which pollen they accept, selectively aborting ovules fertilized by suboptimal pollen.[8] Yep, that's right; greater female choosiness isn't even confined to animals. It's an extremely deep trend in nature.

Given the ubiquity of greater female choosiness in the living world, our default assumption should probably be that it characterizes our own species as well. Sure enough, in many ways, it does. I remember once reading about a man who was arrested for sexually assaulting a peacock. I don't remember ever reading about a woman being arrested for sexually assaulting any kind of bird. And of course, men's wider sexual net doesn't just encompass our flying, feathered friends. Men corner the market on what evolutionary biologists call *mate-choice failure*, with documented cases involving everything from lampposts to trees to vacuum cleaners. We all make mistakes, I guess – but men more often than women.

More rigorous evidence of women's greater choosiness comes from a variety of sources. To start with, when men and women are asked to list what they want in a mate, women's lists are longer – a lot longer. According to an old joke, men only want one thing, but women want everything. In addition, self-report surveys consistently reveal that, when the sexes differ in how important they think a trait is in a mate, women almost always consider it more important.[9] Admittedly, words are cheap. But in this case, men's and women's words map onto their real-world behaviour. For example, on dating apps, women are vastly less likely than men to swipe right on a profile. And among people with a serious mental illness, the men are less likely than the women to have children – exactly as we'd expect if women were generally choosier about their sexual partners.[10]

Consistent with an evolutionary explanation for the sex difference, women's greater choosiness isn't just found in the West. Extensive cross-national surveys have found the difference in every nation where psychologists have looked for it.[11] The difference has even been found in traditional non-state societies. In his ethnography of the Trobriand Islanders of Papua New Guinea, for instance, the anthropologist Bronislaw Malinowski reported that some Trobriand women are considered so unattractive that they're 'absolutely debarred from sexual intercourse and . . . have to resort to solitary means of satisfaction'.[12] Mysteriously enough, though, these women often fall pregnant and have children. The Trobriand Islanders claim this as conclusive proof of virgin birth. More plausibly, it's evidence of women's greater choosiness about their mates. Few women, after all, have secret trysts with the least attractive men in the group.

So, we've got plenty of evidence that women are choosier than men about their sexual partners. Some, however, object to this idea. In my experience, this is usually a result of confusing claims about choosiness with claims about other things. Before going any further, then, let's address some common confusions.

First, to say that women – or females in any species – are choosier than men or other males isn't to say that females are coy, demure, modest, reserved, or passive players in the game of love. In many species, females actively solicit preferred males. For example, in various primates, a love-struck female will jump in front of a male, turn around, and brazenly display her genitals to him. This is rather forward by human standards, but it doesn't mean that females aren't choosy. On the contrary, they're very choosy about which males are recipients of their bold advances.

Second, to say that women are choosier than men isn't to say that women don't like sex. Some people have more refined palates than others, but that doesn't mean they don't like food. The anthropologist Brooke Scelza summed up the evolutionary psychological position well when she observed that women are 'choosy but not chaste'.[13]

With these confusions defused, I think most people would agree that the sexes differ in overall choosiness. Is my work here done? Not quite. An important qualification to everything I've just said is that the sex difference in choosiness in humans is found largely in early courtship and for casual sexual relationships. For established, committed relationships, the gap is much more modest.[14] In fact, some research suggests that it largely evaporates for such relationships, and that both sexes are about as choosy as the other – or to put it more precisely but less romantically, that both sexes are about as choosy as they can get away with, given their own levels of desirability.

This pattern makes good sense in Darwinian terms. In early courtship and for uncommitted sexual liaisons, it's unclear whether the man will stick around and invest in any offspring resulting from the union. The average costs are therefore lower for men than for women, and we'd expect men to be less choosy – the usual story. *Long*-term relationships, however, are a different matter. Falling in love, pairing up, and raising children together entails a large commitment from both parties, and substantially lowers the ceiling number of offspring for men. Men couldn't have evolved to do these things if they didn't also evolve to be roughly as choosy as women about their long-term mates.

So, whereas women are selective across the board, men are selectively selective. They're not always choosy about who they sleep with, but they are choosy about who they fall in love with. This fact is even implicit in everyday folk wisdom: The old adage is that men will *sleep* with anything that moves, not that they'll marry or have children with anything that moves.

And even the idea that men will sleep with anything that moves isn't strictly true. If a man looking for a casual fling could choose between a supermodel and the girl next door, he'd presumably opt for the former, even though both can move. So it's not that men have *no* standards when it comes to casual sexual partners; it's that they're more willing than women to *lower* their standards on the rare occasions when a supermodel isn't an option.[15] Women, in contrast, often *raise* their standards for casual partners, at least when it comes to physical attractiveness.[16]

Still, there *is* a sex difference, and it has important implications. Here's an example. As with other species, greater choosiness in women extends beyond mind and behaviour. According to one prominent theory, female orgasm in our species is a mechanism of female mate choice: Women are more likely to have orgasms with good-looking, high-status guys, which increases the chances of a repeat performance, and thus increases the chances of a good-looking, high-status guy siring the woman's young.[17] If this is right, it might help explain an unfortunate fact about human sexuality, namely that female orgasms are rarer than male ones. One review of the literature reported that for every female orgasm, there are more than 1.5 *male* orgasms, making the gender orgasm gap larger than the gender pay gap.[18] No doubt, this has many causes. But part of the explanation seems to be that female orgasms are harder to trigger than their male equivalents. Females, it seems, are not only pickier about who they'll have sex with; they're pickier about who they'll have orgasms with as well. To be clear, this isn't to suggest that the gender orgasm gap is insurmountable. However, surmounting it might always require extra care and attention. And all of this ultimately traces back to the same selection pressure that gave us acrobatic male birds, death-faking female frogs, and choosy plant reproductive organs: the fact that females invest more than males in their offspring.

Men Put More Weight than Women on a Mate's Looks . . . But Not Always

> One of the things women claim is most important in a man is a sense of humor. In my years as a comedian, I've learned that they're usually referring to the humor of guys like Brad Pitt, Tom Cruise, and Russell Crowe. Apparently, those guys are hilarious.
>
> Jimi McFarland

The fact that women are choosier than men about their romantic partners is one of the best-established findings in evolutionary psychology. Ironically, another of the best-established findings is an exception to that general rule. This is the fact that, on average, men are choosier than women about good looks in a long-term mate.[19]

Men's enthusiastic interest in women's looks isn't exactly a well-guarded secret. It's as familiar to most of us as the blueness of the sky or the wetness of water. At the same time, however, there are nuances to the finding that most people overlook.

First, whereas the sex difference in overall choosiness is largely confined to casual sexual relationships, the sex difference in the preference for good looks is largely confined to committed ones. When a relationship is more than just physical, the physical is less important to women. In contrast, when sex is the only dish on the menu, a partner's looks tend to matter just as much to women as to men, if not more.[20]

Second, it's not the case that men care *only* about a prospective mate's looks, or even that good looks are at the top of most men's priority list. Other traits – including love, kindness, and intelligence – are typically ranked higher than looks by men as well as women.[21]

Third, it's not the case that women are *uninterested* in looks in a long-term mate. If you don't believe me, just flip through the pages of any romance novel ever written – or even just look at the cover. In any case, you might already have noticed that good-looking guys have an easier time attracting romantic interest than their less aesthetically appealing comrades. Conversely, the *absence* of good looks can sometimes outweigh other considerations for women. Contradicting the old joke that there's no such thing as an ugly rich man, Darwin noted in *The Descent* that 'very ugly, though rich men, have been known to fail in getting wives'.[22] Even money, it seems, can't always turn a frog into a prince.

With these three qualifications in mind, the next question is: How do we know that, on average, men are more concerned than women about good looks in a long-term mate? Well, for one thing, we've asked them. We've now got a mountain of self-report studies exploring the issue – enough to bury a small city – and in the vast majority, men report placing more weight than women on a prospective partner's looks. Critics complain that this research is only ever done on students. I've got two responses to this. First, even if it were true, it's not clear it should be a fireable offence. One might argue, in fact, that targeting students provides a tougher test of the hypothesis, given that students tend to be less approving of traditional sex differences, and more likely to favour 'politically correct' responses. Second, the research *hasn't* just been done on students. The good-looks sex difference has now been documented in diverse samples from every age group and walk of life.[23]

Are people confused or lying about their preferences? They don't seem to be. Once again, real-world data corroborate what people are telling us. Men explicitly seek attractiveness in dating ads more than women do, and women more often highlight their own attractiveness. Romantic popularity is more strongly linked to attractiveness for women than men. Women's looks predict their spouse's status and income, whereas men's don't. And despotic male leaders in polygynous societies invariably stock their harems with attractive young women, sometimes banishing them to lower leaders' harems when their looks begin to fade.[24]

Of course, the fact that the sex difference is real doesn't imply it's innate. Several lines of evidence, however, suggest that it is – or rather, that there's an innate contribution. One line is that the difference has persisted across nearly a century of research in the West.[25] To be fair, as the century wore on, both sexes started placing more importance on a spouse's physical appearance. But this probably reflects a change in the nature of marriage, rather than in people's gut-level reactions to good looks: People see sexual attractiveness as a more important attribute in a spouse these days than they did when marriage was more an economic arrangement than a love match.[26] Whatever the reason, despite the changes in absolute levels of the good-looks preference, the sex difference shows no sign of abating.

A second line of evidence is that the difference transcends cultural boundaries. In a massive cross-cultural study – one of the first such studies in psychology – evolutionary psychologist David Buss looked at sex differences in mate preferences in 37 samples from 33 countries covering more than 10,000 participants. In 34 of his 37 samples, men placed more weight than women on a long-term mate's appearance, and in none was the difference reversed.[27] Subsequent studies have replicated Buss's findings with larger samples, more nations, and an even higher hit rate: 45 out of 45 nations in one study, for instance, and 53 out of 53 in another.[28] Importantly, the sex difference in the preference for good looks is no smaller in more gender-equal nations, contrary to what we'd expect if the difference were due to gender inequality, patriarchy, or strict, traditional gender roles.[29]

A third line of evidence is that the sex difference isn't just found in modern nation-states. In a survey of anthropological data from 191 cultures, Clellan Ford and Frank Beach reported that 'in most societies the physical beauty of the female receives more explicit consideration than does the handsomeness of the male. The attractiveness of the man usually depends predominantly upon his skills and prowess rather than upon his physical appearance.'[30] Backing up this observation, a content analysis of folk tales from around the world revealed that, on average, women's appearance was mentioned three times for every one mention of men's.[31] Apparently, the greater importance of women's appearance isn't just a product of modernity.

One complication, however, is that unlike most of the sex differences explored in this book, men's greater concern about a mate's attractiveness doesn't have strong precedents in other animals. On the contrary, in most species, the sex difference goes the other way: Females are more concerned than males about a prospective partner's looks. (I refer you again to our friend the peacock.) As we'll soon see, while this strange inversion in humans does make us exceptional among the animals, it nonetheless fits well with established evolutionary principles. To understand how, though, we need to take a detour and consider another, closely related mate-preference sex difference: the difference in the preferred age of a long-term romantic partner.

Men Prefer Younger Women, Whereas Women Prefer Older Men . . . But Not Always

'Intern Just Happens to Be Beautiful 22-Year-Old Woman', announced a headline from the satirical news site *The Onion*. 'According to reports', continued the article, 'the stylish, fit 5-foot-10 Kestrel was chosen as the best candidate for the job over four coincidentally less attractive 22-year-old women, an unattractive 23-year-old woman, and six men.'

Everyone gets the joke, of course, and no one would doubt, I think, that there's a large helping of truth in the jest. It is worth pointing out that the gag would still work if we flipped the sexes: 'Intern in Female-Dominated Workplace Just Happens to Be Handsome 22-Year-Old Man'. But the flipped version doesn't pack quite the same punch as the original. Why are the two headlines not equally funny? The obvious answer is that we're all aware of yet another sex difference in human mate selection, namely that men and women differ in their preferences regarding a prospective partner's age.

This difference is often summarized as 'Men prefer younger women, whereas women prefer older men.' That's not right, though. Certainly, if you ask heterosexual men and women in their twenties the preferred age of a long-term mate or spouse – as most of the research on this topic has done – the average man does indeed desire a younger woman and the average woman an older man.[32] Even so, sex differences in age preferences are not about 'younger' vs 'older' per se.

To get a handle on what they *are* about, let's look at each sex's preferences in turn. We'll start with men. What's men's ideal age for a long-term partner? To answer this, we need to consider two variables: looks and compatibility. When it comes to looks, men generally prefer traits associated with youthfulness and fertility: the kind of traits possessed by the average 22-year-old intern. Thus, if men's long-term preferences were *only* about looks, men might prefer women of around the intern's age, regardless of how old they were themselves. However, as important as looks often are, they're not the be-all and end-all for most men. Compatibility matters as well. People tend to be more compatible with individuals who are similar to them, and people tend to be more similar to individuals of around their own age. So, while men's physical preferences pull toward youthfulness, compatibility pulls toward same-age pairings.

As a result, the preferred age of a long-term mate for most men is a compromise between their own age and the age of women's peak fertility. For young men, this means a preference for women of around the same age. As the clock ticks, however, and men's age inexorably rises, the preferred age of a long-term mate rises as well – just not as fast as their own age.[33] The upshot is that the gap between men's age and their ideal partner's age gets larger as men get older. Whether such pairings are a realistic option for men is another question – and the bigger the age gap, the less realistic it becomes. It is, though, what most men prefer.

Women, on the other hand, generally prefer someone of around their own age, regardless of what their own age is. If you ask women their ideal *range* of ages for a long-term mate, it usually spans from men somewhat older than themselves to men slightly younger. Within that range, however, the *average* preference is for someone a little older than themselves.[34]

The idea that women prefer older men is sometimes written off as wishful thinking on the part of the older gentleman. But the claim is not that women are attracted to men notably older than themselves, let alone that they prefer old men. If that were the case, teenage girls would plaster their bedroom walls with pin-ups of middle-aged or elderly men, rather than the latest boy band. The claim instead is that women typically prefer someone somewhat older than themselves, on average, but that someone in the same ballpark is generally fine. Women do sometimes pair up with men much older than themselves, but that's usually *despite* the man's age, not because of it. And just to be clear, women are not immune to the charms of youth. Plenty of older women like the idea of a toy boy, and sometimes even the reality. On average, though, youthfulness has a stronger hold on men than it does on women.

Or so I say. What makes me so confident? As with earlier examples, various lines of evidence back me up. For starters, sex differences in age preferences have been found in numerous self-report studies, not just among students in the West but among people of all ages, nationalities, and ethnic backgrounds. Furthermore, these differences are among the largest and most cross-culturally consistent found in the mate-preferences literature.[35] And before you ask, yes: Real-world behaviour again corroborates what people are telling us. For example, in marriage data from multiple nations, husbands tend to be older than their wives, and the older a man is when he marries, the larger the gap between his age and that of his spouse. This pattern isn't just found in the West or in contemporary nation-states; it's also found in non-state societies with little or no contact with the West.[36] Meanwhile, in cultures with bride-price, the highest prices are paid for younger, more fertile brides.[37] And whereas in most professions, earnings rise with age and experience, prostitutes and escorts command higher wages when they're young.[38]

Traditionally, scholars explained the strong emphasis on women's youthfulness in sociocultural terms. The feminist writer Naomi Wolf, for instance, stated in her book *The Beauty Myth* that:

> our eyes are trained to see time as a flaw on women's faces where it is a mark of character on men's. If men's main function were decorative and male adolescence were seen as the peak of male value, a 'distinguished' middle-aged man would look shockingly flawed.[39]

But if it were just that we'd been trained to find older men more attractive – or if it were just that older men were somehow inherently more attractive – then gay men would presumably prefer older partners as well. They don't. Like straight men, they tend to prefer younger ones.[40] Indeed, if anything, youthfulness is even more highly prized among gay men than among straight men. As a gay air steward said in the British mockumentary *Come Fly with Me*, 'I couldn't imagine being 39. That's like 102 in gay years.'

We can't write off the sociocultural approach just yet, though, because other sociocultural explanations are possible. One is that men have learned a social norm that their partners ought to be younger than them. Another is that men want to control their partners for some reason, and that younger partners are easier to control. And a third is that younger women are more responsive to men's romantic interest than older, wiser women, and that this reinforces men's preference for youthfulness. Do any of these explanations hold water?

Nope! In fact, a single finding puts the lie to all three. The finding in question is that whereas men in their twenties and above tend to find younger women more attractive, teenage boys tend to be more attracted to women somewhat *older* than themselves: women in their early twenties.[41] This tells us that men's preference isn't for younger age, but rather for traits associated with fertility. (Women in their early twenties are more fertile than those in their teens.) The finding therefore rules out the social norm theory and controllability theory, both of which assume that men's preference is for someone younger. As for the reinforcement theory, women in their twenties rarely lust after teenage boys, and thus teenage boys' preference for these women couldn't be reinforced by their interest. Apparently, though, the reinforcement is unnecessary, because teenage boys have the preference anyway.

Like men's stronger preference for good looks in a long-term mate, the preference for youthful females is rare in the animal kingdom. In most species, males have no such preference. Indeed, in many primates – including chimps, orangutans, and macaques – males prefer *older* females, presumably because they're more likely to conceive and have more experience looking after the young.[42] Why, then, do human males have this topsy-turvy preference for youthful females?

Most likely, it has its roots in another relatively unique feature of our species: the fact that human females can only have kids for around half their adult lives. Women's fertility comes online in their teens, peaks in their early twenties, then flickers out with menopause, typically before the age of 50. In contrast, men can in principle keep having offspring till the day they die, as long as they can find willing collaborators. In this context, it makes good evolutionary sense that men's mate preferences are centred more strongly on youthfulness than women's; after all, women's *fertility* is centred more strongly on youthfulness than men's. For men, the best bet for a long-term mate is someone who's fairly young. For women, an older mate is fine. In fact, as long as he's not going to drop dead any time soon, an older mate might even be better, as he's had more time to accumulate status and resources.[43]

This all sounds horribly mercenary. Once again, though, the idea is not that people are thinking about these matters. Instead, men and women have a set of inbuilt preferences that lead them to act *as if* they're thinking about them, when most of the time they're not. They're just doing what feels right.

Women Put More Weight on a Mate's Status and Resources

I asked you in Chapter 2 to imagine that you were a participant in a psychology experiment. Well, you must have been a good one, because you've just been invited to take part in another. This time, there are no tricks. You're ushered into a small room and asked to sit at a desk in front of a computer. You're then informed that you can use the computer to message another participant at another university. You can ask the participant anything you want, except whether they're a man or a woman. You're not allowed to ask *that* because your task is to try to figure out their sex based on their answers to other, less direct questions. It's basically a Turing test for sex.

Excited by the challenge, you decide to lead with some personal questions, reasoning that they'll probably be the most diagnostic. Your first question is a doozy: 'Why did you and your most recent partner break up?' The moment you fire off the question, you start to worry that maybe it was a little *too* personal, but your interlocutor seems happy to answer it. 'I broke it off', they respond. 'It was hard. I loved the person; they were fun and funny and really good-looking. But they just weren't very ambitious. They had a job, but it was a dead-end one. That wasn't a big deal at first; we were only in our twenties. Eventually, though, I realized that they had no ambition beyond that job. And I just couldn't get past it. I couldn't see a future for us.'

What's your best guess: Is this person a man or a woman? Of course, it *could* be either. But which is more likely?

You already know the answer, and you already see my point. So far, we've focused largely on traits that men consider more important in a mate, namely good looks and youthful appearance. Now, let's flip the camera, and focus on a cluster of traits that *women* consider more important. The traits in question are social status, competence, and the ability to acquire resources. For women, these things are potent aphrodisiacs. For men . . . not so much.[44] They're nowhere near as big a deal.

How do we know? Well, for a start, we've got people's word for it – that is, we've got the answers they've given us in questionnaire studies. Such studies find the differences not only among students or young adults, but in diverse samples of every age.[45] And rather than creating differences where there are none, questionnaire studies may actually *underestimate* the gaps. The usual protocol in these studies is to give people a list of traits and then ask them how desirable each would be in a long-term mate or spouse, without them having to prioritize any over any others. Where that's the case, both sexes want it all: good looks, good earning potential, everything under the sun. For most mere mortals, however, having it all isn't a realistic option. Most people have to make trade-offs. To bring this annoying reality into the picture, psychologist Norm Li conducted a series of studies in which he gave people a budget of 'mate dollars', and asked them to design a mate. When people had a large budget, they wanted everything, and the sex differences were relatively modest. But when people had a *small* budget – more akin to most people's situation in life (no offence) – the sex differences were significantly larger: Women strongly prioritized status and resources, whereas men strongly prioritized looks. Li concluded that status and resources are necessities for women but luxuries for men, whereas good looks are a necessity for men but a luxury for women.[46] Some years after Li published his seminal work, I was involved in a follow-up study, spearheaded by Andrew Thomas, that replicated the findings in various nations in both the West and the East.[47]

Hopefully by now you've realized that, at least in this domain, self-report measures tend to be reliable. If you're still not convinced, though, I've got good news: The wealth and status sex differences have been amply corroborated by real-world data. Analyses of lonely-hearts personal ads and online dating profiles show that women are more likely than men to signal a desire for a mate with wealth and status, and that men who possess wealth and status attract more romantic attention.[48] Analyses of marriage data suggest that having a good income boosts men's chances of getting married but barely moves the dial for women.[49] And analyses of data from fertility clinics show that women's interest in a mate's status and resources extends even to their choice of sperm donors.[50]

Needless to say, women don't *only* care about a mate's wealth and status, any more than men only care about a mate's looks. Wealth and status are always welcome, of course, but other things can sometimes trump them. For example, based on Internet dating data, Seth Stephens-Davidowitz concluded that 'a male firefighter who earns $60K tends to be more attractive to the average heterosexual woman than a hospitality worker who earns $200K'.[51] Still, even if a mate's wealth and status aren't all that women care about, they do care more than men. And the differences are far from trivial.

Where do they come from? A common view is that sex differences in the preference for wealth and status trace back to the bad old days when women – or at least, middle- and upper-class women – had no other way to make a living than to marry a wealthy man. In that milieu, it's hardly surprising that women prioritized a man's wealth over more 'frivolous' concerns like his jawline. Men, on the other hand, didn't need to worry about a *woman's* wealth because they could earn their own. For that reason, men were free to indulge their fetish for good looks.[52]

Sound reasonable? It does to me. Reasonable or not, though, the facts just don't support it. If sex differences in the preference for wealth and status in a mate were solely about access to resources, we'd expect wealthy women to put less weight on a partner's income than poorer ones. Instead, they usually put more. Meanwhile, poor men don't put any more weight on a partner's income than their more solvent same-sex peers.[53] On top of that, the wealth and status sex differences are extremely robust across time. In the United States, for instance, the differences persisted through the twentieth century, despite women's rapidly increasing economic independence, and feminist insistence that women need men like fish need bicycles.[54]

Nor are sex differences in the preference for wealth and status found only in the Western world. Large-scale surveys have found the differences in almost every nation studied.[55] Furthermore, as with their Western counterparts, non-Westerners' stated preferences translate into real-world outcomes. Multiple studies from multiple nations have found that wealthy, high-status men typically have more sex and more sexual partners than men lower down the food chain; that they're more likely to get married, stay married, and remarry if they get divorced; and that they tend to have more children.[56] None of this holds for wealthy, high-status women. On the contrary, in the developed world at least, the arrow sometimes points the other way: Wealthy, high-status women are *less* likely to get married, stay married, remarry, or have children.[57]

Similar results have been found in the traditional societies studied by anthropologists. Men with higher status and more resources generally have more sexual partners, more wives, a greater choice of wives, younger wives, more affairs, and – unsurprisingly, given all of that – more children. A meta-analysis of 33 non-industrial societies lacking modern birth control found that higher status men have more offspring in every society without exception.[58] And if that's not enough evidence for you, analyses of folk tales and novels from around the world show that women are universally depicted as caring more than men about a mate's status and resources – an odd coincidence if the depictions were purely down to artistic licence rather than a reflection of a universal reality.[59] The cross-cultural ubiquity of the sex differences deals a serious blow to any theory that attempts to explain them in terms of social factors unique to the West.

But the Nurture-Only view is not on the ropes just yet. Sure, sex differences in the preference for wealth and status are close to universal. However, according to Alice Eagly and Wendy Wood's *social role theory*, that's not because the differences are innate. Instead, they're an indirect effect of certain innate *physical* differences. The most important are that, on average, men are larger and stronger than women. As a result, men have always been able to nab the most productive roles in society, and women have been made dependent on men. This dependency led to the cultural evolution, everywhere in the world, of a female preference for a mate with resources. As common as this preference is, though, it's not hard-wired into women's brains, and thus can potentially be undone.[60]

The social-role explanation seems plausible enough at first glance, but it fails a critical test. If it were true, we'd expect that sex differences in the preference for wealth and status in a mate would be larger in countries with lower gender equality: countries where women are more economically dependent on men. Most data suggest, however, that the magnitude of the differences is entirely unrelated to levels of gender equality.[61] This contradicts the view that the differences are a product of women's economic dependence.

And there's still one more line of evidence to consider. This is the fact that the resources and status sex differences aren't just found in humans, but appear in many nonhuman species as well. For example, in many pair-bonding, biparental birds, females prefer mates that ply them with food, or that have resource-rich territories where they can safely raise their young.[62] Likewise, in many primates, high-status, dominant males have more offspring than their lower-status, subordinate peers.[63] For other species, the only realistic explanation for these tendencies is an evolutionary one. The question we then have to ask ourselves is whether, when we find the *same* tendencies in our own species, it's realistic to think that, for us alone, they have a purely sociocultural origin. I hope you agree that the answer is no. The most plausible view is that the same evolutionary forces that created the differences in other species created them as well in ours.

Did Our Ancestors Choose Their Mates?

> Free choice is essential to love. We can't say yes to anyone unless we can also say no . . . as Clare Boothe Luce once explained: 'With the equality of the sexes, there will be a lot more love in the world.'
>
> Gloria Steinem (2014), 'II. Learning Love', para.17

So far so good, but there's a problem. Critics point out that the whole idea that sex differences in mate preferences have an evolutionary origin in our species is based on an unwarranted assumption: the idea that men and women have always been able to choose their own mates. This assumption seems entirely reasonable to people living in modern liberal societies, because in modern liberal societies, that's how things are done. Historically speaking, however, this is anomalous. The norm for human beings, unlike any other species, has always been that parents arrange their children's marriages, or that male-led clans barter and exchange females for political and economic advantage.[64]

Arranged marriages and male coercion of females complicate the picture of our evolved mate preferences. Do they imply, though, that our preferences owe nothing to natural selection, and instead come solely from culture? Surely not. We've already seen that various sex differences in mate preferences have an innate component. This strongly suggests that, throughout most of human evolution, men's and women's mate preferences had a significant impact on their reproductive outcomes. If they didn't, the preferences wouldn't have been subject to selection, and we presumably wouldn't have them.

So, the question is not: Do arranged marriages and male coercion imply that we don't have evolved mate preferences? The question is: How can we reconcile the existence of evolved mate preferences with our long history of arranged marriages and male coercion? In my view, we can do so by pointing to five facts from the anthropological record.

1. ARRANGED MARRIAGES AREN'T UNIVERSAL

Most traditional societies have had arranged marriages.[65] But 'most' isn't 'all', and in a non-trivial minority of societies, brides and grooms have been largely free to choose each other.[66] This leaves at least some elbow room for mate preferences to play a role in shaping people's mating decisions, and thus at least some scope for mate preferences to be shaped by selection.

2. EVEN WHEN PARENTS *DO* ARRANGE THEIR CHILDREN'S MARRIAGES, MATE PREFERENCES OFTEN PLAY A ROLE

In some societies, people have had no choice about who they marry – or rather, their choice has been to marry the person picked out for them or to be exiled or executed. But that's the exception rather than the rule. It's rare for parents to completely disregard their daughters' or sons' views about a potential union, and to force them into a marriage they strongly oppose.[67]

Furthermore, mate preferences don't just switch off the moment people tie the knot. They're still there, bubbling under the surface, and can help determine how many kids the couple has and how long their marriage lasts.

For both reasons, mate preferences can influence mating outcomes even when marriages are arranged.

3. ONLY A MINORITY OF MARRIAGES LAST FOR LIFE IN TRADITIONAL SOCIETIES, AND SUBSEQUENT UNIONS ARE TYPICALLY ARRANGED BY THE BRIDE AND GROOM

A good example comes from the !Kung San hunter-gatherers of the Kalahari Desert. As anthropologist Richard Lee reported, first marriages among the !Kung are arranged by parents, often when the future bride and groom are still children. However, only around half those marriages last, and later ones are generally freely chosen.[68] Wherever we find this pattern, it provides yet another opportunity for people's preferences to exert an influence.

4. MATE PREFERENCES CAN INFLUENCE MATING BEHAVIOUR OUTSIDE MARRIAGE

Even when parents have complete control over who their children marry, and even when divorce is not an option, people can still potentially exercise mate choice. They can do so through premarital sex, affairs, or eloping with a forbidden lover, all of which are reasonably common in the ethnographic record.[69]

5. ARRANGED MARRIAGES AND COERCION OF FEMALES MAY HAVE SELECTED FOR *STRONGER* MATE PREFERENCES, RATHER THAN WEAKER ONES

If we'd always had carte blanche in choosing our mates, even relatively weak mate preferences might have done the job. However, if meddling parents and other third parties were constantly trying to puppet-master our mating decisions, then rather than *shedding* our mate preferences, we might have evolved *stronger* ones – ones that could motivate us to kick up a fuss and fight for what we truly want. Indeed, this is plausibly part of the explanation for the evolution of romantic love in our species, and for the fact that it's such an intense and disruptive emotion: Love may be an adaptation against third-party meddling in our romantic affairs.

For all these reasons, it seems unlikely that arranged marriages and male coercion would lead to the elimination of evolved mate preferences – which is good, because we already know that we *have* evolved mate preferences, so it would be puzzling if it were any other way!

Mate Choice as Selective Breeding

After coming up with his theory of evolution by natural selection, Charles Darwin immediately . . . did nothing. Nothing public, anyway. He knew that his theory would be hugely controversial, so rather than rushing it into print, he spent the next twenty years of his life patiently and laboriously collecting evidence to test it. The result was that, when he finally published his magnum opus *On the Origin of Species* in 1859, readers were buried under an avalanche of evidence for the theory.[70]

The very first piece of evidence was the fact that animal and plant breeders had created new lines of domesticated species by selectively breeding individuals with desired traits: dogs with friendlier dispositions; hens that produce more eggs; corn with larger, tastier kernels. This led Darwin to make a bold inference: If humans can selectively breed domesticated species for traits useful to us, then nature can presumably 'selectively breed' wild species for traits useful to *them* – useful in the sense that they boost individuals' chances of surviving and having offspring. He called the former process *artificial selection* and the latter *natural selection*.

Twelve years after the *Origin*, Darwin unveiled a new theory: his theory of *sexual selection*, which he argued provided an intermediate option between deliberate selection by animal and plant breeders and non-conscious selection by nature. In a sense, said Darwin, animals selectively breed themselves through their choices of sexual partners. On this view, mate preferences aren't just *products* of evolution; they're *causes* of evolution as well, shaping new traits in a species. The classic example, as we've seen, is the peacock's tail. This iridescent, extravagant structure was literally created by the peahen's sexual preferences. It's a rather striking fact that something as abstract and ethereal as a psychological state – a mere preference – could sculpt something as concrete and corporeal as an anatomical feature. But nature is full of surprises, and Darwin turns out to have been right: It happens all the time.

Given that it happens in other species, it seems perfectly plausible it could happen in our own. Indeed, as soon as we accept that humans have reliable, enduring mate preferences, it becomes hard to see how it could *fail* to happen. The process that shaped the peacock's tail has almost certainly given humans a makeover too.

That said, we do need to be careful about applying the peacock rubric to our species, because without appropriate adjustments, it can be highly misleading. The sociobiologist Sarah Hrdy once wrote that,

> to an extraordinary degree, the predilections of the investing sex – females – potentially determine the direction in which the species will evolve. For it is the female who is the ultimate arbiter of *when* she mates and how often and with whom . . . Females, then, are and always have been the chief custodians of the breeding potential of the species.[71]

But although this is true of many species, it isn't true of ours. That's because, unlike most species, humans have *mutual mate choice*: Women choose men, but men choose women as well, and thus both sexes, not just females, determine the direction of human evolution.[72]

This point isn't widely appreciated. It's not uncommon to hear people assert – usually after microdosing sexual selection theory rather than mainlining it – that 'Women are the selectors in our species.' But even a quick glance around the dancefloor of any nightclub reveals the falsity of this proposal: Both sexes dress to impress, not just men. In fact, women generally pay more attention to their appearance than men do to theirs. Why would they bother if men weren't co-selectors in our species? And why would neglected teenage girls complain that the boy of their dreams 'doesn't even know I'm alive'? If males in our species weren't co-selectors, being alive would be all a girl needed to catch her dream boy's eye.

Granted, men traditionally asked women to dance, to date them, or to marry them, leaving women in the driver's seat about whether the partnership would go ahead. That doesn't mean, though, that women alone exercised mate choice. After all, men didn't ask women to dance, date them, or marry them at random; they exercised mate choice in deciding who to ask. And it's not as if women's affirmative answer to any of those questions meant that men were forever committed to the relationship. They could still always cut things off: another common form of mate choice. So, although females are the sole selectors in many species, they're clearly not in ours.

This has an important implication. Just as animal and plant breeders selectively bred domesticated species for the traits they most desired in crops and livestock, so too men and women selectively bred each other for the traits they most desired in a mate. And because men and women desired somewhat different things in a mate, they put each other under somewhat different selective regimens – in the process, further magnifying the sex differences in our species.

Most notably, men's and women's mate preferences helped sculpt women's and men's bodies. To begin with, because men place more weight than women on physical attractiveness in a long-term mate, women were under stronger selection than men for physical attractiveness. And as we'd expect based on sexual selection theory, across the globe, both sexes tend to agree that women are easier on the eye.[73] In effect, when it comes to overall physical attractiveness, women have the larger peacock's tail, reversing the usual sex difference.[74]

Drilling down into the details, men's and women's preferences for specific physical traits may have helped shape the traits in question. Psychologist David Puts argues that women's secondary sexual features – facial femininity, breasts, the hourglass figure, and so on – are largely products of male mate choice for traits associated with youthfulness and fertility.[75] In effect, these attributes are peacock's tails, but found in the female rather than the male of the species. It's a bizarre thought: Not only do men *like* these traits, but the liking helped bring them into existence. Men's preferences helped mould women's appearance, like a slow-acting, collective cosmetic surgeon.

Whether women's preferences did the same to men is less clear. Puts argues that men's secondary sexual features – a chiselled jaw, a muscular torso, a low-pitched voice, and the like – are products not of female mate choice but of male–male competition, with their main function being to intimidate other men rather than to attract women.[76] But although this may be their *primary* function, most women do find these traits attractive, at least in moderation.[77] Thus, my friendly amendment to Puts's suggestion would be that the traits are products of both male–male competition *and* female mate choice, albeit probably more of the former than the latter. Like the roar of the lion and the inflatable red throat pouch of the male frigatebird, they're dual-function adaptations: part deer's antlers and part peacock's tail.

Why Mate Choice Matters

Let's now tiptoe into more controversial territory. Mate preferences not only help shape men's and women's *bodies*, they also help shape their minds. If people want a smart mate, a kind mate, or a funny mate, the species will inevitably evolve to be smarter, kinder, and funnier.[78] Not only that, but we'll evolve a motivation to hone and display the traits that potential mates desire.

You can probably see where I'm going with this. Because the sexes have somewhat different desires, each may have evolved somewhat different traits – and also somewhat different priorities about which traits to hone and display. How might this have played out in our species?

First of all, because a mate's looks are more important to men than to women, women may have evolved to be more concerned about their looks. In his book *The Descent of Man*, Darwin observed that 'Women are everywhere conscious of the value of their own beauty; and when they have the means, they take more delight in decorating themselves with all sorts of ornaments than do men.'[79] Darwin was going well beyond the evidence available at the time, but he seems to have been absolutely right once again. A survey of more than 90,000 people from 93 nations found that, in every single one, women devote more time than men to enhancing their appearance.[80] This cross-cultural unanimity is a telltale sign that we're dealing with more than just a cultural artefact.

So too is the fact that the sex difference appears early in life. As May Ling Halim and colleagues report, even among preschoolers, girls place more importance than boys on their appearance. Moreover, when asked to explain why they like a favourite fictional character, they'll often say it's because she's pretty.[81]

Of course, both sexes enhance their appearance as a way to compete for mates. On average, though, women push this envelope further than men because, on average, men have always been more swayed by a prospective mate's appearance.[82]

An unfortunate side effect of this sex difference is that more women than men struggle with an excessive concern about their looks. To illustrate, one study found that around a quarter of women would rather be severely depressed than obese, and that around one in six would rather be *blind* than obese.[83] I don't think I'm going out on a limb to suggest that these aren't the healthiest priorities. Indeed, placing so much weight on one's appearance contributes to the greater incidence of body dissatisfaction and eating disorders among girls and women than boys and men.

Meanwhile, however, boys and men have their own unhealthy

priorities. To start with, because strength and muscularity are more important to men's mating prospects than women's, men have evolved to be more concerned about these traits. As with its female counterpart, this concern appears early in life. Based on interviews with children aged three to five, Halim and colleagues reported that, even at that tender age, boys care more than girls about being strong. '[D]uring our interviews', the researchers noted, 'some boys would spontaneously flex their muscles for interviewers and lift their chairs to show their physical strength.'[84] Along with the little girl in Chapter 3 who confidently asserted that boys don't have eyelashes, this must be among the cutest statements ever to find its way into a scientific paper.

Unfortunately, though, in later life, the preoccupation stops being cute, and sometimes instead becomes harmful. Just as more women than men are unduly concerned about being slim, more men than women are unduly concerned about being muscular. And just as more women than men have eating disorders, more men than women have muscle dysmorphia or 'bigorexia': an irrational conviction that they're not muscular enough, despite having a normal build or even being buff.

One last example. Because a mate's status and wealth are more important to women than men, men may have evolved a stronger desire to achieve status and wealth.[85] A knock-on effect of this difference is that more men than women struggle with concerns about their standing in the pack – and at the extreme, more men than women give up a balanced life to try to claw their way to the top.

Notice that this immediately suggests an explanation for certain societal gender gaps. These include the fact that, on average, men earn more than women, and the fact that, among the minority of people occupying positions of extreme prestige and power, a large majority are men. The possibility raised by an evolutionary perspective is that, rather than being due solely to discrimination or sexist socialization, these gaps stem in large part from inbuilt differences between the sexes. We'll come back to this thorny issue in Chapter 10. For now, let's just say that although ideas like these are deeply unpopular in certain quarters, if we want to make the world a better place, we shouldn't shy away from the facts. On the contrary, facing the facts is the best way we have to solve our problems and improve our lot. We should keep this firmly in mind as we move on to the next chapter, where we'll confront the dark side of human nature.

7

Breaking Bad

Sex and the Dark Side of Human Nature

The Antisocial Animal

Hollywood isn't exactly known for its originality. When filmmakers hit on a successful formula, they're more likely to beat it to death than to shelve it in pursuit of new artistic horizons.

Still, Hollywood does sometimes change, and one of the biggest changes in recent decades has been the rise of a certain character type: the badass woman. No mere damsel in distress, the badass woman can beat up the bad guys just as well as any man. Indeed, when she's pitted against a man, her victory is virtually a foregone conclusion. Beyond the beatings, the badass woman can match or surpass men in every traditionally male domain: toughness, risk-taking, competitiveness, you name it.

Contrary to what we're sometimes told, the badass woman isn't a recent invention. From Athena to Mulan to Wonder Woman, she's been a recurring feature of storytelling for as long as stories have been told. What's new is not her existence; it's the fact that she's gone from an occasional guest to a frequent visitor.

As a result of the badass woman's ascent on the silver screen, we've also seen the ascent of another character, this one in real life. The character in question is the grumpy guy who's deeply irritated by the rise of the badass woman. Watching the latest female superhero fight off a dozen burly men, this denizen of the interwebs is likely to insist that

'Women couldn't do that!' My first reaction is always to think, well, that's true, they couldn't – but nor could any man. It's pure fantasy in both cases, and it's nice for both sexes to be able to project themselves into the fantasy.

That said, the grumpy guy does get one thing right. There are well-established sex differences in all the areas where badass women kick butt. By expunging these differences from modern movies, filmmakers are effectively setting their offerings in an alternative reality populated by a species that looks like us but isn't really us at all. And while it's nice to visit that reality now and then, it's also sometimes nice to see movies set in the real world.

An additional irritation may be the sense that filmmakers aren't just trying to entertain us; they're trying to remake society. Many seem to have imbibed the academic theory that sex differences are shaped to a large extent by media. As such, media shouldn't just reflect society as it is; it should present it as it ought to be, because life will soon imitate art.

Leaving aside the question of how society ought to be – that's a moral question rather than an empirical one – are filmmakers right about the facts? Are they right that sex differences in aggression, risk-taking, and other stereotypically male traits stem primarily from media or culture? And are they right that presenting an alternative, gender-neutral reality will significantly shrink the gaps?

Of course not! The differences clearly go deeper than culture, and aren't so easily erased. That, at any rate, is the view I've come to after immersing myself in the scientific literature on the topic. In this chapter, I'll walk you through that literature and explain how I reached my conclusion. We'll explore sex differences in a grab bag of antisocial tendencies, including aggression, risk-taking, and sexual misconduct. Everyone knows that the sexes differ in these areas, despite the best efforts of filmmakers to confuse us. But most people don't know why – and nor do they know why the same sex differences are found in most other species. They will by the end of this chapter.

The Strong, Violent Type

Let's start our tour of the dark side with the antisocial trait that looms above all others: aggression. As mentioned, men are more aggressive than women, at least when it comes to face-to-face or *direct aggression*.[1] Men shout more, fight more, and kill more. In experiments, they're more likely to give people electric shocks, and in the real world, they're less likely to back down from a trivial altercation. Even men tamed by modern civilization – men who'd never throw a punch in real life – watch more violent movies, play more violent video games, and have more fantasies about killing other people.[2] To be fair, when it comes to *indirect aggression* – spreading rumours about people, excluding them from the group – we find either no sex difference or that women engage in slightly more.[3] For everything else, though, men are in pole position.

As with most sex differences, the sex difference in aggression gets progressively larger for rarer, more extreme acts: a good example of the tail-of-the-distribution effect.[4] Men are somewhat more likely to engage in verbal aggression; much more likely to engage in physical aggression; much, much more likely to engage in violent crime; and much, much, much more likely to kill someone – or, for that matter, to kill themselves.

It's not that men are vastly more anger-prone than women; the sexes don't particularly differ in how angry they get or how often.[5] Instead, men tend to be less self-controlled, and less concerned about the negative consequences of overt aggression, from ruptured friendships to injuries and imprisonment.[6]

Few would deny that men are the main perpetrators of violence. Who are its main victims? Many assume that it's women – and when it comes to *sexual* violence, they're right.[7] For every other kind of violence, however, men are more often found in the victim column. This pattern is particularly stark when we look at homicide data. In almost every society on Earth, men are more likely than women to be murdered.[8] Most of the time, the killer is a man as well. Women kill much less often, but when they do, the victim is usually a husband or a boyfriend.[9] Apparently, both sexes prefer to kill men.

Now for the usual disclaimer: The fact that, on average, men are more aggressive than women doesn't mean that men are the aggressive sex whereas women are the gentle sex. That would be like saying that, because more men than women have a same-sex sexual orientation, men are the gay sex whereas women are the straight sex. Some members of *both* sexes are highly aggressive, and most members of both are not, at least in the modern world. You know what I'm going to say next, though: Among the minority who *are* highly aggressive, more are XY than XX.

An Unfortunate Inheritance

Where does the aggression sex difference come from? For some the answer is obvious: culture. A standard cultural explanation would be that, in various ways, society encourages male aggression but discourages aggression in females. Parents, teachers, and peers reward boys for aggressive behaviour, at least in its milder forms. And even when they don't reward it, they often turn a blind eye to it in boys in a way they never would with girls: Boys will be boys, after all. Meanwhile, movies and other media constantly model male aggression for impressionable young male minds. The subtext is clear: 'This is the way you should be.'

As always, no one should deny that social factors help shape the sex difference in aggression. But is the difference *entirely* due to social factors? Some would say yes. Writing in *The New York Times*, for instance, psychologist Michael Reichert argued that, although males are more violent than females, this tendency is not innate.[10] However, at least five lines of evidence suggest that Reichert was wrong, and that there's also an innate contribution.

1. STUBBORNNESS OF THE SEX DIFFERENCE IN AGGRESSION

One line of evidence for an innate contribution is the fact that the aggression sex difference persists even in the face of countervailing social pressure. Contrary to the idea that we encourage male aggression, parents and teachers spend a lot more time telling *boys* not to be aggressive than they do girls.[11] This isn't because they approve more of girls' aggression; it's because boys are more often aggressive. But notice the implication: Rather than being *created* by socialization, the sex difference survives even in the face of socialization in the other direction.[12]

To pre-empt a common misunderstanding, this isn't to say that socialization has no effect on the sex difference. Clearly, it does; the size of the difference varies considerably from culture to culture and time to time.[13] The point is that socialization couldn't be the *entire* explanation, because the difference persists even when socialization pushes harder against male than female aggression. Indeed, socialization may often make the difference *smaller* than it would otherwise be, not larger.

2. THE DEVELOPMENTAL TRAJECTORY OF MALE AGGRESSION

A second line of evidence concerns the unfolding of the aggression sex difference over the lifespan. As psychologist John Archer observed, if socialization alone were pulling the strings, we'd expect to find no difference in aggression in infants, followed by a steady increase in the size of the difference across childhood, as socialization makes its mark on our minds. But that's not what we find at all.[14]

First, the sex difference in aggression is apparent from the moment kids are mobile enough to make aggression an option: Boys fight more and lash out more, and engage in more rough-and-tumble play.[15] Importantly, these differences appear long before boys and girls start selectively imitating same-sex role models, and long before they even understand that they're boys or girls.[16]

Second, rather than starting at zero then escalating in boys as the effects of socialization compound, aggression starts out high for both sexes. The most violent category of human being is the toddler, and the only reason we don't worry more about the epidemic of toddler violence is that toddlers are small and cute, and can't do much damage with their tiny fists. From this early summit of violence, both sexes become progressively *less* violent as the years go by. This is a major stumbling block for the theory that children are socialized to be aggressive. To my eye, it suggests instead that they're socialized *not* to be. Throughout the process, however, boys are always more aggressive. Is this because anti-aggression socialization is stronger for girls than for boys? No; as we've already seen, it's usually the opposite. But even if it *were* stronger for girls, the data don't readily fit with a socialization explanation. Rather than the sex difference getting bigger as children absorb the message that female aggression is less acceptable, the gap remains roughly static throughout childhood.

So far so bad for the socialization hypothesis – and it's only downhill from here. The next point where the facts come unstuck from the theory is in the decade or so following the onset of puberty. During this biologically critical window, the aggression sex difference suddenly explodes as men ramp up their aggressive tendencies. The evolutionary psychologists Margo Wilson and Martin Daly dubbed this rapid-onset increase in male misbehaviour the *young-male syndrome*.[17] The most reliable evidence for the syndrome comes from homicide records. In childhood, neither sex is particularly homicidal. In the years after puberty, however, homicide rates suddenly skyrocket for males.[18] Is this because society starts socializing males to be more aggressive? On the contrary, young male aggression is a serious problem facing every society, and thus most try to restrain rather than inflame it.[19] Nevertheless, it persists.

Finally, as young adulthood gives way to middle age, the sex difference in aggression shrinks, largely because men begin mellowing. The socialization explanation gives us no reason to expect this. As we'll see soon, though, an evolutionary explanation does.

3. GETTING HORMONAL

The next line of evidence for an innate contribution to the sex difference in aggression comes from research on the impact of hormones. The star of the show here, of course, is testosterone. When it comes to testosterone's effects on aggression, we can ask two questions. The first is: Are higher levels of testosterone in the bloodstream linked to greater aggression?

The second is: Are higher levels of testosterone in the *womb* linked to greater aggression? Given that males have higher levels than females both in utero and from puberty on, a 'yes' to either question would suggest an innate contribution to men's aggressive streak.

The evidence concerning the first question is less definitive than people tend to think. Levels of circulating testosterone are at best weakly related to male aggression.[20] It is true that circulating testosterone and aggression both rise in the wake of puberty, which seems to implicate the former in the latter. But it's not the case that as soon as the pubertal T starts flowing, boys start fighting everyone they pass on the street, any more than they instantly have a deep voice or the ability to grow a beard.[21] Instead, pubertal testosterone seems to kick off the slow development of a heightened *capacity* for aggression. Importantly, the fact that it does this, rather than kicking off the development of, say, a heightened interest in infants, is presumably an innate feature of male pubertal development, rather than a product of socialization.

Although absolute levels of circulating testosterone don't seem to predict aggression, *changes* in an individual's levels might. According to the *challenge hypothesis*, when men face a threat or compete for mates, their testosterone levels spike, whereas when they form a pair bond or help care for offspring, their testosterone levels plummet.[22] These changes seem to potentiate or inhibit a range of evolutionarily relevant behaviours, including mate seeking, status seeking, and aggression. Innateness minimizers argue that testosterone levels and aggression are strongly influenced by the environment – and they're right. But how could it be otherwise? The only alternative would be for men to be either permanently aggressive or aggressive at random, neither of which would make any adaptive sense. Furthermore, the fact that men secrete testosterone in response to *threats*, rather than in response to, say, babies, is presumably not a product of socialization – and nor, presumably, is the fact that men respond to increased testosterone with a desire to aggress rather than, say, a desire to make pancakes. These responses are built into the male psyche – or at least are stronger in the average man than the average woman.

So much for circulating testosterone. What about prenatal testosterone exposure? Here, the evidence is more straightforward: Individuals exposed to higher levels of testosterone in the womb tend to be more aggressive later in life. The best evidence for this comes from lab studies on nonhuman animals. Females given a large dose of prenatal testosterone are more aggressive than other females, especially if they're also given testosterone at puberty to mimic the usual male double whammy. Conversely, males *starved* of prenatal testosterone are *less* aggressive than other males, even *if* they're given testosterone at puberty. Findings such as these are often explained in terms of the *organizational–activational hypothesis*: the idea that prenatal testosterone begins setting up the brain areas involved in male-typical behaviour, and then pubertal testosterone hones and activates those areas. Both phases are necessary to establish the levels of aggression characteristic of adult males.[23]

Experiments like the above can only be done on nonhuman animals. However, comparable findings are seen in 'natural experiments' involving human beings. One example is that gay men commit fewer violent crimes than straight men, whereas lesbians commit *more* than straight women. Given that, in both cases, these individuals were subject to the same cultural pressures and same-sex role models as their straight counterparts, this pattern is most plausibly explained in terms of sex-atypical prenatal hormones, rather than social factors – just like same-sex sexual orientation itself.[24]

4. SEX DIFFERENCES IN AGGRESSION ACROSS CULTURES

Still not persuaded? Yet another line of evidence for an innate contribution is the fact that greater male aggression is a cross-cultural universal. Indeed, it's one of the best-established cross-cultural universals in the scientific corpus.

The strongest evidence for this is once again homicide data. In every culture and every country where such data are available, the vast majority of homicides are perpetrated by men. Furthermore, although *absolute* levels of homicide vary considerably, the size of the homicide gender gap is surprisingly invariant: Men commit more than 90% of homicides in every society, and are almost always the majority of its victims.[25] And it's not just the basic gap that's preserved across societies; it's also the sex-by-age trend mentioned earlier. The homicide sex difference balloons in early adulthood, then contracts for the remainder of the lifespan.[26]

Scientists haven't just found the aggression sex difference in modern nation-states, either; they've also found it among contemporary hunter-gatherers.[27] This is an important data point given that the hunter-gatherer lifestyle typified most of our evolutionary history, and thus that modern hunter-gatherers most closely approximate humans in their 'natural' state. Scientists have even found the sex difference in cultures that have long since vanished from the Earth. The fossil record shows that ancient skeletons of men have more fractures, dents, and holes in them than ancient skeletons of women. How do we know that the damage came from fighting rather than accidents – from falling out of a tree while collecting honey, for instance, or being gored by a boar while hunting? We know because the damage is concentrated on the left-hand side of the skeletons. This tells us that the injuries were most likely sustained during face-to-face combat: Most humans are right-handed, after all, and thus blows from a right-handed enemy would tend to fall on the left-hand side of the body.[28]

The question this all raises is this: If greater male aggression is due solely to socialization – or even *largely* to socialization – why would we find it in every nation, culture, and time?

This sounds like a rhetorical question, but there are several possible answers. One is that we find greater male aggression in every culture because, in every culture, men are larger and stronger than women. On this view, the *behavioural* sex difference is an indirect effect of evolved *physical* sex differences, rather than a direct effect of evolved psychological ones. But if it were just about physical advantages, men would be more aggressive with women than they are with other men. Moreover, *women* would be just as aggressive with same-sex rivals as men are. In both cases, however, the facts contradict the predictions: Men are more aggressive with other men than with women, and men engage in more same-sex aggression.

A related but more sophisticated suggestion comes from the psychologists Alice Eagly and Wendy Wood.[29] According to their influential *social role theory*, which I introduced in Chapter 6, men and women are assigned different roles in society based on the physical and reproductive differences between them. Because men are larger and stronger than women, and because they don't have to breastfeed the young, societies have always funnelled men into roles involving aggression, such as protector, warrior, and hunter. Involvement in these roles then amps up men's aggressive inclinations, creating the psychological sex difference in this trait. The psychological difference is therefore an indirect echo of the *physical* differences, rather than a direct product of natural selection. If we were to change our social roles, the psychological difference would simply fall away.

Eagly and Wood's theory has an appealing logic. In the end, though, I think it fails as a complete explanation for the aggression sex difference. First, given that selection has endowed men with the physical apparatus for aggression – larger bodies, bigger muscles, and the like – why would it not also endow them with a mind designed for their use? Not to do so would be like giving people sex organs but not a desire for sex. Second, although in some cultures, men's aggression is encouraged, in most, it's not; it's actively *dis*couraged.[30] Despite that, in *all* cultures, men are more aggressive. Finally, and to my mind most decisively, if the social-role account were accurate, we'd expect that the sex difference in aggression would be larger in nations with stricter, more traditional gender roles. It's not. In fact, the difference is often *smaller* in those nations: yet another example of the gender-equality paradox.[31] Taken together, the evidence suggests that social role theory is unable to explain the cross-cultural universality of greater male aggression.

5. SEX DIFFERENCES IN AGGRESSION ACROSS SPECIES

We've got one more line of evidence to consider, and it's arguably the most persuasive. This is the fact that sex differences in aggression aren't just found across cultures; they're found in other species – species that don't have culturally prescribed social roles, socially transmitted stereotypes, or any other staple of the sociocultural explanations.

As with humans, male–male aggression is notably more common in other animals than its female–female equivalent.[32] It'd be easy to fill a library of books with examples of males sparring and scrapping with each other in ways that females basically don't. Male horses and zebras bite and kick each other. Male giraffes club each other with their elongated necks. Male kangaroos engage in 'boxing matches', periodically punctuated with double-foot kicks while balanced on their tails. Male narwhals duel with their unicorn-like tusks. Male bowerbirds vandalize each other's bowers: the ornamental structures they build to impress the females. Male seahorses tail-wrestle each other. And so on and on and on.

To be clear, I'm not suggesting that females are never aggressive. In a sense, 'aggression' is too broad a concept for analysing sex differences in this domain. That's because each sex corners the market on certain forms of aggression. Most obviously, females use aggression to protect their young.[33] When people go hiking in the Malaysian jungles, they always keep an eye out for signs that male elephants are in the area – *or* that *baby* elephants are. The reason for the latter is that if there are baby elephants in the area, there are mothers, and mothers will do anything to protect their young. Whenever someone gets killed by an elephant, the question is always 'male or mother?' Furthermore, as we'll see later, parental aggression isn't the only kind of aggression that females like to dabble in. Still, with the exception of parental aggression in species with no paternal care, males almost always dabble more.

The cross-species similarities don't end there. In humans, males commit 95% of homicides, and are 70 to 80% of homicide victims.[34] In chimpanzees, males commit 92% of chimpicides, and are 73% of chimpicide victims: virtually the same numbers.[35] Nor is this basic pattern unique to humans and chimps. A survey of more than a thousand mammals revealed that, in most, males are more likely than females to kill members of their own species, and that males are more likely to kill other males than they are to kill females.[36] We humans like to think we're unique, and in some ways we obviously are. When it comes to lethal aggression, however, we're just part of a broader trend.

We're also part of a broader trend when it comes to the development of female–male differences in aggression. As with humans, the differences in other species typically appear early in life. I mentioned above that, from a young age, boys are more interested than girls in rough-and-tumble play. What I didn't mention is that this doesn't just apply to humans. The same sex difference is found in other juvenile primates as well.[37] Boy chimps, for instance, spend a lot more time than girl chimps casually assaulting and wrestling each other, all the while laughing their heads off and having a great time.[38] And it's not even just other primates; the same sex difference is found in most mammals.[39] Across species, play functions as practice for the tasks that adult members of the species specialize in . . . including beating each other up. Play-fighting, it seems, is training for real fighting later on. Consistent with this suggestion, in species with high levels of male–male conflict, juvenile males typically engage in more play-fighting than juvenile females.[40] (An exception may be species where both sexes hunt as adults, including lions and other cats. In such species, juveniles of both sexes may evolve to play-fight as training for future hunting.)

In other species, we wouldn't dream of explaining differences like these in sociocultural terms. The only realistic option is natural selection. Why, then, would we assume that, in our case and ours alone, they're products of an entirely different cause, namely socialization and culture? Is it just a coincidence that socialization and culture produced exactly the same sex differences in our species as natural selection did in almost every other?

Psychology is a notoriously difficult field in which to make progress. It's rare to find a slam-dunk case for any claim or theory. But if anything qualifies for the title, it's the claim that sex differences in aggression have a large innate component. Indeed, given the strength of the arguments and evidence, the idea that the differences *don't* have a large innate component should be seen as a radical view. Unless its defenders can give us radical new evidence to support it, we're justified in moving on.

The Evolution of Sex Differences in Aggression

Why, though, did natural selection implant an innate push toward greater male aggression in the human genome? We've touched on the answer already: It's an unfortunate inheritance from our male ancestors, among whom those who were more aggressive tended to have more offspring. To spell out the logic in more detail, let's look at my favourite example of the evolution of aggression in a nonhuman animal: the elephant seal.

Elephant seals are extremely sexually dimorphic; males weigh up to ten times more than females, and are vastly more aggressive. Their extreme dimorphism traces back to the species' unique breeding system. Every year, elephant seals leave the water, haul up on the beach, and gather in vast colonies. The females have two tasks on their to-do list: giving birth to the young conceived during the last breeding season, and getting pregnant again for the next. The males, in contrast, have only one task on *their* to-do list: mate with as many females as possible. What ends up happening is that, while the females go about their business, the males attempt to assemble large harems of females, and defend them from other males. In pursuit of this goal, they adopt an unenviable live-by-the-sword-die-by-the-sword lifestyle. For the duration of the breeding season, they don't eat and they barely sleep. They're dedicated fighting, mating machines. This dedication, however, can pay enormous Darwinian dividends. It's not uncommon for dominant males – known as *beachmasters* – to have fifty or more females in their harem.

In discussing elephant seals with my students, I always ask: Who has more offspring, males or females? The usual answer is males. But it's not so simple. It is true that successful males have many more offspring than any female could ever hope to. However, most males have no offspring; they're elephant seal incels (involuntary celibates). Meanwhile, almost all the females have one pup per year. This means that most females have more offspring than most males. And the skew is not subtle. According to one estimate, 4% of males sire around 85% of the pups in any given breeding season.[41] This creates an intense selection pressure on the males for traits that put them in the 4%. Bigger, meaner, more aggressive males have a better chance of propelling themselves into that rarefied category, so males evolve over the generations to be bigger, meaner, and more aggressive.

The bottom line is that males engage in more aggression than females because the potential payoff of aggression is higher for males – and the potential payoff is higher for males because males can have many more offspring.

As we've seen, humans are no exception to this rule. In the human case, though, there are several complications. These revolve around the fact that we, unlike most mammals, commonly form long-term pair bonds and engage in biparental care. Because these activities reduce the maximum number of offspring that most men can sire, the average payoff for male aggression is lower, and men's willingness to engage in aggression is somewhat curtailed. At the same time, because men often invest heavily in their young, competing with same-sex rivals for the best investors can be a fitness-boosting strategy for women. As a result, women are sometimes known to engage in same-sex aggression over mates. This is especially so when it comes to less physically risky forms of aggression: for example, verbal or indirect aggression as opposed to outright violence. For both reasons, the sex difference in aggression in our species is more modest than that in most mammals – and far more modest than the Mars-and-Venus difference found in elephant seals.

The evolutionary approach to aggression doesn't just explain the raw sex difference. It also explains the trajectory of the difference over the lifespan: the fact that it grows after puberty as men's aggression accelerates, peaks in early adulthood, then shrinks with greater age. Here's what's probably going on. Before puberty, when you're still a child, there's little point risking your neck for status because, by definition, you can't cash in that status for offspring: Children aren't yet sexually mature. *After* puberty, however, the calculus changes, and the risks might well be worth taking – especially if you're a male, because males can potentially rack up so many more offspring. As such, the timing of the sudden increase in male aggression post-puberty fits perfectly with the idea that male aggression is an adaptation for same-sex competition over mates.[42]

As for the subsequent decline in aggression, this probably reflects a built-in tendency to take bigger risks when you've got little to lose, but then to go status quo mode when and if those risks pay off.[43] Consistent with this speculation, when men find a partner and get married, they tend to become less aggressive and less prone to crime – but if they later get divorced or become widowed, they often revert to premarital levels of aggression and criminality.[44] This is a good example of the fact that natural selection doesn't just set up organisms with a fixed propensity for aggression or any other behaviour. Instead, it sets up organisms that calibrate their propensities to their circumstances in ways that typically boost their reproductive fitness – or did, at least, when the tendency evolved.

Reckless Abandon

> Being male is now the single largest demographic risk factor for early mortality in developed countries.
>
> Daniel Kruger and Randy Nesse (2004), p.66

The fact that men engage in more aggression than women – and more of a range of antisocial behaviours – stems in part from another important sex difference: the sex difference in the tendency to take risks. As most people are all-too aware, boys and men are bigger risk-takers than girls and women.[45] This sex difference helps explain various stubborn facts. It helps explain why boy toddlers are more likely than girl toddlers to end up in the emergency room; why men are over-represented on the Wikipedia page of inventors killed by their own inventions; and why more men than women participate in extreme sports – that is, sports extremely likely to kill you, such as base jumping, hang-gliding, and motor racing.[46] It helps explain why men do most of the riskiest jobs in the world – including construction worker, fisherman, logger, taxi driver, and truck driver – and why more than 90% of workplace fatalities are men. And it helps explain why men are more likely than women to accept stupid dares, gamble away their life savings, invest in cryptocurrencies, die while taking extreme selfies, and hit send on an email without reading it through first.[47]

It's quite a résumé . . . and we're only just getting started! Men are more likely than women to get into car accidents, even when you statistically control for the fact that men drive more.[48] This isn't because men are less skilled at handling a vehicle; it's because they more often drive too fast, tailgate, and drive drunk. At the same time, despite their Russian roulette driving habits, men less often wear seatbelts. Not only are men more likely to crash a car, they're more likely to get *hit* by a car while crossing the road. This isn't because motorists try to run men down; it's because men are more likely to try to cross when it's unsafe. Yep, scientists have sat by the side of the road tabulating men's and women's road-crossing habits, and that's what they've observed.[49] And not only are men more likely to be struck by cars, they're more likely to be struck by lightning. This isn't because God hates men; it's because men are more likely to work outdoors and less likely to think 'Hmmm, there's a storm coming; maybe I should go inside.'

Every year, the *British Medical Journal* publishes a light-hearted Christmas edition. The 2014 offering included an article testing the hypothesis that men engage in more 'idiotic risk-taking'. To that end, the authors looked at the demographic makeup of Darwin Award recipients. Darwin Awards are bestowed on individuals whose actions ensure 'the long-term survival of the species, by selectively allowing one less idiot to survive'. Notable recipients include the would-be aviator who strapped helium balloons to a lawn chair then drifted over Los Angeles for 14 hours before being rescued, and the terrorist who put insufficient postage on a letter bomb, then unthinkingly opened it when the parcel was returned to his door. Crunching the numbers, the researchers found that 88% of Darwin Award winners were men, consistent with their 'male idiot theory'.[50]

To be fair, although men take more idiotic risks, they also take more heroic ones. More than 90% of Carnegie Hero Awards go to men, to give just one example.[51] Still, whether idiotic, heroic, or a mixture of both, the root cause of the sex difference is the same: Men are more tolerant of risks.

Some argue that greater male risk-taking is a mirage created by the fact that researchers tend to focus on risks more commonly taken by men: riding motorbikes rather than riding horses; white-water rafting rather than cheerleading; skydiving rather than cosmetic surgery.[52] One way to get around this potential problem is to look not at activities but at outcomes – and when it comes to risk-related outcomes, one stands head-and-shoulders above the rest: accidental fatalities. Not only are the stats on accidental fatalities highly accurate, but they're an evolutionarily relevant metric: Dying tends not to be good for one's fitness. Sure enough, when we look at the data, a clear and consistent sex difference emerges.[53] You know what it is.

One thing you might be wondering, though, is why, given that death is so disastrous for one's fitness, men evolved to dice with it. The answer is that accidental fatalities among men are an unfortunate but rare side effect of levels of risk-taking that, on average, boosted our male ancestors' fitness. Risk-taking is about striking the right balance between caution and taking a chance. If you're too cautious, you'll spend your life hiding under your bed; if you're too risk-prone, you'll fall off a cliff or get eaten by a lion before you leave any descendants. The sweet spot lies somewhere between these two extremes. This is true for both sexes. However, the exact location of the sweet spot differs for men and women. The reason it differs, yet again, is that men have a higher ceiling number of offspring. As a result, taking risks to gain status and ultimately mates can potentially boost men's fitness more than women's, and men's appetite for risk is dialled up higher. By definition, risks don't always pay off: Sometimes you hit the jackpot; sometimes you die. If the jackpot is sufficiently large, though, it can compensate for a non-zero chance of death.

That's the evolutionist's story, anyway. But how do we know that the difference isn't just due to socialization?

To start with, the developmental trajectory of risk-taking fits better with the evolutionary explanation. As with aggression, if the risk-taking sex difference were purely down to socialization, we'd expect it to be absent in very young children, to grow steadily throughout childhood, then eventually to stabilize at a level deemed optimal by the local culture. Instead, the difference is apparent from the moment children can move under their own steam; it swells in early adulthood; then it winds down from that point on.[54] The best evidence for this is again data on accidental fatalities. As Daniel Kruger and Randy Nesse report, for the first ten years of life, 150 boys die for every 100 girls, but after puberty, *300* boys die for every 100 girls.[55] The acceleration of male risk-taking after puberty is so reliable that one study was able to use the onset of the 'accident hump' – that is, the spike in male mortality rates – to show that the age of puberty for boys has been dropping since the mid-1700s.[56] The spike doesn't last forever, however, and to the relief of parents everywhere, the sex difference in accidental fatalities starts shrivelling after the early adult years. None of this is what we'd expect based on a pure sociocultural explanation. On the contrary, the rise and fall of the risk-taking sex difference suggests a significant innate contribution.

Further support for the innateness hypothesis comes from the fact that we find the risk-taking sex difference wherever we find human beings. Survey data from large, multinational studies show that, in every nation without fail, men engage in more risk-taking than women.[57] Real-world data converge on the same conclusion. Across the globe, boys are more likely than girls to be injured or killed while playing, and men are more likely than women to be injured or killed in every context: work, play, random showing off.[58]

And in case you were wondering, the sex difference in risky behaviour isn't just found in nation-states; it's also found in non-state societies.[59]

Among hunter-gatherers, for instance, men target riskier food sources: riskier in the sense that there's a greater chance of coming home empty-handed, and riskier in the sense that your food might fight back and try to kill you.[60] Even more striking, the risk-taking sex difference among hunter-gatherers follows the same developmental trajectory as that in the West: It emerges in early childhood, then escalates in the years after puberty.[61]

A final line of evidence for an innate contribution is that the sex difference in risk-taking is found as well in many nonhuman species – in particular, those where males have a higher reproductive ceiling than females. Our close cousins the chimpanzees are again a perfect example. As with humans, young male chimps are the most risk-prone chimp demographic. And as with humans, young male chimp risk-taking is often aimed at achieving status.[62]

None of this proves beyond a shadow of a doubt that the risk-taking sex difference in humans has evolutionary underpinnings. But in my view, it does prove it beyond a *reasonable* doubt. If you want to adopt the view that, in light of the current evidence, would be the least embarrassing to hold if you turn out to be wrong, the evolutionary view is the one to go for.

Sexual Misconduct and Intimate Partner Abuse

So far, we've explored forms of misbehaviour where men are both the primary perpetrators and primary victims. But no account of the dark side would be complete without also looking at cases that typically cross gender lines, and where the victims are disproportionately women.

These fall into two main categories: sexual misconduct and intimate partner abuse. The gender breakdown for sexual misconduct – which includes sexual harassment, sexual assault, and rape – is straightforward and uncontroversial: Men are overwhelmingly the perpetrators, and women overwhelmingly the victims. The breakdown for intimate partner abuse is more complicated. On the one hand, historically, and in many nations still, men have engaged in more of it. On the other hand, in the modern West, men and women engage in similar levels of physical aggression against partners, and women, if anything, engage in *more* verbal aggression. It's only for *extreme* physical aggression that the old pattern reasserts itself: Men are the main perpetrators, and women the main victims.[63] Still, extreme physical aggression is, by definition, the most damaging form of aggression, and thus while partner abuse is now surprisingly symmetrical in the West, it's fair to say that women still bear the greatest risks when it comes to female–male interactions. The dilemma this puts women in was captured well by the comedian Louis C.K., who once asked: 'How do women still go out with guys, when you consider that there is no greater threat to women than men? . . . [T]ry to imagine that you could only date a half-bear, half-lion. "Oh, I hope this one's nice."'[64]

Let's fast-forward to the explanations. One influential sociocultural explanation is the *patriarchy theory* or *male control theory*. The basic idea is that men use sexual violence and intimate partner abuse to keep women under control. Rape, on this view, isn't about sex but about power; Susan Brownmiller famously described it as 'nothing more or less than a conscious process of intimidation by which *all men* keep *all women* in a state of fear'.[65] Similarly, intimate partner abuse isn't about one person trying to control another person; it's about one *group* trying to control another group. Barbara Raye described it as a 'conspiracy of men to oppress women'.[66] Both behaviours flow from a patriarchal philosophy according to which men are entitled to sex, and can use violence to keep women in their place. And both are motivated by misogyny: men's alleged deep-seated hatred of women.

How does the patriarchy theory fare in light of an evolutionary analysis? The short answer is: Not well. Admittedly, the theory was on shaky ground even before the Darwinian critique took shape. But Darwin hammered the final nails into the coffin.

One of those nails is the fact that, from an evolutionary perspective, it would be decidedly odd if men aimed to benefit all men everywhere – many of whom are rivals, and most of whom they don't know – rather than aiming to benefit themselves and their nearest and dearest, many of whom are women: mothers, wives, daughters, and so on. As David Buss put it,

> Contrary to the view that men or women are united with all members of their own sex for the purpose of oppressing the other sex, each individual shares key interests with particular members of each sex and is in conflict with other members of each sex.[67]

So, whatever role patriarchal attitudes and misogyny play in sexual assault and partner abuse, men don't do these things for the sake of all men, any more than predators hunt prey for their entire species. The men and the predators are doing it for themselves.[68]

But do patriarchal attitudes and misogyny play a significant role in the first place? Here we find more nails for the patriarchy theory's coffin. We'll start with the idea that sexual harassment and rape are about power and misogyny rather than sex. It's probably true that power is part of the kick for some men, and that misogyny is one of the motivations. But there are several reasons to doubt that either are major players. First, sex must be at least *part* of the motivation even when power and misogyny are contributors. After all, power and misogyny don't typically cause erections, and nor do abstract ideas about men's and women's proper place in society. Second, if men's attitudes to women were the main driver of sexual misconduct, then gay men would be less likely to victimize other men than straight men are to victimize women. They're not, though; they engage in similar rates of victimization.[69] This tells us that sexual misconduct isn't driven primarily by men's attitudes to women.

The patriarchy theory of intimate partner abuse faces similar challenges. When men hit their partners, is it because they've internalized a patriarchal belief that it's OK to abuse women? Or is it because they're lashing out in a rage? More often than not, it's the latter. In fact, these days, many men who hit their partners have internalized *anti*-patriarchal beliefs: They *don't* think it's OK to abuse women; they think it's extremely not-OK, but they've lost control. (In case there's any doubt, I'm not suggesting that this in any way excuses their behaviour.) Far from being taught that violence against women is acceptable, boys are taught that they should never hit girls – even in self-defence – while men are expected to protect women, even if it puts them in danger. Patriarchal beliefs and negative attitudes about the entire female half of the species are not the main motivations for violence against women; the main motivations are the same as those for violence against men: trying to control the person, seeking revenge, and reacting to an insult or slight.[70]

Certainly, the fact that most harassers, rapists, and domestic abusers are men, and that most of their victims are women, is consistent with the idea that these behaviours are about all men keeping all women under control. But there's a much more parsimonious and commonsensical explanation for that pattern: Most perpetrators are men because most people committing all crimes are men, and most victims are women because most men are straight. If they were gay, they'd harass, rape, or abuse men instead.

The upshot is that the patriarchy theory isn't a realistic contender for explaining sexual misconduct or intimate partner abuse. Indeed, by placing the blame on culture, the theory mistakes an ally for an enemy. As dissident feminist Camille Paglia put it,

> Society is not the criminal but the force which keeps crime in check. When social controls weaken, man's innate cruelty bursts forth. The rapist is created not by bad social conditioning influences but by a failure of social conditioning.[71]

What's the evolutionary alternative to the patriarchy theory? The most plausible suggestion, in my view, is that sex differences in sexual misconduct and intimate partner abuse aren't adaptations in themselves, but are instead offshoots of other sex differences: differences we've discussed already.[72] For sexual misconduct, the main contributors are men's greater interest in casual sex and sexual variety, coupled with women's greater sexual choosiness. These differences all but guarantee that men sometimes want to have sex with women who'd rather slam their fingers in a door. Combine this with men's greater size, strength, and willingness to use aggression, and you've got a recipe for occasional disaster. As for intimate partner abuse, the story is simpler: The relevant sex differences are men's greater proneness to aggression, coupled again with their greater size and strength.

An evolutionary analysis doesn't just explain the male side of the equation. Importantly, it also helps explain why rape is such a profoundly upsetting experience for women. Because women's obligatory investment in offspring is so large, preserving control over mate choice is an extremely high priority for women. Rape bypasses that choice, and thus is one of the most devastating experiences a woman can suffer.[73] No amount of socialization could make rape any less traumatic for women, because the aversion to sexual coercion is so deeply embedded in human nature.

One line of support for the evolutionary explanation is that, once again, we see comparable behaviour in other animals. In many nonhuman species, males harass females for sex, and in some – including scorpion flies, mallard ducks, and orangutans – males try to force females to copulate with them.[74] Meanwhile, male efforts to control females with aggression are particularly common in primates, as is female resistance to male control.[75] The parallels between humans and other animals strengthen the argument that the impulses driving these behaviours in our species don't come solely from culture.

One reason that people sometimes resist this conclusion is that they assume that if sexual coercion, rape, or partner abuse are natural in any sense, then that must mean they're OK. But as mentioned in earlier chapters, there's simply no reason to think this is true. In fact, it *couldn't* be true. As we've just seen, both sexual coercion and *resistance* to sexual coercion are plausibly products of natural selection. This implies that natural selection can't furnish us with a logically consistent moral system.[76] We can't outsource the task of deciding what's right and wrong to nature. We've got to decide for ourselves.

A second reason that people resist the evolutionary explanation for sexual coercion and partner abuse is that they assume it implies that we're stuck with these things forever. Of course, even if it *did* imply this, the evolutionary explanation could still be true; life sometimes sucks. As it happens, though, it doesn't imply this at all. Whether or not the impulses that drive sexual coercion and partner abuse are part of human nature, we can still curtail these behaviours, and maybe one day even drive them to extinction. To assume otherwise is to commit what I call the *fixed-forever fallacy*. Rather than implying that we're stuck with the status quo, understanding the true causes of the dark side of human nature can help us find interventions to curb it. I'll come back to this point in Chapter 10.

The Dark Side of the Fairer Sex

So far, we've focused on forms of aggression where men hog the limelight. That doesn't mean, however, that women are never aggressive or competitive. On the contrary, a modern evolutionary approach predicts that they will be. Because we're a species with mutual mate choice, competition for status and mates isn't just a male affair. According to scholars of the topic – most of whom are women, incidentally – females in our species compete fervently for power, status, and mates, but generally in subtler, less risky ways than males.[77] Whereas boys are inclined to raise their fists or voices, girls' weapons of choice are more often gossip, cold shoulders, and ostracism. Parents and teachers commonly report that, in secondary school, girls can be just as cruel to each other as boys, if not crueller. And although this 'mean girls' phase tends not to last long, women continue to compete in various ways throughout the rest of their lives.

The fact that both sexes compete for mates has long been recognized in evolutionary psychology. One line of research, for instance, has explored how men and women derogate same-sex rivals as a form of intrasexual competition: in other words, how they try to steer mates or potential mates away from rivals by saying disparaging things about them.[78] Both sexes do this, not just males – exactly as we'd expect in a species where both sexes invest in their young.

Interestingly, though, the sexes sometimes focus on different things when cutting down the competition. Specifically, heterosexual derogators often tailor their derogation efforts to the mate preferences of the other sex. For example, women are more likely than men to castigate same-sex rivals for being promiscuous or unfaithful: something that neither sex likes in a long-term mate, but which men tend to have a bigger bee in their bonnet about. The psychologist Anne Campbell observed that on the rare occasions when women get into physical fights, it's commonly triggered by one woman calling the other promiscuous, albeit usually in less polite terms.[79] When *men* get into physical fights, on the other hand, it's rarely triggered by one *man* calling the other promiscuous. It's fair to say that such an insult would lack bite. In fact, yelling at a man that 'You've slept with hundreds of women!' probably wouldn't be an insult at all. Instead, men are more likely to derogate other men for being physically weak, lacking sexual power, or lacking earning power and status: things that are more often deal-breakers for women than men.

Although the level of female–female competition in our species does make us somewhat unusual among the animals, it's not without precedent. To start with, it's found in many other primates. As Sarah Hrdy points out, female nonhuman primates commonly compete for status and mates, but do so in lower key, less overtly violent ways than males – much like female *human* primates.[80] Beyond the primates, female hyenas are famously aggressive: much more so than the males. And at the extreme, in a handful of species, dominant females harass and terrorize lower-ranking ones to prevent them from having offspring, thus ensuring that they alone pass on their genes.[81] These female reigns of terror are seen, for instance, in cute-but-evil meerkats, not-cute-but-still-evil naked mole rats, and in our old friends, the sex-changing clownfish. (That's another detail that *Finding Nemo* mysteriously overlooked.)

It is true that, for all the female aggression seen in humans and other species, males usually push the aggression envelope further. Still, we shouldn't paint females as the gentle sex and males the aggressive one, and we shouldn't ignore the dark side of human nature as it manifests in either sex. Filmmakers model the badass woman on the badass man. But real-life badass women aren't just copying men's playbook; they're working from a different script.

8
Family Matters

Mum, Dad, and the Green-Eyed Monster

Making a Home with Darwin

So far, we've focused almost entirely on 'adults-only' material – that is, sex, violence, and other topics we generally try to shield our kids from. Let's pivot now to a more family-friendly topic: parenting.

Most people become parents at some point in their lives, and most see it as among the most fulfilling things they ever do. Of course, 'fulfilling' doesn't always mean 'fun'. Parents spend more time than they might prefer nagging three-foot-tall ogres who don't seem to appreciate their progenitors' accumulated wisdom on such matters as whether it's OK to flush their sibling's favourite toy down the toilet. Still, despite the difficulty – or perhaps in part because of it – for most parents, parenting is one of the great sources of meaning in their lives.

But although this is true for both sexes, men and women are not identical in the parental domain. Most notably, women shoulder more of the childcare burden than men, especially during the baby and toddler years.[1] As always, this is an average difference, not a categorical one. But it's also a difference found in every culture and in many other species. Furthermore, it's a particularly important difference from an evolutionary perspective, because it lies behind all the other differences we've looked at so far. Read on to find out how!

Nurturing the Parental Gender Gap

To get things started, let's take our usual tack of outlining the sociocultural approach to explaining the sex difference under discussion, then assessing whether it's up to the task. The two main sociocultural hypotheses for the sex difference in parental care are, first, that women are basically forced into the primary caregiver role by husbands, family, or the weight of tradition, and second, that even if women sometimes take on that role voluntarily, this is only because they've been socialized to do so.[2] Either way, from a Nurture-Only perspective, evolution has nothing to do with it.

We can quickly dispense with the first hypothesis. No doubt, women have sometimes been forced into parenting, especially in earlier centuries. But forcing alone doesn't cut it as an explanation. Even in the modern West, where traditional ways are routinely challenged, women report a stronger desire than men to have children, and a stronger desire to be the primary caregiver.[3] Unless we're going to ignore what women themselves are telling us, we'll have to accept that sex differences in parental participation stem in large part from men's and women's preferences and the choices these lead them to make.

The next question is why men and women prefer the things they prefer and choose the things they choose. That's where the second sociocultural hypothesis comes in. Here's my best effort to frame a Nurture-Only version of it. From their earliest years, girls are encouraged by parents, teachers, and the world in general to be nurturing and to care for others. When they're toddlers, adults shower them with dolls; when they're a little older, adults encourage them to babysit younger kids in a way they rarely do with boys. Meanwhile, children see their mothers and their friends' mothers caring for youngsters, so come to see this as the natural order of things. Fairy stories and media depictions of women hammer home the point. All of this means that girls develop a stronger interest in infants and young children than their brothers. As a result, they spend more time with infants and young children, and soon pick up the knack of caring for them. When they one day have kids of their own, it seems a no-brainer that they, rather than the father, will be the primary parent – after all, they're better equipped for it. But they're better equipped by nurture, not by nature. If boys were given dolls, assigned babysitting duties, and subjected to pro-parenting propaganda, they'd be just as well equipped.

A more extreme spin on the Nurture-Only explanation is the idea that, whereas women were once literally forced into reproductive slavery, in modern societies, they're kept in reproductive slavery with the invisible chains of insidious ideologies: ideologies that claim that women have a maternal instinct, and that they're better suited than men to changing nappies and doing other unpleasant chores that, coincidentally, the men promoting these ideologies would prefer not to have to do themselves. The idea that sex differences in parental care are 'natural' is merely an attempt to brainwash women and prop up the parental status quo. As Chelsea Conaboy argued in *The New York Times*, 'Maternal Instinct Is a Myth That Men Created'.[4]

Consistent with a sociocultural explanation, parental roles in our species are far from fixed. In the not-too-distant past, most well-off women were stay-at-home mums, while most dads had little to do with their kids. Today, most mothers combine work and parenting, and most fathers take an active role in childcare. Some men are even stay-at-home dads, and some women the sole breadwinners. This shift happened much too quickly to reflect a genetic change. It can only be a cultural one. Attributing the parental gender gap to evolution in the face of evidence like this betrays either ignorance or ideological bias.

Or so say the Nurture-Only theorists! Are they right, though? You know my answer, but let's explore the reasons behind it.

Naturing the Parental Gender Gap

We'll begin with the idea that the maternal instinct is simply a way to oppress women and keep them in reproductive slavery. My first response to this proposal is that it's quite an accusation! I'm always surprised that people are so happy to throw around such serious charges so casually, without the slightest wisp of a hint of evidence to back them up. But I'm even more surprised that anyone takes the charges seriously. They're extremely flimsy.

For a start, the modern evolutionary argument is not that women have a maternal instinct whereas men are non-parental; it's that both sexes are parental, but that women are somewhat more so. As such, if the evolutionary explanation is an attempt to oppress women, it's also an attempt to oppress men, albeit to a lesser degree. Leaving that aside, is it realistic to think that anyone who's sceptical of the extreme Nurture-Only theory of parental sex differences is just trying to trap women in the role of primary parent? It's not, if for no other reason than that many scientists advocating the evolutionary explanation are women themselves, not to mention card-carrying feminists.[5]

Granted, it's possible in principle that society brainwashes women into wanting to be the primary caregiver. But it's also possible in principle that society brainwashes gender theorists into *thinking* that it brainwashes women into wanting to be the primary caregiver. Unless we can marshal evidence one way or the other, these possibilities cancel each other out, and don't advance the argument.

The other, less extreme versions of the Nurture-Only view aren't as easily dismissed – but with just a little extra effort, we can dismiss those as well. Consider first the observation that parental roles vary a great deal across cultures and historical periods. For some, this is proof positive that the differences are learned rather than innate. But the conclusion doesn't follow. The variation implies that the differences are not due solely to nature; it *doesn't* imply that they're due solely to nurture instead. Variability in parental contributions falsifies a position that no one holds: the Nature-Only position.

So, what evidence do we have that nature is a contributing factor? The nativist might start by pointing out that, although we see plenty of variation across cultures, the basic sex difference in parental involvement is still found wherever we look. It's found in every major world region, from

Africa to Asia to the Pacific, and in every type of society, from the smallest hunter-gatherer band to the largest sprawling city. It's even found in modern Western nations, where people place a premium on sexual equality and an equitable division of labour between the sexes. If the parental sex difference were just down to culture, why would it be so ubiquitous?

And why would it appear so early in life? As we saw in the previous chapter, from the moment children start playing, girls engage in more play-parenting than boys, while boys engage in more play-fighting. A crude analysis of these data would suggest that women are designed to look after babies, whereas men are designed to beat each other up.

For some sex differences, cross-cultural universality and early appearance clinch the deal for an innate contribution. In this case, however, the sociocultural theorist has a strong counterargument. It comes in the form of Alice Eagly and Wendy Wood's *social role theory*, discussed as well in the last two chapters.[6] From a social-role perspective, the sex difference in parental inclinations – like most psychological sex differences – is not directly innate. Instead, it's a cultural response to certain innate *physical* differences. The most important in this case are that women rather than men get pregnant, and that women rather than men have the equipment for nursing the young. Cultures everywhere have accommodated themselves to these non-negotiable facts by assigning women the role of primary caregivers of their children. Women's engagement in that role cultivates their parental inclinations, creating the psychological sex difference. And having established a societal expectation that women do most of the parenting, we then get the dolls, the babysitting, and the female-targeted pro-parenting propaganda. That's why the difference emerges so early. In short, according to social role theory, the sex difference in parental inclinations is universal not because it's directly innate, but because it's an indirect cultural echo of universal sex differences in reproductive physiology.

The social-role hypothesis has a nice logic to it. It's a compelling position. Nonetheless, for several reasons, I don't think it succeeds as a complete explanation for the sex difference in parental care. To start with, we need to ask why natural selection would create innate *physical* differences related to parenting – most notably, the capacity to nurse offspring – but not also create innate psychological ones. Why would one small part of the body – the brain – be walled off from selection's invisible hand? *We* see an important distinction between body and mind, but natural selection doesn't; the mind, after all, is the activity of the brain, and selection can just as well tinker with what's inside the skull as what's outside. So, why wouldn't it tinker? Why would it leave everything up to culture when, without any innate guidance, culture could easily go off the rails?

On top of that, various lines of evidence indicate, as usual, that although sociocultural factors clearly matter, innate factors matter as well. First, contrary to a pure social-role explanation, the parenting sex difference persists even in the face of social influences pushing in the opposite direction. It's often said that society tells women that they should stay home with their children, or at least prioritize kids over career. But for many in the developed world these days, the opposite is true: 'Society' tells women that they *shouldn't* put children first, or that they shouldn't do it for long.[7] Whereas once upon a time, the career woman was denigrated, today the stay-at-home mum is. Well-to-do parents encourage their daughters to excel at least as much as they encourage their sons.[8] And major societal institutions reinforce their efforts; it's rare for schools or media to extol the joys of motherhood, even as one option among many. Despite the messages and the pressure, however, more mothers than fathers want to take time out from work while the children are young, or want to work part-time, or want to work full-time but in a job that doesn't devour their entire life – all so they'll have more time for their children.[9] Importantly, many women want these things despite feeling that they shouldn't want them. This suggests, as with so many earlier examples, that the sex difference appears *despite* social pressure, not because of it.

A particularly striking illustration of this phenomenon comes from the Israeli communes known as kibbutzim. The founders of these utopian settlements were radical egalitarians who wanted to abolish the nuclear family and establish a perfectly gender-equal society. To that end, they decided that all the children should be housed together and raised communally, rather than living with their biological parents. The early kibbutzniks managed to contort themselves to this blueprint. Later generations, however – generations born into kibbutzim and thus not raised in a nuclear family – reverted to more traditional ways. Parents – mothers in particular – hated the arrangement, and started agitating to have their children live with them. And contrary to the idea that men force women into the role of primary caregiver, in many cases, the women had to fight the more doctrinaire male leaders to take on that very role.[10]

It wasn't that the kibbutzniks had become social conservatives; they still believed in gender equality. But they believed in it as an abstract principle for society as a whole. For themselves, they wanted a special relationship with their children – and more so mothers than fathers.

Another line of evidence for an innate contribution concerns the impact of prenatal hormonal exposure on parental motivation. Most of the research on this topic comes from experiments on other mammals. The nutshell summary is that castrating males in early life, thus depriving them of testosterone, makes them more parental than males with intact tackle. At the same time, giving females large doses of testosterone in early life makes them *less* parental than their non-dosed sisters.[11] Clearly, we can't do experiments like these on human beings. But nature sometimes does it for us, in the form of certain disorders of sexual development. The most important is congenital adrenal hyperplasia or CAH, which as we've seen, involves exposure to high levels of testosterone in the womb. Girls with CAH tend to be less interested in infants, less likely to play with dolls, and less likely to daydream about marriage or motherhood.[12] Prenatal testosterone apparently turns down the volume on their parental desires – and in the normal course of events, does the same for most males.

The contribution of prenatal hormones, along with the tenacity of the parental sex difference, argues strongly against a pure social-role explanation. So too does the fact that the difference is commonly found among a group of individuals who grow up without any culturally created social roles whatsoever: other animals. That's what we'll explore next.

Parenting Across the Animal World

How does human parenting match what we see in the rest of the animal kingdom? The first thing to say is that other animals vary tremendously in their parental arrangements. The most common arrangement is: no parental care at all. That's because most animals are invertebrates, and most invertebrates are non-parental; the females pump out the eggs, the males fertilize them, then both parties go their separate ways. Even among vertebrates, parental care is the exception rather than the rule; most vertebrates are fish, after all, and most fish are non-parental. We humans may have a skewed perception of the prevalence of parental care in other species, because we belong to one of the most parental groups of animals on the planet: mammals. (Birds are our main rivals for that title.)

In the minority of species where we do find parental care, females care for the young in some species, males in others, and both sexes in others still. Of these options, the last one – biparental care – is the least common. Birds are the oddballs here; around 90% of birds are biparental. In most groups, however, uniparental care is the rule. Female-only care is more common than male-only care in insects, reptiles, and mammals; male-only care is more common in teleost fish; and the two options are about equally common in amphibians.[13]

But although female-only care isn't the overwhelming trend among parental animals, it is the general trend – and in our group, the mammals, it really is the overwhelming trend.[14] Because females in all mammalian species lactate, female care is found in all mammals, and thus male-only care is found in none. Biparental care is found in a smattering of mammals, but literally only a smattering.[15] If you pick a mammal at random, odds are you'll have a species where the females handle all of the childcare.

The centrality of maternal care among mammals has left a deep imprint on female mammalian psychology. Female cats respond more swiftly than toms to the cries of distressed kittens, even before they've had kittens of their own.[16] Rat mothers choose their newborn pups over cocaine.[17] And young female monkeys occasionally steal a baby from another troop, or even another species, and adopt it as their own, sometimes spontaneously lactating to feed the tiny hostage.[18] Scientists have yet to spot even a single male monkey embark on a kidnapping spree of this kind.

Closer to our own neck of the phylogenetic woods, girl chimps often treat sticks or logs as surrogate babies: They carry them around, cradle them, and put them to bed in their nests at night. In effect, girl chimps play with dolls. Boy chimps sometimes do too, but less often, and they're more likely to use sticks or logs as weapons.[19] As with humans, chimpanzee sex differences in play-parenting foreshadow adult sex differences in real parenting: Females do much more of it.[20] To be fair, adult male chimps do occasionally adopt orphaned juveniles; we shouldn't unfairly stereotype our furry male cousins.[21] Still, few male chimps are destined to win a father-of-the-year award. The most that most male chimps do for infants and juveniles is refrain from murdering them.

To be clear, I'm not suggesting that the specific skills needed to care for babies are directly innate. They couldn't be; they're much too complex to be inscribed in every detail in the genome. Female mammals have to learn them. However, they're naturally much *keener* to learn them than male mammals. They have an 'instinct to acquire an art', to borrow a phrase from Darwin.[22] Many juvenile female primates, for example, appear to have an inbuilt interest in babies. Juvenile male primates? Not so much. If anything, they have an inbuilt *lack* of interest. Humans are not exempt from this trend. Across cultures, young girls show more interest than young boys in infants, even in the absence of parental encouragement.[23] Female primates' heightened interest in babies presumably motivates them to help care for them, thereby facilitating the development of their parenting skills.[24]

Long story short, sex differences in parenting are found in many non-human animals, including the vast majority of mammals. When we find these differences in other species – species without dolls, fairy stories, or malleable cultural sex roles – we immediately chalk them up to natural selection. When we then find the same differences in our own species, the obvious inference is that they have an evolutionary origin for us too. Sure, it's possible in principle that humans stand apart from all other animals, such that we have the same sex differences for an entirely different reason: culture. However, the fact that this is possible in principle is a bad reason for thinking it's true. The default assumption, in lieu of strong evidence to the contrary, should be that we're continuous with the rest of the living world, and thus that the differences we see in our species have the same origin as those in every other: natural selection.

Evolving Sex

Why, though, did natural selection create the sex difference in parental investment in the first place? For most of the sex differences we've looked at so far – differences in casual sex, aggression, and risk-taking, for instance – the explanation is that the ceiling number of offspring is higher for men than for women. That's *not* the explanation for the sex difference in parental investment. In fact, it's the other way around: The sex difference in parental investment is the primary reason that the ceiling number of offspring is higher for men. The implication is that, in searching for the evolutionary explanation for women's greater parental investment, we're simultaneously searching for the ultimate cause of all the other sex differences. And to crack that case, we're going to need to wind back the clock to the dawn of sex itself, more than a billion years ago.

Doing so, however, takes us into deep waters – literally, as sex first evolved in the oceans. It all began with sexual reproduction. We take it for granted that most animals reproduce sexually, but it's actually something of a mystery. Plenty of organisms have opted for asexual reproduction, and at first glance, this would seem a better bet. For one thing, it means you get to put all your genes into each offspring you produce, rather than only half. For another, reproducing sexually risks breaking up favourable gene combinations: the equivalent of being dealt a royal flush in poker only to have the dealer say, 'Sorry folks, we're going to have to deal again.' Sexual reproduction also entails numerous costs, such as finding and wooing a mate, exposing oneself to sexually transmitted diseases, and – for modern humans – everything from unrequited love to breath fresheners to terrible amateur love poetry.

Why, then, don't we split in half like amoebas? More plausibly, given that we're multicellular organisms, why don't we put all our genes into each of our eggs, thus dispensing with males and doubling the number of genes we each transmit to the next generation? Why, in other words, did life get kinky and start reproducing sexually?

Biologists have come up with many plausible answers to this question, but two stand head and shoulders above the rest. The first is that sexual reproduction creates variability in one's offspring. It's bet-hedging: By diversifying your portfolio of offspring, you increase the chances that at least some of them will be well adapted to the unknown world that awaits.[25]

The second explanation is that, for large organisms like ourselves, sex is about keeping one step ahead of the local parasites. Because parasites are so much smaller than their hosts, they mature more rapidly and start reproducing at an earlier age. This means they can squeeze many generations of evolutionary change into a single host generation. To parasites, long-lived animals like humans are evolving in ultra-slow motion. If we gave up sexual reproduction, we'd pass on all our genes to each offspring (yay), but we'd also pass on parasites pre-adapted to that precise combination of genes and the anti-parasite defences they help create (boo). Sexual reproduction levels the playing field by shuffling the genetic deck and producing offspring that our parasites *aren't* especially well adapted to. Thus, one of the main reasons that sex evolved is to thwart parasites.[26] (Try not to think about that next time you have sex.)

When sexual reproduction first evolved, there was only one type of gamete, and thus there were no sexes. This situation is known as *isogamy*. But isogamy is evolutionarily unstable, and almost always gives way to *anisogamy*: that is, to two types of gametes, and therefore two sexes.[27] To see why, we need to ask: How could an individual organism get ahead in an isogamous population? One option would be to make larger gametes, and to load them up with nutrients. Larger gametes survive better, and the built-in picnic would be like a dowry for one's offspring, nourishing them in their earliest days. Of course, there's a price to be paid for your generosity: Because you don't have an infinite energy budget, making larger gametes means you won't be able to make as many. In some lineages, however, the benefits of this strategy must have started outweighing the costs, and gametes evolved to be larger.

But as soon as larger gametes appeared on the scene, they created a new niche for individuals that produced *smaller* gametes: gametes that specialized in seeking out the larger gametes and riding on their coat-tails. Why pack your own picnic when you can join forces with another gamete that's already packed theirs? Sure, smaller gametes have a shorter life expectancy. But they're also cheaper to produce, which means you can produce more of them. And because they're not weighed down with nutrients for the young, they're more mobile and can focus on seeking out the larger gametes. That's why most sperm have tails, like little animals within the animal.

The real losers in this evolutionary game are organisms that produce intermediate-sized gametes. Taking this approach deprives you of the advantages associated with packing your gametes with a picnic. And although your gametes can always hook up with one of the picnic-packers, you produce fewer of them than individuals specializing in the stripped-back seekers, and thus end up with fewer offspring. Your gametes will be evolutionary losers, and you'll soon go the way of the dodo. The ultimate result is that gametes don't lie on a spectrum between large and small. Selection carves out the middle of the distribution, leaving only the big guys and the little guys: eggs and sperm, respectively.[28]

We're now zeroing in on the ultimate origins of sex differences in parental investment, and thus of all the other standard-issue sex differences. When distinct sexes first evolved, eggs and sperm were the totality of parents' investment in their young. Because eggs were larger, females, by definition, were the higher-investing sex. But little stands still in evolution, and in some lineages, more elaborate forms of parental investment soon evolved. Importantly, they more often evolved in females than males, for the simple reason that females had already started down the high-investment path, and males down the low-investment path.[29] Sticking to these pathways was better for both sexes for the same reason that, if you've started training as a lion tamer, you'll be raking in the cash sooner if you continue mastering that skill than if you go back to the drawing board and start retraining as a tightrope walker. Because natural selection doesn't have foresight, it goes with whatever works best in the short term. Most of the time, that means parental investment for females and seeking out mates for males.

One interesting consequence of this is that, in their physiology and behaviour, organisms often mirror the seeker and provider strategies of their gametes. Individuals that produce small, mobile gametes are themselves often small and mobile: They roam far and wide looking for the large-gamete producers and their stash of large gametes – think tiny male spiders scrambling around in search of the giant females lurking in their webs. Meanwhile, individuals that produce large, sustenance-filled gametes often provide sustenance and care for their young – think female mammals gestating their offspring in their wombs then nursing them after birth. In these ways, fundamental differences between sperm and eggs are often mirrored in the organism's anatomy and behaviour. It all traces back to anisogamy.

That said, it's important to remember that, when it comes to sex differences in overall parental investment, anisogamy is a nudge, not a shove. It biases the coin flip to some degree, but it doesn't rig the outcome. Thus, in many species, males have evolved to provide significant post-gametic investment in their young. In some, this has greatly reduced the size of the sex difference in parental investment; in others, it's wiped out the difference altogether; and in others still, males have become the higher-investing sex. As we'll see in the next section, this is crucial information for understanding *Homo sapiens*.

Father Time

In the acknowledgements section of his book *The Evolution of Parental Care*, the Cambridge zoologist Timothy Clutton-Brock noted ironically that his greatest debt was to his wife, who 'looked after our children while I wrote about parental care'.[30] The tribute calls to mind the traditional sexual division of labour, where men work outside the home and women take care of the kids. As we've seen, women do tend to be more involved in childcare, consistent with what we find in other mammals. But as we've also seen, humans are an outlier among the mammals in our levels of paternal participation. Just for starters, Clutton-Brock knew who his children were, which is more than can be said for males in most mammalian species. And although I don't know Clutton-Brock personally, I'd be willing to wager that his parental contribution went well beyond mere knowing.

My favourite example, however, of the human paternal proclivity is none other than Charles Darwin. By all accounts, Darwin was nothing like the typical (or stereotypical) Victorian father. Far from being a cold and remote patriarch, he was a devoted and loving dad. The Darwin children loved to clamber on him, as juvenile primates often do with willing adults, and they nicknamed him 'the bear'. He, in turn, called them 'the blesseds'. One of his daughters, Henrietta, later wrote that 'To all of us he was the most delightful play-fellow, and the most perfect sympathizer. Indeed, it is impossible adequately to describe how delightful a relation his was to his family, whether as children or in their later life.'[31] Darwin even let his young son Francis draw on the original manuscript of *The Origin of Species* (after the book was published, to be clear).

But although Darwin was a particularly doting dad, dads in all cultures are considerably more doting than the average male chimp or walrus. Men everywhere help provision and provide for their young. Often, in fact, they provide more for their young than anyone other than the mother.[32] Even more bizarre, men everywhere have been known to voluntarily hold their children, feed their children, and play with their children for fun.

As with aggression, men's parental contribution isn't a fixed quantity or impervious to outside influences. Instead, it's upregulated or downregulated in response to current circumstances.[33] I mentioned in Chapter 7 that when competing for status or mates, men's testosterone levels rise, potentiating aggression and other status-related behaviour. The flipside of this is that, when men form pair bonds and help care for children, their testosterone levels fall, fitting them to this less testosterone-charged phase of life.[34]

This built-in flexibility helps explain certain facts that initially seem incompatible with the notion of an evolved paternal psychology. These include, most notably, cross-cultural variation in the extent of men's parental involvement. The best example I know concerns two neighbouring tribes in East Africa: the Hadza and the Datoga. Among the Hadza, men commonly help care for the young: more so than men in most traditional societies. Among the Datoga, on the other hand, parenting is deemed women's work, and men make every effort to avoid it.[35] How can we say that men's parental inclinations are built into human nature when even neighbouring tribes differ so radically – and when in some groups, men are barely involved in the parenting process?

The key, I think, is that Datoga men deliberately isolate themselves from young children, sleeping separately from them and their mothers, and keeping contact to a bare minimum. If they didn't do this, their latent paternal psychology would presumably be activated, and they'd be just as paternal as men in any other group. Why else would the strict separation be necessary? So, while the Datoga example rules out the idea that men are paternal regardless of context, it's perfectly compatible with the idea that men everywhere have the *capacity* to bond with and invest in their young. Even if a culture is set up in such a way that this potentiality is rarely exercised, it's still there, lying dormant in human nature.

The Evolution of Dad

Our paternal potential sets us apart from our fellow mammals. In more than 90% of mammalian species, males invest next to nothing in their offspring. In our species, in contrast, males usually invest a lot. Why are we such mammalian weirdos?

Ultimately, it traces back to the trait that makes us the only animal on the planet capable of even posing such questions: our big brains and hypertrophied intelligence. We saw in Chapter 4 that, as a result of these oversized organs, our offspring are entirely helpless at birth and highly dependent for several decades afterward. This greatly increased the costs of making new human beings – which then ratcheted up the potential evolutionary payoff of male parental care.

It did this in four main ways.[36] The first – and the one that most people think of first – is that paternal care boosted offspring's chances of survival. Each child a man sires shares half his genes, so any genes nudging dad to help keep his kids alive could potentially be selected. Of course, in most mammals, this hasn't happened, presumably because the fitness boost from helping keep the kids alive is usually smaller for males than the boost from seeking additional mates. However, because human offspring require so much more investment than the young of other species – much more than the mother alone could provide – ancestral men who chipped in with the childcare may often have had more surviving offspring than those who pursued the bachelor lifestyle exclusively.

A second reason that paternal care may have been adaptive for our male ancestors is that it led to better outcomes for offspring, over and above mere survival. With two parental providers on tap, offspring may typically have been healthier, grown larger, and acquired more skills than they would have if they only had one. Furthermore, if dad had high status in the group, his kids might have acquired some of that status by association. All of this would have increased the kids' chances of attracting a good mate and producing lots of healthy offspring: their father's grandchildren.

A third reason that paternal care could have boosted the father's fitness – one that's less obvious but arguably more important than the first two – is that it eased the mother's workload, allowing her to have another child sooner. In technical jargon, paternal investment could have shortened the mother's *interbirth interval*. As long as there was a good chance that the investing man would end up siring her next child, this would have boosted his fitness as well as hers. That's partly because you never know what the future holds, and thus selection often favours earlier reproduction over later. And it's partly because, if the relationship persisted, then the couple might have squeezed in more pregnancies than they otherwise would have, thus converting the father's parental input into more of his offspring.

A fourth and final explanation for men's fatherly streak is that it's a product of female mate choice. Following the logic of the peacock's tail, if females preferentially mate with parental males, then males will evolve to be more parental. Not only that, but male parental care will become, in effect, a form of courtship.[37] If this sounds like an unlikely scenario, bear in mind that it has analogues in other species. In various primates, for instance, males attract new females by protecting them and their young.[38] Parental care in these species is a monkey equivalent of the peacock's tail. Is this true of the human monkey? It might be. Women find men who are good with kids more attractive than those who aren't.[39] In principle, this could be a learned preference. However, given the high cost of raising offspring in our species, and thus the large benefit to women of securing a paternal male, it seems entirely plausible that the preference has an evolutionary origin. And if it does, then from the moment it first evolved, women were selectively breeding men to be more paternally inclined.

Some argue that paternal care in our species evolved *purely* as a peacock's tail, rather than as a way to boost the survival and reproductive success of one's offspring – in other words, that it's 100% mating effort and 0% parental effort. I think they're wrong for two reasons. The first is a well-established phenomenon known as the *Cinderella effect*. This refers to the fact that people are more likely to neglect, abuse, or kill stepchildren than they are genetic children.[40] This unfortunate tendency was first discovered by evolutionary psychologists Martin Daly and Margo Wilson, who interpreted it as indirect evidence that people are generally closer to and more willing to invest in their biological offspring. A strong case has been made that this is an evolved propensity in humans, based on its cross-cultural universality and comparability to tendencies found in other species, from mammals to social insects to plants, bacteria, and even viruses.[41] The Cinderella effect raises an important question: If paternal care were *purely* about winning a mate, why would human males have evolved to invest preferentially in their own offspring? The answer is that they wouldn't. Thus, the Cinderella effect pushes us toward the view that male parental care is not purely about winning a mate.

A second finding pushing us in that direction is that men tend to invest more in offspring when paternity confidence is high: when they have good reason to think their partner is faithful, for instance, or they live in a society where promiscuity is rare.[42] Again, this tendency is found across cultures and in other species, suggesting evolutionary underpinnings.[43] And again, the tendency only makes sense if men's parental inclinations evolved at least in part to facilitate investment in their own offspring, rather than just to attract a mate.

Why Do Men Invest Less?

Regardless of the exact details, we can surmise that the costliness of our offspring led to the evolution of extensive male parental care, thus narrowing the parental-care gender gap. Why, though, didn't natural selection close that gap completely, as gender-role progressives might have preferred?

There are two main reasons. The first is what biologists call *mating opportunity cost*. *Opportunity cost* is a pivotal concept in economics; some consider it the most important concept economists have bequeathed to the world. The basic idea is that, unless you're capable of being in two places at once, devoting more time and energy to one activity inevitably means devoting less to another. To put it another way, no one can have it all. *Mating* opportunity cost takes this simple but powerful insight and applies it to mating vs parenting. Specifically, it refers to the fact that devoting more time and energy to parenting means devoting less to seeking mates. Evolutionarily speaking, this is a bigger deal for men than for women, for the usual reason: Men have a higher reproductive ceiling. As a result, men have evolved a stronger mate-seeking instinct than women, and a weaker parental instinct.

The second reason that selection didn't fully close the gender gap in parental care is *paternity uncertainty*. This stems from a profound asymmetry between the sexes in species with internal fertilization, namely that females are more likely than males to end up investing in their own offspring. To put it crudely, if a female invests in a child that came out of her own body, that child is definitely hers; if a *male* invests in a child that came out of his *partner's* body . . . well, it's *probably* his, but there are no guarantees. And if it's not his – if it's some other man's child – that means that his parental efforts are helping a rival male's genes to prosper, rather than helping his own. To the extent that this happens in a species, it reduces the average fitness payoff to males of providing parental care. In some pair-bonding birds, as many as one in three eggs are sired by a male other than the female's partner. This means that the average fitness boost to males of caring for the young is reduced by a third. In humans, the non-paternity rate is much lower, with the best estimates putting it at around 1%.[44] As such, paternity uncertainty may be a relatively modest contributor to the human parental gender gap. Still, in concert with mating opportunity cost, it may help explain why natural selection hasn't fully equalized men's and women's parental contributions.

Before moving to the final topic of the chapter, we should address a question that will have nervously occurred to many readers: What does the evolutionary explanation for the sex difference in parental care imply for gender equality? In an important sense, the answer is: Nothing! The fact that, on average, women evolved to invest more than men in offspring doesn't mean that, for any given couple, the woman should be the primary caregiver and the man the second-in-command. An evolutionary perspective explains the general trend, but it doesn't tell us what we should do. At the same time, however, if the evolutionary analysis is correct, then even in a gender utopia where women are never pressured to be the primary caregivers, more women than men will likely opt for that role. We'll return to this difficult issue in Chapter 10.

Sex Differences in Jealousy

> When we want to read of the deeds that are done for love, whither do we turn? To the murder column.
>
> George Bernard Shaw (attributed)

In many ways, love brings out the best in us. We've all heard stories about the great sacrifices people make to be with the person they love, and about individuals who risk their lives to save a loved one. Love can also bring out the best in us on a more modest, everyday scale. One example is the fact that when something good happens to someone we love, this tends to make us happy. We get a little glow, almost as if it happened to us.

It's a lovely tendency, but like most things in life, it has its limits. Even in the healthiest of relationships, a spouse's or lover's happiness is not necessarily our own. For example, it's rarely the case that upon hearing about a partner's infidelity, we say 'Oh, that's nice! I love my partner, and I'm sure they had fun – so this is great news!' Of course, people are nothing if not varied, and no doubt some people do react in this way. I think we can agree, though, that it's not the norm. Most people are profoundly upset if a romantic partner cheats on them.

As far as we can tell, relationship jealousy is found wherever we have just three ingredients: human beings, love, and extra-pair temptations. Anthropologists have yet to discover a culture where people are immune to the agonies of jealousy. Certainly, some have *claimed* to have found such cultures. Invariably, however, the claims fall apart as further digging reveals, for instance, that infidelity is one of the major causes of divorce, spousal assault, or spousal homicide.[45] All the standard examples of allegedly jealousy-free cultures have ultimately met this fate, including Margaret Mead's Samoa, the wife-sharing Inuit of the Arctic, and the partible-paternity societies of South America.[46]

It is true that some cultures frown on jealousy.[47] But you can't frown on something that doesn't exist. The frowning implies that jealousy is present in all the cultures in question. As a species, we're incurably jealous.

And it's not as if we haven't tried to find a cure. At various times over the centuries, people have attempted to establish free-love communes, where anyone can partner up with anyone else, and no one's supposed to get jealous. Almost without fail, though, these groups quickly disintegrate, because even when social norms tell people that they shouldn't get jealous, and even when people sincerely wish *not* to get jealous, most of the time they still do.

A similar fate often awaits individuals who experiment with polyamorous relationships – that is, relationships where everyone involved is free to have other partners, as long as everything's out in the open. This is vividly illustrated by the following rather heartbreaking post from a Reddit polyamory discussion group.

> My partner and I are pretty new to being poly, opened up a few months ago. We've been married for about 8 years and we knew there would be some growing pains.
>
> She went out for a date night with her new boyfriend and they had sex. She was super communicative, we talked about expectations and boundaries and she kept me in the loop. But despite all that I'm still emotionally devastated. Philosophically I have no issue with anything that happened, and I love and trust my partner. We're secure in our relationship and I don't have any fear of her leaving me or anything.
>
> I just can't get it out of my head. It's like a brainworm. I can't stop picturing her having sex with another man and it tears me apart inside. Every time it pops back into my head I get this massive wave of depression. It feels like remembering that a loved one is dead.
>
> I get this is not a reasonable response, but I don't know what [to] do to mitigate these feelings. Any advice?[48]

In response, various commentators from outside the group proposed that an alternative relationship arrangement might suit him better: one that rhymes with *schmonogamy*. To be fair, some people do seem to be naturally polyamorous, and others seem to be able to make it work. I suspect, though, that both groups will always be greatly outnumbered by people like our Reddit poster, for whom polyamory is the relationship equivalent of torture.

Why are we like this? Why do people everywhere get so upset if a boyfriend, girlfriend, husband, or wife gets involved with someone else? The evolutionary story is straightforward and persuasive. As mentioned, pair bonding tends to be adaptive in our species; those of our ancestors who fell in love and formed enduring relationships tended to have more surviving offspring than those who didn't. For that reason, we evolved to defend our pair bonds. Jealousy motivates us to do just that. It leads us to keep a wary eye on our partners and to prevent them from fraternizing with the enemy – that is, with same-sex rivals who might swoop in and poach them away. This tendency, known in the animal literature as *mate guarding*, increases the pair's chances of staying together and successfully co-rearing children. Thus, jealousy is ultimately about protecting the pair bond, which is ultimately about biparental care.

This is true for both sexes. When we zoom in on the details, however, we discover that men and women aren't in quite the same boat when it comes to a partner's infidelity. For men, the central issue is paternity. As David Buss likes to say, no woman in the history of the world has given birth and thought, 'Hang on, how do I know this is *my* baby and not some other woman's baby?' Men can't be so sure. As we saw earlier, a man who invests in his partner's offspring is probably investing in his own, but there's always a chance that he's not – that he's investing instead in the offspring of his partner's good-looking male co-worker who she insists is just a friend. Any male trait or tendency that makes this outcome less likely has a good chance of being selected.

For women, the situation is different. Whereas if a woman cheats, her partner could end up investing in someone else's child, if her *partner* cheats, that definitely won't happen to her. This doesn't mean, though, that his peccadillos cost her nothing. Being cuckolded isn't a possibility, but being left holding the baby *is*. And that outcome is more likely if her partner falls in love with another woman than if he 'just' sleeps with her.

This creates a selection pressure for any female trait or tendency that preferentially reduces the risk of that.

Based on this line of reasoning, evolutionary psychologists predicted that although both sexes will be prone to jealousy, they'll differ in the strength of their reactions to two aspects of a partner's infidelity: sexual infidelity and emotional infidelity. Sexual infidelity is just what it sounds like: having sex with somebody else. *Emotional* infidelity involves becoming emotionally close to another person, and potentially falling in love with them. The prediction from evolutionary psychology is that men will typically get more upset than women about sexual infidelity, whereas women will typically get more upset than men about emotional infidelity.[49]

This expectation makes good Darwinian sense. For men, a partner's sexual infidelity is the greater danger; although emotional infidelity could lead to sex or the end of the pair bond, sexual infidelity is already a direct threat to his paternity: no further steps required. For women, on the other hand, emotional infidelity is the greater danger; although sex *could* lead to love and abandonment, emotional closeness is more likely to do that than sex alone. The net result is that jealousy is calibrated somewhat differently in men than in women, and has somewhat different functions.

To be clear, most women aren't exactly over the moon about a mate's sexual infidelity, and most men don't dance for joy if a mate gets emotionally close to another guy. On the contrary, most members of both sexes are hugely upset about both scenarios.[50] However, sexual infidelity often looms larger for men than for women, whereas emotional infidelity usually looms larger for women than men.

As with many sex differences, these ones have been documented in various ways. Most famously, Buss and colleagues asked participants which would upset them more: a romantic partner having sex with someone else or a romantic partner falling in love with someone else. The usual finding, appearing in almost every study ever conducted, is that more men than women say that sexual infidelity would upset them more, whereas more women than men say that *emotional* infidelity would.[51]

One common criticism of this research is that by relying on a forced-choice, either–or question, the findings exaggerate the size of the differences.[52] If all men were even just a little more upset about sexual infidelity, and all women just a little more upset about emotional infidelity, the forced-choice format would create the appearance of a Mars-and-Venus sex difference: 100% of men would choose sexual infidelity as the most upsetting option, whereas 100% of women would choose emotional infidelity, despite the tiny differences in actual distress. It's a fair gripe. However, sex differences in jealousy don't just appear when we use the forced-choice format. They appear as well – albeit in an attenuated form – when we ask people how upset they'd be about the two forms of infidelity separately, then give them continuous scales to register their responses.[53]

In any case, the sex differences aren't just found in questionnaire research; they're found in the real world too. In one clever study, the evolutionary psychologist Barry X. Kuhle analysed clips from a reality TV show where people discovered, live on camera, that their partners had been cheating on them. Women were more likely than men to ask their unfaithful partner 'Do you love her?'; men were more likely than women to ask 'Did you fuck him?'[54] Other research suggests that men struggle more than women to forgive a partner's sexual infidelity, and are more likely to break up with a partner who cheats, despite the fact that men cheat more.[55]

Consistent with an evolutionary explanation, sex differences in jealousy are found throughout the world. They're found in Western nations, including even sexually liberal ones like Norway.[56] They're found in non-Western nations, from India to Korea to Japan.[57] They're found in small-scale, non-state societies dotted around the globe.[58] And they're even found in groups like the Himba pastoralists of Namibia, who are officially very tolerant of extramarital affairs and highly disapproving of jealousy.[59]

In short, the differences are real, and the smart money says they're part of human nature, rather than an imposition of culture. It's hard to find a good word to say about jealousy, given how unpleasant it is and how much evil it's inspired over the ages. One thing we *can* say, though – and I don't know if this makes it better or worse – is that, for all its faults, jealousy is intimately bound up with one of the most beautiful aspects of human nature: our tendency to fall in love with each other and to work together to help care for our young.

9

Sex at the Frontier

New Directions in the Evolutionary Psychology of Sex Differences

Human, All Too Human

We're making good progress. We've now explored the central sex differences in our species: the ones predicted by evolutionary principles and comparable to those found in other animals. In this chapter, we'll take a trip to the edge of science, and look at some new directions in the evolutionary psychology of sex differences. Specifically, we'll look at a collection of differences that, though well-established empirically, are less well understood in Darwinian terms. These include sex differences in personality, interests, and career preferences; sex differences in cognitive abilities; sex differences in children's toy preferences; and sex differences in physical and mental health.

Sex Differences in Personality

Personality is a popular concept in psychology and everyday life. It's defined as a person's characteristic patterns of thinking, feeling, and behaving: how resilient they are, how open-minded, how energetic, reliable, and kind. The most popular model of personality in psychology is the Big Five model. Proponents of this approach argue that most variation in people's personalities can be boiled down to just five essential traits.

1. **Neuroticism.** Proneness to depression, anxiety, and other negative emotions; emotional volatility.
2. **Extraversion.** Cheerfulness; sociability; assertiveness.
3. **Openness.** Intellectual curiosity; creativity; openness to experience.
4. **Agreeableness.** Friendliness; compassion; politeness.
5. **Conscientiousness.** Orderliness; self-discipline; industriousness.

Personality is usually measured with self-report questionnaires, which ask people how much they agree with statements such as 'I get stressed out easily', 'I am the life of the party', and 'I get chores done right away.' At first glance, this seems like a dubious way to measure personality – the equivalent of measuring IQ by asking people 'What's your IQ?' But a mountain of research shows that well-constructed personality tests do a good job of measuring personality and predicting important life outcomes.[1]

A consistent finding in personality psychology is that the sexes differ, on average, in all or most of the Big Five traits.[2] Two differences, in particular, stand out. The first is that women score higher than men on the trait of neuroticism. *Neuroticism* is an unfortunate term that refers to people's proneness to negative emotions such as depression and anxiety. *Sensitivity* might be a better, less pejorative label. The good news for anyone struggling with depression and anxiety in early adulthood is that neuroticism peaks at that time, after which both sexes become less neurotic through the remaining adult years. At every age, though, the average woman is more neurotic. As with aggression and risk-taking, the neuroticism sex difference is larger in early adulthood than at any other time of life, but in this case, with women scoring higher. And as with many sex differences, the sex difference in neuroticism is modest near the mean, but more substantial at the extremes of the distribution. The fact that many more women than men are found among the highly neurotic minority, and many more men than women among the most stoical, may contribute to certain exaggerated stereotypes of the sexes.

The second standout personality sex difference is that women score higher than men on the trait of agreeableness. This isn't to say that most women are super-friendly, or that most men are Oscar the Grouch! Most members of both sexes are neither; they fall somewhere in between. However, among the minority who populate the extremes, more women than men are highly agreeable, whereas more men than women are highly disagreeable. Again, this probably contributes to certain well-known stereotypes of the sexes.

Sex differences in the other Big Five traits are smaller and less reliably found. Girls and women tend to be somewhat more conscientious than boys and men – part of the reason they do better at school.[3] Women often score slightly higher on extraversion than men, partly because more men than women are extreme introverts and drag down the male average.[4] And women often score slightly higher than men on openness.

One reason that personality sex differences are generally small is that, for several Big Five traits, the direction of the difference depends on the specific sub-trait – or *facet* – under investigation.[5] For example, when it comes to extraversion, women score higher on the facets of cheerfulness and sociability, whereas men score higher on the facets of excitement seeking and assertiveness. Likewise, when it comes to openness, men score higher on the facet of openness to ideas, whereas women score higher on the facets of openness to emotions and openness to aesthetics. These fine-grained sex differences cancel each other out at the trait level, obscuring some genuine female–male differences in personality.

As with most well-established sex differences, we've got good reason to think that there's an innate contribution to sex differences in personality. First, they're found in all or most nations.[6] Second, they follow a similar developmental trajectory across nations, with the differences solidifying in adolescence, and gender-typical personality profiles appearing in girls before they appear in boys.[7] Third, contrary to a social-role explanation, sex differences in personality are larger, rather than smaller, in more gender-equal nations: one of the largest and most consistent examples of the gender-equality paradox.[8] Finally, we have at least some evidence for comparable sex differences in other species. Among chimps, for instance, males tend to be more aggressive and impulsive, while females are often more neurotic and agreeable.[9]

Plausibly, then, there's an innate contribution to sex differences in personality. If that's right, though, why? I don't have a confident answer to that question, but I do have some unconfident educated guesses. I suspect that the two largest sex differences – those in neuroticism and agreeableness – are offshoots of deeper differences covered in earlier chapters. The sex difference in neuroticism, for example, may help facilitate lower risk-taking among females.[10] Several components of neuroticism – most notably, anxiety – motivate avoidance, and avoidance has the same function as the turtle's shell: self-protection. Greater female agreeableness, meanwhile, may be the flipside of greater male aggression and competitiveness. As for sex differences in conscientiousness, openness to ideas, and the rest, who knows? Perhaps there's an adaptive rationale waiting in the wings; perhaps the differences are just random byproducts of other stuff. To be continued . . .

Sex Differences in Interests and Career Preferences

Another area where the sexes differ is in career-related interests. The main differences here – differences considerably larger than even the largest personality sex differences – are, first, that on average, men are more interested than women in things and things-related jobs (such as computer programming and engineering), and second, that women are more interested than men in people and people-related jobs (such as education and healthcare).[11]

Anyone who responds to this by saying 'But I'm a man, and I'm interested in people' or 'But I'm a woman, and I'm interested in things' has misunderstood the claim. At the same time, though, anyone who responds by saying 'Sounds about right; I'm a man, and I'm more interested in things' or 'Sounds about right; I'm a woman, and I'm more interested in people' has misunderstood the claim as well. You know the drill by now: We're talking about statistical sex differences, not Mars-and-Venus ones. Most people are somewhat interested in both areas; it's only among the minorities at the extremes that we find extreme sex differences.

Strange though it might sound – and it does sound strange to many – we've got good evidence that these differences aren't purely products of culture. First, they're as tenacious as a weed. The people-vs-things sex differences, for instance, were first documented in 1911, and have remained largely static ever since, despite more than half a century of efforts to get more women into male-dominated jobs.[12] Second, the differences have been tied to prenatal hormonal exposure. People with congenital adrenal hyperplasia or CAH – who, as I'm sure you remember by now, are exposed to high levels of testosterone in the womb – have more male-typical occupational interests as children, and more often end up in male-typical occupations as adults.[13] Third, the differences have been found in every nation where psychologists have looked for them. One survey of more than 200,000 people found the differences in 53 out of 53 nations; another survey of nearly half a million people found them in 80 out of 80.[14] This level of cross-cultural unanimity is virtually unheard of in the social sciences. The *size* of the sex differences varies across nations and times, suggesting, as always, that culture makes a crucial contribution. However, the innate push is apparently strong enough that the differences persist even in the face of extensive variation in relevant cultural factors, such as national wealth, education, and levels of gender equality. In fact, not only do they persist, but the differences are larger, rather than smaller, in wealthier, more gender-equal nations, once again clashing with the predictions of a social-role explanation.[15]

Admittedly, the evidence for an innate contribution to sex differences in interests isn't as strong as that for sex differences in sexual inclinations, aggression, or risk-taking: differences that have a stronger grounding in theories from evolutionary biology and clear parallels in other species. Still, the evidence is strong enough that, in my view, it's now less reasonable to hold the Nurture-Only position on interest-related sex differences than to hold one of the Nature-plus-Nurture alternatives.[16] More than that, given the stubborn persistence of the differences across time and cultures, it's more reasonable to hold a *Mainly*-Nature view than a Mainly-Nurture one.

Why might natural selection have implanted these differences in our heads? Again, this question throws us into the realm of speculation, but speculation is fine as long as we remember that that's what it is. A common suggestion is that men's heightened interest in things traces back to ancestral tool use for hunting and warfare, whereas women's heightened interest in people facilitates care of young children and a stronger focus on maintaining social bonds.[17] These ideas don't seem unreasonable to me, but are they actually true? While evolutionary explanations for more fundamental sex differences often have an immediate ring of truth to them, these ones don't; they have an immediate ring of 'Well, I suppose that could be true, but . . .' I'm going to wait till we have more evidence before reaching any definite conclusions.

Sex Differences in Cognitive Abilities

The topic of sex differences is controversial at the best of times. When we start exploring sex differences in cognitive abilities, we turn the controversy dial up to 11. For that reason, let me start by addressing some common concerns.[18]

First, there's no average sex difference in the cognitive ability that matters most to most people: general cognitive ability, also known as general intelligence, also known as IQ.[19] It is true that many IQ tests have been deliberately constructed to produce identical average scores for the sexes. But not all of them have, and even those that haven't reveal no consistent sex difference in intelligence in representative samples.[20]

Second, although the sexes differ in some *specific* cognitive abilities, the differences favour women just as often as they favour men. Thus, if we're going to say that the science is sexist against women, we're also going to have to say that it's sexist against men. Neither claim would make sense, though; the facts are just the facts.

Third, cognitive sex differences tend to be small – much smaller than sex differences in sexual inclinations or career-related interests. When it comes to cognitive abilities, the sexes are much more alike than different.[21]

Enough beating around the bush. What are the relevant cognitive sex differences? Here are my nominations for the Top Six.

1. **Academic Achievement**. Despite not differing in overall intelligence, girls and women do better at school and university than boys and men. Unless prevented from getting an education, they get better grades in almost every subject.[22]
2. **Verbal Abilities**. Females do better than males on most verbal tasks, at least in childhood.[23] As a result, females outnumber males among the most verbally gifted.
3. **Spatial Abilities**. Boys and men do better on most visuospatial tasks.[24] The differences are largest for mental rotation: that is, rotating an object in one's mind's eye. Even there, though, there's plenty of overlap.
4. **Mathematical Abilities**. True to the stereotypes, most females aren't particularly good at maths – but nor are most males. And *contrary* to the stereotypes, average sex differences in maths performance don't always put males ahead. In some countries, boys do slightly better; in others, girls do; and in others still, the differences have largely evaporated.[25] Only two maths-related sex differences are worth writing home about. One is that, just as females outnumber males among the most verbally gifted, males outnumber females among the highest performers in maths.[26] The other is that males are a little more *variable* in their mathematical capabilities, with more males than females occupying not only the top of the range but also the very bottom.[27]

5. **Cognitive Tilt.** Cognitive tilt occurs when a person is notably better at one type of cognitive task than another. The concept is most commonly applied to mathematical vs verbal abilities. The key sex difference here is that more men than women exhibit maths tilt (their maths abilities tower over their verbal abilities), whereas more women than men exhibit verbal tilt (the reverse).[28] In addition, among individuals with exceptional mathematical abilities, the women are more likely than the men to have a balanced intellectual portfolio: in other words, to have exceptional language abilities as well.[29]
6. **Systemizing vs Empathizing.** Systemizing involves understanding and reasoning about systems, including natural systems like atoms and galaxies, abstract systems like logic and maths, and human-made systems like machines and computer programs. Empathizing involves understanding people's thoughts, desires, and feelings, and using this knowledge to predict people's behaviour and respond appropriately. Both sexes are fairly good at both cognitive tasks: much better than any other animal. On average, though, men are somewhat better at systemizing, while women are somewhat better at empathizing.[30] Notice the parallel with interest in things vs people.

Where do sex differences like these ones come from? The standard sociocultural answer is that they're ultimately rooted in stereotypes of the sexes: stereotypes such as that boys are better than girls at maths and science, that girls are better with words and people, and that boys and men are intellectually superior overall. These stereotypes are transmitted like infections via jokes, norms, stories, media, and ads. And in various ways, they function as self-fulfilling prophecies, bringing about their own reality.

First, stereotypes affect how parents treat their children. Expecting that their daughters will be more verbal than their sons, for instance, parents talk to their daughters more – in the process, fast-tracking their language abilities, and creating the very difference they'd expected. At the same time, expecting that their sons will be more interested in science and systemizing, they give them more construction toys, train sets, and science books – again, bringing their expectations to life. Second, stereotypes may affect how teachers treat their students. If teachers expect boys to do better in some subjects and girls in others, they may inadvertently encourage them more in the subjects where they think they'll excel. In this way, teachers turn their expectations into reality: a phenomenon known as the *Pygmalion effect*.[31] Third, stereotypes may affect people's expectations of themselves. For example, the stereotype that maths and science are for boys may persuade some girls that these areas are unlikely to be their fortes, and that they should therefore put their efforts elsewhere.[32] And even if they believe they *could* excel in these areas, unflattering stereotypes of female mathematicians and scientists may still turn girls away. The net effect of all this is that girls and women do less well in advanced maths and science, not because of inherent psychological sex differences, but because they've spent less time honing those skills.

And as if all that weren't enough, stereotypes of the sexes may hamper intellectual performance through a phenomenon known as *stereotype threat*. According to proponents of this idea, stereotype threat happens when people's anxiety about confirming a negative stereotype of the abilities of a group they belong to causes them to perform worse in tests of those abilities, thus ironically confirming the stereotype. As psychologists Gregory Walton and Steven Spencer put it, 'Like the time of a track star running into a stiff headwind, such performances underestimate the true ability of stereotyped students.'[33] It's easy to see how this could work. If you received terrible news right before an exam, you'd probably struggle to concentrate and therefore do badly. Stereotype threat is a low-key version of this phenomenon, except that the terrible news isn't something new or unexpected, but rather the ever-present possibility that you might confirm people's negative stereotypes of your group. When it comes to sex differences, the classic example of stereotype threat is that girls' and women's anxiety about confirming the stereotype that 'girls can't do maths' impairs their maths performance. Presumably, stereotype threat could also impair boys' and men's performance in stereotypically female domains, but people seem less concerned about that.[34]

So, those are some of the most common sociocultural explanations for sex differences in cognitive abilities. The idea that these differences are *entirely* due to sociocultural factors is widely held among psychologists and educators – at least until they look at the evidence. Diane Halpern describes her own journey in this regard in the preface to the first edition of her book *Sex Differences in Cognitive Abilities*.

> [W]hen I started writing this book . . . it seemed clear to me that any between-sex differences in thinking abilities were due to socialization practices, artifacts and mistakes in the research, and bias and prejudice. After reviewing a pile of journal articles that stood several feet high and numerous books and book chapters that dwarfed the stack of journal articles, I changed my mind . . . There are real, and in some cases sizable, sex differences with respect to some cognitive abilities. Socialization practices are undoubtedly important, but there is also good evidence that biological sex differences play a role in establishing and maintaining cognitive sex differences, a conclusion that I wasn't prepared to make when I began reviewing the relevant literature.[35]

What's so wrong with the Nurture-Only version of the story? Well, for a start, many of its central claims fail to withstand scrutiny. Consider, for instance, the idea that people stereotype boys as intellectually superior. This was certainly true in the past, but today is arguable at best. One study found that by four years of age, girls tend to think that boys are academically inferior to them, and that by age seven, boys have caught up and come to the same view.[36] That's right: Boys are behind even in noticing they're behind. Meanwhile, another study found that, contrary to popular belief, teachers often see their female students as academically superior, not just in reading but also in maths – and they see things this way even when aptitude tests show the opposite pattern for their classes.[37] And although boys and men might once have been depicted as more intelligent in stories, media, and ads, now it's usually girls and women: Lisa is smarter than Bart; Marge is smarter than Homer; Hermione is smarter than Ron.

I'm not denying that there are negative stereotypes of girls' and women's abilities in maths and science. But there are lots of stereotypes going in lots of directions, and it's far from clear how common the girls-can't-do-maths-or-science stereotype is these days. Indeed, we've got good reason to think that it's *not* common. One of the best-established findings in social psychology is that stereotypes tend to match the facts – and the fact is that in many countries, girls are doing just as well or even better than boys in both these subjects.[38] It is true that stereotypes of female mathematicians and scientists are sometimes less than flattering. But stereotypes of *male* mathematicians and scientists are hardly flattering either. Culture doesn't tell boys that maths and science are cool; it tells them they're nerdy. All of this flies in the face of the standard sociocultural explanation.

And even when the facts go in the direction presupposed by the sociocultural explanation, we've still got our usual chicken-and-egg problem. Are girls more verbal because their parents talk to them more, or do their parents talk to them more because they're more verbal? Do boys prefer construction toys and train sets because that's what parents give them, or do parents give them that because that's what they prefer? Do stereotypes about sex differences create those differences out of thin air, or do they just dutifully register the statistical associations in people's environments? Where we have good evidence on such matters, the causal arrow often points in the opposite direction to that assumed by the sociocultural approach. Case in point: Although teacher expectations predict boys' and girls' academic outcomes, the main reason for this is not that the expectations function as self-fulfilling prophecies, but rather that teachers aren't stupid, and their impressions of their students' abilities are generally fairly accurate.[39]

In a sense, this shouldn't be surprising. Is it reasonable to think that parents and teachers are unable to see the individual in front of them through the fog of their gender stereotypes? Surely not. Everyone knows that not all boys and girls are the same, so we're clearly capable of perceiving individual differences. Stereotypes only strongly bias our perceptions when we first encounter a person. As soon as we get to know them, we get to know *them*, and the cloud of stereotypes surrounding them largely dissipates.[40]

Another challenge to the sociocultural approach is that some of the mechanisms that supposedly turn the water of stereotypes into the wine of reality have been called into serious question. This is true, most notably, of stereotype threat as applied to women's maths performance. To start with, it's worth reminding ourselves that the sex difference in average maths performance has vanished in many nations, and thus that it's not clear what stereotype threat is even meant to explain. Furthermore, given that girls get better grades than boys in virtually every subject, if stereotype threat were a genuine phenomenon, it'd largely be an issue for boys.

But is it a genuine phenomenon in the first place? Quite possibly not. Most studies demonstrating stereotype threat have small samples. This increases the chances of both false positives and false negatives, with the false positives more often finding their way into print. Compounding the problem, most of the studies aren't preregistered, giving researchers ample scope to fish around for chance findings that could be interpreted within the stereotype-threat framework. What happens when researchers use *large* samples and preregister their studies? Usually, nothing: They find no evidence of stereotype threat.[41] Taking a different path to the same destination, several large meta-analyses have also cast doubt on the phenomenon.[42] One, for instance, found a near-zero effect of stereotype threat on girls' performance in maths, science, and spatial tasks.[43] Of course, near-zero isn't zero, and maybe the effect of stereotype threat is just much smaller than originally claimed. But maybe not. When the authors of the meta-analysis statistically controlled for publication bias, the near-zero effect fell to zero.

As well as these flaws in the sociocultural approach, several lines of evidence suggest a significant innate component. First, many of the differences appear early in life. Sex differences in spatial abilities, for example, may even be present by three months of age.[44] Second, like an unrepentant husband, the differences seem unwilling to change. More precisely, they're willing to change, but only up to a point. As mentioned, men outnumber women among the top performers in maths, while women outnumber men among the top performers on verbal tasks. Efforts to wipe out these differences often have some initial success, closing the gaps to some degree. Soon enough, however, progress grinds to a halt, even in the face of intensifying efforts to eradicate the differences.[45] I call this the *sticking-point phenomenon*, and it seems to be reasonably common.

Third, we have tentative evidence that prenatal hormones help shape at least some common cognitive sex differences. For example, one meta-analysis covering around a quarter of a million people found that gay men exhibit verbal and spatial skills typical of straight women, whereas lesbians exhibit spatial skills (though not verbal skills) typical of straight men.[46] Given that gay men and lesbians are usually exposed to sex-typical socialization and same-sex role models, this points to a role for sex-*atypical* prenatal hormonal exposure – which in turn suggests that *typical* prenatal hormonal exposure helps shape the usual sex differences.

Fourth, most of the differences are found in all or almost all nations.[47] And not only that, but once again, at least some of the differences are larger in more gender-equal nations: the opposite of what we'd expect based on a social-role account.[48]

Fifth and finally, some cognitive sex differences are also found in other animals. For example, males in various species – including mice, rats, and rhesus macaques – have stronger spatial abilities than females.[49] Moreover, experiments show that, in many other mammals, spatial abilities are amplified by testosterone.[50] This doesn't *prove* that the same is true for us – or for wombats or tigers or any other species that hasn't been directly tested. But it does make it the most plausible default position.

As with most of the sex differences discussed in this chapter, the nature–nurture issue is the easy part. The hard part is figuring out why the innate contribution might have evolved. As with earlier examples, there's plenty of conjecture, but I'm not yet persuaded we know. Men's greater spatial and systemizing abilities may have facilitated hunting, tool use, and warfare – or they may just be non-adaptive byproducts of men's higher testosterone levels.[51] Women's greater language abilities and social skills may have facilitated their stronger focus on maintaining social bonds – or they may have some other function, as yet undreamed of.

At this stage, we should resist drawing any hard-and-fast conclusions. One thing I'd like to emphasize, though, is that posing and testing adaptive explanations for cognitive sex differences is a perfectly reasonable endeavour. To some psychologists, the idea that men and women might have evolved somewhat different cognitive abilities sounds like recklessly speculative, straw-grabbing, just-so storytelling. In my view, this is mainly because most psychologists don't know enough about evolution or other animals. Plenty of other species exhibit cognitive sex differences that make good sense in light of differences in how the sexes evolved to meet the adaptive challenges of life. It's possible that we'll one day look at our own species and say the same thing of ourselves.

Toys 'R' Us and Them

In earlier chapters, we touched on sex differences in childhood play: in particular, the fact that boys engage in more rough-and-tumble play than girls, while girls engage in more play-parenting. Another set of play-related sex differences – one that's the focus of a lot of parental angst and hand-wringing – concerns children's toy preferences. Roughly speaking, boys tend to prefer toy vehicles, weapons, and building blocks, whereas girls tend to prefer dolls, homemaking toys, and fashion items. Curiously, sex differences in toy preferences are among the largest found in our species.[52]

Given that toys as we know them today are an evolutionary novelty, the Nurture-Only explanation seems especially compelling in this case. Indeed, to many, it just seems blindingly obvious that boys and girls are socialized to prefer different toys, and that this fully explains the gender disparities. From the moment they're born, children are force-fed sex-stereotypical toys by their parents, other family members, family friends, and – for those who celebrate Christmas – Santa Claus. Playing with 'gender-appropriate' toys wins approval and acceptance; playing with gender-*inappropriate* toys earns disapproval or mockery, especially from other children. Meanwhile, ads and sex-segregated toy aisles cement the message that some toys belong to one gender tribe, and others belong to the other. With all this going on, it's hardly surprising that boys and girls favour different toys.

The Nurture-Only explanation seems plausible enough at first glance. On closer inspection, however, it has more holes in it than a Swiss cheese. First, we've got our old nemesis, the chicken-and-egg problem. Does Santa Claus *create* children's toy preferences by giving them sex-typical toys, or does he give them sex-typical toys because that's what kids generally prefer? Is Santa sexist, in other words, or is he just sensitive to children's desires?

Second, many modern parents are highly tolerant of gender-atypical play, and some even positively welcome it. Despite that, the differences persist. Sometimes, in fact, they persist even in the face of parental *disapproval* of gender-*typical* play. For as long as I can remember, parents have waged war on their sons' love of toy guns and violent video games, and their daughters' love of dolls and pink – and yet they seem no closer to winning that war than ever. No doubt, even the most progressive parents sometimes accidentally convey discomfort with gender-atypical play, especially in boys. But how much effect does this realistically have? Kids are often quite happy to do things their parents *explicitly* disapprove of. How likely is it that they'll be put off things that their parents let slip they're slightly ambivalent about?

Third, the idea that toy ads have a large impact on kids' preferences is much less plausible than most people think. For one thing, the sex difference in toy preferences hasn't particularly grown over the last half century, despite increasingly gendered advertising.[53] For another, ads are nowhere near as persuasive as many people think. Contrary to popular belief – but as marketers and political campaigners know all too well – changing people's minds is extremely difficult.[54] If it weren't, advertisers could sell anything to anyone. They can't; most products fail. And even if toy makers and advertisers *could* conjure sex differences into existence on a whim, why would they? Toy makers would ideally want *both* sexes to covet their offerings, not just one or the other, as this would instantly double the size of their market. Rather than creating sex differences out of nothing, advertisers may simply have got better at catering to kids' pre-existing tastes.

But where did those pre-existing tastes come from? Yet again, several lines of evidence suggest an innate component. To begin with, the differences emerge surprisingly early: long before kids know which toys are stereotypically linked to each sex, and long before kids even understand whether they themselves are female or male.[55] Second, sex differences in toy preferences are found across nations, and are no larger in nations with stricter, more traditional gender roles.[56] And third, at least some of the differences are found in other primates. We saw in Chapter 8 that girl chimps often treat sticks as makeshift dolls, whereas boy chimps do only rarely.[57] On top of that, several studies have found that, given a selection of toys to play with, juvenile female monkeys prefer to play with dolls, whereas juvenile males prefer to play with toy vehicles.[58] (I have to say I find the former result more credible than the latter.)

The most persuasive evidence for an innate contribution, however, concerns the impact of prenatal hormones on kids' play and toy preferences. Exhibit A: Girls with CAH engage in more male-typical play than other girls; have a stronger preference for male-typical toys such as cars, trucks, and building blocks; and are less interested than their same-sex peers in fashion, jewellery, or makeup.[59] Recent evidence suggests that this pattern isn't confined to the West. One study, for instance, looked at play patterns in CAH girls from Iran, and found that they too engage in more male-typical play.[60] Is it that parents across cultures socialize their CAH daughters to be more masculine, perhaps because they're more masculine in appearance? Probably not. In fact, if anything, it's the opposite: Parents tend to give CAH girls more positive feedback when they play with stereotypically *female* toys than male ones. It doesn't matter, though; the girls just like what they like.[61] Prenatal hormones, it seems, can sometimes override postnatal socialization.

Further reinforcing the point, whereas girls exposed to *high* levels of prenatal androgens exhibit more male-typical play, boys exposed to *low* levels – boys with *isolated gonadotropin-releasing-hormone deficiency* (or *IGD*) – exhibit more *female*-typical play. Among other things, they more often play with girls than with other boys; they more often play with dolls than with trucks; and they more often identify with female than male characters in stories.[62]

I'm tempted to leave it there, but we shouldn't dodge the difficult question: *Why* might boys and girls be innately drawn to different toys? Girls' love of dolls is the easiest part to explain; presumably, it's a byproduct of girls' heightened interest in infants, a trait they share with juvenile females of other primate species.[63] Boys' love of toy vehicles is more mysterious; there weren't a lot of racing cars or diggers in hunter-gatherer times. One possibility, though, is that the preference is a byproduct of boys' stronger interest in things and gadgets, and stronger spatial and systemizing abilities. If that's right, then the preference is a behavioural fossil of men's ancestral roles as primary hunters, weapon users, and tool makers. Is this plausible? Yes. Is it true? No idea. Time will tell!

Sex in the Doctor's Office

Let's turn now to a more serious topic. We've seen throughout the book that, from our first breath till our last, females and males are often dealt very different cards in the game of life. Nowhere is this truer than in the domain of physical health, where the odds of developing various diseases tilt heavily to one sex or the other. Among the best-established differences are the following.

1. Men die younger than women in almost every nation on Earth, including in most nations where death during childbirth is still common.

2. Men are more prone than women to heart disease and other cardiovascular disorders, especially before old age.[64]
3. Men are more prone to most cancers, even when controlling for risk factors such as alcohol, diet, smoking, and exposure to carcinogens.[65]
4. Women are more prone than men to autoimmune disorders, including lupus, multiple sclerosis, and rheumatoid arthritis.[66]
5. Women are more prone to pain disorders such as migraines and fibromyalgia.
6. Women are more prone to Alzheimer's disease.

At the risk of stating the obvious, medical conditions are not adaptations. So, how can we make sense of these gaps?

The first thing to say is that sex differences in health are partly due to sex differences in behaviour. The key behavioural difference is that women tend to take better care of their health. Across nations, men smoke more than women, drink more than women, and eat more unhealthy food.[67] One research group wanted to study ten men in the North of England who ate five or more servings of fruit and vegetables a day. They couldn't find any, though, so had to lower their target to three servings.[68] Women are more likely than men to go to the doctor when there's nothing wrong with them; men are more likely than women *not* to go to the doctor when there *is* something wrong. The most extreme example I know of the latter – you might want to make sure you're sitting down for this – is the case of a man who ejaculated via his anus every time he had an orgasm for two years before seeking medical attention. There was clearly something very wrong with the plumbing, but he wasn't concerned enough to visit a doctor for two full orbits of the sun.[69] Another example – again, you might want to make sure you're sitting down – is the case of a man whose increasingly swollen scrotum ended up hanging below his knees after he neglected to get it checked for more than three decades.[70] The psychologist Nicola Graham-Kevan put it well: 'Men literally need to have a leg hanging off before contacting a doctor. Probably married men live longer because their wives push them into it.'[71]

People often assume that the impact of behaviour on health is a contribution of nurture rather than nature. But that's a mistake. Like almost everything, sex differences in health-related behaviour are shaped in part by nature – and to the extent that they are, this is an indirect innate contribution to health-related sex differences. Why might men be innately inclined to take worse care of their health? Several traits we've already covered plausibly play a role. These include, most obviously, men's propensity for taking risks. Men are more likely to accidentally poison themselves, fall to their deaths, drown, die in fires, or blow themselves up, and the main reason for this is that they're *less* likely to take sensible precautions. Additionally, seeking help involves tacitly admitting weakness. Historically – and presumably prehistorically – this was a worse move for men than for women. It ran the risk of making men less attractive to potential mates, and of getting them excluded from same-sex groups engaged in physically demanding tasks such as hunting and warfare. A Darwinian just-so story? Maybe . . . but maybe not. Men's tendency to hide their weaknesses has precedents in other animals. Among chimps, for instance, high-ranking males risk losing status, and open themselves up to attack, if they show any signs of weakness. So, they don't. They do their best to conceal them.[72]

Leaving aside the behavioural contribution, evolutionary theory offers two major tools for explaining sex differences in physical health. The first is the idea that the differences are byproducts of sexual selection. The best example here concerns the sex difference in longevity. As mentioned, men die younger than women in virtually every nation. At birth, the sex ratio is male-biased: that is, more male babies are born than female babies. By sexual maturity, the ratio is approximately equal, and from then on, women increasingly outnumber men. That's why most people in retirement homes are women, and why the oldest person in the world is almost always a woman as well. As one of the founders of evolutionary medicine, Randy Nesse, observed, if we could lower male mortality rates to those of females, we'd save more years of life than if we cured cancer.[73]

I'm often surprised at how many people seem convinced that the sex difference in longevity is due wholly to men's behaviour and social causes: Men live less healthily, take more risks, fight more wars, do more dangerous work, and so on. Factors such as these obviously contribute to the longevity gender gap. But there's no longer any reasonable doubt that the gap is primarily biological.

First, even in groups where men and women lead similarly sheltered lives – Mormons, priests, and nuns, for instance – men die younger.[74] Second, the sex difference in mortality is found even among a group of individuals who've had almost no socialization: infants. More than that, the difference is found in the womb, before kids have had any socialization at all, and before most parents even know the sex of their child. From the moment of conception till their final years on Earth, males are less likely than females to make it to their next birthday.

Third, we have overwhelming evidence that sex hormones play a role in shaping the longevity gender gap. Did you know that there's an environmental intervention that could eliminate the gap entirely? It's called castration. If you castrate male animals prior to puberty, they live about as long as females. This has been demonstrated in various species, including rats, cats, dogs, horses, cows, sheep . . . and humans. In the Korean Chosŏn Dynasty, for example, eunuchs lived longer than intact males of identical social standing.[75] Unfortunately, the castration approach to life extension only works if it's done while you're still a boy – so, my dear male readers, if you've already gone through puberty, I'm sorry to say it's too late. Still, the fact that it was ever possible is yet another line of evidence for an innate contribution to the sex difference in longevity.

Finally, males' habit of dying younger isn't just a Western trend, a modern trend, or even a human trend. In many species, including most mammals, females live to a riper, older age.[76] One study concluded, for instance, that among wild mammals, females live 18.6% longer than their male counterparts. Interestingly, in our species, females live only 7.8% longer.[77] This is consistent with a core theme of this book, namely that sexual dimorphism is relatively modest in our species.[78]

Why, though, might the sex difference in longevity have evolved to begin with? There are two main reasons.[79] The first is that genes can potentially be selected even if they boost their owner's risk of death, just so long as they also boost their owner's reproductive success sufficiently to make the risk worthwhile. Such genes are most likely to be selected if the reproductive boost comes early in life, but the death boost comes only later, when people are unlikely to have more children anyway. This is true for both sexes. However, because males can potentially have more offspring than females, the boost in reproductive success can be considerably larger for males, thus compensating for a larger hit to their survival odds. That's a big part of why males engage in more aggression and risky behaviour, despite the fact that it increases their chances of an early appointment with the Grim Reaper.

The second reason for the longevity gender gap is, in a sense, the flipside of the first. Because fewer males than females make it to each stage of adulthood, genes that boost male survival in later life have less chance of being selected. Why? Because having fewer males means that fewer of those genes are available for natural selection to select. Of course, this process can't get off the ground unless the longevity gap is already present. What it can do, though, is entrench and amplify the gap once it appears. Thus, as soon as males start dying younger, the difference becomes self-reinforcing.

Note that these two processes don't just account for sex differences in life-shortening behaviour. They also account for the fact that greater male mortality is baked into male physiology. Men age faster than women, and are more likely to be cut down by heart attacks, cancers, and many other diseases, even when external risk factors are equalized. The reason, once again, is that genes that raise the risk of these outcomes in later life can be selected if they give an early-life reproductive boost, whereas genes that *lower* later-life risk are less likely to be selected because fewer males make it that far.

So, that's the first possible solution to the mystery of sex differences in physical health. The second is the idea that the differences represent the maladaptive extremes of more general sex differences that, closer to the mean, are adaptive for both sexes. This helps explain many of the disorders that women are more prone to than men. I'll give you two examples. The first is women's greater vulnerability to autoimmune disorders: that is, disorders in which the immune system becomes overly diligent, and starts attacking the body's own cells and tissues. The key to explaining this gender gap is that, on average, women's immune systems are cranked up higher than men's. In the normal range, this is adaptive, and part of the general trend toward greater self-protectiveness in women. But among the minority at the right-hand tail, more women than men have *overactive* immune systems, resulting in more autoimmune disorders.[80]

The second example concerns women's greater proneness to pain disorders such as chronic headaches, migraines, and fibromyalgia. Although there's a popular stereotype that women have a higher pain tolerance than men, a large research literature shows the opposite: that women have a *lower* pain tolerance. Granted, men are usually less willing to admit when they're in pain in a bid to preserve their street cred. However, the sex difference in pain tolerance doesn't just appear in self-reports; it's also found in physiological measurements.[81] Not only that, but it's found in other species – species that don't have social pressure for male stoicism.[82] The implication is that, despite men's stiff upper lip, the difference is real. As with women's stronger immune systems, their lower pain tolerance is presumably part of the general trend toward greater female self-protectiveness.[83] Again, though, it's possible to have too much of a good thing, and among the minority at the extreme of the distribution, more women than men are subject to pain disorders.

Sex on the Psychiatrist's Couch

The sexes don't just differ in their proneness to physical maladies; they differ as well in their proneness to psychological ones. Here are some of the major differences in this area.

1. Women are more prone than men to depression and anxiety disorders. Like many sex differences, these ones are largest in the teen years and early adulthood.[84]

2. Girls and women are more prone to most eating disorders.
3. Boys and men are more prone to ADHD, autism, and learning difficulties.[85]
4. Men are more prone to substance abuse and every kind of addiction.[86]
5. Boys are more likely to be diagnosed with conduct disorder, and men are more likely to be psychopaths or diagnosed with antisocial personality disorder.[87]
6. Men are slightly more likely to develop schizophrenia.[88]
7. Men are much more likely to kill themselves.[89]

To be clear, the sexes don't differ in all psychological problems. Bipolar disorder, for instance, is one of the least sexist disorders on record, with a similar incidence in men and women.[90] Most other mental-health issues, however, are far from gender neutral.

Or so it seems. We should always ask ourselves, though: Are the differences real? As we'll see in the next chapter, people sometimes overlook gender-atypical disorders, in part because they're not expecting them and in part because the disorders present somewhat differently in each sex. This problem is compounded by the fact that the sexes tend to camouflage different symptoms: Females more often camouflage symptoms of ADHD and autism, whereas males more often camouflage symptoms of depression and anxiety. Could it be, then, that although there are sex differences in the frequencies of psychiatric *diagnoses*, there are no sex differences in the frequencies of the underlying disorders?

No. Consider autism. Boys are diagnosed with this condition up to four times as often as girls. Is it plausible that we could have such an enormous disparity in diagnoses if autism were actually equally distributed between the sexes? It's not. It would imply extreme ineptitude on the part of clinicians, doctors, teachers, and others involved in the diagnostic process. And it would be an inexplicable coincidence that we're making the same mistake to roughly the same degree in every nation where autism is diagnosed.

Similar considerations apply to depression. Women are twice as likely as men to be diagnosed with a depressive disorder. Are half of all depressed men overlooked? Are twice as many women as men falsely diagnosed with depression? Neither suggestion is credible. The main reason that men are less often diagnosed with depression is that men less often *suffer* depression.

Sure, it's perfectly plausible – likely, even – that gender gaps in mental health are somewhat overestimated, at least for relatively mild, ambiguous cases. It's entirely *implausible*, however, that there are no gaps at all.

Thus, we're left with our usual conundrum: Where do the differences come from? One popular suggestion is that they're products of traditional sex roles, patriarchy, hegemonic masculinity, and the like. These pervasive social structures put different pressures on men and women, thereby accounting for differences in the kinds of life miseries each sex is most susceptible to.

Could this explain sex differences in the incidence of psychiatric disorders? I don't think so. For one thing, mental-health sex differences aren't unique to any ethnic group, nation, or culture. One pair of meta-analyses, for instance, each covering nearly two million people from 90 nations, found that women everywhere are more prone than men to depression.[91] Other research shows that sex differences in anxiety disorders, ADHD, substance abuse, and indeed most psychological difficulties are universal or very close to it. That's not what we'd expect if the differences were solely due to culture. And it doesn't stop there. Psychologists have documented a gender-equality paradox for sex differences in mental health: They're typically larger in wealthier, more gender-equal nations.[92] This pulls the rug out from under the idea that the differences are due to traditional sex roles, patriarchy, or any of the usual suspects.

It's difficult to avoid the conclusion that sex differences in psychological disorders have a significant biological basis. But this presents us with a puzzle. As with medical disorders, these maladies are almost certainly not adaptations. To start with, adaptationist explanations are most readily applied to traits that we all have in common, whereas serious psychological disorders are rare. In addition, most disorders are associated with lower fitness: in other words, fewer offspring.[93] It's therefore hard to see how genes predisposing people to these disorders could ever get a foothold in the gene pool, let alone stick around if they did. So, the question is: How can we explain the innate contribution to sex differences in psychological problems?

My theory is that, as with many gender gaps in physical health, mental-health sex differences represent the maladaptive extremes of differences that, in the normal range, are adaptive for both sexes.[94] As we saw earlier in the chapter, women score higher than men on the Big Five trait of neuroticism – that is, proneness to negative emotions such as sadness and anxiety. For the majority in the middle of the distribution, the neuroticism sex difference is fairly small and probably adaptive, helping calibrate men's and women's appetite for risk. Among the minority at the right-hand tail, however, the differences are notably larger, with many more women than men suffering from clinical depression and anxiety disorders. Meanwhile, at the other end of the distribution, many more men than women have extremely *low* levels of these emotions. Although having too much anxiety or sadness is clearly a problem, so is having too little. Yet often it's a problem that goes unnoticed. As Randy Nesse notes, 'Patients do not complain of too little anxiety so they do not come to clinic to increase anxiety levels. Instead, they are found in the emergency room, the court room and jail.'[95] But whether too high or too low, sex differences in these psychological problems make perfect sense as soon as we recognize that they're the maladaptive extremes of more general differences that are adaptive in the normal range.

Other mental-health sex differences yield to the same framework. On average, boys are somewhat more active and less attentive than girls; at the extreme, many more boys than girls are diagnosed with ADHD. On average, boys are somewhat less verbally adept than girls; at the extreme, many more boys than girls have language disorders. On average, men are more aggressive and risk-prone than women, and less agreeable and conscientious; at the extreme, more boys than girls are diagnosed with conduct disorder, and more men than women with antisocial personality disorder. In short, sex differences in mental-health problems are byproducts of some of the fundamental sex differences discussed in earlier pages.

Importantly, though, the fact that the non-clinical differences are adaptive doesn't imply that the clinical ones are! Instead, they're a sobering reminder that natural selection favours traits that are adaptive on average, rather than in every case.

* * *

OK, we've done it: We've covered all the standard-issue sex differences. To wrap up the book, let's now shift gears and address a very different question: So what? The fact that many sex differences have an evolutionary origin is interesting, but does it have any practical implications? The short answer is yes, and the best way to see how is to look at the many ways in which getting the differences wrong can create serious problems for individuals and society. That's what we'll do in the next chapter, which is the final chapter of the book.

10

The Peacock's Predicament

Why Sex Differences Matter – and How We Can Learn to Live with Them

> If men and women do by nature want slightly different things, we shall do no good by making them feel that there is something wrong until they want the same.
>
> Janet Radcliffe Richards (1980), p.150

> 'Inherent differences' between men and women, we have come to appreciate, remain cause for celebration, but not for denigration of the members of either sex or for artificial constraints on an individual's opportunity.
>
> Justice Ruth Bader Ginsburg (cited in M. Coyle, 2020)

Everyone is Wrong About Sex Differences

Society is deeply confused and deeply conflicted about sex differences, and it's causing us serious problems. It's causing us problems in our dating lives, our family lives, and our work lives. It's compromising our health and our mental well-being. It's causing us to discriminate against women and against men. And it's leading us into policy errors and moral errors, all the while pitting us against each other and against some of the healthiest aspects of our culture.

Why do we struggle so much with differences between the sexes? My best guess is that it's a side effect of one of the central claims of this book: that sex differences in our species are real but relatively modest. This gives us elbow room to exaggerate the differences or minimize them, depending on personal taste. Both errors are the root of many evils, however, and both lead us to mishandle sex differences as individuals and as a society. In this chapter, we'll survey the harms of both exaggerating and minimizing differences between men and women. We'll then turn to the ultimate question in this area: How should we deal with the differences?

From Sex Differences to Sexism: The Dangers of Exaggerating Sex Differences

Let's start by looking at the dangers of treating men and women as if they were from different planets, and of moralizing the differences between them.

SOCIAL PRESSURE TO CONFORM

An initial danger is that exaggerating and moralizing sex differences creates social pressure to conform to overly restrictive templates of the sexes. Genuine but modest sex differences give rise to exaggerated stereotypes of men and women. These then become enshrined in the norms and the laws of society: norms and laws which force everyone into the mould of the average.

To give a historical example, the fact that women, on average, are more parental than men somehow morphed into the idea that women should shoulder the entire parental burden and forgo the option of a career. The problem with this idea is that it treats a statistical sex difference as a Mars-and-Venus difference, and inevitably means that many women are pressured into a role that doesn't suit them.

The dark flipside of pressure to conform to sex stereotypes is intolerance of those who don't. This can be seen, most notably, in prejudice against sexual minorities. The implicit reasoning seems to be: 'People are usually attracted to the other sex; therefore, people *should* be attracted to the other sex, and anything else is wrong.' In the same way, intolerance of non-conformity adds fuel to the fire of the sexual double standard: 'Women tend to be less interested in casual sex; therefore, women *shouldn't* be interested in casual sex. It's OK for men but not for women.'

In many cases like these, exaggerating and moralizing sex differences leads to sexism against women. As the philosopher David Benatar points out, however, girls and women aren't the only victims of sex-based discrimination. Boys and men often are as well, a phenomenon Benatar calls the *second sexism*.[1] It's easy to think of examples. Whereas women are judged more harshly than men if they defy stereotypes of women – if they sleep around, for instance, or are less-than-perfect parents – *men* are judged more harshly than women if they defy stereotypes of men: if they *don't* sleep around, or if they fail to earn the big bucks. Likewise, whereas women are judged by their appearance more than men, men are judged by their careers more than women. And whereas women are sometimes treated as sex objects, men are sometimes treated as 'success objects'.[2]

We see, then, that evolved sex differences are the dirt in the oyster around which many of our cultural norms develop. Although these norms have their origins in genuine differences between the sexes, they amplify and formalize those differences. Once established, anyone who flouts the rules is stigmatized. And the main catalyst for all of this is our old adversary, the naturalistic fallacy: the unwarranted assumption that what's natural must be good.[3]

NEGATIVE STEREOTYPING

A second danger is that even genuine sex differences can give rise to unfair stereotypes of the sexes. In the last chapter, I mentioned that, on average, women are more neurotic than men, especially in early adulthood. At the centre of the distribution, this difference is fairly small: Plenty of men are more neurotic than plenty of women. At the right-hand tail, however, the difference is significantly larger. This means that, among people who are highly neurotic, women outnumber men by a considerable margin.

Highly neurotic people are rare, but they do stand out. As a result, we may end up stereotyping women in general as highly neurotic – much more so than men – even though most women are not neurotic, and the sex difference in the general population is modest.

Again, this phenomenon affects both sexes, not just women. We saw in Chapter 7 that men commit more than 90% of homicides. People often point to this statistic as proof that men are vastly more aggressive than women. But although most homicides are committed by men, most men don't commit any homicides. I once calculated that, globally, the average man kills approximately 0.00005 people per year, whereas the average woman kills approximately 0.000006. (Notice the extra zero.) That's a huge difference. But it's one found only among a tiny minority of people at the extreme of the aggression distribution, where the differences are much more pronounced.

Here's a good rule of thumb: We shouldn't characterize either sex in terms of behaviour that most members of that sex don't engage in.

STATISTICAL DISCRIMINATION

Negative stereotyping of the sexes isn't walled off from the real world. It can fuel unjust discrimination against the targets of the stereotypes, even when those stereotypes contain a grain of truth.

One set of examples concerns parenting. I suggested earlier that the (accurate but exaggerated) stereotype that women are more parental than men can lead to discrimination against women, as when women are forced into the parental role. As David Benatar notes, however, the same stereotype can also lead to sexism against men, as when men are less likely to win custody of their children. This, argues Benatar, is an example of a common phenomenon: Not only do sex stereotypes lead to discrimination against both sexes, but often the *same* stereotype leads to discrimination against both.[4]

Other examples revolve around education. The stereotype that maths and science are for boys and men may sometimes mean that parents, teachers, and employers underestimate female talent in these areas. Worse than that, in earlier times, false stereotypes about girls' innate inability to do maths or science led to their exclusion from maths and science classrooms, and false stereotypes about their innate intellectual deficits in general led to their exclusion from higher education and public life.

As with earlier examples, though, negative stereotypes don't just affect girls and women. One example affecting boys is grading bias. Many large-scale studies have compared boys' and girls' grades when graded anonymously by strangers with their grades when graded knowingly by their teachers. The most common outcome is that, on average, boys receive worse grades from their teachers, suggesting bias against boys in grading.[5] Much of this is due to the stereotype that boys are worse behaved and less conscientious than girls. Although this stereotype is accurate on average, it creates an expectation of poorer scholastic performance across the board that leads teachers to unfairly downgrade boys' work. Differential marking may also be partly a matter of overcorrection. In an effort to boost girls' confidence in traditionally male subjects such as maths and science, teachers may sometimes inadvertently inflate their marks: an accidental example of the delta bias.[6] To be clear, these effects aren't huge, and the main reason boys do worse at school is that they put in less effort in the classroom. Still, the phenomenon is real, and it may contribute to boys' dissatisfaction with school.

A final example takes us into the courtroom. Research consistently shows that men are treated more harshly than women in the criminal justice system: They receive longer sentences for the same crime, even taking into account factors such as criminal history, type of offence, seriousness of offence, marital status, and childcare responsibilities.[7] Offenders who harm women are especially likely to receive harsh sentences. These biases are mirrored in everyday social perception. As my own and others' research has shown, aggression by men is seen more negatively than that by women, and aggression *toward* women is seen more negatively than that toward men.[8] One survey even reported that people consider a wife stabbing her husband to death to be a less severe crime than a husband stabbing his wife to death.[9] The tendency to punish men more harshly doesn't seem to be a product of recent feminist activism; an analysis of London trials spanning nearly two centuries found that female defendants were treated more leniently throughout the entire period.[10] More than likely, the harsher treatment of men is an example of statistical discrimination: On average, men are more dangerous and prone to criminal behaviour than women, so we end up treating individual men as dangerous and prone to criminal behaviour, even when they're quite possibly not. Meanwhile, the stereotype of women as helpless victims functions as a legal force field for female defendants, protecting them from more severe penalties. The fact that men get longer sentences for the same crime could be seen as sexism against men. But it could also be seen as sexism against women: We view women as childlike innocents who wouldn't hurt a fly (unless the fly deserved it). Interestingly, male judges are more likely than female judges to go easy on female defendants, suggesting that male paternalism is part of the explanation.[11]

OVERLOOKING GENDER-ATYPICAL DISORDERS

Stereotypes give rise to expectations, and expectations sometimes function as blinders, leading us to overlook exceptions to the rule. This causes problems in many areas, but arguably the most important is medicine. As a result of the blinkering power of stereotypes, we may overlook and underdiagnose disorders in the sex that's less susceptible to them. The classic example is that, because men are more prone to heart attacks, medical professionals have sometimes missed the warning signs of heart attacks in women – as have women themselves. But it's not just about women, observes historian of science Londa Schiebinger, 'it's about getting the research right, and it benefits everyone. In osteoporosis, for example, men have been neglected because it is mostly seen as a disease of menopausal women.'[12]

Stereotypes can also blind us to exceptions in the realm of mental health. We've sometimes ignored ADHD, autism, and reading disorders in girls and women, for instance, because of (accurate but exaggerated) stereotypes that these conditions are more common in boys and men.[13]

Similarly, though less often discussed, we've sometimes ignored depression, anxiety disorders, and eating disorders in boys and men because of (accurate but exaggerated) stereotypes that *these* conditions are more common in girls and women.[14] As clinical psychologist Rachel Salk and colleagues observed of depression,

> One possible negative consequence of emphasizing the preponderance of women with depression is that depression becomes a female-stereotyped disorder. Such a stereotype can be harmful to both women and men. The stereotype might lead to over-diagnosis of depression in women, and, potentially, overmedication. For men, the stereotype may mean that their depression is overlooked.[15]

It's worth pointing out that there are limits to the power of stereotypes to obscure reality. Although we may overlook *moderate* instances of health and mental-health problems, we're unlikely to miss severe ones. On the contrary, it's the things that clash most violently with our expectations that stand out to us most in the world. Nonetheless, for milder cases, where there's a significant degree of ambiguity, our expectations may serve as a tie breaker.

Not only do stereotypes lead us to overlook disorders in the sex less prone to them, they lead us to implement suboptimal solutions. One of the big pitfalls of thinking in terms of groups rather than individuals is that when more members of one group than another suffer a given problem, we often end up acting as if *only* members of that group suffer that problem. For example, because more women than men have eating disorders, we sometimes act as if *only* women have them: Almost all the research on these debilitating conditions has been done on women, despite the fact that a non-trivial minority of sufferers are men.[16] Likewise, because more girls and women experience self-esteem and body-image issues, we sometimes act as if *only* girls and women experience these issues: We focus our research attention exclusively on females, and roll out interventions targeting female sufferers alone. If it's not obvious why this is a problem, try flipping the sexes. Imagine that we decided that, because more men than women die of COVID, we should only attempt to reduce COVID deaths among men. Clearly, that would be a medical and moral error; *fewer* women die of COVID, but many still do. The same applies in reverse, though, to disorders where women outnumber men. Our aim should be to reduce as much suffering as possible – and the way to do that is to tackle problems wherever they're found, rather than only in the demographics where they're somewhat more common.

Even if we adopted this policy, however, we still wouldn't be out of the woods. That's because even when we *do* notice gender-atypical health and mental-health problems, we often stigmatize them – even more than we stigmatize gender-typical ones. To illustrate, going bald might be bad for men, but it's a hundred times worse for women. By the same token, conditions such as autism, ADHD, and substance abuse may be stigmatized more in women than men, whereas depression, anxiety disorders, and eating disorders may be stigmatized more in men than women. This is yet another barrier to people seeking the help they need.

OVERLOOKING GENDER-ATYPICAL SOCIAL PROBLEMS

Just as exaggerated stereotypes lead us to overlook gender-atypical medical and psychiatric problems, so too they lead us to overlook gender-atypical societal ones. A good example concerns sexual victimization and intimate partner abuse. As discussed in Chapter 7, the majority of perpetrators of these crimes are men, and the majority of victims are women. Our natural tendency when confronted with facts like these is to 'round up': to convert 'more men than women' to 'only men', and 'more women than men' to 'only women'. Thus, we often view sexual victimization and partner abuse as women's problems, rather than more-women-than-men problems. In doing so, however, we once again treat a statistical sex difference as a Mars-and-Venus difference. Ironically, the tendency to polarize sex differences in this arena is particularly common among gender-role progressives, who usually downplay female–male differences.

Whoever does it, though, polarizing the differences is not a cost-free error. With a male-perpetrator/female-victim model in mind, people often overlook, minimize, or stigmatize sexual victimization and partner abuse suffered by men or perpetrated by women. Police, healthcare workers, and counsellors may fail to spot it or inquire about it. And when men come forward to report that they've been sexually victimized or abused by a partner, their accusations may be taken less seriously. No doubt, the victimization of women is often not taken seriously enough. But the victimization of men may be taken even *less* seriously – another example of Benatar's second sexism.[17]

A further problem with exaggerating sex differences in sexual victimization and partner abuse is that it can distort interventions and policies aimed at addressing these social ills. Media, activists, and awareness campaigns focus almost exclusively on cases that fit the male-perpetrator/female-victim mould. On reflection, this makes little sense. The fact, for instance, that one in four women, but 'only' one in six men, is a victim of intimate partner abuse doesn't imply that only women need help; it implies that one in four women, but only one in six men, need help. The second formulation isn't much harder to grasp than the first. However, the tendency to think in terms of groups rather than individuals blinds many people to the insight.

Our blindness to exceptions to the male-perpetrator/female-victim rule has taken us to some bizarre places. One example is that sexual violence and intimate partner violence were defined in UK law as violence against women and girls. When policymakers belatedly came to the realization that men and boys are sometimes subject to these forms of violence as well, they'd tied their hands and didn't have the vocabulary to sensibly describe this fact. Thus, a policy document dealing with the issue had the laughable title 'Supporting Male Victims of Crimes Considered Violence Against Women and Girls'.[18] As Internet smart alecks immediately asked: What's next? Supporting women and girls at risk of attempting male suicide?

In case this sounds like an attack on feminism, let me just point out that many feminists have taken exactly the line I'm taking. For example,

Lara Stemple and Ilan Meyer argued vigorously against the idea that feminism requires an exclusive concern with female victims of male violence.[19] Aside from the fact that it means we miss many victims – including female victims in same-sex relationships and male victims in same-sex *and* other-sex relationships – it galvanizes traditional, regressive stereotypes of the sexes: stereotypes such as that men are violent sex maniacs, whereas women are helpless victims. As Stemple and Meyer put the point,

> Overreliance on [a male-perpetrator/female-victim paradigm] stigmatizes men who are victimized, risks portraying women as victims, and discourages discussion of abuse that runs counter to the paradigm, such as same-sex abuse and female perpetration of sexual victimization.[20]

I've focused on an example that affects boys and men, but of course plenty of examples affect girls and women. One relates to the 'boy crisis': the fact that, on average, boys are doing worse in school. Because more boys than girls are struggling, we sometimes act as if *only* boys are struggling. But the so-called boy crisis is actually a more-boys-than-girls crisis, and if we focus too intently on boys' difficulties, we may overlook girls in the same boat. Likewise, because more men than women take their own lives, we sometimes act as if only men do. But again, suicide isn't a male problem; it's a more males-than-females problem – and if we lose sight of this, we'll neglect many people in need of help.

With all this in mind, here's another good rule of thumb: The fact that more members of group X than group Y suffer problem Z is a bad reason to act as if *only* members of group X suffer problem Z. Given that it's individuals rather than groups that suffer, we should aim to alleviate problems in all individuals who have them, rather than only in individuals whose groups have a somewhat higher incidence of the problems. Sure, different interventions may sometimes be useful for different groups. But not always – and even when they are, our ultimate goal should be to help the individuals who most need it, not just to iron out group disparities.

Denying Human Nature: The Dangers of Minimizing Sex Differences

While some people are busy exaggerating and moralizing sex differences, others are busy denying them, or at least denying that they have evolutionary roots. Given the dangers of exaggerating sex differences, this might seem like a safe default. But minimizing the differences creates numerous problems of its own, every bit as serious as magnifying them. Let's look at some examples.

SOCIAL PRESSURE TO REJECT TRADITIONAL GENDER ROLES

As we've seen, one danger of exaggerating and moralizing sex differences is that it creates social pressure to conform to a narrow template of what men and women ought to be. But *minimizing* the differences can do exactly the same thing. In our effort to dismantle the restrictive gender straitjackets of past eras, we might end up trying to force people into unisex straitjackets – or we might overshoot the target altogether and end up trying to force people into gender-role-reversed ones.

In the bad old days, people pathologized gender-atypical behaviour. Today, some people seem hell-bent on making the opposite mistake: pathologizing gender-typical behaviour instead. For example, rather than guilt tripping women for prioritizing career over family, some now guilt trip them for prioritizing family over career. Similarly, rather than worrying about boys playing with dolls, some parents now worry about *girls* playing with dolls. I'm exaggerating for effect, of course, but only a little. I once spotted an article in *The Daily Mail* with the rather striking headline: 'How Did I Raise Such a Girly Girl? Feminist Mother Cringes at Her Three-Year-Old Daughter's Love of Princesses, Frills and Pink – And Wishes She Was into Toy Cars Instead.'[21] I remember thinking how strange it is that people who wish their daughters were less girly, and more like boys, are viewed as *pro*-female, rather than anti. And this isn't just a one-off aberration. It's an example of a broader trend, namely that there's disdain in certain quarters for anything traditionally feminine: a rather ironic situation in this age of female empowerment.[22]

Still, it's not only traditional femininity that gets pathologized; traditional masculinity does as well. It's increasingly common for people to talk as if masculinity is inherently bad, and as if every male is a violent offender or sexual predator waiting to happen.[23] School programmes teach boys about their toxic masculinity, while popular media treats masculinity as a problem to be solved, rather than a force to be suitably channelled. Some of this stems from a reasonable concern about harmful behaviours more common among men than women. But some of it is just unfair stereotyping of a kind we wouldn't tolerate for any other group. And given that the harmful behaviours in question are found in some women and not all men, it would be better to target the behaviours themselves, rather than the entire sex in which these behaviours are somewhat more common.

DATING ADVICE FROM DARWIN

Another problem with minimizing sex differences is that it disconnects us from some of the practical advice that could come from a more comprehensive understanding. Nowhere is this clearer than in the minefield of heterosexual relationships.

First, downplaying or denying the differences in this domain can lead to failures of cross-sex mindreading. A good example concerns a phenomenon known as the *sexual over-perception bias*. This is seen in people who jump quickly and confidently to the conclusion that others desire them sexually, such that they routinely mistake a friendly smile or kind word for a barely controlled desire to get down and dirty with them. As you might have noticed, the sexual over-perception bias is more common among men than women.[24] According to evolutionary psychologists Martie Haselton and David Buss, this makes good adaptive sense. For ancestral men, over-inferring sexual interest might have led to some rejections and embarrassment, but it would also have meant a reduced chance of missing any sexual opportunities. *Under*-inferring interest, in contrast, would have meant avoiding the rejections and embarrassment but potentially missing the opportunities as well. From a Darwinian vantage point, what matters is the number of offspring you produce, not the number of rejections you avoid, so for men, selection would have favoured over-inferring sexual interest.

Not so women. For women, neither over-inferring nor under-inferring interest would have had much impact on the evolutionary bottom line: the number of offspring they produce. Men would probably have pursued them anyway, and missed sexual opportunities wouldn't have been especially costly given that the ceiling number of offspring for women is so low. In fact, taking every sexual opportunity would have been a bad move for women, as it would have compromised female choice. Thus, according to Haselton and Buss, while men evolved a lower threshold for inferring sexual interest, women evolved a higher one – leading to thousands of years of mutual misunderstandings, male disappointment, and female consternation. Being aware of the differences could help us sidestep these less-than-fun outcomes.

But although it's important for both sexes to understand the sexual over-perception bias housed in many male skulls, it's also important to keep track of individual differences. The fact that the average man overestimates women's sexual interest doesn't mean that all men do; it just means that enough do to pull the male average above the zero point. Crucially, a significant minority of men do the reverse: They *underestimate* it. A monolithic message that 'men overestimate women's sexual interest' could lead those men to disregard possible signs of interest, resulting in romantic inaction. Who knows how many love stories were never told because shy guys were given advice geared for the sexually overconfident? Ideally, dating advice would be tailored to the individual, not to exaggerated stereotypes of the average man or woman.

Minimizing sex differences in sexual psychology can also deprive us of useful advice for established relationships. People in such relationships sometimes find themselves romantically attracted to individuals other than their long-term partners. This is particularly common among men, for the reasons outlined in Chapter 5. As David Buss points out, if you're not aware of your evolved 'roaming eye', you might more readily fall under its spell. 'Hmmm', you might think, 'I guess I don't love my partner after all. If I did, why would I be interested in this other person? Maybe *this* person is "the one"!' On the other hand, if you understand that you're probably the victim of an evolutionary hallucination – a trick designed to get you to pass on more of your genes – you might reflect on such thoughts more critically: 'Nah, I don't buy it. I'm going to ignore these feelings till they pass, because I know I'll be happier in the long run with my current partner. Who cares what's good for my genes?'[25]

KIDS' STUFF

Romantic relationships are just the start. Understanding typical sex differences can also help us raise and educate our children. Conversely, minimizing or denying the differences means missing out on that help.

To start with, understanding sex differences can help us navigate the job of parenting. As we've seen, a lot of modern parents beat themselves up about their children acting in gender-stereotypical ways: 'Oh no! My son likes play-fighting and toy guns, and my daughter likes dolls and pink! Where have I gone wrong?' The assumption underlying this mindset is that childhood sex differences are due largely to parenting practices and other social influences, and that these things are a cultural hangover from unjust historical gender roles.

But an evolutionary perspective throws a spanner in the works of this hypothesis. As we saw in earlier chapters, we've got good reason to think that there's a strong innate contribution to many childhood sex differences. Knowing this may be good medicine for parents. For one thing, it means they won't be taken by surprise by the differences. They might still want to fight them, but at least they'll know they're not their fault. And they might no longer feel such a strong need to fight them after all. If certain sex differences turn out not to be products of a sexist, patriarchal society, then maybe they're not as terrible as we'd thought. As long as no one's getting hurt, perhaps we can just let kids be kids.

Similar ideas extend to education. A common view among educators is that sex differences in play, toy preferences, and interests are socially constructed, and thus that they can and should be deconstructed. Just as some parents have tried to suppress sex differences in the home, some schools have tried to suppress them in the classroom and playground. What those charged with this task quickly realize, however, is that if you let boys and girls play freely, they play in different ways. As such, eliminating the differences necessitates the establishment of a playground panopticon: Children have to be incessantly monitored, their behaviour micromanaged, and their preferences systematically discounted. The Swedes win the gold medal for taking this approach the furthest.[26] As cultural commentator Christina Hoff Sommers observed, educational reformers in Sweden 'are treating gender-conforming children the way we once treated gender-variant children . . . In their efforts to free children from the constraints of gender, the Swedish reformers are imposing their own set of inviolate rules, standards, and taboos.'[27]

Not only does understanding childhood sex differences help unmask harmful policies, it can guide our efforts to create better ones. Consider, for instance, the fact that boys behave worse than girls in the classroom, and get worse grades in every subject: two central ingredients of the boy crisis.[28] Where do these differences come from? In my view, a big part of the answer is a phenomenon known as *sexual bimaturism*.[29] This refers to the fact that girls typically reach puberty before boys. In essence, they grow up faster. This pattern isn't unique to humans; it's common in species where the ceiling number of offspring is higher for males than females.[30] Sexual bimaturism immediately suggests a reason for boys' poorer behaviour and grades: Boys, in effect, are younger than their female classmates. Recognizing this deep-seated developmental difference hints at novel solutions to the problem. These include policy analyst Richard Reeves's proposal that we 'redshirt' boys: that is, that we generally start them at school a year later than we start the girls.[31] In principle, we could have come up with this idea without an understanding of sexual bimaturism. However, that understanding makes the policy more salient, if for no other reason than that it de-emphasizes other, biologically naive explanations for the gaps, and the policies that those might inspire.

SEX IN THE WORKPLACE

A third area where the science of human sex differences can inform our understanding – and thus where minimizing or denying the differences can hobble it – is the workplace. Three workplace outcomes in particular have grabbed the lion's share of policymakers' attention. I call them the *demonic triad*.

1. **The Gender Pay Gap**. On average, men earn more than women. This doesn't necessarily mean that men are paid more for the same work. For the most part, they're not. Instead, men tend to go into higher-paying professions, work longer hours, and work for more years.[32] The reasons for this are fiercely debated. What's not debated, however – at least among the experts – is that the earnings gap is not due primarily to pay discrimination.
2. **Vertical Gender Segregation**. More men than women make it to the top of the pyramid: Most CEOs and political leaders are men, as are most people at the pinnacle of their professions. It's worth pointing out that, although more men than women make it to the top, more men than women also sink to the bottom – and the overwhelming majority of men don't end up at either the top *or* the bottom. Still, among the small number of individuals who possess extreme power, status, or wealth, men outnumber women.
3. **Horizontal Gender Segregation**. Men and women go into different fields in different numbers. For example, more men than women go into maths-heavy STEM fields like computer science, engineering, and physics, whereas more women than men go into the health sciences, social sciences, and humanities.[33]

How can we explain the demonic triad? For many, the first port of call – and the last – is discrimination. And no doubt, discrimination plays a role. The question is, though: Is it the entire explanation?

Almost certainly not. Several well-established sex differences plausibly contribute to gender gaps in workplace outcomes.[34] Consider first the gender pay gap and the fact that men outnumber women in the top echelons of society. These stubborn facts are probably due in part to some of the sex differences outlined in earlier chapters. In Chapter 6, for instance, we saw that, on average, men have a somewhat stronger drive than women for status and success. In addition, women have a stronger drive than men for a *mate* with status and success. As a result, men may prioritize these things in a job because women prioritize them in a mate – an awkward bind, and one that can't just be legislated away.

In Chapter 7, we saw that men are more willing than women to take risks. Almost by definition, this means a higher chance of great success, but also a higher chance of catastrophic failure. One study found that when an attractive woman was watching, male skateboarders started trying riskier moves on their boards, which led to more impressive stunts but also more wipeouts.[35] This is a good illustration of a pervasive pattern, which applies as well to the world of work. For example, an analysis of entrepreneurs concluded that part of the reason that men start more new businesses than women – and therefore that they succeed *and fail* more than women – is that more men than women are overconfident.[36]

Finally, in Chapter 8, we looked at sex differences in parental involvement: Women tend to be more involved, in large part because they want to be. This too has an impact on workplace outcomes. Many studies, for instance, find either no gender earnings gap among the childless or that women earn slightly more. It's primarily among parents that the gap appears, like a slowly growing fissure in the ice.[37]

My purpose in pointing to sex differences in status-hunger, risk-taking, and parental motivation isn't to deny that other factors contribute to the gender pay gap and vertical gender segregation. It's only to say that it's plausible to think that these differences, wherever they come from, also contribute. More than that, it's *implausible* to think that they don't. How could they not?

The same applies to the fact that more men than women go into some professions, while more women than men go into others. This was the topic of my controversial paper with Lewis Halsey that I mentioned in

Chapter 1.[38] At least two clusters of sex differences, both of which we explored in the last chapter, likely contribute to gender gaps in occupational choice. The first and most important is that the sexes differ, on average, in their career-related interests: Men tend to be more interested than women in working with things and systems, whereas women tend to be more interested than men in working with and helping people.[39] This immediately suggests a reason that more men than women go into fields such as computer science, engineering, and physics: More men than women want to. And it suggests the same reason in reverse for the fact that more women than men go into psychology, education, and the health sciences: They're pursuing what interests them most.

The second potential contributor is that the sexes differ, on average, in their cognitive profiles. Most notably, women do better on most verbal tests, whereas men do better on most tests of spatial ability. This means that, among the minority of people with sufficiently advanced abilities to work in verbally or spatially demanding fields – the humanities or engineering, for instance – the sex ratio is inevitably skewed toward one or the other sex. But it's not just about strengths in isolated domains. Another relevant cognitive sex difference is that, among the minority of people who have exceptional mathematical abilities, the women are more likely than the men to have exceptional language abilities as well.[40] This broadens the range of jobs available to them, and inevitably means that fewer mathematically gifted women pursue careers in maths-heavy fields – not because they have fewer options, but rather because they have more.

We see, then, that psychological sex differences help explain the demonic triad. At the same time, research on the role of discrimination is mixed at best. Many studies fail to find evidence of bias against women, or find evidence of bias in *favour* of women and against men.[41] Consider sex differences in STEM. Psychologists Stephen Ceci and Wendy Williams analysed real-world hiring data, and found little evidence for gender bias in hiring since the 1970s. It is true that women get fewer jobs in maths-heavy STEM fields. But that's only because fewer women apply for them. Those who *do* apply are *more* likely than men to be interviewed, and more likely to be offered the job. One analysis, for instance, reported that only 20% of applications for faculty mathematics positions came from women, but that women were 28% of candidates interviewed, and 32% of those receiving a job offer. The preferential hiring of women isn't because female candidates are superior; the researchers found no overall difference in the strength of female vs male applications.[42] Instead, it reflects a bias in favour of women in STEM hiring.

Backing up the real-world data, Williams and Ceci conducted a tenure-track hiring experiment: the largest such study to date. Professors at leading US universities were asked to evaluate applications for a tenure-track STEM position. The applications were identical for all participants, except that the hypothetical applicant was female for some and male for others. The study revealed a 2:1 preference for the *female* applicants.[43] This finding has since been replicated by other researchers, both in the US and in other countries.[44] Certainly, some hiring experiments suggest bias against women.[45] But these typically involve smaller, less representative samples. The better the study, the more likely it is to show anti-male rather than anti-female bias.[46]

And it's not just hiring that defies the standard narrative. So do journal article acceptances, citations, research grants, and promotions. Although some studies suggest bias in these areas, the effects tend to be small, and just as often favour women as men. With few exceptions, gender fairness is now the rule. Ceci and Williams conclude that for older cohorts, discrimination was a major barrier for women in STEM. For more recent cohorts, however, it's not.[47] It's a minor one at best.

If this isn't the impression you had of what the research shows, it's not your fault. Academics and media are often unreliable witnesses on this topic. When it comes to explaining workplace gender gaps, bias and barriers are always the guests of honour, while alternative explanations rarely get an invitation to the party. Studies finding anti-female bias are shouted from the rooftops; those finding no bias or bias against men are reported in a whisper or simply ignored.[48]

This isn't just poor scholarship; it's potentially harmful. First, exaggerated claims of bias create unnecessary resentment and rancour. Second, they could lead us to burn up time and money on interventions that are doomed to fail because they don't target the true causes of the disparities. We already know, in fact, that some of the most popular interventions – diversity training and implicit bias training – don't work and can even make things worse.[49] Third, when the interventions fail, policymakers are likely to adopt more and more coercive approaches in their effort to eliminate the gaps.[50] Fourth, because workplace sex differences aren't due solely to bias and barriers, eliminating them would necessitate the establishment of new, anti-traditional biases and barriers. Indeed, we've just seen evidence that such biases are already operative in STEM hiring: another case of the delta bias in action. And fifth, if we persuade everyone that male-dominated fields are hypermasculine, sexist hellscapes, we may scare off some girls and young women who would otherwise be interested in pursuing them. All these outcomes can be avoided if we simply tell the truth about the causes of occupational gender gaps.

Finally, it's important to note that, rather than being a roadblock to equality in the workplace, acknowledging sex differences could help us to achieve it. For example, an awareness of sex differences in career-related interests could guide outreach efforts aimed at pitching male-dominated fields to girls and women. One option would be to highlight the fact that, contrary to the stereotypes, these fields sometimes involve working with and helping other people.[51] Amanda Diekman and colleagues put it well. 'It is ironic', they noted, 'that STEM fields hold the key to helping many people, but are commonly regarded as antithetical (or, at best, irrelevant) to such communal goals.'[52]

BAD MEDICINE: WHEN POLITICAL CORRECTNESS KILLS

Some of the strongest arguments for taking sex differences seriously come from medicine. As we've seen, exaggerating sex differences can lead us to overlook medical and psychiatric problems in the less affected sex. The bad news, however, yet again, is that minimizing or ignoring the differences doesn't solve the problem, because doing that can be equally harmful.

First of all, many physical and psychological disorders are not only less common in one sex than the other, they present differently. Failure to recognize this could result in underdiagnosis in the less affected sex. In some cases, the mistake could be fatal. Heart attacks are again a prime example: While chest pain is the classic symptom for men, for women it's shortness of breath.[53] If we're not alert to this difference, we may fail to spot heart attacks in women, not because we *over*estimate the relevant sex differences, but rather because we underestimate them.

The same applies to mental health. Just as heart attacks present differently in women than men, autism and ADHD present differently in girls than boys. Girls with autism less often exhibit repetitive behaviours, for instance, whereas girls with ADHD tend to be less impulsive and disruptive. Meanwhile, depression presents differently in men than women: It more often involves anger, aggression, and substance abuse.[54] As with earlier examples, if we're not aware of these differences, we might overlook the underlying maladies – not just in others, but in ourselves.

Sidelining sex differences can also give rise to what's sometimes called *bikini medicine*: medicine that treats the sexes as if they were identical, other than the bits covered by bikinis.[55] A good example is that we've often tested drugs on men only, then assumed that what works for men will work for women too. This increases the chances of adverse side effects in women, including the worst adverse side effect of them all: death.[56] The blunder stems in part from the traditional assumption that men and women are interchangeable. But it stems as well from researchers' legitimate concern about unfair accusations of sexism. As the journalist Tom Whipple reported in *The Times*,

> Women's health is being put at risk because researchers have ignored gender differences in the brain out of fear of being labelled sexist, scientists have claimed.
>
> Male and female brains can respond differently to drugs for conditions such as stroke, but for years neuroscientists have feared being 'a pariah in the eyes of the neuroscience mainstream' if they highlighted the difference.[57]

Knowledge of sex differences could also help with the provision of psychotherapy. Fewer men than women find talk therapy an appealing prospect, with many preferring activity-based or skills-based programmes. Similarly, many men prefer a problem-focused approach to an emotion-focused one.[58] Rather than assuming that men are wrong to have these preferences, we could aim to make different options available for different people. This isn't to say that we should have distinct female and male therapies; that would be a Mars-and-Venus solution to a fuzzy, statistical problem. However, if we offered a broader range of options, certain forms of therapy would presumably attract more men than women, while others would attract more women than men.

At the same time, many men are reluctant to seek help at all for fear of being seen as weak or having failed as men. In an effort to short-circuit this mentality, the psychologists Martin Seager and John Barry proposed a more male-friendly sales pitch for therapy:

1. *'By seeking help you are taking action, taking control and fighting your problems.'*
2. *'It takes strength and courage to confront and master your problems.'*
3. *'Looking after yourself means protecting your family.'*[59]

Finally, understanding the true origins of mental-health sex differences may be crucial for devising successful interventions. Consider, for instance, the gender gap in suicide. A popular idea in some circles is that men's higher suicide rate is due to patriarchy and traditional masculine gender norms. If that were the case, though, the most patriarchal, traditionally masculine nations would have the highest male suicide rates. Instead, they have the lowest. This suggests that the patriarchy theory is muddled. Actual predictors of suicide include impulsivity, aggression, being unafraid of death, and having a high pain tolerance.[60] All of these traits are more common in men than in women, and at least some may be suitable targets for intervention. In contrast, trying to talk suicidal men out of their alleged patriarchal beliefs and traditional masculinity may amount to little more than political proselytizing. Again, we need to get our facts straight if we want a decent chance of improving people's lives.

HOBBLING OUR ABILITY TO DEAL WITH SOCIAL PROBLEMS

Just as ignoring sex differences can hamper our ability to improve people's health and mental well-being, so too it can hamper our ability to deal with the social problems that beset us.

A good example concerns sexual coercion and intimate partner abuse. As we saw in Chapter 7, these behaviours aren't just creations of culture; they stem from desires and motivations that have evolutionary underpinnings. Many people resist this conclusion, in part because they assume that if it were true, then the behaviours in question would be impossible to change. But this is an example of what I call the *fixed-forever fallacy*. Rather than implying that we're stuck with sexual coercion and intimate partner abuse for all eternity, an evolutionary explanation can help guide the search for effective interventions.

For a start, as with psychotherapy, social interventions based on false explanations of the causes of our problems are unlikely to be effective. To illustrate, many domestic violence interventions are founded on the assumption that intimate partner abuse derives from a patriarchal belief system according to which it's OK for men to use violence to control women.[61] But trying to cure violent men of such beliefs is unlikely to be a successful strategy if men don't hold those beliefs in the first place. As we saw in Chapter 7, most don't.

More generally, an evolutionary perspective tells us that we won't be able to eliminate the propensities motivating sexual coercion and intimate partner abuse simply by changing the cultural messaging around them, because cultural messaging isn't the primary cause of those propensities. Instead, we need to find ways to weaken or neutralize them. Several approaches seem promising. These include teaching people strategies to control their violent impulses and deal with relationship conflicts more constructively.[62] And they include expanding the scope of men's empathy by implanting the habit of thinking 'How would I feel if someone did this to my mother, my sister, or my daughter?'[63] In all such cases, the idea is to work with human nature, rather than deny it.

To be fair, useful interventions can sometimes emerge from inaccurate views of the world. But that relies on us getting lucky. Odds are we'll hit more bullseyes if we're playing in a well-lit room than a poorly lit one. And if we're serious about making the world a better place, understanding the sources of our problems is a better bet than dogged adherence to ideology. The science writer Angela Saini put it well when she observed that 'The facts are what will empower us to transform society for the better.'[64] Needless to say, the process won't always be fun. As the feminist Gloria Steinem once wrote, 'The truth will set you free, but first it will piss you off.'[65] Getting pissed off, however, is a small price to pay if it means taming our social pathologies.

COLLATERAL DAMAGE IN THE WAR AGAINST SEX DIFFERENCES

There's one last harm to consider. If we deny the existence of sex differences that everyone can see with their own two eyes, most people won't believe us anyway. They'll just stop trusting scientists on politically charged topics. And they'll be right to do so; the scientists won't be being trustworthy!

Three Approaches to Sex Differences

I hope I've persuaded you that both exaggerating and minimizing sex differences can cause significant harm, and thus that we should guard against both temptations. Anything less would be acting like the world's worst tightrope walker, worrying so intently about falling to one side of the wire that they end up falling to the other. Hyping or denying sex differences distorts the science, and distorting the science inevitably has costs.

But even if we get the differences right, we've still got another issue to contend with: What should we do about them? In Chapter 1, I introduced three possible answers to this question, which I called *gender-role traditionalism*, *gender-role progressivism*, and *gender-role individualism*. Let's now explore these three 'isms' in greater depth.

GENDER-ROLE TRADITIONALISM

This first ism is also the oldest, and until recently, was the only game in town. Gender-role traditionalism involves both an empirical claim and an ethical one. The empirical claim is that men and women are naturally very different: as different as night and day or as Mars and Venus. The ethical claim is that men and women *should* be very different. Deviations from traditional gender roles go against nature, harming individuals and society as a whole. We should therefore seek to uphold these roles in every sphere of life.

Consider, for instance, children's toys. According to gender-role traditionalists, boys and girls naturally gravitate toward different toys because boys and girls are naturally different. And not only do kids' toy choices *reveal* their inborn preferences, they help guide the development of sex-appropriate interests and skills. It's weird for girls to play with toy trucks or guns, and even weirder for boys to play with dolls. It can warp their minds and confuse them, and thus shouldn't be encouraged. On the contrary, it should be strongly *dis*couraged.

Next, consider occupational gender gaps: the fact, for example, that more men than women go into maths-heavy STEM fields, whereas more women than men stay at home with the kids.[66] To gender-role traditionalists, such gaps are products of natural differences between the sexes, and are therefore right and proper. In fact, if anything, the gaps should be larger, because decades of feminist activism and affirmative action for women have distorted the natural sex ratios in traditionally male fields, such that too many women are in them.

I felt slightly apprehensive writing the last three paragraphs, because I know they could be quoted out of context and made to look like my own views: something that could potentially land me in a lot of hot water. In contrast, I'm not the slightest bit apprehensive about being quoted out of context for the next approach – gender-role progressivism – even though I disagree with that one too. This highlights an important reality, namely that although gender-role traditionalism is far from dead and buried, it no longer has much institutional power, at least in the developed world. There's a new boss calling the shots.

GENDER-ROLE PROGRESSIVISM

The second approach is, in many ways, the mirror image of the first. Like its traditionalist counterpart, gender-role progressivism involves both an empirical claim and an ethical one: an 'is' and an 'ought'. The empirical claim is that the sexes barely differ, and that to the extent that they do, the differences are almost entirely products of discrimination and sexist socialization. The ethical claim is that, given their unjust origins, traditional sex differences ought to be eliminated. Indeed, if anything, they should be reversed to make up for past wrongs.

Gender-role progressivism can be seen in various areas of life. To start with, it can be seen in many parents' uneasy relationship with their children's toy preferences. As far as gender-role progressives are concerned, boys and girls should be no more likely to play with gender-typical toys than gender-atypical ones. More than that, some progressive parents would seem to prefer that their children go with the gender-*atypical* options. As one four-year-old girl said during a psychology study, when left with just a toy truck to play with, 'My mommy would want me to play with this, but I don't want to.'[67] This was in the 1990s, incidentally, so the trend is nothing new. In fact, even in the 1990s, it was nothing new. Right-on parents have been trying to rewrite their children's preferences – and wrecking their children's birthdays – since at least the 1970s.

Gender-role progressivism can also be detected in many people's discomfort with occupational sex differences. This has become a major policy issue in the West, with many millions of dollars devoted each year to trying to shrink the gaps. Strictly speaking, the goal of these efforts isn't a 50:50 sex ratio in every field. If that were the case, policymakers and activists would be just as worried that more women than men go into the social sciences, health sciences, and humanities as they are that more men than women go into computer science, engineering, and physics – *and* they'd be just as worried that more men than women work as garbage collectors as they are that more men than women are CEOs. Clearly, they're not nearly as worried. This tells us that the implicit goal isn't 50% men and 50% women in every field; it's *at least* 50% women in every *desirable* field. This is a good example of the fact that gender-role progressivism isn't necessarily opposed to sex differences in every instance, but is primarily opposed to traditional sex differences and those that favour men.

The progressive approach to gender is a much more recent arrival than its traditionalist counterpart. Indeed, to a large extent, it's a rebellion against gender-role traditionalism. And it's been an extremely successful rebellion, because although it often presents itself as David to the traditionalists' Goliath, in many ways, it's now the status quo.

GENDER-ROLE INDIVIDUALISM

The third and final approach to dealing with sex differences is a very different *type* of approach. Unlike the first two, gender-role individualism doesn't take a position on either the magnitude of the differences, or the extent to which they're shaped by nature or nurture. *Proponents* of gender-role individualism may take such positions, of course, but the approach itself is neutral with respect to these questions. Furthermore, unlike the other approaches, gender-role individualism doesn't take a stand on whether sex differences should be larger, smaller, or exactly as they are today. Rather than aiming for any particular sex ratio in any area, the approach holds simply that we should establish a fair and level playing field, then let the sex ratios set themselves as an aggregate effect of people making informed choices about what they want to do.[68] In other words, it focuses on the process rather than the outcome.

My favourite way to capture the essence of gender-role individualism is with a four-word phrase: Let people be themselves! A less elegant but more precise formulation would be this: Let people be themselves as long as they don't harm others. Why? Because this is the policy that most strongly upholds two fundamental values, namely well-being and freedom.

To see how gender-role individualism would play out in practice, let's return to our two familiar themes: kids' toys and adults' careers. In the toy department, gender-role individualists would be equally aghast at the traditionalist and progressive approaches. Their sympathies in both cases would lie with the kids, some of whom have control-freak adults trying to push them *into* traditional gender roles, and some of whom have control-freak adults trying to push them out of them. The individualists' alternative would be to let kids know all the options, but ultimately to accept their choices. From this perspective, both the traditionalists and the progressives need to learn to live and let live: Traditionalists need to learn to live with gender-atypical behaviour in their children; progressives need to learn to live with gender-typical behaviour.

And what applies to toys applies as well in other areas. The workplace is a good example. As we've seen, traditionalists hold that we should accept or even enlarge occupational gender gaps, whereas progressives hold that we should shrink or even reverse them, at least in desirable professions where men outnumber women. Gender-role individualists, on the other hand, offer a Third Way: the idea that we should do everything we reasonably can to rid the workplace of bias and barriers, but then respect people's right to make their own decisions. Striving for any particular sex ratio in any field effectively involves making choices about who other people should be and what they should do with their lives. But how is this anyone's business other than those people themselves? To the gender-role individualist, the answer is simple: It's not.

Who's Right?

How does the science inform the debate over how to handle sex differences? In an important sense, it doesn't, because the debate is ultimately about values rather than facts. That said, the science of sex differences can help us to evaluate the empirical claims associated with the three approaches, and the probable effects of their implementation.

The first thing to say is that the science clashes with the empirical commitments of both gender-role traditionalism and gender-role progressivism. Contrary to gender-role traditionalists, sex differences in our species are not enormous. They're definitely not Mars-and-Venus differences. For that reason, the insistence that men and women adhere to traditional gender roles inevitably means that many men and women will be forced into roles that don't suit them, or stigmatized for bucking the trend. Not only does this impinge on individual freedom, but it's almost certainly not conducive to happiness.

However, it's not only gender-role traditionalism that butts heads with the modern science. For gender-role progressives, gender gaps are direct evidence of discrimination and sexist socialization. The unstated assumption is that, in the absence of these social factors, the gaps would simply fall away. But this only follows from an extreme Nurture-Only position on the origins of human sex differences: a position that's all but ruled out by the science. As we've seen, sex differences in our species are common, and are not just products of bias and socialization. Many have their roots in the million-year journey of human evolutionary history. As such, short of castrating boys or forcing girls to take testosterone supplements, some common sex differences might never be fully eradicated. This, in turn, implies that eliminating societal gender gaps would come with a hefty price tag. To eliminate gender gaps in occupational choice, for instance, some people would have to be nudged, bribed, manipulated, pressured, or strong-armed into careers less in line with their preferences and talents. This seems like a bad idea; people are surely going to be happier if they follow their own preferences than if they follow policymakers' ideas about what they ought to do – especially given that the policymakers seem less concerned with individual happiness than with simply shrinking the gaps.[69]

In addition to these empirical missteps, gender-role traditionalists and gender-role progressives make several ethical ones. Most notably, both are prone to the naturalistic fallacy. Gender-role traditionalists assume that sex differences are natural, and therefore that they're good. Gender-role progressives assume that sex differences are *bad*, and therefore that they're not natural – or they assume that the *absence* of sex differences is natural, and therefore that the *absence* of sex differences is good, and that that's what we ought to strive for. But all these positions rest on the assumption that what's natural is necessarily good, which, as we've seen, is entirely unwarranted.[70]

As well as committing the naturalistic fallacy, both approaches have an authoritarian streak: One wants to push people *into* traditional gender roles; the other wants to push people out of them. As noted, though, both options are likely to diminish the happiness of the significant minority of individuals who don't fit with the busybodies' template.[71] And even if this weren't the case – even if everyone would be happier if they followed the busybodies' prescriptions – there's still another issue: freedom. Adults should have the right to decide what they want to do and to risk making mistakes. As long as they're adequately informed, and as long as they're not being coerced or causing harm, it's surely no one else's business how they live their lives, any more than it's anyone else's business who they marry or what paintings they hang on their walls. Whether one conforms to or defies traditional gender roles should be up to the individual, not up to activists or policymakers. This is a mindset, perhaps unsurprisingly, that doesn't come naturally to most activists or policymakers. But why should their preferences regarding the overall shape of society take precedence over individuals' preferences regarding their own lives?

Stress-Testing Gender-Role Individualism

> I believe in equal opportunities for women and men . . . I believe feminism is grounded in supporting the choices of women even if we wouldn't make certain choices for ourselves.
>
> Roxane Gay (2014), p.xii

> The idea that we won't be equal until women start making the same choices as men is, frankly, sexist.
>
> Helen Pluckrose on Twitter/X

Does this leave us with gender-role individualism by default? It doesn't. Critics of the individualist approach have two main arguments up their sleeves. The first is that people – women in particular – aren't genuinely free to make their own choices. After all, the preferences that guide those choices are shaped by social forces. It's impossible to step outside our social conditioning and get in touch with our real selves, because there *are* no real selves. There's only what society has made us – and why should we passively accept the way society happens to make us today?

The philosopher Janet Radcliffe Richards provided a powerful retort to this argument in her book *The Sceptical Feminist*.[72] It's true, she notes, that people's preferences are shaped *in part* by social forces. How could it be otherwise? But that doesn't mean that their preferences are illegitimate or not really their own. We need to avoid the trap of discounting people's preferences just because we don't approve of what they prefer. The only reasonable sense in which social forces could take away our freedom to choose is if people aren't aware of all the options, or if they're aware but face significant barriers – external or internal – that prevent them from pursuing the options that most appeal to them. The solution, then, is to do two things: inform and empower. Let people know all the options, then give them the tools to strive for the ones they want. After that, we should leave people to make their own choices, and let the cards fall where they may.

The second worry that people have about the let-people-be-themselves approach to life is that, as nice as it sounds in principle, in practice it amounts to a complacent acquiescence to the gender status quo. This is a problem, argue the critics, because the gender status quo isn't just a product of people being themselves; to a greater or lesser extent, it's a product of social pressure and sex-based injustice. If we overlook this, we'll never confront these social evils, which all but guarantees we'll never root them out.

This concern is perfectly reasonable given our long history of anti-female sexism. But it rests on a misunderstanding. Gender-role individualism doesn't imply that the sex differences we see today are necessarily fine and dandy. On the contrary, there are several reasons that even the most die-hard individualist might hope to see them change.

First, if a sex difference is created or amplified by unjust bias or barriers, then we should want to see that difference disappear. To illustrate, if the sex difference in height were a result of parents feeding their sons more than their daughters, we'd clearly want to eradicate that injustice, in the process eliminating the difference. Note, however, that the problem wouldn't be the sex difference per se, but rather the discrimination that produced it. After all, in the real world, no sane person wants to remedy the height difference, because we all know that it's *not* a product of discrimination.

Importantly, this argument could equally well push us in the opposite direction: If the *absence* of a sex difference were maintained by unjust bias and barriers, we should want to see *that* change, and see the original difference restored. For example, if men and women were the same height, but we discovered that this was because parents were starving their sons or putting their daughters on the rack, we'd want to rectify the injustice and rehabilitate the natural difference – not because what's natural is necessarily good, but because starving or mutilating people is necessarily bad.

A second reason we might hope to see a sex difference vanish is if it causes unnecessary harm. The sex difference in proneness to violence is my go-to example. Men are naturally more violent than women, and male violence is the cause of much needless suffering in the world. We therefore have every right and every reason to stifle it, in the process narrowing the sex difference. Again, though, the rationale for this isn't that *sex differences* are bad; it's that *violence* is bad. After all, another way to narrow the sex difference would be to ensure that women are as violent as men. But that wouldn't make the world a better place; it'd make it a worse one.

As with the earlier argument, this one could equally well push us in the opposite direction: In principle, we might seek to artificially *magnify* sex differences if doing so would reduce unnecessary suffering. Importantly, though, whether aiming to shrink or magnify any sex difference, this would not be inconsistent with gender-role individualism. That's because gender-role individualism is not the view that anyone should be allowed to do anything; it's the view that anyone should be allowed to do anything, *as long as it's not inherently harmful to others*.

What's So Terrible About Sex Differences Anyway?

To the extent that the gender status quo is inherently harmful or a product of injustice, intervention is a moral no-brainer. To the extent that it's not, though, what should we do? Again, the science of sex differences can't directly answer this, as it's a matter of values rather than facts. What it can do, however, is jump-start important discussions by raising questions we might otherwise overlook.

One such question is this: In the absence of harm or injustice, are sex differences necessarily a problem? According to Janet Radcliffe Richards, the answer is simple: No. 'No one', she observes, 'sees anything to complain about when countries have different national dresses, or tribes are skilled in different crafts, and equally there is nothing inherently evil about men's and women's having such differences of activity and appearance either.'[73]

Not only are sex differences not necessarily a problem, in some cases, they might even say something good about society. Throughout this book, we've encountered various examples of the *gender-equality paradox*: the unexpected finding that differences between the sexes are often larger in societies with better social indicators – more wealth, more education, more equality between the sexes. This suggests that, rather than being symptoms of a sick or unjust society, sex differences may sometimes be symptoms of the opposite: a relatively *healthy* one in which people are free to be themselves and fulfil their potential – much to the annoyance of those who'd like to abolish sex differences.

Certainly, we're a clever, flexible species, and we could probably figure out how to eliminate sex differences if we wanted to. But why would we want to? We could wear shoes that are two sizes too small if we wanted to, but why would we want to do that? Our feet would hurt, and unless we had a gun to our head, we'd quickly give up the practice. Likewise, eliminating sex differences would likely require coercive interventions, and the minute we took our foot off the gas, we'd see instinctive drift back to the usual pattern of real but modest sex differences.

So, to return to our earlier question, if a sex difference isn't due to bias or barriers, and if it isn't inherently harmful, what's the problem? Why not let people be themselves, rather than making them miserable by trying to thwart human nature?

Sex at the Crossroads

> [I]n our work and in our living, we must recognize that difference is a reason for celebration and growth, rather than a reason for destruction.
>
> Audre Lorde (2004), p.86

The topic of sex differences is unique in its power to divide opinion. On the one hand, it's among the most fascinating topics in the human sciences. On the other, it's one of the most fraught, as it intersects with difficult questions about tradition, freedom, and women's rights. For every person who's entranced by the topic, there's another who's deeply unsettled by it or even appalled.

Despite the resistance the field has often faced, though, scientists have made considerable headway in unravelling the mysteries of sex differences. Not only that, but we've made considerable headway in thinking through the ethical implications of this growing body of knowledge. Here are my picks for the Top Ten conclusions, both empirical and ethical, that have emerged from the work in this area.

1. A century of research paints a clear picture: Men and women are different.
2. Most psychological sex differences in our species are relatively modest. Some, however, are large, especially among the minority at the extremes. And even small sex differences can often have important societal consequences.
3. Most well-established sex differences aren't due solely to nurture; they're due to nature as well. Indeed, sometimes sex differences appear *despite* nurture, rather than because of it – and sometimes nurture makes sex differences *smaller* than they'd otherwise be, rather than larger.
4. Most sex differences evolved because what's adaptive for men differs from what's adaptive for women. The main reason it differs is that men can potentially have a higher number of offspring.
5. Studying sex differences can lead to misunderstandings and problems. But the solution isn't to lie about the differences; it's to tell the truth carefully. Aside from anything else, the *denial* of sex differences can lead to misunderstandings and problems too.
6. We're not necessarily stuck with what nature gave us. Our genes nudge us in certain directions, but we can often nudge right back.
7. In some cases, however, eliminating sex differences might be impossible, at least without draconian interventions that do more harm than good. We may have to learn to live with the differences.
8. This isn't necessarily a bad thing, though, because sex differences aren't always a sign of social pathology. In fact, in some cases, they may be a sign of social health. The best evidence for this is the gender-equality paradox: the finding that many sex differences are larger, rather than smaller, in wealthier, healthier, more gender-equal nations.
9. We should treat individuals as individuals, rather than as

instantiations of the statistical properties of the groups to which they belong. In other words, we should judge people by the content of their characters, not by their sex chromosomes.

10. We should do all we can to eliminate bias and barriers of every kind. Having done so, however, we should respect people's decisions about their own lives and how they want to live them.

Of course, nothing sits still in science, and future work may necessitate subtle tweaks or even major revisions to the ideas presented in this book. I'm quite confident, though, that the science is sufficiently advanced that the broad outline is substantially correct. And regardless of what future research turns up, I have no doubt that the best way to make the world a better place is to strive for an accurate view of the world, even if it's initially uncomfortable. As long as we keep our ethical wits about us, the science of sex differences poses no threat to women – or to men. The key is to strive for a world where uncoerced differences are celebrated rather than pathologized; where people are accepted and appreciated whether they embrace gender norms or defy them; and where the guiding ethos is that, wherever possible, we should let people be themselves.

Appendix

Effect Sizes for the Standard-Issue Sex Differences

Sex Difference*	Effect Size (Cohen's *d*)†
Physical Sex Differences	
Height ♂	1.5–2
Upper-body strength ♂	2–3
Voice pitch ♀	4
Sexual Psychology	
Partner sex preference (whether one is primarily attracted to men vs women)	2–3
Sex drive ♂	0.5–0.8
Interest in casual sex (sociosexuality) ♂	0.5–0.8
Interest in sexual variety ♂	0.5
Mate Preferences	
Good looks in a long-term mate ♂	0.5
Age preferences	2
Financial prospects in a long-term mate ♀	0.8
Social status in a long-term mate ♀	0.2–0.5
Ambition and industriousness in a long-term mate ♀	0.5

Antisocial Behaviour	
Verbal aggression ♂	0.2
Physical aggression ♂	0.5
Violent crime ♂	1
Homicide ♂	2.5
Indirect aggression ♀ ?	0–0.2
Anger	0
Rough-and-tumble play ♂	0.8
Risk-taking ♂	0.5
Sexual aggression ♂	0.5
Rape ♂	2.5
Verbal partner aggression ♀	0.2
Physical partner aggression	0
Severe physical partner aggression ♂	0.5
Partner homicide ♂	1
Pair Bonding and Parenting	
Sexual jealousy ♂ vs emotional jealousy ♀	0.8
Parental inclinations ♀	?
Personality	
Neuroticism ♀	0.5
Agreeableness ♀	0.5
Extraversion ♀ ?	0–0.2
Conscientiousness ♀ ?	0–0.2
Openness ♀ ?	0–0.2
Career-Related Interests	
Interest in people ♀ vs interest in things ♂	1
Interest in specific occupations	1.5

Cognitive Sex Differences	
Intelligence/IQ	0
Academic achievement ♀	0.2
Verbal abilities ♀	0.2
Spatial abilities ♂	0.2–0.8
Mental rotation ♂	0.5–0.8
Maths abilities ♀ ♂ ?	0–0.2
Systemizing ♂	0.8–1.2
Empathizing ♀	0.8–1
Toy Preferences	
Preference for male-typical toys ♂	1–2
Preference for female-typical toys ♀	0.8–1.5
Mental Health and Related Variables	
Self-esteem ♂	0.2
Body image ♂	0.5
Depression ♀	0.2–0.5
Fear ♀	0.5–1
Anxiety ♀	0.5
Pain threshold/tolerance ♂	0.5–1

* ♀ means females score higher; ♂ means males do. A question mark means it's unclear there's any difference.

† According to a common convention, 0.2 is a small effect, 0.5 a medium effect, and 0.8 a large effect (see Chapter 2 for details). Effect size estimates vary somewhat from study to study, so, to avoid false precision, I've rounded most of them to one of those values. My main source for the estimates is Archer (2019).

Notes

1 A Can of Worms

1 Wright (1994).
2 Stewart-Williams (2018).
3 Stewart-Williams and Thomas (2013a).
4 Löckenhoff et al. (2014).
5 L. Ellis et al. (2023).
6 Jussim (2012).
7 Halpern et al. (2011); Swim (1994).
8 Buss (1989); Buss and Schmitt (1993).
9 Stewart-Williams (2018); Stewart-Williams and Thomas (2013a, 2013b).
10 Stewart-Williams and Thomas (2013a, 2013b).
11 Stewart-Williams and Thomas (2013a, 2013b).
12 Stewart-Williams and Halsey (2021).
13 Stewart-Williams and Thomas (2013a, 2013b).
14 Hare-Mustin and Marecek (1988).
15 Del Giudice (2023a); von Hippel and Buss (2017).
16 Stewart-Williams (2018).
17 Geher and Gambacorta (2010).
18 Stewart-Williams and Thomas (2013a).
19 Del Giudice (2023a); Eagly (1995).
20 Eagly (1995).
21 Stewart-Williams and Thomas (2013b).
22 Gamma bias: Seager and Barry (2019a). Delta bias: Seager and Barry (2020).
23 Stewart-Williams et al. (2021); Stewart-Williams et al. (2024); Stewart-Williams et al. (2022a, 2022b).
24 Bendixen and Kennair (2017); Stemple and Meyer (2014).
25 Netchaeva et al. (2022).
26 T. Reynolds et al. (2020); Stewart-Williams et al. (2022a, 2022b).
27 Haidt (2012); Lukianoff and Haidt (2018).
28 Stewart-Williams and Halsey (2021).
29 L'hospital (2022).
30 C.J. Clark et al. (2023); Duarte et al. (2015).
31 Le Bon (1879), cited in Gould (1981), p.104.
32 Slaves: Bonaparte (1816), cited in Las Cases (1836), p.240. Machines: Bonaparte (1817), cited in Gourgaud (1932), p.118.
33 Stewart-Williams (2010, 2018).
34 Halpern (2012).
35 Stewart-Williams (2010).
36 Susan Pinker (2008).
37 de Beauvoir (1949/1953).

38 Halpern (2012), p.166.
39 Halpern (2012); M.R. Reynolds et al. (2022).
40 Halpern (2012).
41 Liddon and Barry (2021); Stemple and Meyer (2014).
42 Fine (2010, 2017).
43 Stewart-Williams and Halsey (2022).
44 H. Edwards et al. (2024); Liddon and Barry (2021); Reinier et al. (2023).
45 Zucker and Prendergast (2020).
46 Ceci and Williams (2011); Stewart-Williams and Halsey (2021, 2022); W.M. Williams and Ceci (2015).
47 Stewart-Williams and Halsey (2022).
48 Herlitz et al. (2024); Schmitt et al. (2008); Stoet and Geary (2018).
49 Stewart-Williams and Halsey (2021).
50 Radcliffe Richards (1980); Stewart-Williams and Halsey (2021, 2022).

2 What's the Difference?

1 Herrera et al. (2013).
2 Butler (1990).
3 A.E. Martin et al. (2024).
4 Dogs: Carballo et al. (2015). Elephants: McComb et al. (2014).
5 M. Andersson (1994).
6 Sax (2002).
7 Evolution of two sexes (anisogamy): Lehtonen and Parker (2014); Parker et al. (1972). Evolution of sex ratios: R.A. Fisher (1930).
8 Stock (2021).
9 Stewart-Williams and Thomas (2013b).
10 Halpern (2012).
11 Cohen (1977).
12 Stewart-Williams (2020); Stewart-Williams and Thomas (2013a, 2013b).
13 Magnusson (2022).
14 Archer (2004).
15 Stewart-Williams and Thomas (2013b).
16 Lippa (2009).
17 Stewart-Williams and Thomas (2013a, 2013b).
18 Lassek and Gaulin (2009).
19 Rosenfield et al. (2020).
20 Davis and Hines (2020).
21 Su et al. (2009).
22 Archer (2019).
23 Stewart-Williams and Thomas (2013a, 2013b).
24 Archer (2019).
25 Stewart-Williams and Halsey (2021); Stewart-Williams and Thomas (2013b).
26 Hyde and Linn (1988).
27 Petersen (2018); Reilly et al. (2019); Stoet and Geary (2013).
28 Stewart-Williams and Thomas (2013a, 2013b).
29 Durrant (2019).
30 Height, running speed: Lehre et al. (2009). Brain parameters: Ritchie et al. (2018); Wierenga et al. (2022). Energy expenditure: Halsey et al. (2022). Grades: Lehre et al. (2009). Aggression: Archer and Mehdikhani (2003). Risk-taking: Thöni and Volk (2021). Mate preferences: Archer and Mehdikhani (2003). Personality traits: Borkenau et al. (2013). Occupational preferences: Su et al. (2009). Specific cognitive abilities: Hedges and Nowell (1995); Strand et al. (2006). General cognitive ability:

Arden and Plomin (2006); Deary et al. (2003); W. Johnson et al. (2008).

31 Feingold (1994); Hyde and Mertz (2009); Iliescu et al. (2016).

32 Klein et al. (2022); Lippa (2009).

33 Accidental deaths: Kruger and Nesse (2006). Aggression: Archer (2004); Daly and Wilson (1988); M. Wilson and Daly (1985). Alcohol consumption: Britton et al. (2015). Anxiety disorders and depression: Salk et al. (2017). Crime: Loeber et al. (2015). Disgust sensitivity: Berthold et al. (2025). Fireworks-related injuries: Canner et al. (2014). Homicide rates: Daly and Wilson (1988). Interest in casual sex: Petersen and Hyde (2010). Risk-taking: Byrnes et al. (1999). Road deaths: M. Wilson and Daly (1985). Sexual behaviour: Petersen and Hyde (2010). Spatial ability: Lauer et al. (2019).

34 Conroy-Beam et al. (2015); Del Giudice et al. (2012); Eagly and Revelle (2022).

35 Del Giudice et al. (2012). Note that other studies have found smaller effects; e.g., Rammstedt et al. (2025).

36 Cited in Gordon (2012). Of course, the same multivariate method would also lead to the conclusion that individuals within each sex vary greatly from one another, which somewhat weakens the claim that the sexes are virtually different species. So are many individuals within each sex!

37 Mitchell (2018).

38 N.E. Anderson et al. (2019); Ryali et al. (2024).

39 L. Ellis et al. (2023).

3 Born and Bred

1 Discussed in Eagly (2018); Steven Pinker (2016).

2 Bandura (1977).

3 Bem (1981); Bussey and Bandura (1999); Kohlberg (1966).

4 C.L. Martin and Ruble (2004), p.67.

5 Deaux and Major (1987).

6 Fine (2010).

7 Endendijk et al. (2016); Lytton and Romney (1991).

8 Stewart-Williams (2018).

9 Jussim (2012, 2017).

10 Turkheimer (2000).

11 Plomin et al. (2016).

12 Herlitz et al. (2024); Schmitt et al. (2008); Stoet and Geary (2018). Note that Berggren and Bergh (2025) argue that the gender-equality paradox is a statistical artefact, and that gender equality doesn't predict larger sex differences after all.

13 Schmitt (2015).

14 Attitudes to homosexuality: Hildebrandt and Jäckle (2023). Big Five: Costa et al. (2001); Schmitt et al. (2008). Competitiveness: Markowsky and Beblo (2022). Crying: van Hemert et al. (2011). Depression: Salk et al. (2017). Field of study: Charles and Bradley (2009). Gender gap in caring professions: Block et al. (2025). Gender gap in STEM: Stoet and Geary (2018). Interest in people vs things: Lippa (2010a); Stoet and Geary (2022). Interest in STEM subjects: Charles et al. (2014); Else-Quest et al. (2010); Stoet and Geary (2018). Meat-eating: Hopwood et al. (2024). Mental health: O.L.K. Campbell et

al. (2021). Moral judgements: Atari et al. (2020). Narcissism: Jonason et al. (2020). Negative emotions: Else-Quest et al. (2012); Fischer et al. (2004). Occupational interests and aspirations: Stoet and Geary (2022). Patience: Falk and Hermle (2018). Reading ability: Stoet and Geary (2013). Risk-taking: Falk and Hermle (2018); Mata et al. (2016). Self-confidence: Napp and Breda (2022). Self-esteem: Bleidorn et al. (2016). Spatial ability: Lippa et al. (2010); although see Lauer et al. (2019). Subjective well-being: Guo et al. (2023). Suicide mortality: Alothman and Fogarty (2020). Trust: Falk and Hermle (2018). Values: Falk and Hermle (2018); Schwartz and Rubel-Lifschitz (2009). Violence: Archer (2004); Nivette et al. (2019).

15 Giofrè et al. (2025); Pinho-Gomes et al. (2023); Schmitt (2015).
16 Mate preferences: L. Zhang et al. (2019). Casual sex: Lippa (2009); Schmitt (2005). Intimate partner violence: Archer (2006a). Maths performance: Herlitz et al. (2024); Stoet and Geary (2013).
17 Stewart-Williams and Halsey (2021).
18 Herlitz et al. (2024); Stewart-Williams and Halsey (2021).
19 K.M. Cook et al. (2022).
20 Jiang et al. (2020).
21 A. Campbell (2005).
22 Darwin (1871).
23 Archer (2019); Geary (2021).
24 Mate preferences: Buss et al. (2001). Occupational interests: Lippa et al. (2014); Su et al. (2009).
25 Money (1975); Money and Ehrhardt (1972).
26 Colapinto (2000); Diamond and Sigmundson (1997).
27 Reiner (2004); Reiner and Gearhart (2004).
28 Berenbaum and Hines (1992); Kung et al. (2024); Pasterski et al. (2005).
29 Beltz et al. (2011).
30 Hines et al. (2016); Pasterski et al. (2005).
31 Hooven (2021).
32 Hooven (2021).
33 Archer (2019); L. Ellis et al. (2023).
34 Roser et al. (2024).
35 Schmitt and International Sexuality Description Project (2003).
36 Krumer and Musau (2023).
37 Stewart-Williams (2018).
38 M. Andersson (1994).
39 Stewart-Williams and Thomas (2013a).
40 Eagly and Wood (1999); Wood and Eagly (2012).
41 Kenrick and Keefe (1992b), p.120.

4 Nature's Blueprint

1 M. Andersson (1994).
2 Darwin (1871).
3 M. Andersson (1994).
4 Darwin (1860).
5 M. Andersson (1994).
6 R.A. Fisher (1930).
7 Hamilton and Zuk (1982).
8 Zahavi (1975).
9 M. Andersson (1994); Darwin (1871).
10 Darwin (1871).
11 Judson (2002).
12 M. Andersson (1994).

13 M. Andersson (1994).
14 R.D. Alexander et al. (1979).
15 Stewart-Williams and Thomas (2013a).
16 Janicke et al. (2016).
17 Clutton-Brock and Parker (1995); Smuts and Smuts (1993).
18 Smuts (1996).
19 Thornhill (1980).
20 Gowaty (2004).
21 Bateman (1948).
22 Gowaty et al. (2012).
23 Daly and Wilson (1983); Trivers (1985).
24 Johns (1969), p.664, cited in Trivers (1985), p.217.
25 Trivers (1972, 1985). Trivers's theory was foreshadowed by G.C. Williams (1966).
26 Clutton-Brock (1991).
27 Clutton-Brock and Vincent (1991).
28 M. Andersson (1994).
29 Daly and Wilson (1983).
30 Clutton-Brock (1991).
31 M. Andersson (1994); Clutton-Brock and Parker (1992).
32 Fine (2017), p.14.
33 Sociological: L. Andersson et al. (2023). Anthropological: Betzig (2012); J. Brown et al. (2009). Genetic: Labuda et al. (2010).
34 Stewart-Williams and Thomas (2013a, 2013b).
35 R.D. Martin (1990).
36 Kaplan (1994).
37 Hrdy (2009).
38 Hawkes et al. (1989); Hrdy (2009); Sear and Mace (2008).
39 Marlowe (2000).
40 Marlowe (2003a).
41 Stewart-Williams (2018); Stewart-Williams and Thomas (2013a).
42 Marlowe (2003b); Murdock (1967).
43 Stewart-Williams (2018); Stewart-Williams and Thomas (2013a).
44 G.F. Miller (2000).
45 Hone et al. (2012); Jones and Hunter (1993).
46 Puts (2010).
47 Buss (1988); T. Reynolds et al. (2018).
48 Stewart-Williams and Thomas (2013a, 2013b).
49 Betzig (1986).
50 Ross et al. (2023).

5 Sex on the Brain

1 K. Quinn (2015).
2 Archer (2019).
3 Baumeister et al. (2002); Frankenbach et al. (2022).
4 Frankenbach et al. (2022).
5 Frankenbach et al. (2022).
6 Attitudes to casual sex: Oliver and Hyde (1993); Petersen and Hyde (2010). Willingness to engage in casual sex: Lippa (2009); Schmitt (2005); Simpson and Gangestad (1991).
7 Time to consent: Buss and Schmitt (1993); Schmitt and International Sexuality Description Project (2003). Sexual regret: Bendixen et al. (2017).
8 Buss and Schmitt (1993); Schmitt and International Sexuality Description Project (2003).
9 Buss (2016); Warach et al. (2024).
10 Buss (2016).
11 Buss and Schmitt (2011).
12 Symons (1979).
13 B.J. Ellis and Symons (1990).

14 Betzig (1986).
15 Stewart-Williams and Thomas (2013a).
16 R.D. Clark and Hatfield (1989).
17 R.D. Clark (1990); Greitemeyer (2005); Voracek et al. (2005).
18 Baranowski and Hecht (2015); Hald and Høgh-Olesen (2010).
19 Hald and Høgh-Olesen (2010).
20 Baranowski and Hecht (2015).
21 Fine (2017), pp 55–6.
22 Stewart-Williams and Thomas (2013a).
23 Pornography: Petersen and Hyde (2010). Romance novels: Fisher and Cox (2010); Salmon (2012); Symons (1979).
24 Salmon and Symons (2003), p.4.
25 Fein and Schneider (1995); Strauss (2005).
26 Hruska (2015).
27 Symons (1979).
28 Behavioural experiments: Snowden et al. (2024). Brain scans: Putkinen et al. (2023)
29 Haselton and Buss (2000).
30 Buss (2024).
31 Symons (1979).
32 Saad and Gill (2003).
33 Symons (1979).
34 Daly and Wilson (1983).
35 Sohn (2017).
36 Stewart-Williams (2018); Symons (1979).
37 Cited in Perry (2022).
38 Sex drive: Frankenbach et al. (2022). Casual sex: Lippa (2009); Schmitt (2005). Sexual variety: Schmitt and International Sexuality Description Project (2003).
39 Kennair et al. (2009); Thomas et al. (2024).
40 Schmitt (2005).
41 Warwick (2018), p.80.
42 Dixson (2012).
43 Mice: Kinsey et al. (1953), p.669. Fruit flies: Cazalé-Debat et al. (2024).
44 Smuts (1985).
45 Deaner et al. (2005).
46 Lukas and Huchard (2014).
47 Stewart-Williams (2018).
48 Hrdy (1981).
49 Smuts (1985).
50 Buss (2016).
51 Gangestad and Simpson (2000); although see Buss (2024).
52 Betzig (2012); J. Brown et al. (2009).
53 Stewart-Williams (2018).
54 LeVay (2011).
55 Herdt (1981).
56 LeVay (2011).
57 Langstrom et al. (2010).
58 Langstrom et al. (2010).
59 Ganna et al. (2019).
60 Willoughby et al. (2019).
61 E.O. Wilson (1975, 1978).
62 Hamilton (1964).
63 Wright (1994).
64 Bobrow and Bailey (2001).
65 Vasey et al. (2007).
66 Nila et al. (2018).
67 Camperio-Ciani et al. (2004).
68 Zietsch et al. (2021).
69 Felesina and Zietsch (2024); E.M. Miller (2000).
70 Wrangham (2019).
71 Swift-Gallant et al. (2023).
72 Hooven (2021).
73 Frisén et al. (2009); Meyer-Bahlburg et al. (2008).

74 Swift-Gallant (2019).
75 Blanchard (2018).
76 Ablaza et al. (2022); Kabátek and Blanchard (2024).
77 Blanchard (2018).

6 Sex, Love, and Rock 'n' Roll

1 Buss et al. (1990); Lippa (2007); Schwarz and Hassebrauck (2012).
2 Stewart-Williams and Thomas (2013a, 2013b).
3 Dittrich and Rödel (2023).
4 Kralj-Fišer et al. (2025).
5 Godfrey-Smith et al. (2022).
6 Brennan et al. (2009).
7 Kamei and Glabe (2003); Nadeau (2017).
8 Janzen (1977).
9 Buss et al. (1990); Lippa (2007); Schwarz and Hassebrauck (2012).
10 Power et al. (2013).
11 Buss (1989); Buss and Schmitt (1993).
12 Malinowski (1929), p.292.
13 Scelza (2013).
14 Buss and Schmitt (1993); Kenrick et al. (1990).
15 Buss and Schmitt (1993).
16 Buss and Schmitt (1993); Kenrick et al. (1993); Kenrick et al. (1990).
17 G.F. Miller (2000).
18 Döring and Mohseni (2022).
19 Stewart-Williams and Thomas (2013a).
20 Buss and Schmitt (1993).
21 Buss et al. (1990); Stewart-Williams (2020).
22 Darwin (1871), p.385.
23 Schwarz and Hassebrauck (2012).
24 Buss (2016); Feingold (1990).
25 Buss et al. (2001); Walter et al. (2020).
26 cf. Coontz (2005).
27 Buss (1989).
28 Lippa (2007); Thomas et al. (2020); Walter et al. (2020); although see Pillsworth (2008).
29 Walter et al. (2020); L. Zhang et al. (2019).
30 Ford and Beach (1951), p.86.
31 Gottschall et al. (2004).
32 Buss (1989); Walter et al. (2020).
33 Kenrick and Keefe (1992a).
34 Kenrick and Keefe (1992a).
35 Buss (1989); Walter et al. (2020).
36 Kenrick and Keefe (1992a).
37 Borgerhoff Mulder (1988).
38 Griffith et al. (2016); Sohn (2016).
39 Wolf (1991), pp 93–4.
40 Kenrick et al. (1995).
41 Kenrick et al. (1996).
42 Muller et al. (2006).
43 Daly and Wilson (1983).
44 Buss (1989); Schwarz and Hassebrauck (2012); Walter et al. (2020).
45 Schwarz and Hassebrauck (2012).
46 Li et al. (2002).
47 Thomas et al. (2020).
48 R.C. Anderson and Klofstad (2012); Jonason and Thomas (2022); Strassberg and English (2015).
49 Hopcroft (2021).
50 Whyte et al. (2016).
51 Stephens-Davidowitz (2022), p.36.
52 Eagly and Wood (1999).
53 Buss (2024); Ong and Wang (2015).
54 Buss et al. (2001).
55 Buss (1989); Walter et al. (2020).
56 Hopcroft (2006); Nettle and Pollet (2008); Pérusse (1993).

57 Hopcroft (2021, 2022); Y. Zhang and Santtila (2022).
58 von Rueden and Jaeggi (2016).
59 Gottschall et al. (2004).
60 Eagly (1987); Wood and Eagly (2002, 2012).
61 Walter et al. (2020); L. Zhang et al. (2019).
62 M. Andersson (1994).
63 L. Ellis (1995).
64 Apostolou (2007); Westermarck (1921).
65 Apostolou (2007).
66 Schlegel and Barry (1991).
67 Lee (1984); Schlegel and Barry (1991).
68 Lee (1984). See also Hart and Pilling (1960); Malinowski (1929).
69 Malinowski (1929); Pillsworth (2008).
70 Darwin (1859).
71 Hrdy (1981), p.18.
72 Darwin (1871); Stewart-Williams and Thomas (2013a).
73 Darwin (1871); Stewart-Williams (2018); Wassiliwizky et al. (2025).
74 Stewart-Williams (2018); Stewart-Williams and Thomas (2013a).
75 Puts (2010).
76 Puts (2010).
77 Lidborg et al. (2022).
78 G.F. Miller (2000).
79 Darwin (1871), p.384.
80 Kowal et al. (2022).
81 Halim et al. (2024).
82 Buss (1988).
83 Hruschka et al. (2011).
84 Halim et al. (2022), p.2176.
85 Stewart-Williams (2018).

7 Breaking Bad

1 Archer (2004); Eagly and Steffen (1986); Maccoby and Jacklin (1974).
2 Kenrick and Sheets (1993).
3 Archer (2004).
4 Archer (2019).
5 Archer (2004); Brebner (2003).
6 Self-control: Knight et al. (2002). Consequences: A. Campbell (2002).
7 Assumption: Kehr et al. (1997). Sexual violence: Macdowall et al. (2013).
8 United Nations Office on Drugs and Crime (2023).
9 Daly and Wilson (1988).
10 Reichert (2019). See also Wood and Eagly (2012).
11 Maccoby and Jacklin (1980).
12 Stewart-Williams (2018).
13 Steven Pinker (2011).
14 Archer (2009).
15 Baillargeon et al. (2007).
16 Maccoby and Jacklin (1980).
17 M. Wilson and Daly (1985).
18 Daly and Wilson (1988).
19 Low (1989).
20 Book et al. (2001).
21 Archer (2009).
22 Archer (2006b).
23 Hooven (2021).
24 Beaver et al. (2016).
25 Daly and Wilson (1990); United Nations Office on Drugs and Crime (2023).
26 M. Wilson and Daly (1985).
27 Archer (2004); Fry (1998); Hess et al. (2010).
28 Buss (2024).
29 Eagly (1987); Wood and Eagly (2002, 2012).

30 Low (1989).
31 Herlitz et al. (2024); Nivette et al. (2019).
32 Archer (2019).
33 Gómez et al. (2021).
34 United Nations Office on Drugs and Crime (2023).
35 M.L. Wilson et al. (2014).
36 Gómez et al. (2021). An exception is infanticide, which is about as common in females as males.
37 Lonsdorf (2017).
38 de Waal (2022).
39 Marley et al. (2022).
40 Summarized in Archer (2019).
41 Le Boeuf and Reiter (1987).
42 Archer (2019).
43 Kanazawa and Still (2000).
44 Daly and Wilson (2001).
45 Byrnes et al. (1999); Charness and Gneezy (2012); Falk and Hermle (2018); Sutter et al. (2019); M. Wilson and Daly (1985).
46 Wikipedia contributors (n.d.).
47 Dares and gambling: M. Wilson and Daly (1985). Crypto: Nyhus et al. (2024). Selfies: Elgan (2019). Emails: Camilleri et al. (2023).
48 M. Wilson and Daly (1985).
49 Pawlowski et al. (2008).
50 Lendrem et al. (2014).
51 R.C. Johnson (1996).
52 Morgenroth et al. (2018).
53 Kruger and Nesse (2006).
54 Byrnes et al. (1999); Mata et al. (2016).
55 Kruger and Nesse (2006).
56 Goldstein (2011).
57 Mata et al. (2016); Rieger et al. (2015).
58 Kids: Kim et al. (2018); Rosen and Peterson (1990). Adults: Kruger and Nesse (2006).
59 Murdock and Provost (1973); Wood and Eagly (2002).
60 Cosmides and Tooby (1992).
61 Apicella et al. (2017); Lew-Levy et al. (2022).
62 Haux et al. (2023).
63 Archer (2006a, 2019).
64 Cited in Haglund (2013).
65 Brownmiller (1975), p.15.
66 Cited in Young (1999), p.112.
67 Buss (2016), pp 276–7.
68 Malamuth (1996).
69 Felson and Cundiff (2014).
70 Felson (2002).
71 Paglia (1990), p.2.
72 Thornhill and Palmer (2000).
73 Thornhill and Palmer (2000).
74 Clutton-Brock and Parker (1995).
75 Smuts (1985, 1996).
76 Stewart-Williams (2010).
77 Benenson (2013); Blake et al. (2018); A. Campbell (1999); Durante et al. (2012); Fisher (2004); T. Reynolds et al. (2018); Sulikowski et al. (2024); Vaillancourt (2013).
78 Buss (1988).
79 A. Campbell (1995).
80 Hrdy (1981).
81 Freeman (2021).

8 Family Matters

1 L. Ellis et al. (2023); Murdock and Provost (1973); Wood and Eagly (2002).
2 Badinter (2010/2011); Reynaud (2004).

3 Bleske-Rechek and Gunseor (2021); Hakim (2000); Rotkirch (2007).
4 Conaboy (2022). For comparable arguments in academic texts, see Badinter (2010/2011); Reynaud (2004).
5 A good example is Sarah Hrdy. Hrdy, who once described herself as a 'feminist sociobiologist', wrote an excellent book called *Mother Nature: Maternal Instincts and How They Shape the Human Species*. Her publicist had heard she was a feminist, so automatically assumed that she'd be arguing against the notion of maternal instincts. The publicist put out a press release to that effect, which she then had to hastily retract.
6 Eagly (1987); Wood and Eagly (2002, 2012).
7 Rhoads (2004).
8 Endendijk et al. (2016).
9 Hakim (2000, 2006).
10 Tiger and Shepher (1975).
11 Hooven (2021).
12 Ehrhardt and Baker (1974); Leveroni and Berenbaum (1998).
13 Clutton-Brock (1991).
14 Janicke et al. (2016).
15 Clutton-Brock (1991).
16 Konerding et al. (2016).
17 Mattson et al. (2001).
18 Hrdy (2000).
19 Kahlenberg and Wrangham (2010).
20 LaFreniere (2011).
21 de Waal (2022).
22 Darwin (1871), p.56.
23 Blakemore (1990, 1998); C.P. Edwards (1993).
24 Fairbanks (1990); Hrdy (2000).
25 G.C. Williams (1975).
26 Hamilton (2001); Ridley (1993); Van Valen (1973).
27 Lehtonen and Parker (2014); Parker et al. (1972).
28 Lehtonen and Parker (2014); Parker et al. (1972).
29 Schärer et al. (2012).
30 Clutton-Brock (1991), p.xiii.
31 Cited in Darwin (1887), p.57.
32 Hames (1988); Marlowe (2000); Stewart-Williams and Thomas (2013a).
33 Geary (2021).
34 Archer (2006b); Gettler et al. (2011); Holmboe et al. (2017).
35 Muller et al. (2008).
36 Clutton-Brock (1991); Stewart-Williams and Thomas (2013a).
37 Alonzo (2012).
38 van Schaik et al. (2022).
39 Bos and Spencer (2024).
40 Daly and Wilson (1988, 1998).
41 Stewart-Williams (2018).
42 Gaulin and Schlegel (1980).
43 Møller and Birkhead (1993).
44 K.G. Anderson (2006).
45 Daly and Wilson (1988); Daly et al. (1982).
46 Daly and Wilson (1988); Saxon (2012); Stewart-Williams (2018).
47 Scelza (2014).
48 Miserable_Sweet_5245 (2024).
49 Origins: Buss et al. (1992); Daly et al. (1982); Symons (1979). Overview: Sagarin et al. (2012).
50 Stewart-Williams (2020).
51 Buss et al. (1992).
52 Stewart-Williams (2020).
53 Bendixen et al. (2015); Sagarin et al. (2012).

54 Kuhle (2011).
55 Betzig (1989); Buss (2016).
56 Bendixen et al. (2015); Buunk et al. (1996).
57 Buss et al. (1999); Scelza et al. (2020).
58 Scelza et al. (2020).
59 Scelza (2014).

9 Sex at the Frontier

1 Soto (2021).
2 Anglim et al. (2022); Costa et al. (2001); Kajonius and Johnson (2018); Seifert et al. (2024).
3 Verbree et al. (2023).
4 Del Giudice (2023b).
5 Kajonius and Johnson (2018).
6 Costa et al. (2001); Lippa (2008); Schmitt et al. (2008).
7 De Bolle et al. (2015).
8 Herlitz et al. (2024).
9 King et al. (2008); Latzman et al. (2015).
10 Benenson et al. (2021).
11 Lubinski et al. (2023); Su et al. (2009).
12 Thorndike (1911).
13 Beltz et al. (2011); Berenbaum and Beltz (2011); Frisén et al. (2009).
14 53 out of 53: Lippa (2010b). 80 out of 80: Stoet and Geary (2022).
15 Lippa (2010a); Stoet and Geary (2022).
16 Stewart-Williams and Halsey (2022).
17 Geary (2021).
18 Stewart-Williams and Halsey (2021).
19 Halpern (2012); Iliescu et al. (2016); Jensen (1998).
20 Flynn (2012); Jensen (1998).
21 Halpern (2012).
22 Voyer and Voyer (2014).
23 Hyde and Linn (1988); Petersen (2018).
24 Lauer et al. (2019); Maeda and Yoon (2013); Voyer et al. (1995).
25 Hyde and Mertz (2009); Stoet and Geary (2013).
26 Makel et al. (2016); Wai et al. (2010).
27 Del Giudice (2023b).
28 T.R. Coyle et al. (2015); Park et al. (2007).
29 Breda and Napp (2019); Wang et al. (2013).
30 Baron-Cohen (2003).
31 Rosenthal and Jacobson (1968).
32 Hyde (2005).
33 Walton and Spencer (2009), p.1132.
34 Hartley and Sutton (2013).
35 Halpern (2012), p.xxi.
36 Hartley and Sutton (2013).
37 Robinson and Lubienski (2011).
38 Stereotype accuracy: Jussim (2012, 2017). Girls doing as well or better in maths and science: Hyde and Mertz (2009); Stoet and Geary (2013).
39 Jussim and Harber (2005).
40 Koch et al. (2015); Rubinstein et al. (2018).
41 Finnigan and Corker (2016); Flore et al. (2019); Inglis and O'Hagan (2022).
42 Flore and Wicherts (2015); Shewach et al. (2019); Stoet and Geary (2012).
43 Flore and Wicherts (2015).
44 Moore and Johnson (2011); P.C. Quinn and Liben (2008); although see D.I. Miller and Halpern (2014).
45 Makel et al. (2016); Wai et al. (2010).
46 Xu et al. (2017).
47 Academic performance: Voyer and Voyer (2014). Spatial abilities: Lippa

et al. (2010); although see Hoffman et al. (2011).
48 Stoet and Geary (2020).
49 Clint et al. (2012).
50 Summarized in Hampson et al. (1998).
51 Clint et al. (2012).
52 Davis and Hines (2020).
53 Davis and Hines (2020); although see Todd et al. (2018).
54 Mercier (2020).
55 Baron-Cohen (2003).
56 Todd et al. (2018).
57 Kahlenberg and Wrangham (2010).
58 G.M. Alexander and Hines (2002); Hassett et al. (2008); although see Pittet et al. (2023).
59 Berenbaum and Hines (1992); Ehrhardt and Baker (1974); Kung et al. (2024).
60 Khorashad et al. (2018).
61 Pasterski et al. (2005).
62 Shirazi et al. (2022).
63 de Waal (2022).
64 L. Ellis et al. (2023).
65 Jackson et al. (2022).
66 Bernstein et al. (2023).
67 Wardle et al. (2004).
68 Sloan et al. (2010).
69 Ventura et al. (2021).
70 Dowd et al. (2020).
71 Cited in Barry (2022).
72 de Waal (2022).
73 Cited in Mason (2002).
74 Zarulli et al. (2018).
75 Min et al. (2012).
76 Colchero et al. (2016); Lemaître et al. (2020).
77 Lemaître et al. (2020).
78 Stewart-Williams and Thomas (2013a).
79 Clutton-Brock and Isvaran (2007).
80 Benenson et al. (2021).
81 Fillingim (2003).
82 Benenson et al. (2021).
83 Benenson et al. (2021).
84 Salk et al. (2017); Seedat et al. (2009).
85 Ayano et al. (2023); Loomes et al. (2017).
86 Seedat et al. (2009).
87 Seedat et al. (2009).
88 C.M. Brown et al. (2022).
89 Alothman and Fogarty (2020).
90 Diflorio and Jones (2010).
91 Salk et al. (2017).
92 Herlitz et al. (2024).
93 Power et al. (2013).
94 Del Giudice (2018).
95 Nesse (2006), p.91.

10 The Peacock's Predicament

1 Benatar (2012).
2 Farrell (1993).
3 Stewart-Williams (2010, 2018).
4 Benatar (2012).
5 Lavy (2008); Lievore and Triventi (2022); Terrier (2020).
6 Lievore and Triventi (2022).
7 Glaeser and Sacerdote (2003); Spohn (1999); Starr (2015).
8 T. Reynolds et al. (2020); Stewart-Williams (2002).
9 Wolfgang et al. (1985).
10 Bindler and Hjalmarsson (2020).
11 Schanzenbach (2005).
12 Cited in Gibney (2020).
13 ADHD: P.O. Quinn and Madhoo (2014). Autism: Mandy et al. (2012). Special educational needs: Daniel and Wang (2023).

14 Depression: Cochran and Rabinowitz (2003). Anxiety disorders: K. Fisher et al. (2022). Eating disorders: Striegel et al. (2012); Strother et al. (2012).
15 Salk et al. (2017), p.808.
16 Ganson et al. (2025).
17 Benatar (2012).
18 HM Government (2022).
19 Stemple and Meyer (2014).
20 Stemple and Meyer (2014).
21 Fletcher (2015).
22 Radcliffe Richards (1980).
23 Reeves (2022).
24 Haselton and Buss (2000).
25 Buss (2016).
26 Sommers (2012a).
27 Sommers (2012b).
28 Voyer and Voyer (2014).
29 Stewart-Williams (2018).
30 Mealey (2000).
31 Reeves (2022).
32 Blau and Kahn (2017); Bolotnyy and Emanuel (2022); C. Cook et al. (2020); Farrell (2005); Kleven et al. (2025).
33 Ceci et al. (2021); Stewart-Williams and Halsey (2021, 2022).
34 Ceci et al. (2021); Stewart-Williams and Halsey (2021, 2022).
35 Ronay and von Hippel (2010).
36 Kuppuswamy and Mollick (2015).
37 Kleven et al. (2025).
38 Stewart-Williams and Halsey (2021).
39 Lubinski et al. (2023); Su et al. (2009).
40 Breda and Napp (2019); Wang et al. (2013).
41 Ceci et al. (2021); Schaerer et al. (2023); Stewart-Williams and Halsey (2021, 2022).
42 Ceci et al. (2014).
43 W.M. Williams and Ceci (2015).
44 Carlsson et al. (2021); Honeycutt et al. (in press).
45 Moss-Racusin et al. (2012).
46 Ceci et al. (2023); Honeycutt and Jussim (2020).
47 Ceci et al. (2014); Ceci et al. (2023); Ceci and Williams (2011).
48 Ceci et al. (2023); Honeycutt and Jussim (2020).
49 Stewart-Williams and Halsey (2021).
50 Stewart-Williams and Halsey (2022).
51 Stewart-Williams and Halsey (2021, 2022).
52 Diekman et al. (2010), p.1056.
53 Reinier et al. (2023).
54 H. Edwards et al. (2024); Liddon and Barry (2021).
55 Liddon and Barry (2021).
56 Zucker and Prendergast (2020).
57 Whipple (2016).
58 Liddon and Barry (2021).
59 Seager and Barry (2019b), p.241.
60 O'Connor and Kirtley (2018).
61 Liddon and Barry (2021).
62 Karantzas et al. (2023).
63 Buss (2021).
64 Saini (2017), p.237.
65 Steinem (2019).
66 Stewart-Williams and Halsey (2021, 2022).
67 Bussey and Bandura (1992), p.1247.
68 Stewart-Williams and Halsey (2022).
69 Stewart-Williams and Halsey (2021).
70 Stewart-Williams (2010, 2018).
71 Stewart-Williams and Halsey (2021).
72 Radcliffe Richards (1980).
73 Radcliffe Richards (1980), pp 187–8.

References

Ablaza, C., Kabátek, J., & Perales, F. (2022). 'Are sibship characteristics predictive of same sex marriage? An examination of fraternal birth order and female fecundity effects in population-level administrative data from the Netherlands.' *Journal of Sex Research, 59*, pp 671–83. https://doi.org/10.1080/00224499.2021.1974330

Alexander, G.M., & Hines, M. (2002). 'Sex differences in response to children's toys in nonhuman primates (*Cercopithecus aethiops sabaeus*).' *Evolution and Human Behavior, 23*, pp 467–79. https://doi.org/10.1016/S1090-5138(02)00107-1

Alexander, R.D., Hoogland, J.L., Howard, R.D., Noonan, K.M., & Sherman, P.W. (1979). 'Sexual dimorphisms and breeding systems in pinnipeds, ungulates, primates, and humans.' In N.A. Chagnon & W. Irons (eds), *Evolutionary Biology and Human Social Behavior: An Anthropological Perspective*, pp 402–35. Duxbury Press

Alonzo, S.H. (2012). 'Sexual selection favours male parental care, when females can choose.' *Proceedings of the Royal Society B: Biological Sciences, 279*, pp 1784–90. https://doi.org/10.1098/rspb.2011.2237

Alothman, D., & Fogarty, A. (2020). 'Global differences in geography, religion and other societal factors are associated with sex differences in mortality from suicide: An ecological study of 182 countries.' *Journal of Affective Disorders, 260*, pp 67–72. https://doi.org/10.1016/j.jad.2019.08.093

Anderson, K.G. (2006). 'How well does paternity confidence match actual paternity? Evidence from worldwide nonpaternity rates.' *Current Anthropology, 47*, pp 513–20. https://doi.org/10.1086/504167

Anderson, N.E., Harenski, K.A., Harenski, C.L., Koenigs, M.R., Decety, J., Calhoun, V.D., & Kiehl, K.A. (2019). 'Machine learning of brain gray matter differentiates sex in a large forensic sample.' *Human Brain Mapping, 40*, pp 1496–506. https://doi.org/10.1002/hbm.24462

Anderson, R.C., & Klofstad, C.A. (2012). 'For love or money? The influence of personal resources and environmental resource pressures on human mate preferences.' *Ethology, 118*, pp 841–9. https://doi.org/10.1111/j.1439-0310.2012.02077.x

Andersson, L., Jalovaara, M., Saarela, J., & Uggla, C. (2023). 'A matter of time: Bateman's principles and mating success as count and duration across social strata in contemporary Finland.' *Proceedings of the Royal Society B: Biological Sciences, 290*, no.20231061. https://doi.org/10.1098/rspb.2023.1061

Andersson, M. (1994). *Sexual Selection*. Princeton University Press

Anglim, J., Dunlop, P.D., Wee, S., Horwood, S., Wood, J.K., & Marty, A. (2022). 'Personality and intelligence: A meta-analysis.' *Psychological Bulletin, 148*, pp 301–36. https://doi.org/10.1037/bul0000373

Apicella, C.L., Crittenden, A.N., & Tobolsky, V.A. (2017). 'Hunter-gatherer males are more risk-seeking than females, even in late childhood.' *Evolution and Human Behavior, 38*, pp 592–603. https://doi.org/10.1016/j.evolhumbehav.2017.01.003

Apostolou, M. (2007). 'Elements of parental choice: The evolution of parental preferences in relation to in-law selection.' *Evolutionary Psychology, 5*, pp 70–83. https://doi.org/10.1177/147470490700500107

Archer, J. (2004). 'Sex differences in aggression in real-world settings: A meta-analytic review.' *Review of General Psychology, 8*, pp 291–322. https://doi.org/10.1037/1089-2680.8.4.291

Archer, J. (2006a). 'Cross-cultural differences in physical aggression between partners: A social-role analysis.' *Personality and Social Psychology Review, 10*, pp 133–53. https://doi.org/10.1207/s15327957pspr1002_3

Archer, J. (2006b). 'Testosterone and human aggression: An evaluation of the challenge hypothesis.' *Neuroscience and Biobehavioral Reviews, 30*, pp 319–45. https://doi.org/10.1016/j.neubiorev.2004.12.007

Archer, J. (2009). 'Does sexual selection explain human sex differences in aggression?' *Behavioral and Brain Sciences, 32*, pp 249–66. https://doi.org/10.1017/S0140525X09990951

Archer, J. (2019). 'The reality and evolutionary significance of human psychological sex differences.' *Biological Reviews, 94*, pp 1381–415. https://doi.org/10.1111/brv.12507

Archer, J., & Mehdikhani, M. (2003). 'Variability among males in sexually selected attributes.' *Review of General Psychology*, 7, pp 219–36. https://doi.org/10.1037/1089-2680.7.3.219

Arden, R., & Plomin, R. (2006). 'Sex differences in variance of intelligence across childhood.' *Personality and Individual Differences*, 41, pp 39–48. https://doi.org/10.1016/j.paid.2005.11.027

Atari, M., Lai, M.H.C., & Dehghani, M. (2020). 'Sex differences in moral judgements across 67 countries.' *Proceedings of the Royal Society B: Biological Sciences*, 287, no.20201201. https://doi.org/10.1098/rspb.2020.1201

Ayano, G., Demelash, S., Gizachew, Y., Tsegay, L., & Alat, R. (2023). 'The global prevalence of attention deficit hyperactivity disorder in children and adolescents: An umbrella review of meta-analyses.' *Journal of Affective Disorders*, 339, pp 860–66. https://doi.org/10.1016/j.jad.2023.07.071

Badinter, E. (2011). *The Conflict: How Modern Motherhood Undermines the Status of Women* (trans. A. Hunter). Henry Holt and Company (original work published 2010)

Baillargeon, R.H., Zoccolillo, M., Keenan, K., Côté, S., Pérusse, D., Wu, H.-X., Boivin, M., & Tremblay, R.E. (2007). 'Gender differences in physical aggression: A prospective population-based survey of children before and after 2 years of age.' *Developmental Psychology*, 43, pp 13–26. https://doi.org/10.1037/0012-1649.43.1.13

Bandura, A. (1977). *Social Learning Theory*. Prentice Hall

Baranowski, A.M., & Hecht, H. (2015). 'Gender differences and similarities in receptivity to sexual invitations: Effects of location and risk perception.' *Archives of Sexual Behavior*, 44, pp 2257–65. https://doi.org/10.1007/s10508-015-0520-6

Baron-Cohen, S. (2003). *The Essential Difference: Male and Female Brains and the Truth About Autism*. Basic Books

Barry, J. (2022). 'You can't reduce domestic abuse by telling people that life is a power struggle between men and women. Interview with Professor Nicola Graham-Kevan.' *Male Psychology: The Magazine*. https://www.centreformalepsychology.com/male-psychology-magazine-listings/you-cant-reduce-domestic-abuse-by-telling-people-that-life-is-a-power-struggle-between-men-and-women-interview-with-professor-nicola-graham-kevan

Bateman, A.J. (1948). 'Intra-sexual selection in *Drosophila*.' *Heredity*, 2, pp 349–68. https://doi.org/10.1038/hdy.1948.21

Baumeister, R.F., Catanese, K.R., & Vohs, K.D. (2002). 'Is there a gender difference in strength of sex drive? Theoretical views, conceptual distinctions, and a review of relevant evidence.' *Personality and Social Psychology Review, 5*, pp 242–73. https://doi.org/10.1207/S15327957PSPR0503_5

Beaver, K.M., Connolly, E.J., Schwartz, J.A., Boutwell, B.B., Barnes, J.C., & Nedelec, J.L. (2016). 'Sexual orientation and involvement in nonviolent and violent delinquent behaviors: Findings from the National Longitudinal Study of Adolescent to Adult Health.' *Archives of Sexual Behavior, 45*, pp 1759–69. https://doi.org/10.1007/s10508-016-0717-3

Beltz, A., Swanson, J., & Berenbaum, S. (2011). 'Gendered occupational interests: Prenatal androgen effects on psychological orientation to Things versus People.' *Hormones and Behavior, 60*, pp 313–17. https://doi.org/10.1016/j.yhbeh.2011.06.002

Bem, S.L. (1981). 'Gender schema theory: A cognitive account of sex typing.' *Psychological Review, 88*, pp 354–64. https://doi.org/10.1037/0033-295X.88.4.354

Benatar, D. (2012). *The Second Sexism: Discrimination against Men and Boys*. Wiley-Blackwell

Bendixen, M., Asao, K., Wyckoff, J.P., Buss, D.M., & Kennair, L.E.O. (2017). 'Sexual regret in US and Norway: Effects of culture and individual differences in religiosity and mating strategy.' *Personality and Individual Differences, 116*, pp 246–51. https://doi.org/10.1016/j.paid.2017.04.054

Bendixen, M., & Kennair, L.E.O. (2017). 'Advances in the understanding of same-sex and opposite-sex sexual harassment.' *Evolution and Human Behavior, 38*, pp 583–91. https://doi.org/10.1016/j.evolhumbehav.2017.01.001

Bendixen, M., Kennair, L.E.O., & Buss, D.M. (2015). 'Jealousy: Evidence of strong sex differences using both forced choice and continuous measure paradigms.' *Personality and Individual Differences, 86*, pp 212–16. https://doi.org/10.1016/j.paid.2015.05.035

Benenson, J.F. (2013). 'The development of human female competition: Allies and adversaries.' *Philosophical Transactions of the Royal Society B: Biological Sciences, 368*, no.20130079. https://doi.org/10.1098/rstb.2013.0079

Benenson, J.F., Webb, C.E., & Wrangham, R.W. (2021). 'Self-protection as an adaptive female strategy.' *Behavioral and Brain Sciences, 45*, e128. https://doi.org/10.1017/S0140525X21002417

Berenbaum, S. (2017). 'Born this way? A spirited polemic takes aim at biological sex differences but misses opportunities to highlight relevant science.' *Science, 355*, p.254. https://doi.org/10.1126/science.aal1938

Berenbaum, S.A., & Beltz, A.M. (2011). 'Sexual differentiation of human behavior: Effects of prenatal and pubertal organizational hormones.'

Frontiers in Neuroendocrinology, 32, pp 183–200. https://doi.org/10.1016/j.yfrne.2011.03.001

Berenbaum, S.A., & Hines, M. (1992). 'Early androgens are related to childhood sex-typed toy preferences.' *Psychological Science, 3*, pp 203–6. https://doi.org/10.1111/j.1467-9280.1992.tb00028.x

Berggren, M., & Bergh, R. (2025). 'Simpson's gender-equality paradox.' *Proceedings of the National Academy of Sciences, 122*, e2422247122. https://doi.org/10.1073/pnas.2422247122

Bernstein, S.R., Kelleher, C., & Khalil, R.A. (2023). 'Gender-based research underscores sex differences in biological processes, clinical disorders and pharmacological interventions.' *Biochemical Pharmacology, 215*, no.115737. https://doi.org/10.1016/j.bcp.2023.115737

Berthold, A., Bearth, A., Ammann, J., & Siegrist, M. (2025). 'Not so different anymore? Women's and men's disgust sensitivity becomes similar with increasing age.' *Physiology and Behavior, 294*, no.114884. https://doi.org/10.1016/j.physbeh.2025.114884

Betzig, L.L. (1986). *Despotism and Differential Reproduction: A Darwinian View of History*. Aldine

Betzig, L. (1989). 'Causes of conjugal dissolution: A cross-cultural study.' *Current Anthropology, 30*, pp 654–76. https://doi.org/10.1086/203798

Betzig, L. (2012). 'Means, variances, and ranges in reproductive success: Comparative evidence.' *Evolution and Human Behavior, 33*, pp 309–17. https://doi.org/10.1016/j.evolhumbehav.2011.10.008

Bindler, A., & Hjalmarsson, R. (2020). 'The persistence of the criminal justice gender gap: Evidence from 200 years of judicial decisions.' *Journal of Law and Economics, 63*, pp 297–339. https://doi.org/10.1086/707482

Blake, K.R., Bastian, B., Denson, T.F., Grosjean, P., & Brooks, R.C. (2018). 'Income inequality not gender inequality positively covaries with female sexualization on social media.' *Proceedings of the National Academy of Sciences, 115*, pp 8722–7. https://doi.org/10.1073/pnas.1717959115

Blakemore, J.E.O. (1990). 'Children's nurturant interactions with their infant siblings: An exploration of gender differences and maternal socialization.' *Sex Roles, 22*, pp 43–57. https://doi.org/10.1007/BF00288153

Blakemore, J.E.O. (1998). 'The influence of gender and parental attitudes on preschool children's interest in babies: Observations in natural settings.' *Sex Roles, 38*, pp 73–94. https://doi.org/10.1023/A:1018764528694

Blanchard, R. (2018). 'Fraternal birth order, family size, and male homosexuality:

Meta-analysis of studies spanning 25 years.' *Archives of Sexual Behavior, 47*, pp 1–15. https://doi.org/10.1007/s10508-017-1007-4

Blau, F.D., & Kahn, L.M. (2017). 'The gender wage gap: Extent, trends, and explanations.' *Journal of Economic Literature, 55*, pp 789–865. https://doi.org/10.1257/jel.20160995

Bleidorn, W., Arslan, R.C., Denissen, J.J.A., Rentfrow, P.J., Gebauer, J.E., Potter, J., & Gosling, S.D. (2016). 'Age and gender differences in self-esteem: A cross-cultural window.' *Journal of Personality and Social Psychology, 111*, pp 396–410. https://doi.org/10.1037/pspp0000078

Bleske-Rechek, A., & Gunseor, M.M. (2021). 'Gendered perspectives on sharing the load: Men's and women's attitudes toward family roles and household and childcare tasks.' *Evolutionary Behavioral Sciences, 16*, pp 201–19. https://doi.org/10.1037/ebs0000257

Block, K., Olsson, M.I.T., van Grootel, S., Schuster, C., Meeussen, L., Van Laar, C., Martiny, S., Croft, A., Sun, M.S., Wee, S., Ainsaar, M., Aarntzen, L., Adamus, M., Anderson, J., Atkinson, C., Avicenna, M., Bąbel, P., Barth, M., Benson-Greenwald, T.M., . . . Schmader, T. (2025). 'The gender gap in the care economy is larger in highly developed countries: Sociocultural explanations for paradoxical findings.' *American Psychologist*, advance online publication. https://doi.org/10.1037/amp0001512

Bobrow, D., & Bailey, J.M. (2001). 'Is male homosexuality maintained via kin selection?' *Evolution and Human Behavior, 22*, pp 361–8. https://doi.org/10.1016/S1090-5138(01)00074-5

Bolotnyy, V., & Emanuel, N. (2022). 'Why do women earn less than men? Evidence from bus and train operators.' *Journal of Labor Economics, 40*, pp 283–323. https://doi.org/10.1086/715835

Book, A.S., Starzyk, K.B., & Quinsey, V.L. (2001). 'The relationship between testosterone and aggression: A meta-analysis.' *Aggression and Violent Behavior, 6*, pp 579–99. https://doi.org/10.1016/S1359-1789(00)00032-X

Borgerhoff Mulder, M. (1988). 'Kipsigis bridewealth payments.' In L. Betzig, M. Borgerhoff Mulder, & P. Turke (eds), *Human Reproductive Behaviour: A Darwinian Perspective*, pp 65–82. Cambridge University Press

Borkenau, P., McCrae, R.R., & Terracciano, A. (2013). 'Do men vary more than women in personality? A study in 51 cultures.' *Journal of Research in Personality, 47*, pp 135–44. https://doi.org/10.1016/j.jrp.2012.12.001

Bos, P.A., & Spencer, H. (2024). 'Attractive caregiving: Women's preference for men that care for children and the role of nurturance motivation and menstrual cycle phase.' *Evolutionary Psychological Science, 10*, pp 110–21. https://doi.org/10.1007/s40806-024-00391-6

Brebner, J. (2003). 'Gender and emotions.' *Personality and Individual Differences, 34*, pp 387–94. https://doi.org/10.1016/S0191-8869(02)00059-4

Breda, T., & Napp, C. (2019). 'Girls' comparative advantage in reading can largely explain the gender gap in math-related fields.' *Proceedings of the National Academy of Sciences, 116*, pp 15435–40. https://doi.org/10.1073/pnas.1905779116

Brennan, P.L.R., Clark, C.J., & Prum, R.O. (2009). 'Explosive eversion and functional morphology of the duck penis supports sexual conflict in waterfowl genitalia.' *Proceedings of the Royal Society B: Biological Sciences, 277*, pp 1309–14. https://doi.org/10.1098/rspb.2009.2139

Britton, A., Ben-Shlomo, Y., Benzeval, M., Kuh, D., & Bell, S. (2015). 'Life course trajectories of alcohol consumption in the United Kingdom using longitudinal data from nine cohort studies.' *BMC Medicine, 13*, no.47. https://doi.org/10.1186/s12916-015-0273-z

Brown, C.M., Wong, Q., Thakur, A., Singh, K., & Singh, R.S. (2022). 'Origin of sex-biased mental disorders: Do males and females experience different selective regimes?' *Journal of Molecular Evolution, 90*, pp 401–17. https://doi.org/10.1007/s00239-022-10072-2

Brown, J., Laland, K.N., & Borgerhoff Mulder, M. (2009). 'Bateman's principles and human sex roles.' *Trends in Ecology and Evolution, 24*, pp 297–304. https://doi.org/10.1016/j.tree.2009.02.005

Brownmiller, S. (1975). *Against Our Will: Men, Women and Rape*. Ballantine Books

Buss, D.M. (1988). 'The evolution of human intrasexual competition: Tactics of mate attraction.' *Journal of Personality and Social Psychology, 54*, pp 616–28. https://doi.org/10.1037/0022-3514.54.4.616

Buss, D.M. (1989). 'Sex differences in human mate preferences: Evolutionary hypotheses tested in 37 cultures.' *Behavioral and Brain Sciences, 12*, pp 1–49. https://doi.org/10.1017/S0140525X00023992

Buss, D.M. (2016). *The Evolution of Desire: Strategies of Human Mating* (rev. edn). Basic Books

Buss, D.M. (2021). *When Men Behave Badly: The Hidden Roots of Sexual Deception, Harassment, and Assault*. Little, Brown Spark

Buss, D.M. (2024). *Evolutionary Psychology: The New Science of the Mind* (7th edn). Routledge

Buss, D.M., Abbott, M., Angleitner, A., Asherian, A., Biaggio, A., Blanco-Villasenor, A., Bruchon-Schweitzer, M., Ch'U, H.-Y., Czapinski, J., Deraad, B., Ekehammar, B., El Lohamy, N., Fioravanti, M., Georgas, J., Gjerde, P., Guttman, R., Hazan, F., Iwawaki, S., Janakiramaiah, N., . . . Yang, K.-S. (1990). 'International preferences in selecting mates: A study of 37 cultures.' *Journal of Cross-Cultural Psychology, 21*, pp 5–47. https://doi.org/10.1177/0022022190211001

Buss, D.M., Larsen, R.J., Westen, D., & Semmelroth, J. (1992). 'Sex differences in jealousy: Evolution, physiology, and psychology.' *Psychological Science, 3*, pp 251–5. https://doi.org/10.1111/j.1467-9280.1992.tb00038.x

Buss, D.M., & Schmitt, D.P. (1993). 'Sexual strategies theory: An evolutionary perspective on human mating.' *Psychological Review, 100*, pp 204–32. https://doi.org/10.1037/0033-295X.100.2.204

Buss, D.M., & Schmitt, D.P. (2011). 'Evolutionary psychology and feminism.' *Sex Roles, 64*, pp 768–87. https://doi.org/10.1007/s11199-011-9987-3

Buss, D.M., Shackelford, T.K., Kirkpatrick, L.A., Choe, J.C., Lim, H.K., Hasegawa, M., Hasegawa, T., & Bennett, K. (1999). 'Jealousy and the nature of beliefs about infidelity: Tests of competing hypotheses about sex differences in the United States, Korea, and Japan.' *Personal Relationships, 6*, pp 125–50. https://doi.org/10.1111/j.1475-6811.1999.tb00215.x

Buss, D.M., Shackelford, T.K., Kirkpatrick, L.A., & Larsen, R.J. (2001). 'A half century of mate preferences: The cultural evolution of values.' *Journal of Marriage and Family, 63*, pp 491–503. https://doi.org/10.1111/j.1741-3737.2001.00491.x

Bussey, K., & Bandura, A. (1992). 'Self-regulatory mechanisms governing gender development.' *Child Development, 63*, pp 1236–50. https://doi.org/10.2307/1131530

Bussey, K., & Bandura, A. (1999). 'Social cognitive theory of gender development and differentiation.' *Psychological Review, 106*, pp 676–713. https://doi.org/10.1037/0033-295X.106.4.676

Butler, J. (1990). *Gender Trouble: Feminism and the Subversion of Identity*. Routledge

Buunk, B.P., Angleitner, A., Oubaid, V., & Buss, D.M. (1996). 'Sex differences in jealousy in evolutionary and cultural perspective: Tests from the Netherlands, Germany, and the United States.' *Psychological Science, 7*, pp 359–63. https://doi.org/10.1111/j.1467-9280.1996.tb00389.x

Byrnes, J.P., Miller, D.C., & Schafer, W.D. (1999). 'Gender differences in risk taking: A meta-analysis.' *Psychological Bulletin, 125*, pp 367–83. https://doi.org/10.1037/0033-2909.125.3.367

Camilleri, T., Rockey, S., & Dunbar, R. (2023). *The Social Brain: The Psychology of Successful Groups*. Penguin

Campbell, A. (1995). 'A few good men: Evolutionary psychology and female adolescent aggression.' *Ethology and Sociobiology, 16*, pp 99–123. https://doi.org/10.1016/0162-3095(94)00072-F

Campbell, A. (1999). 'Staying alive: Evolution, culture, and women's intrasexual aggression.' *Behavioral and Brain Sciences, 22*, pp 203–14. https://doi.org/10.1017/S0140525X99001818

Campbell, A. (2002). *A Mind of Her Own: The Evolutionary Psychology of Women*. Oxford University Press

Campbell, A. (2005). 'Feminism and evolutionary psychology.' In J.H. Barkow (ed.), *Missing the Revolution: Darwinism for the Social Sciences*, pp 63–99. Oxford University Press

Campbell, O.L.K., Bann, D., & Patalay, P. (2021). 'The gender gap in adolescent mental health: A cross-national investigation of 566,829 adolescents across 73 countries.' *SSM – Population Health, 13*, no.100742. https://doi.org/10.1016/j.ssmph.2021.100742

Camperio-Ciani, A., Corna, F., & Capiluppi, C. (2004). 'Evidence for maternally inherited factors favouring male homosexuality and promoting female fecundity.' *Proceedings of the Royal Society B: Biological Sciences, 271*, pp 2217–21. https://doi.org/10.1098/rspb.2004.2872

Canner, J.K., Haider, A.H., Selvarajah, S., Hui, X., Wang, H., Efron, D.T., Haut, E.R., Velopulos, C.G., Schwartz, D.A., Chi, A., & Schneider, E.B. (2014). 'US emergency department visits for fireworks injuries, 2006–2010.' *Journal of Surgical Research, 190*, pp 305–11. https://doi.org/10.1016/j.jss.2014.03.066

Carballo, F., Freidin, E., Putrino, N., Shimabukuro, C., Casanave, E., & Bentosela, M. (2015). 'Dog's discrimination of human selfish and generous attitudes: The role of individual recognition, experience, and experimenters' gender.' *PLOS ONE, 10*, e0116314. https://doi.org/10.1371/journal.pone.0116314

Carlsson, M., Finseraas, H., Midtbøen, A.H., & Rafnsdóttir, G.L. (2021). 'Gender bias in academic recruitment? Evidence from a survey experiment in the Nordic region.' *European Sociological Review, 37*, pp 399–410. https://doi.org/10.1093/esr/jcaa050

Cazalé-Debat, L., Scheunemann, L., Day, M., Fernandez-d.V. Alquicira, T., Dimtsi, A., Zhang, Y., Blackburn, L.A., Ballardini, C., Greenin-Whitehead,

K., Reynolds, E., Lin, A.C., Owald, D., & Rezaval, C. (2024). 'Mating proximity blinds threat perception.' *Nature, 634*, pp 635–43. https://doi.org/10.1038/s41586-024-07890-3

Ceci, S.J., Ginther, D.K., Kahn, S., & Williams, W.M. (2014). 'Women in academic science: A changing landscape.' *Psychological Science in the Public Interest, 15*, pp 75–141. https://doi.org/10.1177/1529100614541236

Ceci, S.J., Kahn, S., & Williams, W.M. (2021). 'Stewart-Williams and Halsey argue persuasively that gender bias is just one of many causes of women's underrepresentation in science.' *European Journal of Personality, 35*, pp 40–44. https://doi.org/10.1177/0890207020976778

Ceci, S.J., Kahn, S., & Williams, W.M. (2023). 'Exploring gender bias in six key domains of academic science: An adversarial collaboration.' *Psychological Science in the Public Interest, 24*, pp 15–73. https://doi.org/10.1177/15291006231163179

Ceci, S.J., & Williams, W.M. (2011). 'Understanding current causes of women's underrepresentation in science.' *Proceedings of the National Academy of Sciences, 108*, pp 3157–62. https://doi.org/10.1073/pnas.1014871108

Charles, M., & Bradley, K. (2009). 'Indulging our gendered selves? Sex segregation by field of study in 44 countries.' *American Journal of Sociology, 114*, pp 924–76. https://doi.org/10.1086/595942

Charles, M., Harr, B., Cech, E., & Hendley, A. (2014). 'Who likes math where? Gender differences in eighth-graders' attitudes around the world.' *International Studies in Sociology of Education, 24*, pp 85–112. https://doi.org/10.1080/09620214.2014.895140

Charness, G., & Gneezy, U. (2012). 'Strong evidence for gender differences in risk taking.' *Journal of Economic Behavior and Organization, 83*, pp 50–58. https://doi.org/10.1016/j.jebo.2011.06.007

Clark, C.J., Jussim, L., Frey, K., Stevens, S.T., al-Gharbi, M., Aquino, K., Bailey, J.M., Barbaro, N., Baumeister, R.F., Bleske-Rechek, A., Buss, D., Ceci, S., Del Giudice, M., Ditto, P.H., Forgas, J.P., Geary, D.C., Geher, G., Haider, S., Honeycutt, N., . . . von Hippel, W. (2023). 'Prosocial motives underlie scientific censorship by scientists: A perspective and research agenda.' *Proceedings of the National Academy of Sciences, 120*, e2301642120. https://doi.org/10.1073/pnas.2301642120

Clark, R.D. (1990). 'The impact of AIDS on gender differences in willingness to engage in casual sex.' *Journal of Applied Social Psychology, 20*, pp 771–82. https://doi.org/10.1111/j.1559-1816.1990.tb00437.x

Clark, R.D., & Hatfield, E. (1989). 'Gender differences in receptivity to sexual offers.' *Journal of Psychology and Human Sexuality*, 2, pp 39–55. https://doi.org/10.1300/J056v02n01_04

Clint, E.K., Sober, E., Garland, T., Jr, & Rhodes, J.S. (2012). 'Male superiority in spatial navigation: Adaptation or side effect?' *Quarterly Review of Biology*, 87, pp 289–313. https://doi.org/10.1086/668168

Clutton-Brock, T.H. (1991). *The Evolution of Parental Care*. Princeton University Press

Clutton-Brock, T.H., & Isvaran, K. (2007). 'Sex differences in ageing in natural populations of vertebrates.' *Proceedings of the Royal Society B: Biological Sciences*, 274, pp 3097–104. https://doi.org/10.1098/rspb.2007.1138

Clutton-Brock, T.H., & Parker, G.A. (1992). 'Potential reproductive rates and the operation of sexual selection.' *Quarterly Review of Biology*, 67, pp 437–56. https://doi.org/10.1086/417793

Clutton-Brock, T.H., & Parker, G.A. (1995). 'Sexual coercion in animal societies.' *Animal Behaviour*, 49, pp 1345–65. https://doi.org/10.1006/anbe.1995.0166

Clutton-Brock, T.H., & Vincent, A.C.J. (1991). 'Sexual selection and the potential reproductive rates of males and females.' *Nature*, *351*, pp 58–60. https://doi.org/10.1038/351058a0

Cochran, S.V., & Rabinowitz, F.E. (2003). 'Gender-sensitive recommendations for assessment and treatment of depression in men.' *Professional Psychology: Research and Practice*, 34, pp 132–40. https://doi.org/10.1037/0735-7028.34.2.132

Cohen, J. (1977). *Statistical Power Analysis for the Behavioral Sciences*. Academic Press

Colapinto, J. (2000). *As Nature Made Him: The Boy Who Was Raised as a Girl*. HarperCollins

Colchero, F., Rau, R., Jones, O.R., Barthold, J.A., Conde, D.A., Lenart, A., Nemeth, L., Scheuerlein, A., Schoeley, J., Torres, C., Zarulli, V., Altmann, J., Brockman, D.K., Bronikowski, A.M., Fedigan, L.M., Pusey, A.E., Stoinski, T.S., Strier, K.B., Baudisch, A., . . . Vaupel, J.W. (2016). 'The emergence of longevous populations.' *Proceedings of the National Academy of Sciences*, *113*, e7681–90. https://doi.org/10.1073/pnas.1612191113

Conaboy, C. (2022). 'Maternal instinct is a myth that men created.' *The New York Times*. https://www.nytimes.com/2022/08/26/opinion/sunday/maternal-instinct-myth.html

Conroy-Beam, D., Buss, D.M., Pham, M.N., & Shackelford, T.K. (2015).

'How sexually dimorphic are human mate preferences?' *Personality and Social Psychology Bulletin, 41*, pp 1082–93. https://doi.org/10.1177/0146167215590987

Cook, C., Diamond, R., Hall, J.V., List, J.A., & Oyer, P. (2020). 'The gender earnings gap in the gig economy: Evidence from over a million rideshare drivers.' *Review of Economic Studies, 88*, pp 2210–38. https://doi.org/10.1093/restud/rdaa081

Cook, K.M., De Asis-Cruz, J., Lopez, C., Quistorff, J., Kapse, K., Andersen, N., Vezina, G., & Limperopoulos, C. (2022). 'Robust sex differences in functional brain connectivity are present in utero.' *Cerebral Cortex, 33*, pp 2441–54. https://doi.org/10.1093/cercor/bhac218

Coontz, S. (2005). *Marriage: A History: From Obedience to Intimacy, or How Love Conquered Marriage*. Penguin

Cosmides, L., & Tooby, J. (1992). 'Cognitive adaptations for social exchange.' In J.H. Barkow, L. Cosmides, & J. Tooby (eds), *The Adapted Mind: Evolutionary Psychology and the Generation of Culture*, pp 163–228. Oxford University Press

Costa, P.T., Terracciano, A., & McCrae, R.R. (2001). 'Gender differences in personality traits across cultures: Robust and surprising findings.' *Journal of Personality and Social Psychology, 81*, pp 322–31. https://doi.org/10.1037/0022-3514.81.2.322

Coyle, M. (2020). '5 of Ruth Bader Ginsburg's most powerful Supreme Court opinions.' *PBS NewsHour.* https://www.pbs.org/newshour/nation/5-of-ruth-bader-ginsburgs-most-powerful-supreme-court-opinions

Coyle, T.R., Snyder, A.C., & Richmond, M.C. (2015). 'Sex differences in ability tilt: Support for investment theory.' *Intelligence, 50*, pp 209–20. https://doi.org/10.1016/j.intell.2015.04.012

Daly, M., & Wilson, M. (1983). *Sex, Evolution, and Behavior: Adaptations for Reproduction* (2nd edn). Willard Grant

Daly, M., & Wilson, M. (1988). *Homicide*. Aldine de Gruyter

Daly, M., & Wilson, M. (1990). 'Killing the competition: Female–female and male–male homicide.' *Human Nature, 1*, pp 81–107. https://doi.org/10.1007/BF02692147

Daly, M., & Wilson, M. (1998). *The Truth About Cinderella: A Darwinian View of Parental Love*. Yale University Press

Daly, M., & Wilson, M. (2001). 'Risk-taking, intrasexual competition, and homicide.' In J.A. French, A.C. Kamil, & D.W. Leger (eds), *Nebraska*

Symposium on Motivation, vol.47, pp 1–36. University of Nebraska Press

Daly, M., Wilson, M., & Weghorst, S.J. (1982). 'Male sexual jealousy.' *Ethology and Sociobiology, 3*, pp 11–27. https://doi.org/10.1016/0162-3095(82)90027-9

Daniel, J., & Wang, H. (2023). 'Gender differences in special educational needs identification.' *Review of Education, 11*, e3437. https://doi.org/10.1002/rev3.3437

Darwin, C. (1859). *On the Origin of Species by Means of Natural Selection.* Murray

Darwin, C. (1860). 'Letter no. 2743 to Asa Gray.' *Darwin Correspondence Project*. University of Cambridge. https://www.darwinproject.ac.uk/letter/DCP-LETT-2743.xml

Darwin, C. (1871). *The Descent of Man, and Selection in Relation to Sex*. Murray

Darwin, C. (1887). *The Life and Letters of Charles Darwin*, vol.1. John Murray

Davis, J.T.M., & Hines, M. (2020). 'How large are gender differences in toy preferences? A systematic review and meta-analysis of toy preference research.' *Archives of Sexual Behavior*, 49, pp 373–94. https://doi.org/10.1007/s10508-019-01624-7

de Beauvoir, S. (1953). *The Second Sex* (trans. H.M. Parshley). Knopf (original work published 1949)

De Bolle, M., De Fruyt, F., McCrae, R.R., Löckenhoff, C.E., Costa, P.T., Jr, Aguilar-Vafaie, M.E., Ahn, C.-k., Ahn, H.-n., Alcalay, L., Allik, J., Avdeyeva, T.V., Bratko, D., Brunner-Sciarra, M., Cain, T.R., Chan, W., Chittcharat, N., Crawford, J.T., Fehr, R., Ficková, E., . . . Terracciano, A. (2015). 'The emergence of sex differences in personality traits in early adolescence: A cross-sectional, cross-cultural study.' *Journal of Personality and Social Psychology, 108*, pp 171–85. https://doi.org/10.1037/a0038497

de Waal, F.B.M. (2022). *Different: Gender Through the Eyes of a Primatologist.* Norton

Deaner, R.O., Khera, A.V., & Platt, M.L. (2005). 'Monkeys pay per view: Adaptive valuation of social images by rhesus macaques.' *Current Biology, 15*, pp 543–8. https://doi.org/10.1016/j.cub.2005.01.044

Deary, I.J., Thorpe, G., Wilson, V., Starr, J.M., & Whalley, L.J. (2003). 'Population sex differences in IQ at age 11: The Scottish mental survey 1932.' *Intelligence, 31*, pp 533–42. https://doi.org/10.1016/S0160-2896(03)00053-9

Deaux, K., & Major, B. (1987). 'Putting gender into context: An interactive model of gender-related behavior.' *Psychological Review, 94*, pp 369–89. https://doi.org/10.1037/0033-295X.94.3.369

Del Giudice, M. (2018). *Evolutionary Psychopathology: A Unified Approach*. Oxford University Press

Del Giudice, M. (2023a). 'Ideological bias in the psychology of sex and gender.' In C.L. Frisby, W.T. O'Donohue, R.E. Redding, & S.O. Lilienfeld (eds), *Political Bias in Psychology: Nature, Scope, and Solutions*, pp 743–78. Springer. https://doi.org/10.1007/978-3-031-29148-7_28

Del Giudice, M. (2023b). 'The S-Index: Summarizing patterns of sex differences at the distribution extremes.' *Personality and Individual Differences, 205*, no.112088. https://doi.org/10.1016/j.paid.2023.112088

Del Giudice, M., Booth, T., & Irwing, P. (2012). 'The distance between Mars and Venus: Measuring global sex differences in personality.' *PLOS ONE, 7*, e29265. https://doi.org/10.1371/journal.pone.0029265

Diamond, M., & Sigmundson, H.K. (1997). 'Sex reassignment at birth: Long-term review and clinical implications.' *Archives of Pediatrics and Adolescent Medicine, 151*, pp 298–304. https://doi.org/10.1001/archpedi.1997.02170400084015

Diekman, A.B., Brown, E.R., Johnston, A.M., & Clark, E.K. (2010). 'Seeking congruity between goals and roles: A new look at why women opt out of science, technology, engineering, and mathematics careers.' *Psychological Science, 21*, pp 1051–7. https://doi.org/10.1177/0956797610377342

Diflorio, A., & Jones, I. (2010). 'Is sex important? Gender differences in bipolar disorder.' *International Review of Psychiatry, 22*, pp 437–52. https://doi.org/10.3109/09540261.2010.514601

Dittrich, C., & Rödel, M.-O. (2023). 'Drop dead! Female mate avoidance in an explosively breeding frog.' *Royal Society Open Science, 10*, no.230742. https://doi.org/10.1098/rsos.230742

Dixson, A.F. (2012). *Primate Sexuality: Comparative Studies of the Prosimians, Monkeys, Apes, and Humans* (2nd edn). Oxford University Press. https://doi.org/10.1093/acprof:osobl/9780199544646.001.0001

Döring, N., & Mohseni, M.R. (2022). 'Der gender orgasm gap. Ein kritischer forschungsüberblick zu geschlechterdifferenzen in der orgasmus-häufigkeit beim heterosex [The gender orgasm gap: A critical research review on gender differences in orgasm frequency during heterosex].' *Zeitschrift für Sexualforschung, 35*, pp 73–87. https://doi.org/10.1055/a-1832-4771

Dowd, K., Patel, B., Blumenthal, Z., Rodriguez-Unda, N., & Bird, E. (2020). 'Acute management of Fournier's gangrene in the setting of massive lymphedema.' *Urology Case Reports, 28*, no.101013. https://doi.org/10.1016/j.eucr.2019.101013

Duarte, J.L., Crawford, J.T., Stern, C., Haidt, J., Jussim, L., & Tetlock, P.E. (2015). 'Political diversity will improve social psychological science.' *Behavioral and Brain Sciences, 38*, e130. https://doi.org/10.1017/S0140525X14000430

Durante, K.M., Griskevicius, V., Simpson, J.A., Cantú, S.M., & Tybur, J.M. (2012). 'Sex ratio and women's career choice: Does a scarcity of men lead women to choose briefcase over baby?' *Journal of Personality and Social Psychology, 103*, pp 121–34. https://doi.org/10.1037/a0027949

Durrant, R. (2019). 'Evolutionary approaches to understanding crime: Explaining the gender gap in offending.' *Psychology, Crime and Law, 25*, pp 589–608. https://doi.org/10.1080/1068316X.2018.1558224

Eagly, A.H. (1987). *Sex Differences in Social Behavior: A Social Role Interpretation*. Lawrence Erlbaum Associates

Eagly, A.H. (1995). 'The science and politics of comparing men and women.' *American Psychologist, 50*, pp 145–58. https://doi.org/10.1037/0003-066X.50.3.145

Eagly, A.H. (2018). 'The shaping of science by ideology: How feminism inspired, led, and constrained scientific understanding of sex and gender.' *Journal of Social Issues, 74*, pp 871–88. https://doi.org/10.1111/josi.12291

Eagly, A.H., & Revelle, W. (2022). 'Understanding the magnitude of psychological differences between women and men requires seeing the forest and the trees.' *Perspectives on Psychological Science, 17*, pp 1339–58. https://doi.org/10.1177/17456916211046006

Eagly, A.H., & Steffen, V.J. (1986). 'Gender and aggressive behavior: A meta-analytic review of the social psychological literature.' *Psychological Bulletin, 100*, pp 309–30. https://doi.org/10.1037/0033-2909.100.3.309

Eagly, A.H., & Wood, W. (1999). 'The origins of sex differences in human behavior: Evolved dispositions versus social roles.' *American Psychologist, 54*, pp 408–23. https://doi.org/10.1037/0003-066X.54.6.408

Edwards, C.P. (1993). 'Behavioral sex differences in children of diverse cultures: The case of nurturance to infants.' In M.E. Pereira & L.A. Fairbanks (eds), *Juvenile Primates: Life History, Development, and Behavior*, pp 327–38. University of Chicago Press

Edwards, H., Wright, S., Sargeant, C., Cortese, S., & Wood-Downie, H. (2024). 'Research review: A systematic review and meta-analysis of sex differences in narrow constructs of restricted and repetitive behaviours and interests in autistic children, adolescents, and adults.' *Journal of Child Psychology and*

Psychiatry, 65, pp 4–17. https://doi.org/10.1111/jcpp.13855

Ehrhardt, A.A., & Baker, S.W. (1974). 'Fetal androgens, human central nervous system differentiation, and behavior sex differences.' In R.C. Friedman, R.M. Richart, R.L. Vande Wiele, & L.O. Stern (eds), *Sex Differences in Behavior*, pp 33–51. Wiley

Elgan, M. (2019). 'People are falling off buildings in search of the perfect Instagram shot.' *Fast Company*. https://www.fastcompany.com/90287323/people-are-falling-off-buildings-in-search-of-the-perfect-instagram-shot

Ellis, B.J., & Symons, D. (1990). 'Sex differences in sexual fantasy: An evolutionary psychological approach.' *Journal of Sex Research, 27*, pp 527–55. https://doi.org/10.1080/00224499009551579

Ellis, L. (1995). 'Dominance and reproductive success among nonhuman animals: A cross-species comparison.' *Ethology and Sociobiology, 16*, pp 257–333. https://doi.org/10.1016/0162-3095(95)00050-U

Ellis, L., Palmer, C.T., Hopcroft, R., & Hoskin, A.W. (2023). *The Handbook of Sex Differences*, vols 1–4. Routledge

Else-Quest, N.M., Higgins, A., Allison, C., & Morton, L.C. (2012). 'Gender differences in self-conscious emotional experience: A meta-analysis.' *Psychological Bulletin, 138*, pp 947–81. https://doi.org/10.1037/a0027930

Else-Quest, N.M., Hyde, J.S., & Linn, M.C. (2010). 'Cross-national patterns of gender differences in mathematics: A meta-analysis.' *Psychological Bulletin, 136*, pp 103–27. https://doi.org/10.1037/a0018053

Endendijk, J.J., Groeneveld, M.G., Bakermans-Kranenburg, M.J., & Mesman, J. (2016). 'Gender-differentiated parenting revisited: Meta-analysis reveals very few differences in parental control of boys and girls.' *PLOS ONE, 11*, e0159193. https://doi.org/10.1371/journal.pone.0159193

Fairbanks, L.A. (1990). 'Reciprocal benefits of allomothering for female vervet monkeys.' *Animal Behaviour, 40*, pp 553–62. https://doi.org/10.1016/S0003-3472(05)80536-6

Falk, A., & Hermle, J. (2018). 'Relationship of gender differences in preferences to economic development and gender equality.' *Science, 362*, eaas9899. https://doi.org/10.1126/science.aas9899

Farrell, W. (1993). *The Myth of Male Power*. Simon & Schuster

Farrell, W. (2005). *Why Men Earn More: The Startling Truth Behind the Pay Gap – And What Women Can Do About It*. Simon & Schuster

Fausto-Sterling, A. (1992). *Myths of Gender: Biological Theories About Women and Men*. Basic Books

Fein, E., & Schneider, S. (1995). *The Rules: Time-Tested Secrets for Capturing the Heart of Mr. Right*. Warner Books

Feingold, A. (1990). 'Gender differences in effects of physical attractiveness on romantic attraction: A comparison across five research paradigms.' *Journal of Personality and Social Psychology, 59*, pp 981–93. https://doi.org/10.1037/0022-3514.59.5.981

Feingold, A. (1994). 'Gender differences in variability in intellectual abilities: A cross-cultural perspective.' *Sex Roles, 30*, pp 81–92. https://doi.org/10.1007/BF01420741

Felesina, T., & Zietsch, B. (2024). 'The desirable dad hypothesis: Male same-sex attraction as the product of selection for paternal care via antagonistic pleiotropy.' *Archives of Sexual Behavior, 53*, pp 1731–45. https://doi.org/10.1007/s10508-023-02780-7

Felson, R.B. (2002). *Violence and Gender Reexamined*. American Psychological Association. https://doi.org/10.1037/10470-000

Felson, R.B., & Cundiff, P. (2014). 'Sexual assault as a crime against young people.' *Archives of Sexual Behavior,* 43, pp 273–84. https://doi.org/10.1007/s10508-013-0127-8

Fillingim, R.B. (2003). 'Sex-related influences on pain: A review of mechanisms and clinical implications.' *Rehabilitation Psychology,* 48, pp 165–74. https://doi.org/10.1037/0090-5550.48.3.165

Fine, C. (2010). *Delusions of Gender: The Real Science Behind Sex Differences*. Norton

Fine, C. (2017). *Testosterone Rex: Myths of Sex, Science, and Society*. Norton

Finnigan, K.M., & Corker, K.S. (2016). 'Do performance avoidance goals moderate the effect of different types of stereotype threat on women's math performance?' *Journal of Research in Personality, 63*, pp 36–43. https://doi.org/10.1016/j.jrp.2016.05.009

Fischer, A.H., Rodriguez Mosquera, P.M., van Vianen, A.E.M., & Manstead, A.S.R. (2004). 'Gender and culture differences in emotion.' *Emotion,* 4, pp 87–94. https://doi.org/10.1037/1528-3542.4.1.87

Fisher, K., Seidler, Z.E., King, K., Oliffe, J.L., Robertson, S., & Rice, S.M. (2022). 'Men's anxiety, why it matters, and what is needed to limit its risk for male suicide.' *Discover Psychology*, 2, no.18. https://doi.org/10.1007/s44202-022-00035-5

Fisher, M.L. (2004). 'Female intrasexual competition decreases female facial attractiveness.' *Proceedings of the Royal Society B: Biological Sciences, 271*, S283–5. https://doi.org/10.1098/rsbl.2004.0160

Fisher, M., & Cox, A. (2010). 'Man change thyself: Hero versus heroine development in Harlequin romance novels.' *Journal of Social, Evolutionary, and Cultural Psychology*, 4, pp 305–16. https://doi.org/10.1037/h0099281

Fisher, R.A. (1930). *The Genetical Theory of Natural Selection*. Clarendon Press

Fletcher, S. (2015). 'How did I raise such a girly girl? Feminist mother cringes at her three-year-old daughter's love of princesses, frills and pink – and wishes she was into toy cars instead.' *Daily Mail*. https://www.dailymail.co.uk/femail/article-3292230/Feminist-mother-cringes-three-year-old-daughter-s-love-princesses-frills-pink.html

Flore, P.C., Mulder, J., & Wicherts, J.M. (2019). 'The influence of gender stereotype threat on mathematics test scores of Dutch high school students: A registered report.' *Comprehensive Results in Social Psychology, 3*, pp 140–74. https://doi.org/10.1080/23743603.2018.1559647

Flore, P.C., & Wicherts, J.M. (2015). 'Does stereotype threat influence performance of girls in stereotyped domains? A meta-analysis.' *Journal of School Psychology, 53*, pp 25–44. https://doi.org/10.1016/j.jsp.2014.10.002

Flynn, J.R. (2012). *Are We Getting Smarter? Rising IQ in the Twenty-First Century*. Cambridge University Press

Ford, C.S., & Beach, F.A. (1951). *Patterns of Sexual Behavior*. Harper & Row

Frankenbach, J., Weber, M., Loschelder, D.D., Kilger, H., & Friese, M. (2022). 'Sex drive: Theoretical conceptualization and meta-analytic review of gender differences.' *Psychological Bulletin, 148*, pp 621–61. https://doi.org/10.1037/bul0000366

Freeman, A.R. (2021). 'Female–female reproductive suppression: Impacts on signals and behavior.' *Integrative and Comparative Biology, 61*, pp 1827–40. https://doi.org/10.1093/icb/icab027

Frisén, L., Nordenström, A., Falhammar, H., Filipsson, H., Holmdahl, G., Janson, P.O., Thorén, M., Hagenfeldt, K., Möller, A., & Nordenskjöld, A. (2009). 'Gender role behavior, sexuality, and psychosocial adaptation in women with congenital adrenal hyperplasia due to CYP21A2 deficiency.' *Journal of Clinical Endocrinology and Metabolism, 94*, pp 3432–9. https://doi.org/10.1210/jc.2009-0636

Fry, D.P. (1998). 'Anthropological perspectives on aggression: Sex differences and cultural variation.' *Aggressive Behavior, 24*, pp 81–95. https://doi.org/10.1002/(SICI)1098-2337(1998)24:2<81::AID-AB1>3.0.CO;2-V

Gangestad, S.W., & Simpson, J.A. (2000). 'The evolution of human mating: Trade-offs and strategic pluralism.' *Behavioral and Brain Sciences, 23*, pp 573–87. https://doi.org/10.1017/S0140525X0000337X

Ganna, A., Verweij, K.J.H., Nivard, M.G., Maier, R., Wedow, R., Busch, A.S., Abdellaoui, A., Guo, S., Sathirapongsasuti, J.F., Lichtenstein, P., Lundström, S., Långström, N., Auton, A., Harris, K.M., Beecham, G.W., Martin, E.R., Sanders, A.R., Perry, J.R.B., Neale, B.M., & Zietsch, B.P. (2019). 'Large-scale GWAS reveals insights into the genetic architecture of same-sex sexual behavior.' *Science, 365*, eaat7693. https://doi.org/10.1126/science.aat7693

Ganson, K.T., Mitchison, D., Rodgers, R.F., Murray, S.B., Testa, A., & Nagata, J.M. (2025). 'Eating disorders among an online sample of Canadian and American boys and men.' *Eating Behaviors, 57*, no.101980. https://doi.org/10.1016/j.eatbeh.2025.101980

Gaulin, S.J.C., & Schlegel, A. (1980). 'Paternal confidence and paternal investment: A cross-cultural test of a sociobiological hypothesis.' *Ethology and Sociobiology, 1*, pp 301–9. https://doi.org/10.1016/0162-3095(80)90015-1

Gay, R. (2014). *Bad Feminist: Essays*. Corsair

Geary, D.C. (2021). *Male, Female: The Evolution of Human Sex Differences* (3rd edn). American Psychological Association. https://doi.org/10.1037/0000181-000

Geher, G., & Gambacorta, D. (2010). 'Evolution is not relevant to sex differences in humans because I want it that way! Evidence for the politicization of human evolutionary psychology.' *EvoS Journal, 2*, pp 32–47. https://doi.org/10.59077/BFWV5169

Gettler, L.T., McDade, T.W., Feranil, A.B., & Kuzawa, C.W. (2011). 'Longitudinal evidence that fatherhood decreases testosterone in human males.' *Proceedings of the National Academy of Sciences, 108*, pp 16194–9. https://doi.org/10.1073/pnas.1105403108

Gibney, E. (2020). 'The researcher fighting to embed analysis of sex and gender into science.' *Nature, 588*, p.209. https://doi.org/10.1038/d41586-020-03336-8

Giofrè, D., Geary, D.C., & Halsey, L.G. (2025). 'The sexy and formidable male body: Men's height and weight are condition-dependent, sexually selected traits.' *Biology Letters, 21*, no.20240565. https://doi.org/10.1098/rsbl.2024.0565

Glaeser, E.L., & Sacerdote, B. (2003). 'Sentencing in homicide cases and the role of vengeance.' *Journal of Legal Studies, 32*, pp 363–82. https://doi.org/10.1086/374707

Godfrey-Smith, P., Scheel, D., Chancellor, S., Linquist, S., & Lawrence, M. (2022). 'In the line of fire: Debris throwing by wild octopuses.' *PLOS ONE, 17*, e0276482. https://doi.org/10.1371/journal.pone.0276482

Goldstein, J.R. (2011). 'A secular trend toward earlier male sexual maturity: Evidence from shifting ages of male young adult mortality.' *PLOS ONE, 6*, e14826. https://doi.org/10.1371/journal.pone.0014826

Gómez, J.M., Verdú, M., & González-Megías, A. (2021). 'Killing conspecific adults in mammals.' *Proceedings of the Royal Society B: Biological Sciences, 288*, no.20211080. https://doi.org/10.1098/rspb.2021.1080

Gordon, C. (2012). 'Men and women's differences extend to personality, study claims.' *HuffPost*. https://www.huffpost.com/entry/men-and-womens-difference-personality_n_1194613

Gottschall, J., Martin, J., Quish, H., & Rea, J. (2004). 'Sex differences in mate choice criteria are reflected in folktales from around the world and in historical European literature.' *Evolution and Human Behavior, 25*, pp 102–12. https://doi.org/10.1016/S1090-5138(04)00007-8

Gould, S.J. (1981). *The Mismeasure of Man*. Norton

Gourgaud, G.B. (1932). *The St. Helena Journal of General Baron Gourgaud, 1815–1818: Being a Diary Written at St. Helena During a Part of Napoleon's Captivity* (trans. S. Gillard). John Lane

Gowaty, P.A. (2004). 'Sex roles, contests for the control of reproduction, and sexual selection.' In P.M. Kappeler & C.P. van Schaik (eds), *Sexual Selection in Primates: New and Comparative Perspectives*, pp 37–54. Cambridge University Press. https://doi.org/10.1017/CBO9780511542459

Gowaty, P.A., Kim, Y.-K., & Anderson, W.W. (2012). 'No evidence of sexual selection in a repetition of Bateman's classic study of *Drosophila melanogaster*.' *Proceedings of the National Academy of Sciences, 109*, pp 11740–45. https://doi.org/10.1073/pnas.1207851109

Greitemeyer, T. (2005). 'Receptivity to sexual offers as a function of sex, socioeconomic status, physical attractiveness, and intimacy of the offer.' *Personal Relationships, 12*, pp 373–86. https://doi.org/10.1111/j.1475-6811.2005.00121.x

Griffith, J.D., Capiola, A., Balotti, B., Hart, C.L., & Turner, R. (2016). 'Online female escort advertisements: The cost of sex.' *Evolutionary Psychology, 14*, no.1474704916651270. https://doi.org/10.1177/1474704916651270

Guo, J., Basarkod, G., Perales, F., Parker, P.D., Marsh, H.W., Donald, J., Dicke, T., Sahdra, B.K., Ciarrochi, J., Hu, X., Lonsdale, C., Sanders,

T., & del Pozo Cruz, B. (2023). 'The equality paradox: Gender equality intensifies male advantages in adolescent subjective well-being.' *Personality and Social Psychology Bulletin, 50*, pp 147–64. https://doi.org/10.1177/01461672221125619

Haglund, D. (2013). '"We're the no.1 threat to women!" The feminist comedy of Louis C.K.' *Slate*. https://slate.com/culture/2013/04/louis-c-k-feminism-oh-my-god-on-hbo-proves-comic-a-feminist.html

Haidt, J. (2012). *The Righteous Mind: Why Good People Are Divided by Politics and Religion*. Pantheon/Random House

Hakim, C. (2000). *Work-Lifestyle Choices in the 21st Century: Preference Theory*. Oxford University Press

Hakim, C. (2006). 'Women, careers, and work-life preferences.' *British Journal of Guidance and Counselling, 34*, pp 279–94. https://doi.org/10.1080/03069880600769118

Hald, G.M., & Høgh-Olesen, H. (2010). 'Receptivity to sexual invitations from strangers of the opposite gender.' *Evolution and Human Behavior, 31*, pp 453–8. https://doi.org/10.1016/j.evolhumbehav.2010.07.004

Halim, M.L.D., Russo, L.N., Echave, K.N., Tawa, S., Sakamoto, D.J., & Portillo, M.A. (2024). '"She's so pretty": The development of valuing personal attractiveness among young children.' *Child Development, 95*, pp 1659–75. https://doi.org/10.1111/cdev.14104

Halim, M.L.D., Sakamoto, D.J., Russo, L.N., Echave, K.N., Portillo, M.A., & Tawa, S. (2022). 'Early gender differences in valuing strength.' *Archives of Sexual Behavior, 51*, pp 2169–82. https://doi.org/10.1007/s10508-021-02185-4

Halpern, D.F. (2012). *Sex Differences in Cognitive Abilities* (4th edn). Psychology Press. https://doi.org/10.4324/9780203816530

Halpern, D.F., Straight, C.A., & Stephenson, C.L. (2011). 'Beliefs about cognitive gender differences: Accurate for direction, underestimated for size.' *Sex Roles, 64*, pp 336–47. https://doi.org/10.1007/s11199-010-9891-2

Halsey, L.G., Careau, V., Pontzer, H., Ainslie, P.N., Andersen, L.F., Anderson, L.J., Arab, L., Baddou, I., Bedu-Addo, K., Blaak, E.E., Blanc, S., Bonomi, A.G., Bouten, C.V.C., Bovet, P., Buchowski, M.S., Butte, N.F., Camps, S.G.J.A., Close, G.L., Cooper, J.A., . . . Speakman, J.R. (2022). 'Variability in energy expenditure is much greater in males than females.' *Journal of Human Evolution, 171*, no.103229. https://doi.org/10.1016/j.jhevol.2022.103229

Hames, R.B. (1988). 'The allocation of parental care among the Ye-Kwana.' In

L. Betzig, M. Borgerhoff Mulder, & P. Turke (eds), *Human Reproductive Behavior: A Darwinian Perspective*, pp 237–52. Cambridge University Press

Hamilton, W.D. (1964). 'The genetical evolution of social behaviour: I & II.' *Journal of Theoretical Biology*, 7, pp 1–52. https://doi.org/10.1016/0022-5193(64)90038-4

Hamilton, W.D. (2001). *Narrow Roads of Gene Land: The Collected Papers of W.D. Hamilton*, vol.2: *The Evolution of Sex*. Oxford University Press

Hamilton, W.D., & Zuk, M. (1982). 'Heritable true fitness and bright birds: A role for parasites?' *Science*, *218*, pp 384–7. https://doi.org/10.1126/science.7123238

Hampson, E., Rovet, J.F., & Altmann, D. (1998). 'Spatial reasoning in children with congenital adrenal hyperplasia due to 21–hydroxylase deficiency.' *Developmental Neuropsychology*, *14*, pp 299–320. https://doi.org/10.1080/87565649809540713

Hare-Mustin, R.T., & Marecek, J. (1988). 'The meaning of difference: Gender theory, postmodernism, and psychology.' *American Psychologist*, *43*, pp 455–64. https://doi.org/10.1037/0003-066X.43.6.455

Hart, C.W., & Pilling, A.R. (1960). *The Tiwi of North Australia*. Holt, Rinehart & Winston

Hartley, B.L., & Sutton, R.M. (2013). 'A stereotype threat account of boys' academic underachievement.' *Child Development*, *84*, pp 1716–33. https://doi.org/10.1111/cdev.12079

Haselton, M.G., & Buss, D.M. (2000). 'Error management theory: A new perspective on biases in cross-sex mind reading.' *Journal of Personality and Social Psychology*, *78*, pp 81–91. https://doi.org/10.1037/0022-3514.78.1.81

Hassett, J.M., Siebert, E.R., & Wallen, K. (2008). 'Sex differences in rhesus monkey toy preferences parallel those of children.' *Hormones and Behavior*, *54*, pp 359–64. https://doi.org/10.1016/j.yhbeh.2008.03.008

Haux, L.M., Engelmann, J.M., Arslan, R.C., Hertwig, R., & Herrmann, E. (2023). 'Chimpanzee and human risk preferences show key similarities.' *Psychological Science*, *34*, pp 358–69. https://doi.org/10.1177/09567976221140326

Hawkes, K., O'Connell, J.F., & Blurton Jones, N. (1989). 'Hardworking Hadza grandmothers.' In V. Standen & R. Foley (eds), *Comparative Socioecology*, pp 341–66. Basil Blackwell

Hedges, L.V., & Nowell, A. (1995). 'Sex differences in mental test scores, variability and numbers of high-scoring individuals.' *Science*, *269*, pp 41–5. https://doi.org/10.1126/science.7604277

Herdt, G. (1981). *Guardians of the Flutes: Idioms of Masculinity*. McGraw-Hill

Herlitz, A., Hönig, I., Hedebrant, K., & Asperholm, M. (2024). 'A systematic review and new analyses of the gender-equality paradox.' *Perspectives on Psychological Science, 20*, pp 503–39. https://doi.org/10.1177/17456916231202685

Herrera, A.M., Shuster, S.G., Perriton, C.L., & Cohn, M.J. (2013). 'Developmental basis of phallus reduction during bird evolution.' *Current Biology, 23*, pp 1065–74. https://doi.org/10.1016/j.cub.2013.04.062

Hess, N., Helfrecht, C., Hagen, E., Sell, A., & Hewlett, B. (2010). 'Interpersonal aggression among Aka hunter-gatherers of the Central African Republic.' *Human Nature, 21*, pp 330–54. https://doi.org/10.1007/s12110-010-9094-0

Hildebrandt, A., & Jäckle, S. (2023). 'Particularly in highly developed and more gender egalitarian societies: Sex differences in attitudes towards homosexuality.' *Journal of Sex Research, 61*, pp 1400–13. https://doi.org/10.1080/00224499.2023.2198500

Hines, M., Pasterski, V., Spencer, D., Neufeld, S., Patalay, P., Hindmarsh, P.C., Hughes, I.A., & Acerini, C.L. (2016). 'Prenatal androgen exposure alters girls' responses to information indicating gender-appropriate behaviour.' *Philosophical Transactions of the Royal Society B: Biological Sciences, 371*, no.20150125. https://doi.org/10.1098/rstb.2015.0125

HM Government (2022). 'Supporting male victims of crimes considered violence against women and girls [policy paper].' Crown. https://data.parliament.uk/DepositedPapers/Files/DEP2022-0294/Supporting_Male_Victims_March_2022.pdf

Hoffman, M., Gneezy, U., & List, J.A. (2011). 'Nurture affects gender differences in spatial abilities.' *Proceedings of the National Academy of Sciences, 108*, pp 14786–8. https://doi.org/10.1073/pnas.1015182108

Holmboe, S.A., Priskorn, L., Jørgensen, N., Skakkebaek, N.E., Linneberg, A., Juul, A., & Andersson, A.-M. (2017). 'Influence of marital status on testosterone levels: A ten year follow-up of 1113 men.' *Psychoneuroendocrinology, 80*, pp 155–61. https://doi.org/10.1016/j.psyneuen.2017.03.010

Hone, D.W.E., Naish, D., & Cuthill, I.C. (2012). 'Does mutual sexual selection explain the evolution of head crests in pterosaurs and dinosaurs?' *Lethaia, 45*, pp 139–56. https://doi.org/10.1111/j.1502-3931.2011.00300.x

Honeycutt, N., Careem, A., Lewis, N.A., Jr, & Jussim, L. (in press). 'Are STEM faculty biased against female applicants? A robust replication and extension of Moss-Racusin and colleagues (2012).' *Meta-Psychology*

Honeycutt, N., & Jussim, L. (2020). 'A model of political bias in social science research.' *Psychological Inquiry, 31*, pp 73–85. https://doi.org/10.1080/1047840X.2020.1722600

Hooven, C. (2021). *T: The Story of Testosterone, the Hormone That Dominates and Divides Us*. Henry Holt and Company

Hopcroft, R.L. (2006). 'Sex, status, and reproductive success in the contemporary United States.' *Evolution and Human Behavior, 27*, pp 104–20. https://doi.org/10.1016/j.evolhumbehav.2005.07.004

Hopcroft, R.L. (2021). 'High income men have high value as long-term mates in the U.S.: Personal income and the probability of marriage, divorce, and childbearing in the U.S.' *Evolution and Human Behavior, 42*, pp 409–17. https://doi.org/10.1016/j.evolhumbehav.2021.03.004

Hopcroft, R.L. (2022). 'Husband's income, wife's income, and number of biological children in the U.S.' *Biodemography and Social Biology, 67*, pp 71–83. https://doi.org/10.1080/19485565.2022.2037070

Hopwood, C.J., Zizer, J.N., Nissen, A.T., Dillard, C., Thompkins, A.M., Graça, J., Waldhorn, D.R., & Bleidorn, W. (2024). 'Paradoxical gender effects in meat consumption across cultures.' *Scientific Reports, 14*, no.13033. https://doi.org/10.1038/s41598-024-62511-3

Hrdy, S.B. (1981). *The Woman That Never Evolved*. Harvard University Press

Hrdy, S.B. (2000). *Mother Nature: Maternal Instincts and How They Shape the Human Species*. Ballantine Books

Hrdy, S.B. (2009). *Mothers and Others: The Evolutionary Origin of Mutual Understanding*. Harvard University Press

Hruschka, D.J., Brewis, A.A., Wutich, A., & Morin, B. (2011). 'Shared norms and their explanation for the social clustering of obesity.' *American Journal of Public Health, 101*, S295–300. https://doi.org/10.2105/AJPH.2010.300053

Hruska, J. (2015). 'New analysis shows over 99 percent of the women on Ashley Madison were fake.' *Extreme Tech*. https://www.extremetech.com/internet/213019-new-analysis-shows-over-99-percent-of-the-women-on-ashley-madison-were-fake

Hyde, J.S. (2005). 'The gender similarities hypothesis.' *American Psychologist, 60*, pp 581–92. https://doi.org/10.1037/0003-066X.60.6.581

Hyde, J.S., & Linn, M.C. (1988). 'Gender differences in verbal ability: A meta-analysis.' *Psychological Bulletin, 104*, pp 53–69. https://doi.org/10.1037/0033-2909.104.1.53

Hyde, J.S., & Mertz, J.E. (2009). 'Gender, culture, and mathematics performance.' *Proceedings of the National Academy of Sciences, 106*, pp 8801–7. https://doi.org/10.1073/pnas.0901265106

Iliescu, D., Ilie, A., Ispas, D., Dobrean, A., & Clinciu, A.I. (2016). 'Sex differences in intelligence: A multi-measure approach using nationally representative samples from Romania.' *Intelligence, 58*, pp 54–61. https://doi.org/10.1016/j.intell.2016.06.007

Inglis, M., & O'Hagan, S. (2022). 'Stereotype threat, gender and mathematics attainment: A conceptual replication of Stricker & Ward.' *PLOS ONE, 17*, e0267699. https://doi.org/10.1371/journal.pone.0267699

Jackson, S.S., Marks, M.A., Katki, H.A., Cook, M.B., Hyun, N., Freedman, N.D., Kahle, L.L., Castle, P.E., Graubard, B.I., & Chaturvedi, A.K. (2022). 'Sex disparities in the incidence of 21 cancer types: Quantification of the contribution of risk factors.' *Cancer, 128*, pp 3531–40. https://doi.org/10.1002/cncr.34390

Janicke, T., Häderer, I.K., Lajeunesse, M.J., & Anthes, N. (2016). 'Darwinian sex roles confirmed across the animal kingdom.' *Science Advances, 2*, e1500983. https://doi.org/10.1126/sciadv.1500983

Janzen, D.H. (1977). 'A note on optimal mate selection by plants.' *American Naturalist, 111*, pp 365–71. https://doi.org/10.1086/283166

Jensen, A.R. (1998). *The G Factor: The Science of Mental Ability*. Praeger

Jiang, R., Calhoun, V.D., Cui, Y., Qi, S., Zhuo, C., Li, J., Jung, R., Yang, J., Du, Y., Jiang, T., & Sui, J. (2020). 'Multimodal data revealed different neurobiological correlates of intelligence between males and females.' *Brain Imaging and Behavior, 14*, pp 1979–93. https://doi.org/10.1007/s11682-019-00146-z

Johnson, R.C. (1996). 'Attributes of Carnegie medalists performing acts of heroism and of the recipients of these acts.' *Ethology and Sociobiology, 17*, pp 355–62. https://doi.org/10.1016/S0162-3095(96)00059-3

Johnson, W., Carothers, A., & Deary, I.J. (2008). 'Sex differences in variability in general intelligence: A new look at the old question.' *Perspectives on Psychological Science, 3*, pp 518–31. https://doi.org/10.1111/j.1745-6924.2008.00096.x

Jonason, P.K., & Thomas, A.G. (2022). 'Being more educated and earning more increases romantic interest: Data from 1.8 M online daters from 24 nations.' *Human Nature, 33*, pp 115–31. https://doi.org/10.1007/s12110-022-09422-2

Jonason, P.K., Żemojtel-Piotrowska, M., Piotrowski, J., Sedikides, C., Campbell, W.K., Gebauer, J.E., Maltby, J., Adamovic, M., Adams, B.G., Kadiyono, A.L., Atitsogbe, K.A., Bundhoo, H.Y., Bălţătescu, S., Bilić, S., Brulin, J.G.,

Chobthamkit, P., Del Carmen Dominguez, A., Dragova-Koleva, S., El-Astal, S., . . . Yahiiaev, I. (2020). 'Country-level correlates of the Dark Triad traits in 49 countries.' *Journal of Personality, 88*, pp 1252–67. https://doi.org/10.1111/jopy.12569

Jones, I.L., & Hunter, F.M. (1993). 'Mutual sexual selection in a monogamous seabird.' *Nature, 362*, pp 238–39. https://doi.org/10.1038/362238a0

Judson, O. (2002). *Dr. Tatiana's Sex Advice to All Creation: The Definitive Guide to the Evolutionary Biology of Sex*. Henry Holt and Company

Jussim, L. (2012). *Social Perception and Social Reality: Why Accuracy Dominates Bias and Self-Fulfilling Prophecy*. Oxford University Press

Jussim, L. (2017). 'Précis of *Social Perception and Social Reality: Why Accuracy Dominates Bias and Self-Fulfilling Prophecy*.' *Behavioral and Brain Sciences, 40*, e1. https://doi.org/10.1017/S0140525X1500062X

Jussim, L., & Harber, K.D. (2005). 'Teacher expectations and self-fulfilling prophecies: Knowns and unknowns, resolved and unresolved controversies.' *Personality and Social Psychology Review, 9*, pp 131–55. https://doi.org/10.1207/s15327957pspr0902_3

Kabátek, J., & Blanchard, R. (2024). 'Birth order and family size of UK Biobank subjects identified as asexual, bisexual, heterosexual, or homosexual according to self-reported sexual histories.' *Archives of Sexual Behavior, 54*, pp 35–50. https://doi.org/10.1007/s10508-024-03004-2

Kahlenberg, S.M., & Wrangham, R.W. (2010). 'Sex differences in chimpanzees' use of sticks as play objects resemble those of children.' *Current Biology, 20*, R1067–8. https://doi.org/10.1016/j.cub.2010.11.024

Kajonius, P.J., & Johnson, J. (2018). 'Sex differences in 30 facets of the five factor model of personality in the large public (N = 320,128).' *Personality and Individual Differences, 129*, pp 126–30. https://doi.org/10.1016/j.paid.2018.03.026

Kamei, N., & Glabe, C.G. (2003). 'The species-specific egg receptor for sea urchin sperm adhesion is EBR1, a novel ADAMTS protein.' *Genes and Development, 17*, pp 2502–7. https://doi.org/10.1101/gad.1133003

Kanazawa, S., & Still, M.C. (2000). 'Why men commit crimes (and why they desist).' *Sociological Theory, 18*, pp 434–47. https://doi.org/10.1111/0735-2751.00110

Kaplan, H. (1994). 'Evolutionary and wealth flows theories of fertility: Empirical tests and new models.' *Population and Development Review, 20*, pp 753–91. https://doi.org/10.2307/2137661

Karantzas, G.C., Curtis, A., Knox, L., Staiger, P.K., Head, T., Toumbourou, J.W., Gruenert, S., Romano, D., & Miller, P.G. (2023). 'Do relationship education programs reduce relationship aggression? A meta-analytic study.' *Clinical Psychology Review, 104*, no.102285. https://doi.org/10.1016/j.cpr.2023.102285

Kehr, N., Daly, M., & Wilson, M. (1997). 'Homicide in Canada: Perception and reality.' In M. Riedel & J. Boulahanis (eds), *Lethal Violence: Proceedings of the 1995 Meeting of the Homicide Research Group, Ottawa, Canada*, pp 89–96. University of Michigan Library

Kennair, L.E.O., Schmitt, D., Fjeldavli, Y.L., & Harlem, S.K. (2009). 'Sex differences in sexual desires and attitudes in Norwegian samples.' *Interpersona: An International Journal on Personal Relationships, 3*, pp 1–32. https://doi.org/10.5964/ijpr.v3isupp1.67

Kenrick, D.T., Gabrielidis, C., Keefe, R.C., & Cornelius, J.S. (1996). 'Adolescents' age preferences for dating partners: Support for an evolutionary model of life-history strategies.' *Child Development, 67*, pp 1499–511. https://doi.org/10.1111/j.1467-8624.1996.tb01810.x

Kenrick, D.T., Groth, G., Trost, M.R., & Sadalla, E.K. (1993). 'Integrating evolutionary and social exchange perspectives on relationships: Effects of gender, self-appraisal, and involvement level on mate selection criteria.' *Journal of Personality and Social Psychology, 64*, pp 951–69. https://doi.org/10.1037/0022-3514.64.6.951

Kenrick, D.T., & Keefe, R.C. (1992a). 'Age preferences in mates reflect sex differences in human reproductive strategies.' *Behavioral and Brain Sciences, 15*, pp 75–91. https://doi.org/10.1017/S0140525X00067595

Kenrick, D.T., & Keefe, R.C. (1992b). 'Authors' response [Response to commentaries on "Age preferences in mates reflect sex differences in human reproductive strategies"]'. *Behavioral and Brain Sciences, 15*, pp 119–33. https://doi.org/10.1017/S0140525X00067595

Kenrick, D.T., Keefe, R.C., Bryan, A., Barr, A., & Brown, S. (1995). 'Age preferences and mate choice among homosexuals and heterosexuals: A case for modular psychological mechanisms.' *Journal of Personality and Social Psychology, 69*, pp 1166–72. https://doi.org/10.1037/0022-3514.69.6.1166

Kenrick, D.T., Sadalla, E.K., Groth, G., & Trost, M.R. (1990). 'Evolution, traits, and the stages of human courtship: Qualifying the parental investment model.' *Journal of Personality, 58*, pp 97–116. https://doi.org/10.1111/j.1467-6494.1990.tb00909.x

Kenrick, D.T., & Sheets, V. (1993). 'Homicidal fantasies.' *Ethology and Sociobiology, 14*, pp 231–46. https://doi.org/10.1016/0162-3095(93)90019-E

Khorashad, B.S., Roshan, G.M., Reid, A.G., Aghili, Z., Moghadam, M.D., Khazai, B., Hiradfar, M., Afkhamizadeh, M., Ghaemi, N., Talaei, A., Abbaszadegan, M.R., Aarabi, A., Dastmalchi, S., & Van de Grift, T.C. (2018). 'Childhood sex-typed behavior and gender change in individuals with 46,XY and 46,XX disorders of sex development: An Iranian multicenter study.' *Archives of Sexual Behavior*, 47, pp 2287–98. https://doi.org/10.1007/s10508-018-1281-9

Kim, A., Song, H., Park, N., Choi, S., & Cho, J. (2018). 'Injury pyramid of unintentional injuries according to sex and age in South Korea.' *Clinical and Experimental Emergency Medicine, 5*, pp 84–94. https://doi.org/10.15441/ceem.17.205

King, J.E., Weiss, A., & Sisco, M.M. (2008). 'Aping humans: Age and sex effects in chimpanzee (*Pan troglodytes*) and human (*Homo sapiens*) personality.' *Journal of Comparative Psychology, 122*, pp 418–27. https://doi.org/10.1037/a0013125

Kinsey, A.C., Pomeroy, W.B., Martin, C.E., & Gebhard, P.H. (1953). *Sexual Behavior in the Human Female*. Saunders

Klein, V., Laan, E., Brunner, F., & Briken, P. (2022). 'Sexual pleasure matters (especially for women): Data from the German Sexuality and Health Survey (GeSiD).' *Sexuality Research and Social Policy, 19*, pp 1879–87. https://doi.org/10.1007/s13178-022-00694-y

Kleven, H., Landais, C., & Leite-Mariante, G. (2025). 'The Child Penalty Atlas.' *Review of Economic Studies, 92*, pp 3174–207. https://doi.org/10.1093/restud/rdae104

Knight, G.P., Guthrie, I.K., Page, M.C., & Fabes, R.A. (2002). 'Emotional arousal and gender differences in aggression: A meta-analysis.' *Aggressive Behavior, 28*, pp 366–93. https://doi.org/10.1002/ab.80011

Koch, A.J., D'Mello, S.D., & Sackett, P.R. (2015). 'A meta-analysis of gender stereotypes and bias in experimental simulations of employment decision making.' *Journal of Applied Psychology, 100*, pp 128–61. https://doi.org/10.1037/a0036734

Kohlberg, L. (1966). 'A cognitive-developmental analysis of children's sex role concepts and attitudes.' In E.E. Maccoby (ed.), *The Development of Sex Differences*, pp 82–173. Stanford University Press

Konerding, W.S., Zimmermann, E., Bleich, E., Hedrich, H.-J., & Scheumann,

M. (2016). 'Female cats, but not males, adjust responsiveness to arousal in the voice of kittens.' *BMC Evolutionary Biology, 16*, no.157. https://doi.org/10.1186/s12862-016-0718-9

Kowal, M., Sorokowski, P., Pisanski, K., Valentova, J.V., Varella, M.A.C., Frederick, D.A., Al-Shawaf, L., García, F.E., Giammusso, I., Gjoneska, B., Kozma, L., Otterbring, T., Papadatou-Pastou, M., Pfuhl, G., Stöckli, S., Studzinska, A., Toplu-Demirtaş, E., Touloumakos, A.K., Bakos, B.E., . . . Zumárraga-Espinosa, M. (2022). 'Predictors of enhancing human physical attractiveness: Data from 93 countries.' *Evolution and Human Behavior, 43*, pp 455–74. https://doi.org/10.1016/j.evolhumbehav.2022.08.003

Kralj-Fišer, S., Cargnelutti, F., Li, D., & Kuntner, M. (2025). 'Unravelling evolutionary dynamics of female sexual cannibalism and male reproductive strategies in spiders.' *Integrative Zoology*, advance online publication. https://doi.org/10.1111/1749-4877.13027

Kruger, D.J., & Nesse, R.M. (2004). 'Sexual selection and the male:female mortality ratio.' *Evolutionary Psychology, 2*, pp 66–85. https://doi.org/10.1177/147470490400200112

Kruger, D.J., & Nesse, R.M. (2006). 'An evolutionary life-history framework for understanding sex differences in human mortality rates.' *Human Nature, 17*, pp 74–97. https://doi.org/10.1007/s12110-006-1021-z

Krumer, A., & Musau, A. (2023). 'Golden tears: A cross-country study of crying in the Olympics.' *Emotion, 24*, pp 27–38. https://doi.org/10.1037/emo0001247

Kuhle, B.X. (2011). 'Did you have sex with him? Do you love her? An in vivo test of sex differences in jealous interrogations.' *Personality and Individual Differences, 51*, pp 1044–7. https://doi.org/10.1016/j.paid.2011.07.034

Kung, K.T.F., Louie, K., Spencer, D., & Hines, M. (2024). 'Prenatal androgen exposure and sex-typical play behaviour: A meta-analysis of classic congenital adrenal hyperplasia studies.' *Neuroscience and Biobehavioral Reviews, 159*, no.105616. https://doi.org/10.1016/j.neubiorev.2024.105616

Kuppuswamy, V., & Mollick, E.R. (2015). *Gender Differences in Serial Founding Rates* (Working Paper No.2623746). SSRN. https://ssrn.com/abstract=2623746

L'hospital, A. (2022). '"C'est devenu le tabou ultime": Quand Sciences Po censure Darwin ["It has become the ultimate taboo": When Sciences Po censors Darwin].' *L'Express*. https://www.lexpress.fr/actualite/c-est-devenu-le-tabou-ultime-quand-sciences-po-censure-darwin_2175789.html

Labuda, D., Lefebvre, J.-F., Nadeau, P., & Roy-Gagnon, M.-H. (2010). 'Female-to-male breeding ratio in modern humans: An analysis based on historical recombinations.' *American Journal of Human Genetics, 86*, pp 353–63. https://doi.org/10.1016/j.ajhg.2010.01.029

LaFreniere, P. (2011). 'Evolutionary functions of social play: Life histories, sex differences, and emotion regulation.' *American Journal of Play, 3*, pp 464–88.

Langstrom, N., Rahman, Q., Carlstrom, E., & Lichtenstein, P. (2010). 'Genetic and environmental effects on same-sex sexual behavior: A population study of twins in Sweden.' *Archives of Sexual Behavior, 39*, pp 75–80. https://doi.org/10.1007/s10508-008-9386-1

Las Cases, E. de (1836). *Memoirs of the Life, Exile, and Conversations of the Emperor Napoleon*, vol.2 (trans. E.K. O'Meara). Henry Colburn

Lassek, W.D., & Gaulin, S.J.C. (2009). 'Costs and benefits of fat-free muscle mass in men: Relationship to mating success, dietary requirements, and native immunity.' *Evolution and Human Behavior, 30*, pp 322–8. https://doi.org/10.1016/j.evolhumbehav.2009.04.002

Latzman, R.D., Freeman, H.D., Schapiro, S.J., & Hopkins, W.D. (2015). 'The contribution of genetics and early rearing experiences to hierarchical personality dimensions in chimpanzees (*Pan troglodytes*).' *Journal of Personality and Social Psychology, 109*, pp 889–900. https://doi.org/10.1037/pspp0000040

Lauer, J.E., Yhang, E., & Lourenco, S.F. (2019). 'The development of gender differences in spatial reasoning: A meta-analytic review.' *Psychological Bulletin, 145*, pp 537–65. https://doi.org/10.1037/bul0000191

Lavy, V. (2008). 'Do gender stereotypes reduce girls' or boys' human capital outcomes? Evidence from a natural experiment.' *Journal of Public Economics, 92*, pp 2083–105. https://doi.org/10.1016/j.jpubeco.2008.02.009

Le Boeuf, B.J., & Reiter, J. (1987). 'Lifetime reproductive success in northern elephant seals.' In T.H. Clutton-Brock (ed.), *Reproductive Success: Studies of Selection and Adaptation in Contrasting Breeding Systems*, pp 344–62. University of Chicago Press

Lee, R.B. (1984). *The Dobe !Kung*. Holt, Rinehart & Winston

Lehre, A.-C., Lehre, K.P., Laake, P., & Danbolt, N.C. (2009). 'Greater intrasex phenotype variability in males than in females is a fundamental aspect of the gender differences in humans.' *Developmental Psychobiology, 51*, pp 198–206. https://doi.org/10.1002/dev.20358

Lehtonen, J., & Parker, G.A. (2014). 'Gamete competition, gamete limitation, and the evolution of the two sexes.' *Molecular Human Reproduction, 20*, pp 1161–8. https://doi.org/10.1093/molehr/gau068

Lemaître, J.-F., Ronget, V., Tidière, M., Allainé, D., Berger, V., Cohas, A., Colchero, F., Conde, D.A., Garratt, M., Liker, A., Marais, G.A.B., Scheuerlein, A., Székely, T., & Gaillard, J.-M. (2020). 'Sex differences in adult lifespan and aging rates of mortality across wild mammals.' *Proceedings of the National Academy of Sciences, 117*, pp 8546–53. https://doi.org/10.1073/pnas.1911999117

Lendrem, B.A.D., Lendrem, D.W., Gray, A., & Isaacs, J.D. (2014). 'The Darwin Awards: Sex differences in idiotic behaviour.' *BMJ: British Medical Journal, 349*, g7094. https://doi.org/10.1136/bmj.g7094

LeVay, S. (2011). *Gay, Straight, and the Reason Why: The Science of Sexual Orientation.* Oxford University Press

Leveroni, C.L., & Berenbaum, S.A. (1998). 'Early androgen effects on interest in infants: Evidence from children with congenital adrenal hyperplasia.' *Developmental Neuropsychology, 14*, pp 321–40. https://doi.org/10.1080/87565649809540714

Lew-Levy, S., Andersen, M.M., Lavi, N., & Riede, F. (2022). 'Hunter-gatherer children's object play and tool use: An ethnohistorical analysis.' *Frontiers in Psychology, 13*, no.824983. https://doi.org/10.3389/fpsyg.2022.824983

Li, N.P., Bailey, J.M., Kenrick, D.T., & Linsenmeier, J.A.W. (2002). 'The necessities and luxuries of mate preferences: Testing the tradeoffs.' *Journal of Personality and Social Psychology, 82*, pp 947–55. https://doi.org/10.1037/0022-3514.82.6.947

Lidborg, L.H., Cross, C.P., & Boothroyd, L.G. (2022). 'A meta-analysis of the association between male dimorphism and fitness outcomes in humans.' *eLife, 11*, e65031. https://doi.org/10.7554/eLife.65031

Liddon, L., & Barry, J.A. (2021). *Perspectives in Male Psychology: An Introduction.* Wiley-Blackwell.

Lievore, I., & Triventi, M. (2022). 'Do teacher and classroom characteristics affect the way in which girls and boys are graded?' *British Journal of Sociology of Education, 44*, pp 97–122. https://doi.org/10.1080/01425692.2022.2122942

Lippa, R.A. (2007). 'The preferred traits of mates in a cross-national study of heterosexual and homosexual men and women: An examination of biological and cultural influences.' *Archives of Sexual Behavior, 36*, pp 193–208. https://doi.org/10.1007/s10508-006-9151-2

Lippa, R.A. (2008). 'Sex differences and sexual orientation differences in personality: Findings from the BBC Internet survey.' *Archives of Sexual Behavior, 37*, pp 173–87. https://doi.org/10.1007/s10508-007-9267-z

Lippa, R.A. (2009). 'Sex differences in sex drive, sociosexuality, and height across 53 nations: Testing evolutionary and social structural theories.' *Archives of Sexual Behavior, 38*, pp 631–51. https://doi.org/10.1007/s10508-007-9242-8

Lippa, R.A. (2010a). 'Gender differences in personality and interests: When, where, and why?' *Social and Personality Psychology Compass, 4*, pp 1098–110. https://doi.org/10.1111/j.1751-9004.2010.00320.x

Lippa, R.A. (2010b). 'Sex differences in personality traits and gender-related occupational preferences across 53 nations: Testing evolutionary and social-environmental theories.' *Archives of Sexual Behavior, 39*, pp 619–36. https://doi.org/10.1007/s10508-008-9380-7

Lippa, R.A., Collaer, M.L., & Peters, M. (2010). 'Sex differences in mental rotation and line angle judgments are positively associated with gender equality and economic development across 53 nations.' *Archives of Sexual Behavior, 39*, pp 990–97. https://doi.org/10.1007/s10508-008-9460-8

Lippa, R.A., Preston, K., & Penner, J. (2014). 'Women's representation in 60 occupations from 1972 to 2010: More women in high-status jobs, few women in things-oriented jobs.' *PLOS ONE, 9*, e95960. https://doi.org/10.1371/journal.pone.0095960

Löckenhoff, C.E., Chan, W., McCrae, R.R., De Fruyt, F., Jussim, L., De Bolle, M., Costa, P.T., Sutin, A.R., Realo, A., Allik, J., Nakazato, K., Shimonaka, Y., Hřebíčková, M., Graf, S., Yik, M., Ficková, E., Brunner-Sciarra, M., Leibovich de Figueroa, N., Schmidt, V., . . . Terracciano, A. (2014). 'Gender stereotypes of personality: Universal and accurate?' *Journal of Cross-Cultural Psychology, 45*, pp 675–94. https://doi.org/10.1177/0022022113520075

Loeber, R., Farrington, D.P., Hipwell, A.E., Stepp, S.D., Pardini, D., & Ahonen, L. (2015). 'Constancy and change in the prevalence and frequency of offending when based on longitudinal self-reports or official records: Comparisons by gender, race, and crime type.' *Journal of Developmental and Life-Course Criminology, 1*, pp 150–68. https://doi.org/10.1007/s40865-015-0010-5

Lonsdorf, E.V. (2017). 'Sex differences in nonhuman primate behavioral development.' *Journal of Neuroscience Research, 95*, pp 213–21. https://doi.org/10.1002/jnr.23862

Loomes, R., Hull, L., & Mandy, W.P.L. (2017). 'What is the male-to-female ratio in autism spectrum disorder? A systematic review and meta-analysis.' *Journal of the American Academy of Child and Adolescent Psychiatry, 56*, pp 466–74. https://doi.org/10.1016/j.jaac.2017.03.013

Lorde, A. (2004). *Conversations with Audre Lorde*. University Press of Mississippi

Low, B.S. (1989). 'Cross-cultural patterns in the training of children: An evolutionary perspective.' *Journal of Comparative Psychology, 103*, pp 311–19. https://doi.org/10.1037/0735-7036.103.4.311

Lubinski, D., Benbow, C.P., McCabe, K.O., & Bernstein, B.O. (2023). 'Composing meaningful lives: Exceptional women and men at age 50.' *Gifted Child Quarterly, 67*, pp 278–305. https://doi.org/10.1177/00169862231175831

Lukas, D., & Huchard, E. (2014). 'The evolution of infanticide by males in mammalian societies.' *Science, 346*, pp 841–4. https://doi.org/10.1126/science.1257226

Lukianoff, G., & Haidt, J. (2018). *The Coddling of the American Mind: How Good Intentions and Bad Ideas Are Setting Up a Generation for Failure*. Penguin

Lytton, H., & Romney, D.M. (1991). 'Parents' differential socialization of boys and girls: A meta-analysis.' *Psychological Bulletin, 109*, pp 267–96. https://doi.org/10.1037/0033-2909.109.2.267

Maccoby, E., & Jacklin, C.N. (1974). *The Psychology of Sex Differences*. Stanford University Press

Maccoby, E.E., & Jacklin, C.N. (1980). 'Sex differences in aggression: A rejoinder and reprise.' *Child Development, 51*, pp 964–80. https://doi.org/10.2307/1129535

Macdowall, W., Gibson, L.J., Tanton, C., Mercer, C.H., Lewis, R., Clifton, S., Field, N., Datta, J., Mitchell, K.R., Sonnenberg, P., Erens, B., Copas, A.J., Phelps, A., Prah, P., Johnson, A.M., & Wellings, K. (2013). 'Lifetime prevalence, associated factors, and circumstances of non-volitional sex in women and men in Britain: Findings from the third National Survey of Sexual Attitudes and Lifestyles (Natsal-3).' *Lancet, 382*, pp 1845–55. https://doi.org/10.1016/S0140-6736(13)62300-4

Maeda, Y., & Yoon, S.Y. (2013). 'A meta-analysis on gender differences in mental rotation ability measured by the Purdue Spatial Visualization Tests: Visualization of Rotations (PSVT:R).' *Educational Psychology Review, 25*, pp 69–94. https://doi.org/10.1007/s10648-012-9215-x

Magnusson, K. (2022). 'Interpreting Cohen's *d* effect size: An interactive visualization.' *R Psychologist*. https://rpsychologist.com/cohend/

Makel, M.C., Wai, J., Peairs, K., & Putallaz, M. (2016). 'Sex differences in the right tail of cognitive abilities: An update and cross cultural extension.' *Intelligence, 59*, pp 8–15. https://doi.org/10.1016/j.intell.2016.09.003

Malamuth, N.M. (1996). 'The confluence model of sexual aggression: Feminist and evolutionary perspectives.' In D.M. Buss & N.M. Malamuth (eds), *Sex, Power, Conflict: Evolutionary and Feminist Perspectives*, pp 269–95. Oxford University Press. https://doi.org/10.1093/oso/9780195095814.003.0012

Malinowski, B. (1929). *The Sexual Life of Savages in North-Western Melanesia: An Ethnographic Account of Courtship, Marriage, and Family Life among the Natives of the Trobriand Islands, British New Guinea*. Harcourt Brace

Mandy, W., Chilvers, R., Chowdhury, U., Salter, G., Seigal, A., & Skuse, D. (2012). 'Sex differences in autism spectrum disorder: Evidence from a large sample of children and adolescents.' *Journal of Autism and Developmental Disorders, 42*, pp 1304–13. https://doi.org/10.1007/s10803-011-1356-0

Markowsky, E., & Beblo, M. (2022). 'When do we observe a gender gap in competition entry? A meta-analysis of the experimental literature.' *Journal of Economic Behavior and Organization, 198*, pp 139–63. https://doi.org/10.1016/j.jebo.2022.03.030

Marley, C.L., Pollard, T.M., Barton, R.A., & Street, S.E. (2022). 'A systematic review of sex differences in rough and tumble play across non-human mammals.' *Behavioral Ecology and Sociobiology, 76*, no.158. https://doi.org/10.1007/s00265-022-03260-z

Marlowe, F. (2000). 'Paternal investment and the human mating system.' *Behavioural Processes, 51*, pp 45–61. https://doi.org/10.1016/S0376-6357(00)00118-2

Marlowe, F.W. (2003a). 'A critical period for provisioning by Hadza men: Implications for pair bonding.' *Evolution and Human Behavior, 24*, pp 217–29. https://doi.org/10.1016/S1090-5138(03)00014-X

Marlowe, F.W. (2003b). 'The mating system of foragers in the Standard Cross-Cultural Sample.' *Cross-Cultural Research, 37*, pp 282–306. https://doi.org/10.1177/1069397103254008

Martin, A.E., Guevara Beltran, D., Koster, J., & Tracy, J.L. (2024). 'Is gender primacy universal?' *Proceedings of the National Academy of Sciences, 121*, e2401919121. https://doi.org/10.1073/pnas.2401919121

Martin, C.L., & Ruble, D. (2004). 'Children's search for gender cues: Cognitive perspectives on gender development.' *Current Directions in Psychological Science, 13*, pp 67–70. https://doi.org/10.1111/j.0963-7214.2004.00276.x

Martin, R.D. (1990). *Primate Origins and Evolution: A Phylogenetic Reconstruction*. Princeton University Press

Mason, B. (2002). 'Men die young – even if old.' *New Scientist*. https://www.newscientist.com/article/dn2586-men-die-young-even-if-old/

Mata, R., Josef, A.K., & Hertwig, R. (2016). 'Propensity for risk taking across the life span and around the globe.' *Psychological Science, 27*, pp 231–43. https://doi.org/10.1177/0956797615617811

Mattson, B.J., Williams, S., Rosenblatt, J.S., & Morrell, J.I. (2001). 'Comparison of two positive reinforcing stimuli: Pups and cocaine throughout the postpartum period.' *Behavioral Neuroscience, 115*, pp 683–94. https://doi.org/10.1037/0735-7044.115.3.683

McComb, K., Shannon, G., Sayialel, K.N., & Moss, C. (2014). 'Elephants can determine ethnicity, gender, and age from acoustic cues in human voices.' *Proceedings of the National Academy of Sciences, 111*, pp 5433–8. https://doi.org/10.1073/pnas.1321543111

Mealey, L. (2000). *Sex Differences: Developmental and Evolutionary Strategies*. Academic Press

Mercier, H. (2020). *Not Born Yesterday: The Science of Who We Trust and What We Believe*. Princeton University Press

Meyer-Bahlburg, H.F.L., Dolezal, C., Baker, S.W., & New, M.I. (2008). 'Sexual orientation in women with classical or non-classical congenital adrenal hyperplasia as a function of degree of prenatal androgen excess.' *Archives of Sexual Behavior, 37*, pp 85–99. https://doi.org/10.1007/s10508-007-9265-1

Miller, D.I., & Halpern, D.F. (2014). 'The new science of cognitive sex differences.' *Trends in Cognitive Sciences, 18*, pp 37–45. https://doi.org/10.1016/j.tics.2013.10.011

Miller, E.M. (2000). 'Homosexuality, birth order, and evolution: Toward an equilibrium reproductive economics of homosexuality.' *Archives of Sexual Behavior, 29*, pp 1–34. https://doi.org/10.1023/A:1001836320541

Miller, G.F. (2000). *The Mating Mind: How Sexual Choice Shaped the Evolution of Human Nature*. Vintage Books

Min, K.-J., Lee, C.-K., & Park, H.-N. (2012). 'The lifespan of Korean eunuchs.' *Current Biology, 22*, R792–3. https://doi.org/10.1016/j.cub.2012.06.036

Miserable_Sweet_5245. (2024). 'Having a hard time getting over partner having sex [online forum post].' *Reddit*. https://www.reddit.com/r/polyamory/comments/1einfqp/having_a_hard_time_getting_over_partner_having_sex/

Mitchell, K. (2018). *Innate: How the Wiring of Our Brains Shapes Who We Are*. Princeton University Press. https://doi.org/10.1515/9780691184999

Møller, A.P., & Birkhead, T.R. (1993). 'Certainty of paternity covaries with paternal care in birds.' *Behavioral Ecology and Sociobiology, 33*, pp 261–8. https://doi.org/10.1007/BF02027123

Money, J. (1975). 'Ablatio penis: Normal male infant sex-reassigned as a girl.' *Archives of Sexual Behavior, 4*, pp 65–71. https://doi.org/10.1007/BF01541887

Money, J., & Ehrhardt, A.A. (1972). *Man and Woman, Boy and Girl: The Differentiation and Dimorphism of Gender Identity from Conception to Maturity*. Johns Hopkins University Press

Moore, D.S., & Johnson, S.P. (2011). 'Mental rotation of dynamic, three-dimensional stimuli by 3-month-old infants.' *Infancy, 16*, pp 435–45. https://doi.org/10.1111/j.1532-7078.2010.00058.x

Morgenroth, T., Fine, C., Ryan, M.K., & Genat, A.E. (2018). 'Sex, drugs, and reckless driving: Are measures biased toward identifying risk-taking in men?' *Social Psychological and Personality Science, 9*, pp 744–53. https://doi.org/10.1177/1948550617722833

Moss-Racusin, C.A., Dovidio, J.F., Brescoll, V.L., Graham, M.J., & Handelsman, J. (2012). 'Science faculty's subtle gender biases favor male students.' *Proceedings of the National Academy of Sciences, 109*, pp 16474–9. https://doi.org/10.1073/pnas.1211286109

Muller, M.N., Marlowe, F.W., Bugumba, R., & Ellison, P.T. (2008). 'Testosterone and paternal care in East African foragers and pastoralists.' *Proceedings of the Royal Society B: Biological Sciences, 276*, pp 347–54. https://doi.org/10.1098/rspb.2008.1028

Muller, M.N., Thompson, M.E., & Wrangham, R.W. (2006). 'Male chimpanzees prefer mating with old females.' *Current Biology, 16*, pp 2234–8. https://doi.org/10.1016/j.cub.2006.09.042

Murdock, G.P. (1967). *Ethnographic Atlas*. University of Pittsburgh Press

Murdock, G.P., & Provost, C. (1973). 'Factors in the division of labor by sex: A cross-cultural analysis.' *Ethnology, 12*, pp 203–25. https://doi.org/10.2307/3773347

Nadeau, J.H. (2017). 'Do gametes woo? Evidence for their nonrandom union at fertilization.' *Genetics, 207*, pp 369–87. https://doi.org/10.1534/genetics.117.300109

Napp, C., & Breda, T. (2022). 'The stereotype that girls lack talent: A worldwide investigation.' *Science Advances, 8*, eabm3689. https://doi.org/10.1126/sciadv.abm3689

Nesse, R.M. (2006). 'Darwinian medicine and mental disorders.' *International Congress Series, 1296*, pp 83–94. https://doi.org/10.1016/j.ics.2006.03.037

Netchaeva, E., Sheppard, L.D., & Balushkina, T. (2022). 'A meta-analytic review of the gender difference in leadership aspirations.' *Journal of Vocational Behavior, 137*, no.103744. https://doi.org/10.1016/j.jvb.2022.103744

Nettle, D., & Pollet, T.V. (2008). 'Natural selection on male wealth in humans.' *American Naturalist, 172*, pp 658–66. https://doi.org/10.1086/591690

Nila, S., Barthes, J., Crochet, P.-A., Suryobroto, B., & Raymond, M. (2018). 'Kin selection and male homosexual preference in Indonesia.' *Archives of Sexual Behavior,* 47, pp 2455–65. https://doi.org/10.1007/s10508-018-1202-y

Nivette, A., Sutherland, A., Eisner, M., & Murray, J. (2019). 'Sex differences in adolescent physical aggression: Evidence from sixty-three low-and middle-income countries.' *Aggressive Behavior,* 45, pp 82–92. https://doi.org/10.1002/ab.21799

Nyhus, E.K., Frank, D.-A., Król, M.K., & Otterbring, T. (2024). 'Crypto cravings: Gender differences in crypto investment intentions and the mediating roles of financial overconfidence and personality.' *Psychology and Marketing, 41*, pp 447–64. https://doi.org/10.1002/mar.21921

O'Connor, R.C., & Kirtley, O.J. (2018). 'The integrated motivational–volitional model of suicidal behaviour.' *Philosophical Transactions of the Royal Society B: Biological Sciences,* 373, no.20170268. https://doi.org/10.1098/rstb.2017.0268

Oliver, M.B., & Hyde, J.S. (1993). 'Gender differences in sexuality: A meta-analysis.' *Psychological Bulletin, 114*, pp 29–51. https://doi.org/10.1037/0033-2909.114.1.29

Ong, D., & Wang, J. (2015). 'Income attraction: An online dating field experiment.' *Journal of Economic Behavior and Organization, 111*, pp 13–22. https://doi.org/10.1016/j.jebo.2014.12.011

Paglia, C. (1990). *Sexual Personae: Art and Decadence from Nefertiti to Emily Dickinson*. Yale University Press

Park, G., Lubinski, D., & Benbow, C.P. (2007). 'Contrasting intellectual patterns predict creativity in the arts and sciences: Tracking intellectually precocious youth over 25 years.' *Psychological Science, 18*, pp 948–52. https://doi.org/10.1111/j.1467-9280.2007.02007.x

Parker, G.A., Baker, R.R., & Smith, V.G.F. (1972). 'The origin and evolution of gamete dimorphism and the male–female phenomenon.' *Journal of Theoretical Biology, 36*, pp 529–53. https://doi.org/10.1016/0022-5193(72)90007-0

Pasterski, V.L., Geffner, M.E., Brain, C., Hindmarsh, P., Brook, C., & Hines, M. (2005). 'Prenatal hormones and postnatal socialization by parents as determinants of male-typical toy play in girls with congenital adrenal hyperplasia.' *Child Development, 76*, pp 264–78. https://doi.org/10.1111/j.1467-8624.2005.00843.x

Pawlowski, B., Atwal, R., & Dunbar, R.I.M. (2008). 'Sex differences in everyday risk-taking behavior in humans.' *Evolutionary Psychology, 6*, pp 29–42. https://doi.org/10.1177/147470490800600104

Perry, L. (2022). *The Case Against the Sexual Revolution: A New Guide to Sex in the 21st Century*. Polity Press

Pérusse, D. (1993). 'Cultural and reproductive success in industrial societies: Testing the relationship at the proximate and ultimate levels.' *Behavioral and Brain Sciences, 16*, pp 267–322. https://doi.org/10.1017/S0140525X00029939

Petersen, J. (2018). 'Gender difference in verbal performance: A meta-analysis of United States state performance assessments.' *Educational Psychology Review, 30*, pp 1269–81. https://doi.org/10.1007/s10648-018-9450-x

Petersen, J.L., & Hyde, J.S. (2010). 'A meta-analytic review of research on gender differences in sexuality, 1993–2007.' *Psychological Bulletin, 136*, pp 21–38. https://doi.org/10.1037/a0017504

Pillsworth, E.G. (2008). 'Mate preferences among the Shuar of Ecuador: Trait rankings and peer evaluations.' *Evolution and Human Behavior, 29*, pp 256–67. https://doi.org/10.1016/j.evolhumbehav.2008.01.005

Pinho-Gomes, A.-C., Peters, S.A.E., & Woodward, M. (2023). 'Gender equality related to gender differences in life expectancy across the globe gender equality and life expectancy.' *PLOS Global Public Health*, 3, e0001214. https://doi.org/10.1371/journal.pgph.0001214

Pinker, Steven (2011). *The Better Angels of Our Nature: Why Violence Has Declined*. Penguin

Pinker, Steven (2016). *The Blank Slate: The Modern Denial of Human Nature* (rev. edn). Penguin

Pinker, Susan (2008). *The Sexual Paradox: Troubled Boys, Gifted Girls, and the Real Difference Between the Sexes*. Scribner

Pittet, F., Heng, V., Atufa, J., & Bliss-Moreau, E. (2023). 'Monkeys do not show sex differences in toy preferences through their individual choices.' *Biology of Sex Differences, 14*, no.3. https://doi.org/10.1186/s13293-023-00489-9

Plomin, R., DeFries, J.C., Knopik, V.S., & Neiderhiser, J.M. (2016). 'Top 10 replicated findings from behavioral genetics.' *Perspectives on Psychological Science, 11*, pp 3–23. https://doi.org/10.1177/1745691615617439

Power, R.A., Kyaga, S., Uher, R., MacCabe, J.H., Langstrom, N., Landen, M., McGuffin, P., Lewis, C.M., Lichtenstein, P., & Svensson, A.C. (2013). 'Fecundity of patients with schizophrenia, autism, bipolar disorder, depression, anorexia nervosa, or substance abuse vs their unaffected siblings.' *JAMA Psychiatry, 70*, pp 22–30. https://doi.org/10.1001/jamapsychiatry.2013.268

Putkinen, V., Nazari-Farsani, S., Karjalainen, T., Santavirta, S., Hudson, M., Seppälä, K., Sun, L., Karlsson, H.K., Hirvonen, J., & Nummenmaa, L. (2023). 'Pattern recognition reveals sex-dependent neural substrates of sexual perception.' *Human Brain Mapping*, 44, pp 2543–56. https://doi.org/10.1002/hbm.26229

Puts, D.A. (2010). 'Beauty and the beast: Mechanisms of sexual selection in humans.' *Evolution and Human Behavior, 31*, pp 157–75. https://doi.org/10.1016/j.evolhumbehav.2010.02.005

Quinn, K. (2015). 'Here's what happens when you send 40 unsuspecting guys a preemptive V-pic.' *Thrillist*. https://www.thrillist.com/sex-dating/los-angeles/we-sent-a-preemptive-v-pic-before-dudes-could-send-dick-pics-heres-what-happened

Quinn, P.C., & Liben, L.S. (2008). 'A sex difference in mental rotation in young infants.' *Psychological Science, 19*, pp 1067–70. https://doi.org/10.1111/j.1467-9280.2008.02201.x

Quinn, P.O., & Madhoo, M. (2014). 'A review of attention-deficit/hyperactivity disorder in women and girls: Uncovering this hidden diagnosis.' *Primary Care Companion for CNS Disorders, 16*, PC-13r01596. https://doi.org/10.4088/PCC.13r01596

Radcliffe Richards, J. (1980). *The Sceptical Feminist: A Philosophical Enquiry*. Routledge

Rammstedt, B., Roemer, L., Roth, M., Zabal, A., & Lechner, C.M. (2025). *Revisiting Gender Differences in Personality: New Evidence on Big Five Domains and Facets with Large-Scale Samples from 27 Nations*. OSF Preprints. https://doi.org/10.31219/osf.io/ysd3p_v1

Reeves, R.V. (2022). *Of Boys and Men: Why the Modern Male Is Struggling, Why It Matters, and What To Do About It*. Brookings Institution Press

Reichert, M.C. (2019). 'It's dangerous to be a boy.' *The New York Times*. https://www.nytimes.com/2019/03/30/opinion/sunday/boys-men-violence.html

Reilly, D., Neumann, D.L., & Andrews, G. (2019). 'Gender differences in reading and writing achievement: Evidence from the National Assessment of

Educational Progress (NAEP).' *American Psychologist, 74*, pp 445–58. https://doi.org/10.1037/amp0000356

Reiner, W.G. (2004). 'Psychosexual development in genetic males assigned female: The cloacal exstrophy experience.' *Child and Adolescent Psychiatric Clinics, 13*, pp 657–74. https://doi.org/10.1016/j.chc.2004.02.009

Reiner, W.G., & Gearhart, J.P. (2004). 'Discordant sexual identity in some genetic males with cloacal exstrophy assigned to female sex at birth.' *New England Journal of Medicine, 350*, pp 333–41. https://doi.org/10.1056/NEJMoa022236

Reinier, K., Dizon, B., Chugh, H., Bhanji, Z., Seifer, M., Sargsyan, A., Uy-Evanado, A., Norby, F.L., Nakamura, K., Hadduck, K., Shepherd, D., Grogan, T., Elashoff, D., Jui, J., Salvucci, A., & Chugh, S.S. (2023). 'Warning symptoms associated with imminent sudden cardiac arrest: A population-based case-control study with external validation.' *Lancet Digital Health, 5*, e763–73. https://doi.org/10.1016/S2589-7500(23)00147-4

Reynaud, E. (2004). 'Holy virility: The social construction of masculinity.' In P.F. Murphy (ed.), *Feminism and Masculinities*, pp 136–48. Oxford University Press

Reynolds, M.R., Hajovsky, D.B., & Caemmerer, J.M. (2022). 'The sexes do not differ in general intelligence, but they do in some specifics.' *Intelligence, 92*, no.101651. https://doi.org/10.1016/j.intell.2022.101651

Reynolds, T., Baumeister, R.F., & Maner, J.K. (2018). 'Competitive reputation manipulation: Women strategically transmit social information about romantic rivals.' *Journal of Experimental Social Psychology, 78*, pp 195–209. https://doi.org/10.1016/j.jesp.2018.03.011

Reynolds, T., Howard, C., Sjåstad, H., Zhu, L., Okimoto, T.G., Baumeister, R.F., Aquino, K., & Kim, J. (2020). 'Man up and take it: Gender bias in moral typecasting.' *Organizational Behavior and Human Decision Processes, 161*, pp 120–41. https://doi.org/10.1016/j.obhdp.2020.05.002

Rhoads, S.E. (2004). *Taking Sex Differences Seriously*. Encounter Books

Ridley, M. (1993). *The Red Queen: Sex and the Evolution of Human Nature*. Penguin

Rieger, M.O., Wang, M., & Hens, T. (2015). 'Risk preferences around the world.' *Management Science, 61*, pp 637–48. https://doi.org/10.1287/mnsc.2013.1869

Ritchie, S.J., Cox, S.R., Shen, X., Lombardo, M.V., Reus, L.M., Alloza, C., Harris, M.A., Alderson, H.L., Hunter, S., Neilson, E., Liewald, D.C.M., Auyeung, B., Whalley, H.C., Lawrie, S.M., Gale, C.R., Bastin, M.E., McIntosh, A.M., & Deary, I.J. (2018). 'Sex differences in the adult human brain: Evidence from 5216 UK Biobank participants.' *Cerebral Cortex, 28*, pp 2959–75. https://doi.org/10.1093/cercor/bhy109

Robinson, J.P., & Lubienski, S.T. (2011). 'The development of gender achievement gaps in mathematics and reading during elementary and middle school: Examining direct cognitive assessments and teacher ratings.' *American Educational Research Journal, 48*, pp 268–302. https://doi.org/10.3102/0002831210372249

Ronay, R., & von Hippel, W. (2010). 'The presence of an attractive woman elevates testosterone and physical risk taking in young men.' *Social Psychological and Personality Science, 1*, pp 57–64. https://doi.org/10.1177/1948550609352807

Rosen, B.N., & Peterson, L. (1990). 'Gender differences in children's outdoor play injuries: A review and an integration.' *Clinical Psychology Review, 10*, pp 187–205. https://doi.org/10.1016/0272-7358(90)90057-H

Rosenfield, K.A., Sorokowska, A., Sorokowski, P., & Puts, D.A. (2020). 'Sexual selection for low male voice pitch among Amazonian forager-horticulturists.' *Evolution and Human Behavior, 41*, pp 3–11. https://doi.org/10.1016/j.evolhumbehav.2019.07.002

Rosenthal, R., & Jacobson, L. (1968). *Pygmalion in the Classroom*. Holt, Rinehart & Winston

Roser, M., Appel, C., & Ritchie, H. (2024). 'Human height.' *Our World in Data*. https://ourworldindata.org/human-height

Ross, C.T., Hooper, P.L., Smith, J.E., Jaeggi, A.V., Smith, E.A., Gavrilets, S., Zohora, F.t., Ziker, J., Xygalatas, D., Wroblewski, E.E., Wood, B., Winterhalder, B., Willführ, K.P., Willard, A.K., Walker, K., von Rueden, C., Voland, E., Valeggia, C., Vaitla, B., . . . Mulder, M.B. (2023). 'Reproductive inequality in humans and other mammals.' *Proceedings of the National Academy of Sciences, 120*, e2220124120. https://doi.org/10.1073/pnas.2220124120

Rotkirch, A. (2007). '"All that she wants is a(nother) baby"? Longing for children as a fertility incentive of growing importance.' *Journal of Evolutionary Psychology, 5*, pp 89–104. https://doi.org/10.1556/jep.2007.1010

Rubinstein, R.S., Jussim, L., & Stevens, S.T. (2018). 'Reliance on individuating information and stereotypes in implicit and explicit person perception.' *Journal of Experimental Social Psychology, 75*, pp 54–70. https://doi.org/10.1016/j.jesp.2017.11.009

Ryali, S., Zhang, Y., de los Angeles, C., Supekar, K., & Menon, V. (2024). 'Deep learning models reveal replicable, generalizable, and behaviorally relevant sex differences in human functional brain organization.' *Proceedings of the National Academy of Sciences, 121*, e2310012121. https://doi.org/10.1073/pnas.2310012121

Saad, G., & Gill, T. (2003). 'An evolutionary psychology perspective on gift giving among young adults.' *Psychology and Marketing, 20*, pp 765–84. https://doi.org/10.1002/mar.10096

Sagarin, B.J., Martin, A.L., Coutinho, S.A., Edlund, J.E., Patel, L., Skowronski, J.J., & Zengel, B. (2012). 'Sex differences in jealousy: A meta-analytic examination.' *Evolution and Human Behavior, 33*, pp 595–614. https://doi.org/10.1016/j.evolhumbehav.2012.02.006

Saini, A. (2017). *Inferior: How Science Got Women Wrong – And the New Research That's Rewriting the Story*. Beacon Press

Salk, R.H., Hyde, J.S., & Abramson, L.Y. (2017). 'Gender differences in depression in representative national samples: Meta-analyses of diagnoses and symptoms.' *Psychological Bulletin, 143*, pp 783–822. https://doi.org/10.1037/bul0000102

Salmon, C.A. (2012). 'The pop culture of sex: An evolutionary window on the worlds of pornography and romance.' *Review of General Psychology, 16*, pp 152–60. https://doi.org/10.1037/a0027910

Salmon, C., & Symons, D. (2003). *Warrior Lovers: Erotic Fiction, Evolution and Female Sexuality*. Yale University Press

Sax, L. (2002). 'How common is intersex? A response to Anne Fausto-Sterling.' *Journal of Sex Research, 39*, pp 174–8. https://doi.org/10.1080/00224490209552139

Saxon, L. (2012). *Sex at Dusk: Lifting the Shiny Wrapping from Sex at Dawn*. CreateSpace

Scelza, B.A. (2013). 'Choosy but not chaste: Multiple mating in human females.' *Evolutionary Anthropology, 22*, pp 259–69. https://doi.org/10.1002/evan.21373

Scelza, B.A. (2014). 'Jealousy in a small-scale, natural fertility population: The roles of paternity, investment and love in jealous response.' *Evolution and Human Behavior, 35*, pp 103–8. https://doi.org/10.1016/j.evolhumbehav.2013.11.003

Scelza, B.A., Prall, S.P., Blumenfield, T., Crittenden, A.N., Gurven, M., Kline, M., Koster, J., Kushnick, G., Mattison, S.M., Pillsworth, E., Shenk, M.K., Starkweather, K., Stieglitz, J., Sum, C.-Y., Yamaguchi, K., & McElreath,

R. (2020). 'Patterns of paternal investment predict cross-cultural variation in jealous response.' *Nature Human Behaviour,* 4, pp 20–26. https://doi.org/10.1038/s41562-019-0654-y

Schaerer, M., du Plessis, C., Nguyen, M.H.B., van Aert, R.C.M., Tiokhin, L., Lakens, D., Clemente, E.G., Pfeiffer, T., Dreber, A., Johannesson, M., Clark, C.J., & Uhlmann, E.L. (2023). 'On the trajectory of discrimination: A meta-analysis and forecasting survey capturing 44 years of field experiments on gender and hiring decisions.' *Organizational Behavior and Human Decision Processes, 179*, no.104280. https://doi.org/10.1016/j.obhdp.2023.104280

Schanzenbach, M. (2005). 'Racial and sex disparities in prison sentences: The effect of district-level judicial demographics.' *Journal of Legal Studies, 34*, pp 57–92. https://doi.org/10.1086/425597

Schärer, L., Rowe, L., & Arnqvist, G. (2012). 'Anisogamy, chance and the evolution of sex roles.' *Trends in Ecology and Evolution, 27*, pp 260–64. https://doi.org/10.1016/j.tree.2011.12.006

Schlegel, A., & Barry, H. (1991). *Adolescence: An Anthropological Inquiry*. Free Press

Schmitt, D.P. (2005). 'Sociosexuality from Argentina to Zimbabwe: A 48-nation study of sex, culture, and strategies of human mating.' *Behavioral and Brain Sciences, 28*, pp 247–75. https://doi.org/10.1017/S0140525X05000051

Schmitt, D.P. (2015). 'The evolution of culturally-variable sex differences: Men and women are not always different, but when they are . . . it appears not to result from patriarchy or sex role socialization.' In T.K. Shackelford & R.D. Hansen (eds), *The Evolution of Sexuality*, pp 221–56. Springer. https://doi.org/10.1007/978-3-319-09384-0_11

Schmitt, D.P., & International Sexuality Description Project (2003). 'Universal sex differences in the desire for sexual variety: Tests from 52 nations, 6 continents, and 13 islands.' *Journal of Personality and Social Psychology, 85*, pp 85–104. https://doi.org/10.1037/0022-3514.85.1.85

Schmitt, D.P., Realo, A., Voracek, M., & Allik, J. (2008). 'Why can't a man be more like a woman? Sex differences in Big Five personality traits across 55 cultures.' *Journal of Personality and Social Psychology, 94*, pp 168–82. https://doi.org/10.1037/0022-3514.94.1.168

Schwartz, S.H., & Rubel-Lifschitz, T. (2009). 'Cross-national variation in the size of sex differences in values: Effects of gender equality.' *Journal of Personality and Social Psychology, 97*, pp 171–85. https://doi.org/10.1037/a0015546

Schwarz, S., & Hassebrauck, M. (2012). 'Sex and age differences in mate-selection preferences.' *Human Nature, 23*, pp 447–66. https://doi.org/10.1007/s12110-012-9152-x

Seager, M.J., & Barry, J.A. (2019a). 'Cognitive distortion in thinking about gender issues: Gamma bias and the gender distortion matrix.' In J.A. Barry, R. Kingerlee, M.J. Seager, & L. Sullivan (eds), *The Palgrave Handbook of Male Psychology and Mental Health*, pp 87–104. Palgrave Macmillan. https://doi.org/10.1007/978-3-030-04384-1_5

Seager, M.J., & Barry, J.A. (2019b). 'From stereotypes to archetypes: An evolutionary perspective on male help-seeking and suicide.' In J.A. Barry, R. Kingerlee, M.J. Seager, & L. Sullivan (eds), *The Palgrave Handbook of Male Psychology and Mental Health*, pp 227–48. Palgrave Macmillan. https://doi.org/10.1007/978-3-030-04384-1_12

Seager, M.J., & Barry, J.A. (2020). 'Delta bias in how we celebrate gender-typical traits and behaviours.' *Psychreg Journal of Psychology, 4*, pp 166–9. https://doi.org/fksz

Sear, R., & Mace, R. (2008). 'Who keeps children alive? A review of the effects of kin on child survival.' *Evolution and Human Behavior, 29*, pp 1–18. https://doi.org/10.1016/j.evolhumbehav.2007.10.001

Seedat, S., Scott, K.M., Angermeyer, M.C., Berglund, P., Bromet, E.J., Brugha, T.S., Demyttenaere, K., de Girolamo, G., Haro, J.M., Jin, R., Karam, E.G., Kovess-Masfety, V., Levinson, D., Medina Mora, M.E., Ono, Y., Ormel, J., Pennell, B.-E., Posada-Villa, J., Sampson, N.A., . . . Kessler, R.C. (2009). 'Cross-national associations between gender and mental disorders in the World Health Organization World Mental Health Surveys.' *Archives of General Psychiatry, 66*, pp 785–95. https://doi.org/10.1001/archgenpsychiatry.2009.36

Seifert, I.S., Rohrer, J.M., & Schmukle, S.C. (2024). 'Using within-person change in three large panel studies to estimate personality age trajectories.' *Journal of Personality and Social Psychology, 126*, pp 150–74. https://doi.org/10.1037/pspp0000482

Shewach, O.R., Sackett, P.R., & Quint, S. (2019). 'Stereotype threat effects in settings with features likely versus unlikely in operational test settings: A meta-analysis.' *Journal of Applied Psychology, 104*, pp 1514–34. https://doi.org/10.1037/apl0000420

Shirazi, T.N., Self, H., Rosenfield, K.A., Dawood, K., Welling, L.L.M., Cárdenas, R., Bailey, J.M., Balasubramanian, R., Delaney, A., Breedlove, S.M., & Puts, D.A. (2022). 'Low perinatal androgens predict recalled childhood gender nonconformity in men.' *Psychological Science, 33*, pp 343–53. https://doi.org/10.1177/09567976211036075

Simpson, J.A., & Gangestad, S.W. (1991). 'Individual differences in sociosexuality: Evidence for convergent and discriminant validity.' *Journal of Personality and Social Psychology, 60*, pp 870–83. https://doi.org/10.1037/0022-3514.60.6.870

Sloan, C., Gough, B., & Conner, M. (2010). 'Healthy masculinities? How ostensibly healthy men talk about lifestyle, health and gender.' *Psychology and Health, 25*, pp 783–803. https://doi.org/10.1080/08870440902883204

Smuts, B.B. (1985). *Sex and Friendship in Baboons*. Aldine

Smuts, B. (1996). 'Male aggression against women: An evolutionary perspective.' In D.M. Buss & N.M. Malamuth (eds), *Sex, Power, Conflict: Evolutionary and Feminist Perspectives*, pp 231–68. Oxford University Press. https://doi.org/10.1093/oso/9780195095814.003.0011

Smuts, B.B., & Smuts, R.W. (1993). 'Male aggression and sexual coercion of females in nonhuman primates and other mammals: Evidence and theoretical implications.' *Advances in the Study of Behavior, 22*, pp 1–63. https://doi.org/10.1016/S0065-3454(08)60404-0

Snowden, R.J., Midgley, P., & Gray, N.S. (2024). 'Automatic distraction by sexual images: Gender differences.' *Sexes, 5*, pp 778–95. https://doi.org/10.3390/sexes5040050

Sohn, K. (2016). 'Men's revealed preferences regarding women's ages: Evidence from prostitution.' *Evolution and Human Behavior, 37*, pp 272–80. https://doi.org/10.1016/j.evolhumbehav.2016.01.002

Sohn, K. (2017). 'Men's revealed preference for their mates' ages.' *Evolution and Human Behavior, 38*, pp 58–62. https://doi.org/10.1016/j.evolhumbehav.2016.06.007

Sommers, C.H. (2012a). 'Sweden's new gender-neutral pronoun: *Hen*.' *Slate*. https://slate.com/human-interest/2012/04/hen-swedens-new-gender-neutral-pronoun-causes-controversy.html

Sommers, C.H. (2012b). 'You can give a boy a doll, but you can't make him play with it.' *The Atlantic*. https://www.theatlantic.com/sexes/archive/2012/12/you-can-give-a-boy-a-doll-but-you-cant-make-him-play-with-it/265977/

Soto, C.J. (2021). 'Do links between personality and life outcomes generalize? Testing the robustness of trait–outcome associations across gender, age, ethnicity, and analytic approaches.' *Social Psychological and Personality Science, 12*, pp 118–30. https://doi.org/10.1177/1948550619900572

Spohn, C. (1999). 'Gender and sentencing of drug offenders: Is chivalry dead?' *Criminal Justice Policy Review, 9*, pp 365–99. https://doi.org/10.1177/088740349900900305

Starr, S.B. (2015). 'Estimating gender disparities in federal criminal cases.' *American Law and Economics Review, 17*, pp 127–59. https://doi.org/10.1093/aler/ahu010

Steinem, G. (2014). *As If Women Matter: The Essential Gloria Steinem Reader*. Rupa Publications

Steinem, G. (2019). *The Truth Will Set You Free, but First It Will Piss You Off! Thoughts on Life, Love and Rebellion*. Random House

Stemple, L., & Meyer, I.H. (2014). 'The sexual victimization of men in America: New data challenge old assumptions.' *American Journal of Public Health, 104*, e19–26. https://doi.org/10.2105/AJPH.2014.301946

Stephens-Davidowitz, S. (2022). *Don't Trust Your Gut: Using Data to Get What You Really Want in Life*. Dey Street Books

Stewart-Williams, S. (2002). 'Gender, the perception of aggression, and the overestimation of gender bias.' *Sex Roles, 46*, pp 177–89. https://doi.org/10.1023/A:1019665803317

Stewart-Williams, S. (2010). *Darwin, God, and the Meaning of Life: How Evolutionary Theory Undermines Everything You Thought You Knew*. Cambridge University Press. https://doi.org/10.1017/CBO9780511778827

Stewart-Williams, S. (2018). *The Ape That Understood the Universe: How the Mind and Culture Evolve*. Cambridge University Press. https://doi.org/10.1017/9781108348140

Stewart-Williams, S. (2020). 'Are humans peacocks or robins?' In L. Workman, W. Reader, & J. Barkow (eds), *Cambridge Handbook of Evolutionary Perspectives on Human Behavior* (2nd edn), pp 342–52. Cambridge University Press. https://doi.org/10.1017/9781108131797.029

Stewart-Williams, S., Chang, C.Y.M., Wong, X.L., Blackburn, J.D., & Thomas, A.G. (2021). 'Reactions to male-favoring vs female-favoring sex differences: A pre-registered experiment and Southeast Asian replication.' *British Journal of Psychology, 112*, pp 389–411. https://doi.org/10.1111/bjop.12463

Stewart-Williams, S., & Halsey, L.G. (2021). 'Men, women and STEM: Why the differences and what should be done?' *European Journal of Personality, 35*, pp 3–39. https://doi.org/10.1177/0890207020962326

Stewart-Williams, S., & Halsey, L.G. (2022). 'Not biology or culture alone: Response to El-Hout et al. (2021).' *European Journal of Personality, 36*, pp 991–6. https://doi.org/10.1177/08902070211022477

Stewart-Williams, S., Leong, C.X.R., Seto, S.A., Thomas, A.G., & Wong, X.L. (2024). 'The harm hypothesis: How perceived harm to women shapes reactions to research on sex differences.' *International Journal of Psychology, 59*, pp 495–504. https://doi.org/10.1002/ijop.13101

Stewart-Williams, S., & Thomas, A.G. (2013a). 'The ape that thought it was a peacock: Does evolutionary psychology exaggerate human sex differences?' *Psychological Inquiry, 24*, pp 137–68. https://doi.org/10.1080/1047840X.2013.804899

Stewart-Williams, S., & Thomas, A.G. (2013b). 'The ape that kicked the hornet's nest: Response to commentaries on "The ape that thought it was a peacock".' *Psychological Inquiry, 24*, pp 248–71. https://doi.org/10.1080/1047840X.2013.823831

Stewart-Williams, S., Wong, X.L., Chang, C.Y.M., & Thomas, A.G. (2022a). 'People react more positively to female- than to male-favoring sex differences: A direct replication of a counterintuitive finding.' *PLOS ONE, 17*, e0266171. https://doi.org/10.1371/journal.pone.0266171

Stewart-Williams, S., Wong, X.L., Chang, C.Y.M., & Thomas, A.G. (2022b). 'Reactions to research on sex differences: Effect of sex favoured, researcher sex and importance of sex-difference domain.' *British Journal of Psychology, 113*, pp 960–86. https://doi.org/10.1111/bjop.12580

Stock, K. (2021). *Material Girls: Why Reality Matters for Feminism*. Fleet

Stoet, G., & Geary, D.C. (2012). 'Can stereotype threat explain the gender gap in mathematics performance and achievement?' *Review of General Psychology, 16*, pp 93–102. https://doi.org/10.1037/a0026617

Stoet, G., & Geary, D.C. (2013). 'Sex differences in mathematics and reading achievement are inversely related: Within- and across-nation assessment of 10 years of PISA data.' *PLOS ONE, 8*, e57988. https://doi.org/10.1371/journal.pone.0057988

Stoet, G., & Geary, D.C. (2018). 'The gender-equality paradox in science, technology, engineering, and mathematics education.' *Psychological Science, 29*, pp 581–93. https://doi.org/10.1177/0956797617741719

Stoet, G., & Geary, D.C. (2020). 'Sex-specific academic ability and attitude patterns in students across developed countries.' *Intelligence, 81*, no.101453. https://doi.org/10.1016/j.intell.2020.101453

Stoet, G., & Geary, D.C. (2022). 'Sex differences in adolescents' occupational aspirations: Variations across time and place.' *PLOS ONE, 17*, e0261438.

https://doi.org/10.1371/journal.pone.0261438

Strand, S., Deary, I.J., & Smith, P. (2006). 'Sex differences in Cognitive Abilities Test scores: A UK national picture.' *British Journal of Educational Psychology, 76*, pp 463–80. https://doi.org/10.1348/000709905X50906

Strassberg, D.S., & English, B.L. (2015). 'An experimental study of men's and women's personal ads.' *Archives of Sexual Behavior, 44*, pp 2249–55. https://doi.org/10.1007/s10508-014-0428-6

Strauss, N. (2005). *The Game: Penetrating the Secret Society of Pickup Artists*. Canongate Books

Striegel, R.H., Bedrosian, R., Wang, C., & Schwartz, S. (2012). 'Why men should be included in research on binge eating: Results from a comparison of psychosocial impairment in men and women.' *International Journal of Eating Disorders, 45*, pp 233–40. https://doi.org/10.1002/eat.20962

Strother, E., Lemberg, R., Stanford, S.C., & Turberville, D. (2012). 'Eating disorders in men: Underdiagnosed, undertreated, and misunderstood.' *Eating Disorders, 20*, pp 346–55. https://doi.org/10.1080/10640266.2012.715512

Su, R., Rounds, J., & Armstrong, P.I. (2009). 'Men and things, women and people: A meta-analysis of sex differences in interests.' *Psychological Bulletin, 135*, pp 859–84. https://doi.org/10.1037/a0017364

Sulikowski, D., Williams, M., Nair, G., Shepherd, B., Wilson, A., Tran, A., & Wagstaff, D. (2024). 'Off with her hair: Intrasexually competitive women advise other women to cut off more hair.' *Personality and Individual Differences, 216*, no.112406. https://doi.org/10.1016/j.paid.2023.112406

Sutter, M., Zoller, C., & Glätzle-Rützler, D. (2019). 'Economic behavior of children and adolescents: A first survey of experimental economics results.' *European Economic Review, 111*, pp 98–121. https://doi.org/10.1016/j.euroecorev.2018.09.004

Swift-Gallant, A. (2019). 'Individual differences in the biological basis of androphilia in mice and men.' *Hormones and Behavior, 111*, pp 23–30. https://doi.org/10.1016/j.yhbeh.2018.12.006

Swift-Gallant, A., Aung, T., Rosenfield, K., Dawood, K., & Puts, D. (2023). 'Organizational effects of gonadal hormones on human sexual orientation.' *Adaptive Human Behavior and Physiology, 9*, pp 344–70. https://doi.org/10.1007/s40750-023-00226-x

Swim, J.K. (1994). 'Perceived versus meta-analytic effect sizes: An assessment of the accuracy of gender stereotypes.' *Journal of Personality and Social Psychology, 66*, pp 21–36. https://doi.org/10.1037/0022-3514.66.1.21

Symons, D. (1979). *The Evolution of Human Sexuality*. Oxford University Press

Terrier, C. (2020). 'Boys lag behind: How teachers' gender biases affect student achievement.' *Economics of Education Review*, 77, no.101981. https://doi.org/10.1016/j.econedurev.2020.101981

Thomas, A.G., Harrison, S., Stewart-Williams, S., & Workman, L. (2024). 'Polygamous interest in a mononormative nation: The roles of sex and sociosexuality in polygamous interest in a heterosexual sample from the UK.' *Archives of Sexual Behavior*, 53, pp 611–27. https://doi.org/10.1007/s10508-023-02749-6

Thomas, A.G., Jonason, P.K., Blackburn, J.D., Kennair, L.E.O., Lowe, R., Malouff, J., Stewart-Williams, S., Sulikowski, D., & Li, N.P. (2020). 'Mate preference priorities in the East and West: A cross-cultural test of the mate preference priority model.' *Journal of Personality*, 88, pp 606–20. https://doi.org/10.1111/jopy.12514

Thöni, C., & Volk, S. (2021). 'Converging evidence for greater male variability in time, risk, and social preferences.' *Proceedings of the National Academy of Sciences*, 118, e2026112118. https://doi.org/10.1073/pnas.2026112118

Thorndike, E.L. (1911). *Individuality*. Houghton Mifflin

Thornhill, R. (1980). 'Rape in *Panorpa* scorpionflies and a general rape hypothesis.' *Animal Behaviour*, 28, pp 52–9. https://doi.org/10.1016/S0003-3472(80)80007-8

Thornhill, R., & Palmer, C.T. (2000). *A Natural History of Rape: Biological Bases of Sexual Coercion*. MIT Press

Tiger, L., & Shepher, J. (1975). *Women in the Kibbutz*. Harcourt Brace Jovanovich

Todd, B.K., Fischer, R.A., Di Costa, S., Roestorf, A., Harbour, K., Hardiman, P., & Barry, J.A. (2018). 'Sex differences in children's toy preferences: A systematic review, meta-regression, and meta-analysis.' *Infant and Child Development*, 27, e2064. https://doi.org/10.1002/icd.2064

Trivers, R.L. (1972). 'Parental investment and sexual selection.' In B. Campbell (ed.), *Sexual Selection and the Descent of Man: 1871–1971*, pp 136–79. Aldine Press

Trivers, R.L. (1985). *Social Evolution*. Benjamin/Cummings

Turkheimer, E. (2000). 'Three laws of behavior genetics and what they mean.' *Current Directions in Psychological Science*, 9, pp 160–64. https://doi.org/10.1111/1467-8721.00084

United Nations Office on Drugs and Crime. (2023). *Global Study on Homicide*.

https://www.unodc.org/unodc/en/data-and-analysis/global-study-on-homicide.html

Vaillancourt, T. (2013). 'Do human females use indirect aggression as an intrasexual competition strategy?' *Philosophical Transactions of the Royal Society B: Biological Sciences, 368*, no.20130080. https://doi.org/10.1098/rstb.2013.0080

van Hemert, D.A., van de Vijver, F.J.R., & Vingerhoets, A.J.J.M. (2011). 'Culture and crying: Prevalences and gender differences.' *Cross-Cultural Research, 45*, pp 399–431. https://doi.org/10.1177/1069397111404519

van Schaik, C.P., Bshary, R., Wagner, G., & Cunha, F. (2022). 'Male anti-predation services in primates as costly signalling? A comparative analysis and review.' *Ethology, 128*, pp 1–14. https://doi.org/10.1111/eth.13233

Van Valen, L. (1973). 'A new evolutionary law.' *Evolutionary Theory, 1*, pp 1–30.

Vasey, P.L., Pocock, D.S., & VanderLaan, D.P. (2007). 'Kin selection and male androphilia in Samoan *fa'afafine*.' *Evolution and Human Behavior, 28*, pp 159–67. https://doi.org/10.1016/j.evolhumbehav.2006.08.004

Ventura, F.L., Nguyen, C.M., Dang, A., Baliss, M., & Sonstein, L.K. (2021). 'A curious case of rectal ejaculation.' *Cureus, 13*, e17330. https://doi.org/10.7759/cureus.17330

Verbree, A.-R., Hornstra, L., Maas, L., & Wijngaards-de Meij, L. (2023). 'Conscientiousness as a predictor of the gender gap in academic achievement.' *Research in Higher Education, 64*, pp 451–72. https://doi.org/10.1007/s11162-022-09716-5

von Hippel, W., & Buss, D.M. (2017). 'Do ideologically driven scientific agendas impede the understanding and acceptance of evolutionary principles in social psychology?' In J.T. Crawford & L. Jussim (eds), *The Politics of Social Psychology*, pp 7–25. Routledge. https://doi.org/10.4324/9781315112619-2

von Rueden, C.R., & Jaeggi, A.V. (2016). 'Men's status and reproductive success in 33 nonindustrial societies: Effects of subsistence, marriage system, and reproductive strategy.' *Proceedings of the National Academy of Sciences, 113*, pp 10824–9. https://doi.org/10.1073/pnas.1606800113

Voracek, M., Hofhansl, A., & Fisher, M.L. (2005). 'Clark and Hatfield's evidence of women's low receptivity to male strangers' sexual offers revisited.' *Psychological Reports, 97*, pp 11–20. https://doi.org/10.2466/pro.97.1.11-20

Voyer, D., & Voyer, S.D. (2014). 'Gender differences in scholastic achievement: A meta-analysis.' *Psychological Bulletin, 140*, pp 1174–204. https://doi.org/10.1037/a0036620

Voyer, D., Voyer, S., & Bryden, M.P. (1995). 'Magnitude of sex differences in spatial abilities: A meta-analysis and consideration of critical variables.' *Psychological Bulletin, 117*, pp 250–70. https://doi.org/10.1037/0033-2909.117.2.250

Wai, J., Cacchio, M., Putallaz, M., & Makel, M.C. (2010). 'Sex differences in the right tail of cognitive abilities: A 30 year examination.' *Intelligence, 38*, pp 412–23. https://doi.org/10.1016/j.intell.2010.04.006

Walter, K.V., Conroy-Beam, D., Buss, D.M., Asao, K., Sorokowska, A., Sorokowski, P., Aavik, T., Akello, G., Alhabahba, M.M., Alm, C., Amjad, N., Anjum, A., Atama, C.S., Atamtürk Duyar, D., Ayebare, R., Batres, C., Bendixen, M., Bensafia, A., Bizumic, B., . . . Zupančič, M. (2020). 'Sex differences in mate preferences across 45 countries: A large-scale replication.' *Psychological Science, 31*, pp 408–23. https://doi.org/10.1177/0956797620904154

Walton, G.M., & Spencer, S.J. (2009). 'Latent ability: Grades and test scores systematically underestimate the intellectual ability of negatively stereotyped students.' *Psychological Science, 20*, pp 1132–9. https://doi.org/10.1111/j.1467-9280.2009.02417.x

Wang, M.-T., Eccles, J.S., & Kenny, S. (2013). 'Not lack of ability but more choice: Individual and gender differences in choice of careers in science, technology, engineering, and mathematics.' *Psychological Science, 24*, pp 770–75. https://doi.org/10.1177/0956797612458937

Warach, B., Bornstein, R.F., Gorman, B.S., & Moyer, A. (2024). 'The current state of affairs in infidelity research: A systematic review and meta-analysis of romantic infidelity prevalence and its moderators.' *Personal Relationships, 31*, pp 1001–26. https://doi.org/10.1111/pere.12571

Wardle, J., Haase, A.M., Steptoe, A., Nillapun, M., Jonwutiwes, K., & Bellisle, F. (2004). 'Gender differences in food choice: The contribution of health beliefs and dieting.' *Annals of Behavioral Medicine, 27*, pp 107–16. https://doi.org/10.1207/s15324796abm2702_5

Warwick, H. (2018). *A Prickly Affair: The Charm of the Hedgehog*. Penguin

Wassiliwizky, E., Zietsch, B.P., & Ullén, F. (2025). 'The gender attractiveness gap.' *bioRxiv*. https://doi.org/10.1101/2025.05.21.655261

Westermarck, E.A. (1921). *The History of Human Marriage* (5th edn). Macmillan

Whipple, T. (2016). 'Sexism fears hamper brain research.' *The Times*. https://www.thetimes.co.uk/article/sexism-fears-hamper-brain-research-rx6w39gbw

Whyte, S., Torgler, B., & Harrison, K.L. (2016). 'What women want in their sperm donor: A study of more than 1000 women's sperm donor selections.' *Economics and Human Biology, 23*, pp 1–9. https://doi.org/10.1016/j.ehb.2016.06.001

Wierenga, L.M., Doucet, G.E., Dima, D., Agartz, I., Aghajani, M., Akudjedu, T.N., Albajes-Eizagirre, A., Alnæs, D., Alpert, K.I., Andreassen, O.A., Anticevic, A., Asherson, P., Banaschewski, T., Bargallo, N., Baumeister, S., Baur-Streubel, R., Bertolino, A., Bonvino, A., Boomsma, D.I., . . . Tamnes, C.K. (2022). 'Greater male than female variability in regional brain structure across the lifespan.' *Human Brain Mapping, 43*, pp 470–99. https://doi.org/10.1002/hbm.25204

Wikipedia contributors (n.d.). 'List of inventors killed by their own inventions.' In Wikipedia. https://en.wikipedia.org/wiki/List_of_inventors_killed_by_their_own_inventions

Williams, G.C. (1966). *Adaptation and Natural Selection: A Critique of Some Current Evolutionary Thought*. Princeton University Press

Williams, G.C. (1975). *Sex and Evolution*. Princeton University Press

Williams, W.M., & Ceci, S.J. (2015). 'National hiring experiments reveal 2:1 faculty preference for women on STEM tenure track.' *Proceedings of the National Academy of Sciences, 112*, pp 5360–65. https://doi.org/10.1073/pnas.1418878112

Willoughby, E.A., Love, A.C., McGue, M., Iacono, W.G., Quigley, J., & Lee, J.J. (2019). 'Free will, determinism, and intuitive judgments about the heritability of behavior.' *Behavior Genetics, 49*, pp 136–53. https://doi.org/10.1007/s10519-018-9931-1

Wilson, E.O. (1975). *Sociobiology: The New Synthesis*. Belknap Press

Wilson, E.O. (1978). *On Human Nature*. Harvard University Press

Wilson, M., & Daly, M. (1985). 'Competitiveness, risk taking, and violence: The young male syndrome.' *Ethology and Sociobiology, 6*, pp 59–73. https://doi.org/10.1016/0162-3095(85)90041-X

Wilson, M.L., Boesch, C., Fruth, B., Furuichi, T., Gilby, I.C., Hashimoto, C., Hobaiter, C.L., Hohmann, G., Itoh, N., Koops, K., Lloyd, J.N., Matsuzawa, T., Mitani, J.C., Mjungu, D.C., Morgan, D., Muller, M.N., Mundry, R., Nakamura, M., Pruetz, J., . . . Wrangham, R.W. (2014). 'Lethal aggression in *Pan* is better explained by adaptive strategies than human impacts.' *Nature, 513*, pp 414–17. https://doi.org/10.1038/nature13727

Wolf, N. (1991). *The Beauty Myth: How Images of Beauty Are Used Against*

Women. Morrow

Wolfgang, M., Figlio, R.M., Tracy, P.E., & Singer, S.J. (1985). *The National Survey of Crime Severity (NCJ-96017)*. US Government Printing Office

Wood, W., & Eagly, A.H. (2002). 'A cross-cultural analysis of the behavior of women and men: Implications for the origins of sex differences.' *Psychological Bulletin, 128*, pp 699–727. https://doi.org/10.1037/0033-2909.128.5.699

Wood, W., & Eagly, A.H. (2012). 'Biosocial construction of sex differences and similarities in behavior.' In J.M. Olson & M.P. Zanna (eds), *Advances in Experimental Social Psychology*, vol.46, pp 55–123. Elsevier. https://doi.org/10.1016/B978-0-12-394281-4.00002-7

Wrangham, R. (2019). *The Goodness Paradox: The Strange Relationship Between Virtue and Violence in Human Evolution*. Pantheon

Wright, R. (1994). *The Moral Animal: The New Science of Evolutionary Psychology*. Pantheon

Xu, Y., Norton, S., & Rahman, Q. (2017). 'Sexual orientation and neurocognitive ability: A meta-analysis in men and women.' *Neuroscience and Biobehavioral Reviews, 83*, pp 691–6. https://doi.org/10.1016/j.neubiorev.2017.06.014

Young, C. (1999). *Ceasefire! Why Women and Men Must Join Forces to Achieve True Equality*. Free Press

Zahavi, A. (1975). 'Mate selection: A selection for a handicap.' *Journal of Theoretical Biology, 53*, pp 205–14. https://doi.org/10.1016/0022-5193(75)90111-3

Zarulli, V., Barthold Jones, J.A., Oksuzyan, A., Lindahl-Jacobsen, R., Christensen, K., & Vaupel, J.W. (2018). 'Women live longer than men even during severe famines and epidemics.' *Proceedings of the National Academy of Sciences, 115*, e832–40. https://doi.org/10.1073/pnas.1701535115

Zhang, L., Lee, A.J., DeBruine, L.M., & Jones, B.C. (2019). 'Are sex differences in preferences for physical attractiveness and good earning capacity in potential mates smaller in countries with greater gender equality?' *Evolutionary Psychology, 17*, no.1474704919852921. https://doi.org/10.1177/1474704919852921

Zhang, Y., & Santtila, P. (2022). 'Social status predicts different mating and reproductive success for men and women in China: Evidence from the 2010–2017 CGSS data.' *Behavioral Ecology and Sociobiology, 76*, no.101. https://doi.org/10.1007/s00265-022-03209-2

Zietsch, B.P., Sidari, M.J., Abdellaoui, A., Maier, R., Långström, N., Guo, S.,

Beecham, G.W., Martin, E.R., Sanders, A.R., & Verweij, K.J.H. (2021). 'Genomic evidence consistent with antagonistic pleiotropy may help explain the evolutionary maintenance of same-sex sexual behaviour in humans.' *Nature Human Behaviour,* 5, pp 1251–8. https://doi.org/10.1038/s41562-021-01168-8

Zucker, I., & Prendergast, B.J. (2020). 'Sex differences in pharmacokinetics predict adverse drug reactions in women.' *Biology of Sex Differences,* 11, no.32. https://doi.org/10.1186/s13293-020-00308-5

Index

Note: Italic page numbers indicate figures.